JORDAN JUNIOR HIGH SCHOOL

THIS BOOK LOANED TO

NAME   DATE   TEACHER

Books by Carleton S. Coon

THE SEVEN CAVES *(1957)*
THE STORY OF MAN *(1954–62)*
THE ORIGIN OF RACES *(1962)*

These are BORZOI BOOKS
published by Alfred A. Knopf in New York

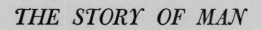

THE STORY OF MAN

THE STORY OF
MAN

*From the First Human to Primitive Culture
and Beyond*

Second Edition, Revised

by CARLETON S. COON

LINE DRAWINGS BY RICHARD ALBANY
PHOTOGRAPHS BY REUBEN GOLDBERG

NEW YORK   ALFRED A. KNOPF   1962

L. C. catalog card number: 62–11055

⚜ THIS IS A BORZOI BOOK, ⚜
PUBLISHED BY ALFRED A. KNOPF, INC.

A portion of Chapter I originally appeared in *The New York Times Magazine* for March 19, 1961.

PUBLISHED NOVEMBER 8, 1954
SECOND PRINTING, NOVEMBER 1954
THIRD PRINTING, APRIL 1955
FOURTH PRINTING, FEBRUARY 1958
SECOND EDITION, APRIL 1962
SECOND PRINTING, OCTOBER 1962

T O

HOMO SAPIENS

WISHING HIM GOOD LUCK ON HIS NEXT ADVENTURE

THIS is the story of man
who alone of beasts mastered the wild-fire,
became a skilled hunter and healer,
a tiller of earth and a herdsman,
and conquered the cold and the sea
while the power of the sun altered him.
Wheel-making, smelting, and writing,
he hammered out empires with iron,
circled his planet with cannon,
found and took a new world—
whence he challenges space with his atoms
while facing the ultimate challenge

—HIMSELF.

PREFACE

ONE CAN have little more to say after having written a history of the world, even as short and limited a one as this. I am exhausted, and amazed at my foolhardiness. So many years have I spent on it that I cannot remember all the people who helped me. If I fail to mention anyone who deserves it, my apologies are offered. Of those who tried to educate me, four men contributed particularly to what went into the planning and execution of this volume. The late Charles T. Copeland tried to teach me to write, and the late Earnest Hooton inspired me as he did dozens of others to make anthropology my career. Eliot Chapple taught me about social anthropology, and William Crozier taught both Chapple and me about scientific method.

More immediately I am indebted to the trustees of the University Museum of the University of Pennsylvania, and its director, Froelich Rainey, for letting me do mostly what I wanted to do during the last six years. It was Rainey's idea that I should install a Hall of Man. The plan of organization of that exhibit is the table of contents of this book. I hope that a scheme which has been accorded success visually will also carry an intelligible verbal message. During the summers of 1952 and 1953 I appeared in a television program entitled *Summer School*, which CBS broadcast over a national network under the direction of Robert Forrest. Arnold Rabin, a talented young television writer, prepared the script on the basis of preliminary drafts of this manuscript. The need of condensation imposed by this medium helped both Rabin and me screen and focus the ideas that went into this book.

Hallam Movius and Bruce Howe helped me specifically with the chapters on Old World prehistory, Stanley Garn, Russell Newman, J. Lawrence Angel, William L. Straus, and Kenneth Oakley on the subjects of evolution and race. Froelich Rainey and J. Louis Giddings helped with the Eskimo section, Ward Goodenough with the Polynesian sketch, and Alfred Kidder II with the American Indian chapter. Kidder has also, in his usual saint-like fashion, taken over the onerous task of proof-reading during my convenient absence in Afghanistan. To Boies Penrose I am indebted for information about the Age of Gunpowder, to William Crozier for checking the last chapter for scientific accuracy, and to President Gaylord P. Harnwell of the University of Pennsylvania for a friendly warning not to carry my mathematical analysis too far.

Earnest Hooton designed the lower jaw that we used in reconstructing the life model of Rhodesian man, and Loren Eiseley, William L. Straus, J. Lawrence Angel, Neil Tappan, Sherwood Washburn, and Lawrence Oschinsky advised and helped me on the four reconstructions that appear in the illustrations. These lively busts of long dead men and women were made in the plaster room of our museum by Antoinette Gentile under the direction of Emily Pettinos and myself and the eagle eye of that master caster, Domenico Consani. Richard Albany's sharp and simple line drawings and Reuben Goldberg's consummate use of lighting in photographing otherwise dead objects help to relieve my pedestrian literary effort. My wife designed the maps—she and my assistant Jane Goodale helped me from start to finish, and other useful helpers were my students Dexter Perkins, Jr., and Theresa Howard Carter, as well as Charles Wiley, Cynthia Griffin, Geraldine Bruckner, and Caroline Dosker, all of the University Museum staff. Elizabeth Stifler typed the manuscript several times. In citing all of these people I have omitted the titles of "Doctor" and "Professor," Miss and Mrs., because I think of them as human beings and not as academic or marital slots. Bare of titles we came into the world, and in the same fashion we shall leave it.

Those of my friends who have attained distinction do not need to have their titles mentioned, and the others will, I hope, soon achieve it.

I now turn to another category of friends, equally important in the production of whatever this book may turn out to be. Harold Strauss, the editor-in-chief of Alfred A. Knopf, Inc., worked almost as much on the manuscript as I did, and taught me literary humility. Sidney Jacobs, of the manufacturing department, screened my illustrations with a gimlet eye, and Herbert Weinstock, of the same fraternity, went through my manuscript once like an ice storm, breaking off rotten limbs with loud crashes. Harry Ford is responsible for the quality of layout and production. To these four men I am deeply indebted, as I am to my older and less severe friend Jonathan Cape, who will bring out the English edition, and who cured me (I hope) of the professorial habit of being "jocular," a polite British adjective for "academically facetious," or in plain American, corny.

CARLETON S. COON

January 12, 1954
Devon, Pennsylvania

PREFACE TO SECOND EDITION

Since 1954 great advances have been made in our knowledge of human evolution and man's differentiation into races, and new discoveries in archæology have changed some of our concepts of prehistory. To bring *The Story of Man* up to date, and to make it consistent with my forthcoming book, *The Origin of Races,* I have rewritten a considerable part of the text and changed a few maps and pictures. But I have not changed anything just for novelty. This is a Solera product, not a raw vintage.

CARLETON S. COON

January 5, 1962
West Gloucester, Massachusetts

CONTENTS

LIST OF PLATES

*(Unless otherwise identified, all photographs
are by* REUBEN GOLDBERG*)*

EARLY MEN AND THEIR TOOLS
(FOLLOWING PAGE 40)

RACE
(FOLLOWING PAGE 200)

LIST OF DRAWINGS
IN THE TEXT

NOTE: All line drawings except the French cave figure, the Nilotic Negro, the Wu ship, and the pod corn, whether made directly from artifacts or from information provided by others, have been prepared specially for this book by Richard Albany. Unless otherwise noted, the drawings from French cave art have been made possible by the magnificent and tireless work of Abbé Henri Breuil, and those from Spanish cave art by that of Father Hugo Obermeier. The Egyptian drawings were made from material furnished by Dr. Rudolph Anthes and Mr. Henry Fischer. The Hall of Tara plan is after MacAlester; the early cannon and the coking oven are after Forbes; the gazelle silhouettes are after Ugo Mochi; and the Homeric scenes are after Notor. The Upper Paleolithic wall engraving was taken from Paolo Graziosi's *Paleolithic Art* and the Nilotic Negro was drawn from a photograph by Cipriani.

LIST OF MAPS

(By LIAM DUNNE)

THE STORY OF MAN

INTRODUCTION

TOWARD AN UNDERSTANDING
OF HISTORY

So SIMPLE and so basic is the aim of this book that its
first sentence must be a warning to the reader not to look behind
the words for hidden meanings or academic profundities. This aim
is to describe the main events of human history from the time that
man appeared on the face of the earth until the present moment,
when he has the power to destroy it. For the best part of a century historians have been struggling to break the shackles of conventional history. Some have followed the framework of economics
through time; others those of art, social structure, science, and
other disciplines and combinations of disciplines. I shall approach
history with the tools of an anthropologist: human biology, archæology, and the study of living cultures, particularly those of
"primitive" men. Because anthropologists have had some success
in finding out how cultures work I hope to find some meaning in
history, which is nothing but a record of all the cultures of the
world since man first became a reasoning animal and taught his
children to chip flint.

One advantage of the anthropological approach over some
others is that it needs few technical words. The only one used in
this book which the educated lay reader might misunderstand is
institution. In anthropological language an institution is a group
of people. It is organized for some purpose, follows rules, and has
a structure—in its simplest form that of a leader and a few followers, in its most complicated form a world federation of nations.
An individual belongs to several institutions, such as his family,
business organization, church, clubs, community, and nation.[1] If

[1] For a more detailed and precise definition see C. S. Coon, *A Reader in General Anthropology,* Henry Holt & Company, New York, 1949, pp. 604–9.

we remember that for present purposes *institution* means *people*, and not ideas, rules, practices, or customs, as the word is generally used, what follows should be understood without difficulty.

Our next logical step is to define the unit of history. This is a historical event. In cosmic history, events are the explosion of a star, the birth of a planet, the formation of its atmosphere, the advance and retreat of an ice sheet on its surface, and the rise of a new species of animal. In human history comparable events are the critical landmarks of the evolution of man from lower primates; of his elimination of all other erect primate species; of his conquest of the forces of nature, from fire to atomic energy; of his division into races in response to variations in heat and light as he came to occupy all terrestrial environments; of his growth in numbers; of his specialization in different arts and crafts; of his division of labor on the bases of sex, age, and occupation; of his advances in transport and communication; of his participation in an increasing number of institutions; and of his growing knowledge of the nature of the universe of which he is part. The landmarks of these sequences, like cosmic events, are non-repetitive, progressive, and cumulative, and like them they follow cosmic laws.

Events in other disciplines are measured in terms of the expenditure of energy in time and space. The events of human history which we shall review are also those which involve the expenditure of energy by the human organism in these dimensions.

The organism itself is a unique bipedal mammal, equipped with grasping hands that are capable of fine work, with fine-focusing stereoscopic eyes, with a brain unique for its large size, and with vocal organs capable of producing the sounds needed in speech. This organism had already evolved, in its essential form, a half million years ago, and has since then been modified in certain physiological respects as a result of its adaptation to extremes of light and heat as it moved into the different climates of the earth's surface. Other modifications, particularly brain growth, accompanied its rising capacities for working, thinking, communicating, and organizing itself socially.

The environment in which this organism has lived and grown—

until now it has conquered the earth—consists of land, air, and water and all of the plants and other animals that live in and on these media. Increasingly man has learned how to use natural materials for basic cutting tools, and to fabricate from them secondary tools and other products, in order to feed himself and his kind, to protect himself from the elements, and to send messages back and forth between individuals and groups. Man's gradual conquest of nature has caused him to live in groups of increasing size and complexity, until now the world of men verges on an intricate unity.

At the same time man has used up many of the materials on the earth's surface until parts of it lie bare and ravished. To a cosmic geographer with only an objective interest in man, our species might appear to be nothing but a highly organized skin cancer destroying the surface of the earth with growing rapidity, until, early in the seventh decade of the twentieth century, a moment of climax is approaching. The whole surface of the earth and even its atmosphere are in danger of destruction. The stages in this course of gradual deterioration at the hand of man may be used inversely as an objective measure of cultural advance in human history.

Culture itself is a term that many anthropologists either kick about as a football of debate, or worship as a sacred cow. Its definitions are almost as numerous as anthropologists. For present purposes we may consider culture in general to be the sum total of the ways in which human beings live, transmitted from generation to generation by learning. It includes the relations between people in pairs and in groups, man's work activities involving natural materials, and his expenditure of energy in the realm of symbols, including speech, music, the visual arts, and the human body itself. Culture is the sum total of the things that people do as a result of having been so taught.

A specific culture is a set of procedures by which a people living in a place over a span of time conduct their lives. Every element in such a culture is integrated with every other element so that the whole forms a unit just as functional as a cell or a living organism. Cultures meet along spatial frontiers, as do the peoples who live according to their tenets. Cultures borrow, blend, and change with the passage of time. During the span of the twenty thousand generations of human beings who lived through the Middle and Upper Pleistocene periods, until ten thousand years ago, the upward curve of human culture moved slowly and almost imperceptibly, but nevertheless cumulatively, until, within the last three hundred generations that have passed since the beginning of agriculture, its acceleration has reached a staggering speed. Nevertheless, during this time the human organism has remained the same.

Progressive changes in culture have increased both the number of persons who can live off a piece of landscape, and the complexity of their division of labor. Among man's primate relatives, males and females do much the same things in the course of a day, and old monkeys and apes seldom outlive their prime; among our remote kin there is no division of labor on the basis of sex or of age. Early man, equipped with tools and speech, divided up the tasks needed for survival, so that men hunted while women gathered and cared for the young. Where and when an abundance of food and a stability of residence permitted, old people survived long enough to serve as tutors to the young, and healers to all who needed comfort; hence an age division of labor also appeared while man was still a hunter.

During this long hunting phase of human existence a third division of labor, based on differences in occupation, began to appear, to a certain extent in tool-making, but more in the arts of healing and of dealing with disturbances in human relations caused by changes in the weather. This segmentation was not great enough to affect the basic structure of human groups. Hunters lived in bands of from two to twenty or so families, all usually related to one another. In each band, while families were independent, the leadership was vested in one man in his prime, distinguished for his skill at providing meat, in preventing and settling quarrels, and in conducting foreign affairs with the leaders of other bands occupying neighboring hunting territories.

In such a band everyone knew everyone else and protocol was simple. Over the hundreds of thousands of years that man lived as a hunter he perfected his capacity to be intimate with the members of his band, and formal with outsiders. Young men learned ways of behaving toward women, children, and old people which would make life easiest for all concerned, and hence would enhance the survival value of the band as a whole.

As man progressively conquered the forces of nature, and as a division of labor on the basis of work techniques increased, more and more people were brought into mutual contact. For each type of organization that arose in addition to those of family and band, some kind of leadership, and a pattern of orderly behavior, created themselves. The shop of smiths, the crew of a boat, the members of a trading expedition, a war party, all had to have structure, with a leader, followers, and rules of procedure. As these institutions grew in size and numbers, they also grew increasingly formal. While it is easy for members of a small intimate band to get along together on a personal informal basis of natural give and take, when people belong to different families and different face-to-face groups, such as neighborhoods or sections of a village, trouble can arise if rules are not formulated and observed. This is still true because human beings are still biologically hunters. Each of us has his group of intimates among whom he can relax, and he deals with other people in a more formal manner.

The institutions that arose as culture increased in complexity grew up around specific patterns of activity, such as teaching, manufacturing, trading, and attending religious meetings. The band expanded into the tribe and the tribe into a nation, the nation into an empire, the empires into leagues, and the leagues into the United Nations, until at the same time that the earth's cancer-crisis had arrived, the peoples of the earth were on the verge of becoming a single nation. Which would come first, destruction or union, was already a moot question in 1960.

The acceleration of culture was itself speeded up in the last third of the nineteenth century when science, which had been the toy of ecclesiastics and of academicians, was made to serve industry, which had formerly been in the hands of artisans. The marriage of science and technology, which was consummated after the former had been separated from religion and from academic protocol, made science grow, until man came to understand the physical nature of the earth and stars, and to grope toward an understanding of the immutable laws that govern the universe, something which intuitive men had approached from time immemorial and had expressed in symbols suited to the ages in which they had lived. A climax in science thus approached at the same time as the climaxes in earth-destruction and social structure; the three peaks were part of a single picture.

All of this shows that human history has followed a number of natural laws. One is the biological law that once a species has evolved, it will not change into another species for a long time. That is why the biological capacities of man are geared to the life of a hunter, and hence why the most satisfactory civilizations are those that permit the full expression of those capacities. Another is the law of least effort, as Henry Adams realized a half-century ago. It is this law that explains the cohesion and internal structure of social systems and configurations of symbols, such as languages. A third law is that of acceleration, or of cumulative increase. Just as a stone falls at a fixed rate of acceleration, so culture piles up in the same fashion. When the stone approaches the ground, a moment of physical climax is at hand. When man's culture outgrows the fixed dimensions of the earth, a moment of human as well as physical climax faces man. What we are going to do about it is the question that the whole world is asking.

Our hope of answering it depends to a certain extent on our understanding of the nature of man and of the steps by which he has arrived at this point of climax. If this book can contribute something toward a beginning of the understanding that is needed in this moment of darkness, I shall be extremely happy, for I too wish to survive the events that lie ahead, and to live in peace with my fellow men of all colors, creeds, and cultures, and with my conscience. But let us get on with the narrative. Whatever its outcome, the story of man, being unique and dramatic, is well worth the telling.

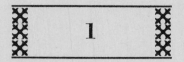

THE EARLIEST MEN

Four Phases of History

H U M A N history falls naturally into four phases. In the first, five races of an extinct form of man, *Homo erectus,* inhabited the land surfaces of the Old World south of the winter frost line, except in China, where one race dwelt north of it. By the time phase one began, these men had already learned to make recognizable tools and probably to speak, and before long some of them had learned to keep warm with fire and to cook food. By the middle of this phase at least one race of Homo erectus had evolved into a race of our present species, and before it was over Homo erectus had vanished from the earth. This was essentially a biological phase of history, in which the possession of a superior capacity for culture gave *Homo sapiens* a decisive immediate advantage, and an opportunity for the future.

In phase two, man learned to dress skins and to sew warm clothing. Now he moved into the rich hunting grounds that covered the cold parts of the Old World, and crossed Bering Strait into the Americas. Unlike other animals, he occupied all zoological realms. Toward the end of this phase of history he invented the bow and arrow and domesticated a hunting companion, the dog. Now that hunting was easier than before, he had time to begin specializing in arts and crafts, and his skill grew. During this period man's biological make-up still needed to be perfect for food-getting, but nature and culture were in balance.

In the third phase he tamed the barnyard animals, began cultivating plants, invented pottery, built wagons, smelted copper, invented writing, and embarked on a rapid sequence of cultural advances that moved swiftly to horses, iron, money, cannon, printing, deep-water ships, coke, steam engines, electricity, and all of the modern inventions that have led us into the global travel, communications, and trade of the present day. During this phase he wasted the materials of the earth and found the means to destroy it and himself. Culture ran rampant at nature's expense and to the peril of nature, culture, and man himself. At the end of phase three nearly all previous stages of human culture coexisted.

We now stand on the threshold of phase four of history, faced with a triple choice. Either the world will be destroyed, or nature will regain its balance at man's expense, or man will restore nature without loss of his cultural heritage when he learns to unify the cultures of the world, just as his ancestor made man a single species. As he unified the human species at the highest biological level then in existence, so must we unify man at the highest cultural level existing today, or evolution will come to an end.

Our story starts at the beginning of the Ice Age, about seven hundred thousand years ago. Phase one consumed over six hundred and fifty thousand years, or over ninety per cent of the known span of human history. The second phase began during the fourth glacial advance and lasted over twenty thousand years; the third, now ending, began about 7000 B.C. and took less than two per cent of the whole. No one knows how long the fourth phase will take.

This chapter and Chapter Two are concerned with the first, longest, and least known of the three completed phases of history. In it human beings acquired the basic habits of dealing with one another which still guide the behavior of individuals, communities, and nations. These habits are human nature, which can best be understood by learning how it came into being. But first we must tell how our human ancestors evolved out of apes, through an earlier form of two-legged primates, the Australopithecines.

Adventure on the Ground

M o r e than thirteen million years ago, long before the first appearance of man on earth, his remote tree-living ancestors took their first step in a human direction. They came to the ground. Although monkey-like in bodies and limbs, these ancestors were ape-like in the form of their molar teeth, but they had short, blunt canines, suitable for fighting and shearing. Our ancestors' teeth were suited mainly for grinding.

Somewhere in the tropical regions of the Old World, probably in Africa, a band of these ancient animals lived in a forest. Every morning at daybreak they awoke, and the males began calling to their families to follow them to the feeding grounds. There they spent most of the day, picking fruit, peeling and eating it, and robbing birds' nests of their eggs and fledglings. As time went on, however, the fruit became scarcer, and when the animals tried to move to another part of the forest they found their way blocked. Every way that they turned they came to the edge of the trees, and all about them was grass. They were trapped. As the fruit and fledglings failed them, they had no choice but to climb down to the ground.

In their frantic search for food they learned to lift up stones to collect insects and grubs, and to dig ground squirrels and moles out of their burrows. Having acquired a taste for meat, they came to relish the flesh of antelope and of other large hoofed animals that grazed on the plain, but all that they could catch with their own hands were helpless fawns, newborn and abandoned when their mothers were startled by lions. While the beasts of prey raced after their fully grown victims, the apes quickly snatched up the helpless fawns, avoiding vultures, hyenas, and other scavengers with which they had begun to compete for such easily gathered meat. Life on the ground was as dangerous as it was exciting. In the trees they had feared only falling and the snake. On the ground their only primate competitors were monkeys, the ancestors of the baboons, which still run about on all fours, lifting stones, picking berries, nibbling buds and shoots, and stealing an occasional baby antelope.

Meanwhile other apes that had come down to the ground with our ancestors found their way back to the shrinking border of the forest where they climbed back into the trees, and some of them evolved into the living apes. Only the ones that stayed in the open grew to be Australopithecines, and some eventually became men.

In certain ways the baboons resemble us more than the apes do, but only because the apes are very specialized in locomotion. Our chemistry is more ape-like than monkey-like in many details, such as the transfusion blood-groups and the amino acids excreted in our urine. At one stage the fetus of a chimpanzee has a foot resembling a man's in that its great toe points forward for walking rather than sidewise for grasping. Only as it approaches its birth size does its foot acquire the appearance of a hand. At no stage does the human foot resemble an ape's. The chimpanzee fetus has hair on its head like a man, and human-style eyebrows.

The apes, then, have changed more in certain respects than we have. They have specialized in forest living, while we can live in many environments. All along the evolutionary line our ancestors remained unspecialized in all but those features that prepared them for human living, in forests and on grasslands, plains, and mountains. As we know from the histories of extinct reptiles, birds, and mammals, lack of specialization is the key to survival and to success in competition with other kinds of animals.

When man first appeared in the world, he possessed five special features, some old and some new, and some a combination of both, which gave him the chance to become master of the earth. These were his erect posture, his free-moving arms and hands, his sharp-focusing eyes, a brain eventually capable of fine judgment and decision as well as of keen perception, and the power of speech. All of these he shared to some extent with the monkeys and apes, but the total combination was his alone, and this combination of gifts became in itself something unique.

On Standing Erect

W H I L E they are resting or on the lookout for foes, tree-living monkeys sit up straight in the branches, and baboons, perched on rocks, do the same. Not long ago I visited a lady baboon in the Philadelphia Zoo. She had recently given birth to a son. While the mother rested on the floor of the cage, the baby walked over her body, hopped to a shelf, and walked along this to its end. This baboon had not yet been taught to run on all fours. At this early age he was experimenting with the posture and gait of men.

Habits like sitting erect and now and then taking a few steps on his hind limbs alone gave man's ancestor a foretaste of the erect posture, but to give up running on all fours forever was a much more serious thing. It was as great an adventure as that of bats when their ancestors first took off in flight in the murk of some ancient cave, or of the first seals that slid off the wet rocks to feed and to sleep in the water, returning to the shore only to breed and to give birth to their young. In many respects man's shift to erect walking is comparable to the development of organs of flight in birds. In both birds and men the fore and hind limbs have grown different from each other in form and in use. This is rare among vertebrates. Both birds and men have to teach their young how to move about, birds by flying and human beings by walking.

When the primates who left the forest long ago began to adapt themselves to life on the ground, they moved into more than one kind of terrain. Some of them went to live in rocky places, as the Barbary apes and baboons still do. They are climbers, having substituted cliffs for trees. From their stony perches they can look out over the landscape in search of something to eat. But our ancestors had no fangs. They could kill only with weapons. Weapons must be made with tools, and tool-making requires planning and learning. Planning and learning need brain power superior to that of most primates. Tool-making places a premium on a good brain, and hunting with weapons affected posture, because an animal holding weapons has to run erect. If he wants to carry his tools, weapons, and meat away from the scene of action, he must also learn to walk and to stand erect. So tool-making may have touched off the chain of events that led to the erect posture.

Now that he had changed his habits of position and motion, he had to acquire a number of new features through the modification of old ones. An arched spinal column became S-shaped, and a weak pelvis grew strong enough to support the weight of the entire trunk, head, and upper limbs. His legs had to grow longer, straighter, and stronger, and his feet had to become so stiffened

and strengthened that they could sustain the weight of his entire
body on lengthy journeys. Once he had become a hunter, as the
ancestors of the apes never did, there was no turning back. From
then on these changes had to be made rapidly, like the growth of
the first bird's wings, or we would not be here.

Free-Moving Arms and Grasping Hands

STANDING and walking erect freed man's hands from the
burden of locomotion. In this respect he gained an advantage over
the birds, bats, and sea mammals, whose forelimbs, converted into
wings and flippers, were still not free. They had merely traded
walking for flying and swimming. Of all the creatures only man
has hands exclusively devoted to work, to signaling, to folding
in prayer, and to the hundreds of other things he does with them.
As in the case of erect posture, this great step had a primate beginning. When not climbing or walking, apes and monkeys use
their hands for picking up objects, feeding themselves, and groom-
ing one another.

The human arms and hands can be rotated in two nearly complete and overlapping spheres. By moving his arms a man can
reach anything within arm's length above, beside, behind, or in
front of him, and by a flip of the wrist he can turn his palm up or
down. No matter what the position of his hand in relation to the
forearm, he can open and contract his fingers. Holding an object
in one hand, he can work on it with the other. No other primate
fully shares these abilities. If the finest of contemporary engineers
were to sit down for weeks to design a perfect tool for grasping
and for fine manipulation, they could come out with nothing
better than the human hand.

Sharp-Focusing Eyes

A MAN cannot, however, work with an object held in his hand
unless he can see it clearly and in fine perspective. We are able to

do this because of our direct inheritance of primate vision. Primates need good eyes to be able to know where they are and where they are going. Tropical forest trees are very tall. If a monkey misses a hand hold and falls out of the branches that form his highroad, he may drop more than a hundred feet, and to his death. This is natural selection of the strictest category. What is good for monkeys in trees is even better for men on the ground.[1]

In the trees the most important aspect of primate vision is its stereoscopic quality: the fact that the two eyes are placed side by side and pointed in one direction. The images of the two overlap, and as the eyes themselves are separated, the slight difference of angle between their axes brings the combined image out in bold relief. Thus the monkey can see where to grip with his hands and feet. If he picks a fruit and holds it up to peel it with his teeth, he can focus sharply on it while holding it a foot or so beyond his nose. He focuses the center of the image on a pair of sensitive spots, one in the base of each eye, and can look the fruit over for defects. Because the center of each eye records color, he can tell if it is ripe. In order to focus on an object held in the hand as close as this, his eyes have to converge a little, making him momentarily cross-eyed. Overlapping images, focusing on a pair of sensitive spots, color vision, and the ability to become slightly cross-eyed when necessary are essential features of human vision, making it possible for man to work and to read. In this one feature he is no better equipped than a monkey, who could work and read too if he had the rest of man's special biological equipment.

A Reasoning Brain

O f this the essential part is a mass of pallid gray material packed into the skull like a sheet of sponge rubber into a football casing. Laid out on a dissecting slab, a human brain looks much less im-

[1] Binocular vision is primarily adapted for fine perception within hand reach, while the judgment of distance depends on the perception of such details as differences of texture. See Gerhardt von Bonin, "The Isocortex of Tarsius," *Journal of Comparative Neurology*, Vol. 95, No. 3, December 1951.

pressive than a heart or even a kidney, which may be why the ancients thought the heart, rather than this inconspicuous organ, to be the seat of the intelligence and emotions. Although we know better, we still have much to learn about how brains work.

When we place a monkey's brain on the slab beside a man's, we see little difference in over-all shape. This is because in both specimens the brainstem, in which automatic actions are controlled, is developed to take care of the special movements of the primate eye, shared by monkey and man, and because the cerebellum is particularly developed to provide for the fine balance that both arboreal life and erect walking require.

It is the size, rather than the shape, of man's brain, both absolutely and in relation to his body bulk, that makes it unique. Several Dutch neurologists who have done much research on this problem have come to the conclusion that the brains of mammals have evolved by a repetitive process of doubling the number of their gray cells.[2] In the brain-to-body size ratio, computed on this basis and corrected by special formulæ for all sorts of outside factors such as total body size itself, they fit all mammals into five progressive classes of brain development. Modern man alone occupies the top berth. When he began the process of becoming human, he started on the same level as some of the other primates, a notch below his present position.

There can be little doubt that the skills his hands and eyes began to acquire with the onset of cultural life placed a premium on a capacity for intelligence, and hence on a larger brain. The larger brain size is more suited to the needs of a cultural being than the smaller because it gives more free space for association, doubt or hesitation, and creative thought. However, the enlargement of the association area which went with an increase in total brain size slowed down the learning process of the youthful primate, and increased the length of time the infant was obliged to remain dependent on its parents. At birth the human brain is only twenty-three per cent of its adult size, while among the apes the

    [2] The key reference to this field is: S. T. Bok, "Cephalization and the Boundary Values of the Brain and Body Size in Mammals," in *Proc. Kon. Ned. Akad. v. Wetenschap*, Amsterdam, Vol. 13, 1939, pp. 512–25.

figures are: forty per cent for the orang, forty-five for the chimpanzee, and fifty-nine for the gorilla. These ratios help explain why the baby chimpanzee learns more rapidly than a human child until the time arrives when the human infant has begun to talk, and thus to learn primarily by speech communication rather than by visual stimuli.

The more simply an animal lives, the sooner it needs to be relieved of the care of its young, and the sooner its young needs to be able to shift for itself. Man did not permanently acquire a full-sized brain until he had gone far enough along the cultural path to be able to nurse his big-brained children, who must have seemed to him slow and stupid, long enough to permit their survival into maturity. It is quite possible that more than one big-brained strain arose and died out before this mutation had occurred in a population able to preserve it and to take advantage of its capacities.

The Power of Speech

No matter how large a creature's brain, he would be unable to do what we call thinking unless he had in the meantime learned to talk. The second ability cannot have lagged overlong, however, for—like the habit of sitting erect, the possession of the opposable thumb and fine vision, and like the shape of the brain itself—the germ of speech went back to life in the trees. If you live in the country, the noises that awaken you are usually the songs of birds. If you sleep within a few blocks of the Washington Zoo, it may be the liquid reveille of the male gibbon, his throat blown out like the skin of a bagpipe, which you hear. Creatures that live in the trees or fly in the air can afford to be noisy, for they have no enemies to fear except the snake, which can detect their presence by the warmth of their bodies, whether they are noisy or silent. Unless they have been long under man's protection, like the sheep, or fear no rivals, like the lion, ground-living animals that break into sound do so only on special occasions, such as mating time, when the sex urge overcomes the instinct for self-preservation.

By these chirpings and roarings animals communicate with one another. They can warn and command, but they cannot transmit past experience. Among the most competent of vocalists are the gibbons, whose vocabulary has been shown to possess at least nine sets of sounds with specific meanings. Sound number one: "Keep away from my wife!" Sound number two: "Let's go get some fruit!" These are simple imperatives. Because of the superiority of the human brain,[3] human languages include much larger vocabularies and more complex ideas, expressed in units known as words. Not only do we speak and hear words, but we produce them silently when we think. The kind of thinking which creates culture is the use of words. Without words one is without communicable thought. The earliest forms of human speech must have begun when man's brain had no more intellectual capacity than that of a gibbon, capable only of a few commands and warnings, and limited entirely to immediate interpersonal relations. Qualities of objects of various classes, such as safe and dangerous, large and small; ways of referring to other persons, such as husband and wife, father and son, in their absence; and methods of expressing the idea that a given action has been finished, rather than left incomplete—these mechanisms of expression must have followed, with the eventual addition of further abstractions.

From what we have learned of the systems of communication of the most primitive living peoples, we know that each language is a complete and satisfactory system of communication which faithfully mirrors the cultural needs of those who speak it. Only situations that those particular people are likely to face can be readily expressed. All languages, nevertheless, are so constructed that growth is possible. As a culture changes, new words are added and old ones lost or given new meanings. As a culture becomes more complex, its grammar is likely to grow simpler to permit more rapid change.

For our present purpose the most important thing to know about language is that it enables human beings to exchange cultural experiences and thus to create more culture. Culture can accumu-

---

[3] Whether or not man's organs of speech are superior to those of some of the lower primates is under debate.

late because language is capable of change. Language can change because its center lies in the association area of the brain, where the increase in brain size, the last vital change in human evolution, gave it room for expansion.

The five gifts that man received from nature during his early formative period gave him superior powers of transportation, in his legs and feet; of communication, in his brain and organs of speech; and of work, in his hands, eyes, and brain. During man's entire history his steady progress in transport, communication, and handling materials has let him rise to the mastery of the world.

Of Chewing and Fighting

O F almost any organ of the bodies of men and other mammals it may be said that it serves more than one purpose. Long before he began to talk, man's ancestor was using his mouth for eating and his teeth for fighting. The teeth of tree-living monkeys are simple and unspecialized compared to those of a beaver or horse, for their principal use is neither felling trees nor cropping grass, but chewing relatively soft food placed in their mouths by their hands. Both the apes and monkeys who left the forest to live on the ground soon were obliged to chew tougher foods such as raw roots and meat. Because they still fed themselves with their hands, no change in the shape of their teeth was needed, but only in the size. Thus the teeth of baboons are larger than those of their cousins in the trees. Without question man's ancestors acquired large teeth for the same reason.

Every primate, including man, uses four pairs of muscles for chewing his food, not counting the muscles that open the jaw and operate the tongue. The longest and strongest, which is the temporal, pulls the jaw straight upward. The masseter, a shorter but very strong muscle attached to the outside of the jaw, not only helps the temporal with up-and-down motion, but is also, on account of its position, able to produce some side-to-side and front-and-back movement. Sidewise motion is the principal task of the internal pterygoid, a muscle concealed inside the neck which connects the jaw to the back of the palate, while the external pterygoid, smallest of the four, thrusts the jaw forward.

By using these four muscles, the primates that have unspecialized teeth are able to move the working surfaces of their lower teeth against those of the uppers in a combination up-and-down, back-and-forth, and side-to-side motion eminently suited for reducing their food to the proper state for digestion. Those of us who have what our dentists call perfect occlusion share this motion with the tree-dwelling monkeys, and the chances are good that our remote ancestors who first came to the ground did too.

The ground-living monkeys and the apes, however, cannot move their jaws freely forward and sidewise because of an obstruction. As their chewing has to be largely up and down, they need bigger teeth than the rest of us to do a given amount of work. The obstruction consists of one specialized tooth on either side of the mouth, the upper canine, or eyetooth. While the rest of the teeth of the two jaws meet each other in line, each upper canine overlaps two lower teeth in such a fashion that whenever the mouth is closed this special tooth sharpens itself on the others. This action gives it two permanently knife-like edges. Although these fangs are also used by the chimpanzees for peeling the tough rinds of large tropical fruits, they provide all of the apes and baboons with pairs of deadly weapons for fighting. Even a spidery gibbon can inflict a nasty cut on a zoo-keeper's hand, and it can kill a rival for its mate's attentions by slashing its jugular with quick thrusts of these dental daggers. Among the baboons and larger apes the canines are even more deadly; in fact the male orang has developed a kind of armor, in the form of a thick leathery collar about his face and neck, to protect himself against them.

It seems likely that the ancestors of the apes and those of the baboons acquired these fighting canines after they came to live on the ground, where for the first time they encountered natural enemies to fight with, and where they developed a harem type of social organization unlike that of tree-living monkeys. As with walruses, deer, and other kinds of mammals that quarrel over females, natural weapons soon appear to help the stronger and more aggressive males rid themselves of their rivals.

We cannot be certain whether or not our ancestors ever grew these built-in stilettos, but if they did they lost them once they had learned to defend themselves with sticks and stones, reserving their jaws for the less colorful but commoner business of mastication. This does not mean that our simian ancestors were any less aggressive than those of the apes; they were only less specialized and brighter.

Fossil Apes

W H I L E this study of teeth has been based on those of living monkeys, apes, and men, that is not the limit of our evidence. The remains of fossil primates, including Australopithecines, have been found in Europe, Africa, Asia, and Indonesia. Among these remains teeth are particularly numerous, because tooth enamel lasts longer in the earth than bone. Some of the species that have been described so far are known through teeth alone. Those that have a bearing on the immediate evolution of the apes and men go back to the Miocene and Pliocene divisions of Cenozoic time, which began (roughly) twenty-five and thirteen million years ago.

One such extinct primate was Proconsul, who lived in East Africa. He came in three species: gibbon-sized, chimpanzee-sized, and gorilla-sized. His canines were long, and his limb bones so shaped that he had apparently just begun returning to the trees, swinging hand over hand. Another, Sivapithecus of northern India, known to us only from teeth and jaws, had canines nearly as short as man's, and a rudimentary chin. While these two species come closest of any yet unearthed to our idea of the ancestors of apes and men, many others fall into the same general class. Among them was Oreopithecus, a stocky ape who lived in the swamps of central Italy. His brain was chimpanzee-sized, his canine teeth of moderate length. But his other teeth differed from man's in many details. His position on the primate family tree is undecided. At any rate, evolution was working overtime during the Miocene and Pliocene among the primates. One of these apes, or one like them, sired the two-legged, large-toothed man-apes of the Early Pleistocene. Among them, without much doubt, were our ancestors.

The Pleistocene or Age of Ice

T H E Pleistocene epoch began about one million years ago and lasted until about eight thousand years before the Christian era. Mountains rose rapidly and the earth cooled off. Climatic differences between the tropics and the lands far from the equator were intensified. The earth had entered a period of climatic pulsations, in marked contrast to the peaceful sameness of the Miocene and Pliocene. The cold that flowed down from the poles and high places drove before it whole galaxies of mutually dependent plant and animal life. Near the equator itself, wet forest shrank into grassland and grassland withered to desert, the procession reversing itself as more rain fell. During the first half of the epoch local glaciers formed on the newly raised mountain chains, on the Alps, Himalayas, and Rockies. At the beginning of the Middle Pleistocene, a half million years ago, great icecaps formed on the land masses of Greenland, Scandinavia, and Antarctica. From Greenland the ice sheet crawled westward and southward to cover much of Canada and the northeastern United States. From Scandinavia it blanketed northwestern Europe, while from Antarctica it had nowhere to go, and tumbled into the sea.

Three times the ice sheets advanced, and three times they melted. Each time that they came forward, the ice on the center of the sheets piled up to a thickness of several miles. Much of the earth's water was thus immobilized, and the oceans of the world shrank to about three hundred feet less than their present depth, baring shorelines now under water. Each time they melted, the oceans filled again, and the waters lapped at shorelines now on dry land. Some of this sea water frozen on high shores is still trapped on top of Greenland and Antarctica. Since the end of the Pleistocene, when the ice last retreated, minor shifts in climate have raised and lowered the shorelines as much as six feet.

This alternating succession of glacial and interglacial periods gives us a timetable on which to measure the goings and comings of the various kinds of men who lived through the best part of a million years of history. While the time span was too short for the

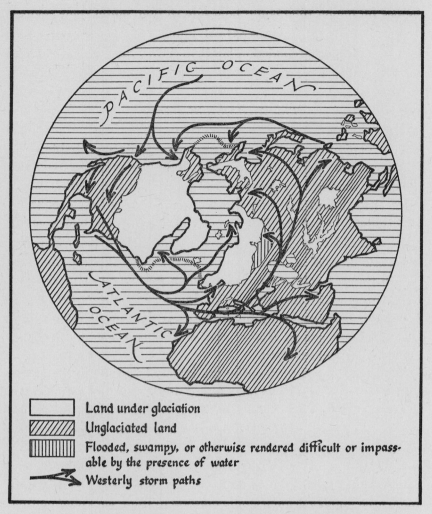

Land under glaciation

Unglaciated land

Flooded, swampy, or otherwise rendered difficult or impassable by the presence of water

Westerly storm paths

ESTIMATED MAXIMUM EXTENT OF THE LAST (WURM) GLACIATION IN THE NORTHERN HEMISPHERE. *After Flint, Movius, and other sources*

evolution of most lines of animals, the climatic changes of the Pleistocene drove them about from continent to continent, so that in each place the sequence of arrivals and departures provides a local schedule for dating human skeletons and the cultural remains of man. These changes also stimulated human beings who found themselves living in a variety of climates to invent new tools and devices by which they could continue to live, while their bodies responded to new conditions of heat, light, and dampness after the fashion of all warm-blooded animals, and thus races were created.

The Australopithecines

A T the beginning of the Pleistocene epoch it is probable that several genera and species of erect, man-like primates were in existence, sharing the parts of the earth's surface which were warm enough and rich enough in game and vegetable foods to keep them alive. As the Pleistocene period wore on, new species arose, and old ones disappeared. Some may have been trapped in pockets of cold or desiccation caused by the climatic changes then in progress. Others may have been pushed to extinction by competition with more competent human or sub-human rivals. Still others were absorbed by mixture. At the end of the Pleistocene only one genus, *Homo,* and of this one species, *sapiens,* is known to have survived.

It appears logical to describe the kinds of fossil man-like creatures and men which have been found in Pleistocene deposits, not in the order of their known or suspected geological age nor in that of the dates of their discovery, but in their order of evolutionary progression, because this is the order in which they evolved in earlier times. When a whole group of animals is represented by a single specimen or by a small number of specimens taken from a single area and covering a single episode in time, we know neither when this group came into being nor when it became extinct. Unless it is still alive, we know only that it existed in that place at that time. It would be stretching the law of chance to the breaking point to suppose that every fossil species found had evolved immediately before the life span of the one individual out of millions which happened to be preserved for posterity, or that it passed into extinction immediately afterward.

Because of its climatic alternations the Early Pleistocene was a time of rapid evolution among mammals, particularly the large ones—elephants, horses, oxen, and camels—and some of the middle-sized ones—the apes and two-legged primates. Only one species of large mammal alive today is left over from the Pliocene, the hippopotamus. Only two species first appeared after the end of the Early Pleistocene, the spotted hyena and Homo sapiens. Modern horses, stags, reindeer, and rhinoceros were in existence a half million years ago. The first recognizable man, Homo erectus, goes back to the beginning of the Middle Pleistocene. Before that, all we know of our own line is a group of man-apes, the Australopithecines, some of which resembled man more than others did.

The oldest man-ape yet found left the braincase and piece of face discovered by a Frenchman, Yves Coppens, in the central Sahara, near Lake Chad, in 1961. Its brain was small, its face large, and its anatomical details are said to be the closest to man's of any known Australopithecine. Its antiquity is certified by the presence, in the same deposit, of a very ancient elephant that can have lived no later than the dawn of the Pleistocene.

Next in probable age are two specimens. One is a piece of skull and a tooth from the Jordan Valley, near Lake Tiberias, in Israel, discovered in 1959. It is undescribed. The second, found in 1960, is a broken skull, jawbone, foot, and finger bones of a fourteen-year-old child, excavated in Olduvai Gorge, Tanganyika, Central Africa. Both these finds were accompanied by crude stone tools and the remains of small game, indicating that these man-apes had not yet begun full-scale hunting. The Olduvai youth's foot suggests that he had begun to walk erect, but his finger bones are flattened like those of tree-borne apes. His brain was as large as those of the largest apes, although his body was pygmy-sized. His teeth were essentially human, but large. He and his Palestinian contemporary may have lived some seven hundred thousand years ago.

The first relic of the man-apes to be recognized as such was found in South Africa in 1924. It was a child's skull. Raymond Dart, who described it, called it Australopithecus, the Southern Ape, whence the name Australopithecine for the whole sub-family. Since 1924 South African workers have found dozens more, cemented by water action in the fill of caves and crevices in the Transvaal. They come in two sizes. The earlier ones are small,

like the Olduvai child, the latter ones as large as full-grown men.
We do not know their exact age, but the smaller ones are perhaps
as old as the Olduvai child, and the larger ones came later, living
toward the end of the Early Pleistocene and even into the Middle
Pleistocene, when true men caused their extinction. Tools have
been found only with the later group.

Back in Olduvai Gorge, Tanganyika, Lewis Leakey, who has
been digging there for over thirty years, found, in 1959, the skull
of one of the large man-apes directly over the child's skeleton.
He called the specimen Zinjanthropus, or East African man. In
Java, in a deposit also containing human remains and dated at
the turning point between the Early and Middle Pleistocene,
Ralph von Koenigswald discovered the first of three known pieces
of oversized jawbone which probably belonged to a man-ape
similar to those in Africa. If this is true, other Australopithecines
must eventually turn up between Palestine and Java.

The earliest of these animals, those from Chad, Olduvai, and
South Africa, are more human-looking than the latest ones, at
least in Africa. Their teeth are more like ours, while their successors' teeth are specialized for grinding coarse, gritty food, such
as roots. Also the big ones had no larger brains, in proportion to
body size, than had the small ones, and both were equally poor
hunters. The only conclusion that we can draw from still fragmentary evidence is that Homo erectus, who first appeared in the
Middle Pleistocene, is more likely to have been descended from
the early Australopithecines than from the late ones, where and
when we do not know. We know only that by five hundred thousand years ago he had taken their place in the Old World tropics,
and the Australopithecines were on the road to extinction.[4]

[4] On July 22, 1961, the National Geographic Society announced a date of
1,750,000 years old for Zinjanthropus, based on the argon-potassium method of
analysis. This date has since been invalidated by tests made in Heidelberg, Germany, on the basalt underlying the Olduvai deposits. They are 1,300,000 years
old. The old volcanic soils in which Zinjanthropus lay may have been secondarily
deposited. Now we are back where we started.

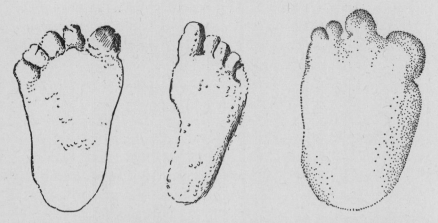

FOOTPRINTS OF THE NEANDERTHAL, CRO-MAGNON, AND ABOMINABLE SNOWMAN. SNOWMAN PRINT WAS FOUND IN SNOW BY ERIC SHIPTON, THE OTHERS IN CAVE MUD BY BARON ALBERTO BLANC.

Of Giant Apes and Snowmen

I n the 1930's, Ralph von Koenigswald, who discovered the first man-ape jaw in Java and some human remains to be described shortly, combed the Chinese drugstores of several Oriental cities, in search of fossil teeth. For centuries the Chinese have used the bones of fossil animals to cure their ills, in the belief that courage, strength, and virility come from the powdered remains of large, strong, and potent animals. Their cure for toothache is powdered teeth. Out of thousands of teeth, von Koenigswald found, in Hong Kong, six of particular interest.

They are human-like in form, but six times as large, in volume, as those of living men. Between the stubs of the roots, gnawed by cave porcupines, he detected powdered yellow earth, which told him that the teeth had come from caves near the Yangtze gorges. He called the animal to whom the teeth had belonged Giganto-pithecus, the giant ape. For years some paleontologists believed that Gigantopithecus was an ancestor of man, but in the late 1950's Chinese scientists found three jaws of this animal, which was an aberrant ape. It lived in the Pleistocene, too late to be our ancestor.

An even more famous and fabulous animal is the Yeti, or

Abominable Snowman. His tracks have been found in snow and mud in the Himalayas, and he has been reported as far north as Mongolia. Eyewitnesses have described him as tall, two-legged, tawny-coated, maned, big-muzzled, and big-toothed. Several expeditions to Nepal and Soviet Central Asia have failed to find this elusive animal, whose numerous tracks are so far unique. Even if it turns out to be a primate it is more likely to be a survival of Gigantopithecus than an Australopithecine.

On Classifying Fossil Men

R E T U R N I N G from these evolutionary false alarms to actual specimens of fossil men, we find no agreement of minds as to how the latter shall be classified, and classification is needed before we can understand how each is related to the others. In general, however, there are two schools of thought. One would split all known specimens into four or more genera, as different as cats and lions, and six or more species, as different as horses, zebras, and donkeys. According to this concept Homo sapiens is but one of many species. He appeared about thirty-five thousand years ago and spread rapidly to the corners of the earth, while the other genera and species conveniently disappeared.

The other school calls all fossil men *Homo*, and divides this genus into two successive species, Homo erectus, the earlier one, and Homo sapiens, who evolved out of local groups of Homo erectus at various times and in different places. According to this interpretation, Homo erectus became extinct, not by extermination, but by evolving into someone else—in this case, modern man. In this book I shall follow the second school.[5]

Bits and parts of Homo erectus have been found in Java, China, North Africa, and East Africa. Early fossil remains of Homo sapiens have been found in the same places, as well as in Europe, western Asia, and central Asia. Later ones have turned up in Australia, New Guinea, and America. These fossil men occupied

[5] Full documentation of this point of view, and of the details of human evolution mentioned in the next few sections, may be found in my *The Origin of Races*, Alfred A. Knopf, New York, 1962.

the same regions as the living races of man, who is probably descended from all of them. In other words, each of the major living races—the African Negro, Bushman, Caucasoid, Mongoloid, and Australoid—has had its own evolutionary history, but not one of them has become a separate, local species because no race of man has ever been out of contact with its neighbors long enough to evolve independently.

Homo erectus forms an anatomical link between a still unidentified Australopithecine ancestor and Homo sapiens. As his name implies, he stood and walked erect, but he was not as clever as the wise man, Homo sapiens, or he would still be here. Homo erectus made and used tools, and all of his races eventually used fire. Every specimen yet found in a living site—and not just washed into a mudbank—was mingled with the split bones of adult animals, which he slew and ate.

A moot question in my profession is, how can we tell Homo erectus from Homo sapiens? Not by the bones of his body, from the neck down. We have few such bones of Homo erectus, and most of their peculiarities are racial, not evolutionary. Nor directly by his behavior, which zoologists find important in distinguishing species among other animals, because his social life went unrecorded, and even his tools grade imperceptibly into those of Homo sapiens. But human behavior must have changed during the course of human evolution, or Homo erectus would still be among us. Human behavior has its control tower in the brain, stimulated and tempered by the glands. While little is known of his glands, we have the shell of his brain, the skull. In it differences between the two species are found.

A Homo erectus skull looks like a shallow, narrow dishpan turned upside down. It has everted rims most of the way around, and flaring handles on the forward half of either side. A Homo sapiens skull looks like an inverted, rimless bowl, with flush handles. The rims of an erectus skull consist of three parts: a brow ridge in front, which protects the eyeballs from blows from above; a crest behind, to which powerful neck muscles are attached; and adjoining crests over each earhole which extend to the side and rear. The handles are the bony arches under which powerful temporal muscles are flexed as they raise the jaw.

In the sapiens skull the braincase itself protects the eyeballs because it rises steeply above them. The neck muscles need no

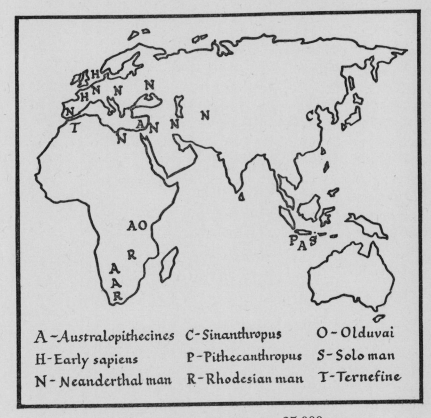

FINDS OF FOSSIL MAN BEFORE 35,000 B.C.

A – Australopithecines	C – Sinanthropus	O – Olduvai
H – Early sapiens	P – Pithecanthropus	S – Solo man
N – Neanderthal man	R – Rhodesian man	T – Ternefine

powerful brace because the head and face are in better balance, and the weaker jaw muscles can do with flatter arches as they need less room to work in.

Inside an erectus skull the brain space is relatively small, ranging from 775 cubic centimeters to 1225 cubic centimeters. The bottom of this range exceeds that of the Australopithecines and the top of it overlaps the span of Homo sapiens, which varies widely from below 1100 cc. to over 1800 cc.

The erectus brain, as revealed by the inner surface of the skull, was flattish at the bottom and only gently curved above. Homo sapiens's brain is more humped in the middle and bent downward at either end. But in the infant erectus skull, the brain is shaped much as in Homo sapiens. This means that while Homo sapiens's brain grows larger than its ancestor's, it retains the infantile form of its ancestor's brain into adult life.

A few erectus skulls also contain the bony seat of the pituitary or master gland, which seems to have been nearly four times as large as in most modern men.

In general, the teeth of Homo erectus are larger than those of Homo sapiens, but not in all cases. What is more critical than tooth size is the ratio between brain size and palate size. This ratio forms a steady progression from the Australopithecines to Homo erectus to Homo sapiens, meaning, on the whole, that the brighter we are, the less we have to chew.

By using a combination of skull shape, brain size, brain shape, and the brain-to-palate ratio, we can usually tell whether a skull was erectus or sapiens, although there are borderline cases, as there should be in any series in which one species is evolving into another.

The History of Homo Erectus

ACCORDING to my diagnosis we have in the world, at the time of writing, a dozen skulls of Homo erectus from the Middle Pleistocene, or five hundred thousand to one hundred and fifty thousand years ago, and also eight others from the Upper Pleistocene, or one hundred and fifty to ten thousand years ago. These figures do not include a number of specimens which are either incomplete or fragmentary, and therefore cannot be diagnosed.

The first erectus skull to be discovered was a skullcap found by a Dutch physician named Eugène Dubois in 1891. It lay in a layer of volcanic tufa deposited by water action in the banks of the Solo River in Java. With it was a diseased thighbone and three teeth, two of which turned out later to have belonged to an orangutan.

During the Middle Pleistocene, roughly three hundred thousand years ago, a volcanic eruption had gassed or otherwise killed an entire local fauna. Then the river washed the bones seaward and deposited them on its flood banks, after which it conveniently buried them in ash. The date was established by identifying the animal bones that accompanied the human remains. Paleontologists know at what part of the Pleistocene different species of mammals became extinct in different regions, and this knowledge gives the student of fossil man a convenient time scale.

Dubois called the new creature *Pithecanthropus erectus,* the erect ape-man. Except for a diseased growth, the thighbone was perfectly modern. Pithecanthropus was man-sized and did indeed walk erect. His brain, however, was small, no more than 900 cc. in cranial capacity, his brow ridges massive, and his forehead sloping.

Forty years later Ralph von Koenigswald resumed the search for remains of Java's Pleistocene population. During the 1930's he found four more Pithecanthropus specimens. Two were skullcaps of the same age and type as Dubois's original find. A fourth was that of a one-year-old infant, eggshell-thin, and the fifth was a massive and brutal skull which he named *Pithecanthropus robustus.* Both it and the infant were older than the other Pithecanthropi. They lived at the very beginning of the Middle Pleistocene, at the same time as the Australopithecine, called Meganthropus, which von Koenigswald found in the same deposit. As the island was then intermittently connected with the Asiatic mainland, it is likely that these creatures populated a wider area than Java itself. If we are lucky someone may find a facsimile of robustus in a late Lower Pleistocene deposit in southeast Asia.

A larger series of the skeletal remains of half-brained men was collected, between 1927 and the outbreak of World War II, in the famous cave of Choukoutien some thirty-seven miles from Peking, by a team of excavators headed successively by Davidson Black and Franz Weidenreich. Pieces of fifteen skulls, seven thighbones, two upper arm bones, one collarbone, and one small bone from the wrist gave Weidenreich enough data to analyze. Because the Chinese government wanted the originals to remain in Peking, Weidenreich carried casts of the specimens with him to New York when he was forced to leave. Soon afterward an attempt was made to ship the originals to America for safekeeping via the S.S. *President Harrison,* but it was too late. The train carrying the bones to the coast was seized by the Japanese, and no one knows what has become of them.

So good were Weidenreich's casts and so assiduous his labors on them in the American Museum of Natural History in New York that before his death in 1948 he had been able to produce a series of definitive monographs which leaves Sinanthropus in the enviable position of being our best-known fossil man. He was probably more heavily built than Pithecanthropus, and his thighbones were more bowed. The marrow canals in the centers of his limb bones were unusually small, and the walls of the bones dense and thick.

The brain of Sinanthropus, known from five more or less complete skullcaps, was larger than that of Pithecanthropus, ranging from 1015 cc. to 1255 cc., while Pithecanthropus's run only from 775 to 900 cc. His skull was as craggy and bony and his teeth as large as those of Pithecanthropus erectus, but in these tokens of brutality robustus outclassed him.

Although all erectus skulls look more or less alike, this is because they all belong to the same general evolutionary grade. Nevertheless certain racial features appear as early as the time of Sinanthropus, about three hundred and sixty thousand years ago. Pithecanthropus's forehead slopes in almost a single plane from the center of his brow ridge to the crown of his head. In Sinanthropus the brow ridge stands out like a shelf and the forehead rises steeply, for a short way, behind it. Also the high cheekbones of the modern Mongoloid were already present in Sinanthropus. Like theirs, his face was flattish.

From China we turn to Africa for our next Middle Pleistocene specimen, a Homo erectus skullcap discovered in Olduvai Gorge by Lewis Leakey in 1960. It lay above Zinjanthropus and the Olduvai child, and is provisionally dated at four hundred thousand years ago. It differs from those of Java and China in one principal respect. Its brow ridges, while equally large, form twin arches over its eye sockets and sweep to the rear on either side. The Javanese and Chinese brow ridges are nearly straight bars of bone.

In the shape of his brow ridges the Olduvai erectus resembles both Caucasoids and Negroes. In North Africa three lower jaws of the same geological age, found at Ternefine, Algeria, were accompanied by one small piece of skull bone which looks like an erectus specimen, but we cannot be sure. No skull of Homo erectus has yet been found in Europe or in western Asia.

Homo erectus vanished from the earth during the latter part of the Upper Pleistocene. In some places he simply evolved into Homo sapiens. In others he may have been killed off by advancing waves of sapiens hunters who were more efficient than he, and in still others he was simply absorbed into the sapiens ranks through mixture. In some parts of the world he lasted longer than in other parts. As might be expected, he survived longest in the out-of-the-way refuge areas, and the most sheltered refuges of our planet lie in the southern hemisphere.

In Java, at a site called Ngandong on the Solo River, eleven braincases and two shinbones were found in 1931 by a Dutch geologist named G. ter Haar. All of the skulls had had their faces cut off and, from all but one, their brains removed. These skulls are given an Upper Pleistocene date, possibly Late Upper Pleistocene, between seventy-five and thirty-five thousand years ago.

The Solo skulls, as they are called, resemble those of Pithecanthropus in shape, but are larger. Their braincases duplicate in size those of Sinanthropus, who lived as much as three hundred thousand years earlier. Either the Solo people were descended from Pithecanthropus, or both Pithecanthropus and Solo were immigrants from the southeastern Asiatic mainland. In either case they were probably related.

The other great refuge area is Africa south of the equator. In 1921 a very late specimen of Homo erectus was brought to light in an open-air mine at Broken Hill, Northern Rhodesia. The miners had dug a section through a hill, in which was a cave. The cave was packed with animal bones, some of which had been brought there by man. At the very bottom of the cave shaft they found human bones. These included one skull complete except for its lower jaw, the upper jaw of a second individual, a sacrum, shinbone, and both ends of a thighbone.

Homo rhodesiensis, or Rhodesian man, as the specimen was named, was a large, heavy-boned man standing about five feet ten and weighing over one hundred and sixty pounds. His leg bones and sacrum were completely modern, and could have belonged to a local Negro. The skull housed a brain of 1280 cc., in the lower half of the modern male size range, and a little large for Homo erectus. The eyebrow ridges are huge, the forehead nearly horizontal, the eye sockets cavernous and square-rimmed, the face extremely long, the nose flattish. His brow ridges are, however, shaped like those of the much earlier Homo erectus from Olduvai Gorge, and his facial configuration is an oversized caricature of the features of living Negroes. While the age of the Rhodesian skull is uncertain, mineral analysis and the accompanying implements indicate that it was probably no more than thirty thousand years old, or even a little younger.

A similar specimen was found in 1953 on the surface of a wind-eroded site near the village of Hopefield, on Saldanha Bay, Cape Province, South Africa. It consists only of a braincase and the corner of a jawbone. Although it adds nothing to our knowledge of Rhodesian man's anatomy, it proves that he was not unique, and helps to date him. The associated animal bones and implements give Saldanha Bay man a date of no more than forty thousand years ago.

Broken Hill man and Saldanha Bay man show no substantial advance over the Olduvai man of the Early Middle Pleistocene. Like Java, Central and South Africa were regions of evolutionary lag during most of the latter half of the Pleistocene. The survival of Homo erectus in these antipodal Edens was not disturbed until no earlier than about thirty thousand years ago, almost a quarter of a million years after the first appearance of Homo sapiens in regions nearer the center of evolutionary activity.

The Rise and Spread of Homo Sapiens

HOMO SAPIENS first appeared in the world at different times in different places. This is only to be expected, because it follows the rules of nature which govern animal life in general. During the Pleistocene, evolution proceeded more rapidly in Europe, west Asia, and China than it did in Java and South Africa, and man was no exception.

The oldest human specimen from Europe is the famous Heidelberg jaw, dug out of a sand pit in west Germany in 1907. It is a heavy, chinless jaw, with teeth of modern size. As no part of the cranium was found with it, we do not know whether to call it erectus or sapiens. Its age is now believed to be about three hundred and sixty thousand years, the same as that of Sinanthropus.

Dated at two hundred and fifty thousand years ago are two skulls which are complete enough to be allocated to a species, and both are primitive examples of Homo sapiens. One is the Swanscombe skull from England, the other the Steinheim skull from Germany.

In 1935 a dentist named A. T. Marston, who is also an amateur archæologist, discovered the whole back portion of a human skull in the second interglacial gravels of the one-hundred-foot terrace of the Thames River at Swanscombe, a few miles downriver from London. Mr. Marston had the great good sense to call for professionals from the British Museum to photograph the specimen in its original setting before removing it from the gravel in which it had lain for a quarter of a million years. Competent geologists determined that the gravel over it had never been disturbed. Subsequent laboratory tests showed that the fluorine content of the bone was the same as that of extinct mammals of that period. The fluorine test was developed in England by Kenneth Oakley in the 1940's to tell whether two fossil bones found in one place are of the same age. It cannot be used for absolute dating because, though fluorine is constantly being laid down in the soil, the rate of its deposition varies greatly in different places.

The Swanscombe specimen is the rear and central portion of the skullcap of a woman, consisting, more specifically, of three bones, the occipital and both parietals. These are enough to show that her brain as well as her skull were of modern size and form. Her cranial capacity was about 1325 cc., near the average for modern European women. We know nothing of her face, forehead, or jaw, but information on these items is supplied by the second skull of that period, that of Steinheim.

The Steinheim skull, found in a gravel pit near Stuttgart in 1933, is complete except for the lower jaw, but it was badly bent and damaged in the soil, and has never been fully restored. The brain size, low for Homo sapiens, is between 1150 and 1175 cc., but it is not too low; many living women have smaller brains. The shape of the skull is completely modern except that it bears a sharp, thin, projecting visor over the eye sockets; this brow ridge would be hard to duplicate among European women today. There is nothing noteworthy about the face and teeth except that the nose was broad.

These two skulls establish the existence of Homo sapiens in Europe a quarter of a million years ago. No sapiens skulls of equal antiquity have been found elsewhere.

Between the date of these skulls and the beginning of the final or Würm glaciation, Europeans changed little from the Steinheim-Swanscombe model. Two female skullcaps from Fontéchevade, France, were notable for a lack of brow ridges. Skulls from Germany, Yugoslavia, and elsewhere had brow ridges. A primitive form of Homo sapiens, one that was European in race, inhabited Europe continuously until the beginning of the first advance of the last ice sheet, about seventy-five thousand years ago. Then the mysterious Neanderthals took their place, but before we discuss them, let us plot the first appearances of Homo sapiens in other parts of the world.

In China the turning point came at about one hundred and fifty thousand years ago. A late Middle Pleistocene skull from Mapa, South China, was still essentially erectus, while an early Middle Pleistocene one from Tze Yang was essentially sapiens. Both bear the racial hallmarks of Sinanthropus and the Mongoloids. After Tze Yang a sequence of a half-dozen other skulls leads us to the Upper Cave people of Choukoutien, who lived near the end of the Pleistocene and were modern Mongoloids.

In Java two skulls from a place called Wadjak, also dated near the end of the Pleistocene, are primitively sapiens and resemble modern Australian aborigines. In North Borneo a fully sapiens

Australoid skull, excavated in Niah Cave, has been dated by
radiocarbon at nearly forty thousand years ago. Farther north, in
southeast Asia, an Australoid kind of Homo sapiens probably
appeared somewhat earlier.

The oldest sapiens skulls from Africa were probably a set of
four which Lewis Leakey excavated at Kanjera, Kenya, in 1932.
They are extremely long and low vaulted, and have no more brow
ridges than Fontéchevade. Racially they seem to be Negro. For
thirty years a controversy has raged over the age of these skulls,
and many attempts have been made to date them by fluorine
tests, comparisons with fauna, and archæological associations.
They are probably Upper Pleistocene and may be contemporary
with Saldanha Bay man, although this is not sure.

In North Africa we have nothing to work with before about
10,000 B.C., when Caucasoids invaded Barbary from either Palestine or Spain, and sired the modern Berbers. Then or a little later
other Caucasoids moved south to the White Highlands of Kenya
and Tanganyika where their possible descendants, the spear-
brandishing Masai, the lordly Watusi, and other lean, thin-nosed
"Hamites" still live. No certain Pleistocene date can be attributed
to the ancestors of the Bushmen and Hottentots. We can only
speculate about who they were and where they originated. South
Africa, their present home, is unlikely because they do not resemble the Rhodesian or Saldanha Bay men. The most plausible
theory today is still the old one that they evolved in North Africa
and were driven south by the Hamites, but this can be neither
proved nor disproved until more digging is done in Barbary.

The Neanderthals

A N equally great mystery is the racial history of the famous
Neanderthals, and the mystery is not lessened by the fact that we
know much about them. At the beginning of the first Würm
glaciation, about seventy-five thousand years ago, they appeared
in western Europe, Italy, the Crimea, Palestine, Iraq, and central
Asia. Because only a very few have been found, despite much

search, in central and eastern Europe, we divide them into two groups, a western and an eastern. In both regions they lived through the first Würm advance, and when the ice retreated momentarily for a ten-thousand-year breathing spell, between forty and thirty thousand years ago, the Neanderthals disappeared, to be replaced by the ancestors of living Europeans and Near Easterners.

Where did the Neanderthals come from, and why did they fade away? The problem can be brought within sight of solution only after we have disposed of the popular image of Neanderthal man, that he was a squat, slouching, low-browed, stupid, and vicious brute, wooing his women by clubbing them over the head and eating his deceased parents.

This misconception began to arise with the discovery of the original Neanderthal skull in west Germany. The Neander, whence the name, is a small watercourse flowing through a handsome little valley in the Rhineland country, near Düsseldorf. There a faceless skullcap was unearthed in a gravel pit in 1856, two years before Darwin announced the theory of evolution.

The time could not have been riper for the discovery of a low-browed skull with massive bony ridges shading what was left of its eye sockets. It was called everything from an ape to a Russian soldier left behind in the Napoleonic Wars. Thus was first created the fantasy of the cave-dwelling brute.

This feral image was reinforced in 1911–13 by the French anatomist-paleontologist Marcellin Boule, who described a nearly complete skeleton of a Neanderthal man unearthed in the cave of La Chapelle-aux-Saints in the Dordogne country. According to Boule, Mr. Neanderthal was a stunted, barrel-chested brute, who walked with his knees permanently bent, his arms reaching forward, and his head thrust out on a short, slanting neck. His skull was long and low, his forehead almost flat, and his huge eye sockets overhung by a beetling, bony visor of continuous brow ridges. His nose (the bones of which had been broken off, presumably to extract the brain) was low and flattened, his jaws protruded in the form of a muzzle, and he had no chin. On broad, stubby feet he shambled about from cave to cave. From such a brute only the most dismal sort of social behavior could be expected.

In 1955, two professors of anatomy, William L. Straus, Jr., of Johns Hopkins and A. J. E. Cave of St. Bartholomew's in London, obtained permission to examine the La Chapelle remains in the Musée de l'Homme, Paris. They found that the skeleton, which had belonged to a male forty to fifty years old, was rotten with arthritis. This disease had affected the hinges of La Chapelle's lower jaw, his neck, and much of his body. The forward thrust of his head noted by Boule was due, in part at least, to a wry neck, and the stunted stature and stooping posture were due to arthritic lesions in his vertebral column. In his youth La Chapelle had been as tall as the average Frenchman living in the Dordogne today.

The western Neanderthals stood up straight and held their heads in a normal position, but they were, as Boule said, stocky, heavy people, with long trunks, deep chests, and short arms and legs. Their forearms and shins were particularly short, as are those of several peoples living in the Arctic today, from Lapland to Greenland, and of the Canoe Indians of Tierra del Fuego. All of these peoples are adapted, in one way or another, to live in the cold, and Neanderthal probably was physiologically adapted to the rigors of life near the edge of the ice.

The heads of the European Neanderthals were also peculiarly shaped, for their skulls were long, wide, and low, looking somewhat drooping or melted down over the ears, like a Dali soft watch. Yet the brains inside were as large as, or larger than, those of most Europeans living today. Their faces were long and drawn forward in the center line; their noses, as we now know, were large and salient; their jaws deep and protruding. Some, like La Chapelle, were chinless, but others, like La Ferrassie, another French specimen, had as much chin as do many living people.

The flatness of their skulls and the protrusion of their jaws have led some anthropologists to consider these western Neanderthals to be a race of Homo erectus which invaded Europe from some unknown cradle-land, supplanting the less hardy sapiens Europeans who had lived there since early in the Middle Pleistocene. This theory is currently popular, but it falls foul of three facts.

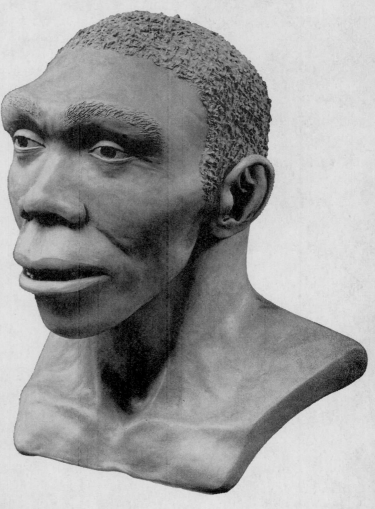

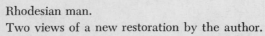

Rhodesian man.
Two views of a new restoration by the author.

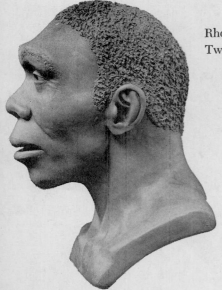

PLATE I

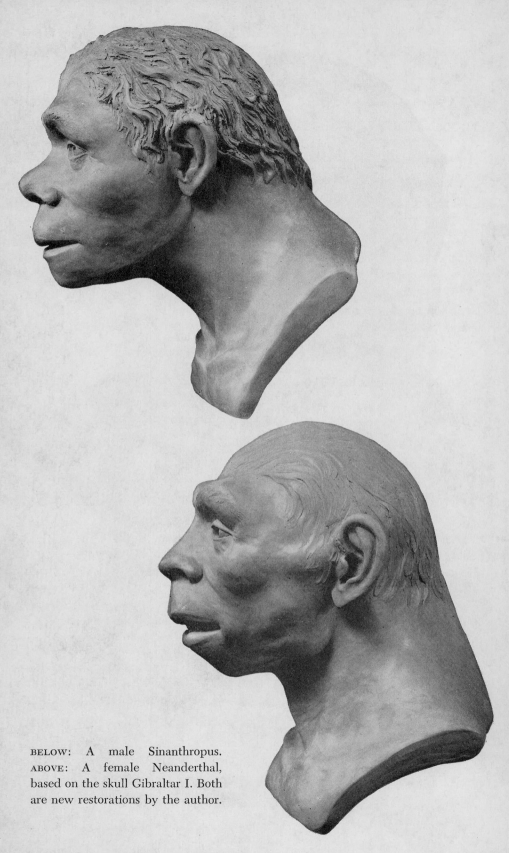

BELOW: A male Sinanthropus. ABOVE: A female Neanderthal, based on the skull Gibraltar I. Both are new restorations by the author.

PLATE II

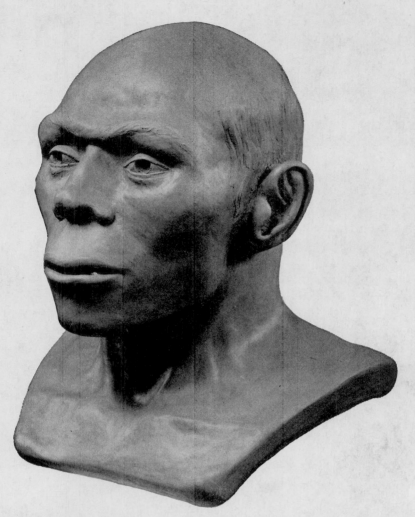

Palestine man. A new restoration of Skhul V, one of
the Neanderthaloids found in the Cave of the Kids at
Mount Carmel. He represents either an evolutionary
stage between Neanderthal and modern man, or a
cross of the two.

In the plastolene reconstructions shown in Plates I, II, and III, the
skulls and jaws were restored, and then the missing portions were
filled in by imagination. Then the muscles were laid on, and finally the
skin and hair were conjured up. The form of the soft parts, including
lips, nose tips, ears, and hair, are wholly conjectural.

PLATE III

The Sorcerer of Lourdes. An Upper Paleolithic
cave painting showing a man disguised as a deer.
After Bandi et Maringer, *L'Art Préhistorique*, with
permission.

PLATE IV

A second-interglacial hand ax. Found on the banks of the Thames, England. Striking testimony to the artistic and technical skill of our ancestors half a million years ago. Height, 5½".

PLATE V

Lower and Middle Paleolithic industries. (1) A flake scraper from the site and period of Swanscombe man. Hgt., 3″. (2) A chopping tool of fossil wood, collected in Burma by Hallam L. Movius, Jr. Hgt., 3″. (3) A Middle Paleolithic core with striking platform and flake scars. Width, 5½″. (4) A double-bladed knife from Bisitun, Iran. Hgt., 2½″. (5) A Neanderthal spear point from the same site. Hgt., 2½″.

PLATE VI

Upper Paleolithic industries. (1) A blade core, Aurignacian, France. Hgt., 4½″. (2) An end scraper on a blade, Turaif, Saudi Arabia. Hgt., 3¼″. (3) A backed blade, France. Hgt., 2¼″. (4) A burin, Turaif, Saudi Arabia. The working edge is up. Hgt., 2″. (5) Bone needles made with burins, France. Hgts., 1½″, 1⅞″, 1¾″.

PLATE VII

Neolithic tools. (1) Blade core. Note half of broken blade still in place. The break spoiled the core. Belt Cave, Iran. Hgt., 4½″. (2) Sickle blade from same site. Shiny streaks at right are silica deposit from cutting wheat. Hgt., 2¾″. (3) Stone chisel, side view. Belt Cave. Hgt., 3″. (4) Flint knife from Scandinavia, resembling Solutrean mammoth-hunters' blades. Hgt., 7¾″. (5) Bone fork from lowest Neolithic level. Belt Cave, about 6000 B.C. Length, 4½″. (6) Polished-stone axhead. Belt Cave. Hgt., 2½″.

PLATE VIII

We know of no erectus populations on the borders of Europe as late as seventy-five thousand years ago. The stone implements which the Neanderthals made were fashioned in the same styles as those of their local predecessors. Some of their predecessors, like the Saccopastore skulls in Italy and the Krapina finds in Yugoslavia, foreshadowed the anatomical peculiarities of the Neanderthals. To this it may be added that the western Neanderthals were efficient hunters, buried some of their dead, and fed a crippled, toothless old man, La Chapelle-aux-Saints, for years after he had stopped bringing in his share of meat to the community. None of the Homo erectus skulls was buried, nor is there any evidence among them of solicitude for the aged and maimed.

In my opinion the bulk of the evidence suggests that the western Neanderthals evolved out of their sapiens predecessors and that they owe their anatomical peculiarity partly to cold adaptation and partly to the fact that they bred for tens of thousands of years in isolation, as a closed community.

The eastern Neanderthals made the same kinds of implements and apparently led similar lives. One skeleton, from Shanidar Cave in Iraq, was that of a man in his late forties who had been born with a withered right arm. Some Neanderthal surgeon had amputated it above the elbow. The cripple had been fed by his fellows until he died, killed by rockfall from the roof of his cave. On the grounds of behavior alone, the Shanidar folk merit the title Homo sapiens.

Despite their cultural similarity they differed from the western Neanderthals in that they were taller and sparer, and their braincases were high and more modern in shape, without the Dali touch. Their faces also had more forehead and more chin. Whatever influences steered the western Neanderthals into their anatomical peculiarities apparently passed their eastern cousins by.

Some of the eastern Neanderthals, particularly those living in Palestine, looked much more modern than the others, and it now seems probable that modern man, as he appeared in Europe at the end of the Neanderthal regime, was descended from those very Near Easterners, or from others like them. It also now appears, in view of recent discoveries, that the western Neanderthals did

not become utterly extinct, but were absorbed by newly established populations of hunters, particularly in Spain and Italy. Although the Neanderthal mystery has not been completely solved,
it is on the way to solution.

An Outline of Early Human History

THE PICTURE that we trace from a study of the scanty remains of man and his erect primate kin from the end of the Pliocene to the melting of the first installment of the Würm ice sheet,
covering nearly a million years, is dependent on too few finds to
warrant full confidence in any fixed scheme of interpretation. Yet
as I write new caves and river-banks are being dug, new information is pouring in, and the general lines of human evolution are
taking shape. We can be a little bolder than we were ten years
ago.

From some kind of a Miocene ape, probably living in Africa,
both living apes and men are descended. The apes' ancestors,
after a trial period on the ground, swung back into the trees. Ours
stayed below, rose onto their hind legs, made tools, walked,
talked, and became hunters.

Our ancestors were probably but one of several erect species,
the Australopithecines, which became extinct about a half million years ago, or a little later, after one of them had evolved into
Homo—man. The first man we know is Homo erectus, who lived
in Java, China, East Africa, North Africa, and probably elsewhere
in the warmer parts of the Old World. Homo erectus was divided
into geographical races, at least five of which were transformed
by standard, evolutionary processes into Homo sapiens, some
races sooner than others.

In this chapter we have concentrated on the biological aspects
of human evolution, but in man biology has been inseparable
from culture ever since our ancestors began to make tools. From
then on natural selection favored those who could use culture to
their best advantage. It is to the cultural aspects of human evolution that we next turn.

2

OF FLINT, FIRE, AND EARLY SOCIETY

O U R study of the bones of slightly over a hundred individuals who lived in Middle and Upper Pleistocene times—and over half of these are of one subspecies, Neanderthal—has led us to a logical reconstruction of the snail-pace course of human history before and during that period. So few are the bones and so dubious the exact dates of many of them that more than one interpretation is possible. It would be an unhappy world if all my colleagues felt obliged to agree with me or I with them. The earth holds many surprises, and we may all be wrong.

Had I only casts, pictures, and descriptions of these bones to work with, I would feel more hesitation than I do in offering this reconstruction. Although early man's bones are scarce, the product of his handiwork is abundant. His basic cutting tools, made of pebbles, quartzite, fossil wood, and flint, run into millions, for they were made of materials less perishable than his bones and more numerous than his bodies. Each person who lived to middle age in that ancient time must have used hundreds or even thousands of them because while the material of which they were made is imperishable it is also fragile. The tools give me confidence. They tell the same story that I have read from the bones. Like the cleverly fashioned hilt on a fine sword, this story fits the less controversial remainder of the story of man, from Late Pleistocene times to the present, which will be told in later chapters.

Early Cutting Tools, a Logical Premise

W E can suppose on logical grounds that some kind of cutting tool was made and used by our ancestors as soon as they had acquired their special combination of erect posture, slender fingers, short canine teeth, and at least a half-sized brain, for the simple reason that human beings are not equipped by nature to live without them. Tools are our substitutes for the lion's fangs and claws, the elephant's trunk, and the long muzzle and special teeth of the grazing animals.

Monkeys who live in trees need no tools because they can pick fruit and rob birds' nests with their hands. Apes do not need them because they live on shoots and stalks, and on fruits, which they can pick by hand and peel with their canines. Baboons do not need tools because they have short, stubby hands with strong fingers and thick nails, and long muzzles with sharp canine teeth. In the deserts where they live, the soil is loose and easy to dig. They can dig their favorite root, called Welwitzia, without trouble, and open up the burrows of gophers, voles, and snakes. They can find other animal food by turning over stones, under which lurk lizards, grubs, worms, insects, and scorpions, hiding from the heat of the sun.

The first tool used by man was probably a pointed stick used to dig out roots and small game. To fell and sharpen a sapling requires a tool with some kind of edge. This tool can be a broken pebble, a piece of fossil wood, which naturally breaks up into rectangular pieces, or, best of all, a piece of broken flint. Scraps of flint may be picked up off the ground or dug out of riverbanks, where early men must have gone to drink and to ambush drinking animals.

When flint is shattered, it has an edge like a broken beer bottle, a disagreeable weapon. It is harder than any metal used before the invention of steel. An arrowhead made of flint will penetrate the flesh of an animal more deeply than a comparable arrowhead made of metal, as was proved by experiments made nearly fifty years ago at the University of California in which the testers hung up sides of beef and shot into them, using the same bow for both kinds of arrow.

Flint usually comes in nodules. Some of these shatter naturally from heat, others are smashed by stones falling from the lips of washed-out banks. Most flints must be broken by dropping a rock.

But in the very beginning, useful flints could, in places, be picked up off the ground ready for service. A little observation would show how the pieces with cutting edges were formed, and the next step was obvious. Drop a rock, break the flint, pick out a piece with a good edge, walk over to a sapling, cut it down, and point its end. After this, throw the flint away, or keep it if you think of it. Now you have a digging stick.

The earliest tools known come from living sites in Africa and Asia. Their date is late Lower Pleistocene. We know they are tools because they are found with broken animal bones. Alleged tools found in gravel banks are hard to tell from naturally fractured stones. The only possible test is to make a statistical analysis of the fracture scars to see whether they follow a pattern or occur at random.

That man could have used unshaped flints for his essential and only cutting tools is more than a theory. Living human beings, members of a tribe in east-central Australia studied and photographed by Charles A. Mountford, do exactly that thing today. Mountford's excellent moving pictures, *Walk About* and *Tsurunga*, establish this fact. With unworked flints these living fossils of mankind make digging sticks, spears, and bark vessels carved in one piece from a kettle-shaped section of tree trunk. There is no logical reason why woodworking of this degree of simplicity may not hark back to nearly the very beginning of man's life on the ground.

With a pointed stick a man can not only dig out roots and burrowing animals: he can brain a tortoise and pry open its shell, and kill a snake, rat, or other small and relatively slow-moving animal. In the simplest surviving societies this is exactly what women still do with sticks. Without reasonable doubt, collecting slow game, as such animals are collectively called, was once part of man's general daily routine of food-gathering, which included root-digging and berry-picking as well. At the beginning of man's cultural life such a routine was probably standard for both men and women. However, in every shift of occupation of which we know throughout history, women have taken over the jobs formerly held by men as the men have moved on to something new and more specialized. Women would keep on collecting slow game long after men had become hunters, devoting their energy and skill to the pursuit of those large and swift ungulates, sheep, goats, deer, oxen, horses, and antelope, those succulent grass-chewers whose flesh still forms a part of our daily diet.

By the time man began true hunting, he had already learned the use of weapons. The same digging stick, a little longer and considerably sharper, could do service as a spear. A man who

WILD OXEN. FRENCH CAVE ART.

spends his whole life casting a simple one-piece spear can become almost incredibly skillful. Natives of Tasmania, who used such weapons, could cast them a distance of forty yards to pass through a knothole in a board even though the hole was less than an inch wider than the thickness of the spear itself. The simple spear made it possible to kill animals weighing over one hundred pounds from a distance that a clever man, creeping upwind, could reasonably reach.

Once he had made his kill, the hunter was faced with the problem of handling the carcass. Let us suppose that we are dealing with very early hunters who had not yet learned to cook, and who were primarily interested in the corpus delicti as a source of food rather than of secondary products such as skins, ivory, antler, horn, or bone. Most of the Pleistocene animals whose bones show evidence of human attention were large. Wild oxen, wild horses, red deer (a close relative of the American elk), the mammoth, are all animals too heavy to be carried off in one piece by man. Either the hunter and his companions were obliged to eat the meat on the spot, or they cut it up to share the load.

In Africa today, when pygmies wound an elephant, they follow it until it dies, and then the whole band—men, women, and children—assemble around the body to eat as much of it as they can while it is still edible. In Tierra del Fuego the Indians from far

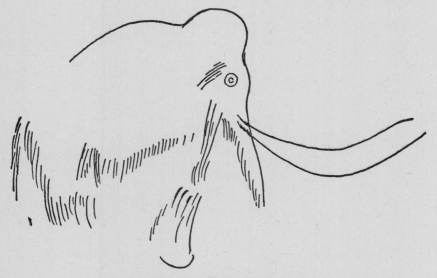

MAMMOTH. FRENCH CAVE ART.

and wide used to collect on the beach to consume the flesh of a stranded whale. Such a banquet can last for several weeks.

Elephants and whales are special cases. The horse, ox, deer, or gazelle is not large enough to warrant moving camp to the site of the kill, which may be too far from shelter and water. Furthermore, the women and children do not accompany hunters. They are off on their own business, gathering vegetable foods and slow game. If they are obliged to drop their work and rush to the scene for a single meal each time an animal is killed, they will gather no vegetable food and will serve no useful purpose in the economy of family life.

A man who is able to make a spear already has cutting tools. If

he can make a scraper he can also produce a knife, or the same
piece of flint will serve both purposes. With his knife he can cut
the animal into quarters and remove the head. Even a dead horse
can be carried home if it is converted into five parcels. Before
shouldering their loads, the hunters can cut out the fat behind the
eyeballs and eat it to give them strength on their journey, along
with the heart, liver, and other soft and easily digested internal
organs, rich in vitamins. This is exactly what living Stone Age
hunters still do. Once in the camp with the women and children,
a man with a knife can divide the meat according to age-old principles of protocol, so that each person gets the share he or she
needs to provide for the maximum survival value of the group.
For an animal such as man, whose teeth are not adapted for shearing and tearing tough raw meat and tendons, some kind of knife
is necessary for efficient eating. For social eating, of which the
essential element is sharing, some kind of cutting tool is needed to
facilitate the division of food, unless the meat is very well cooked
in advance. As man ate meat before he learned to cook it, it is
hard to visualize a human situation that involved hunting in which
knives were not available. Without knives, using this word in its
broadest sense, there could be no human beings.

The Properties of Flint

O N C E human beings had begun deliberately shaping flint into
scrapers and knives, they learned the properties of flint, which is
a kind of impure natural glass not formed, like obsidian, by the
action of heat, but by the mutual attraction of minute particles of
silica scattered in chalk and limestone. In the process of being
drawn together these particles group themselves in concentric
layers, like the growth layers of a pearl, and the outer surface of
the lump or nodule of flint which is thus formed is covered by a
white chalky crust. This outer layer is too soft to furnish a cutting
edge; it must be removed as a prelude to professional tool-making.
These nodules vary in size from that of a chestnut to that of a
pumpkin, and hence the maximum size of tools made in any re-

gion is dependent on the size of the available flint. While one finds many irregular nodules, some of which resemble freak potatoes, the basic form is globular.

To break a nodule of flint into pieces that can be further modified into tools, the tool-maker strikes the surface of the material with some kind of hammer, such as a pebble or a stick, at such an angle that a flattish flake is removed. The shape of the flake can be controlled because the growth-layer pattern of the nodule gives it a grain comparable to that of wood. Like wood, flint splits with the grain. At the point of impact the force of the blow is strong enough to cut across the grain, but as the force weakens along the line of cleavage, it curves toward the grain, which it joins and follows until it breaks off. This shift of direction gives the butt-end of the flake a characteristically bulbous appearance, and the scar from which it was removed a corresponding concavity, similar to the pattern that you see when you shoot a bullet through a heavy plate of glass. The curvature of the flake and the size and position of the bulb are factors that the expert tool-maker understands. He can control them by his choice of nodule and by the force and direction of each blow.

After the crust has been trimmed off and a number of flakes removed, the central nucleus of the nodule which remains is called the core. The flint-worker has a choice of making his tools of the flakes, of the core, or of both. Whichever he plans to use, he rarely knocks off with a single blow or series of blows a piece that is shaped exactly to his purpose. A bit of trimming here and there, done with gentler blows than those struck in the flake removal, will convert the raw blank into a finished tool.

Its cutting edge may be perfect at the beginning, but a little use will nick it, for though flint is harder than most metals it is also very brittle. Striking a bone when cutting meat will produce a nick. In order to repair the edge, the flint-worker will remove a series of small flakes all along it. This process of sharpening is known as retouching. Nearly all the finished implements that archæologists find, among thousands of unused flakes discarded in the flint-working process, have been retouched, and many have also been broken. Probably the life of an average implement was but a few working days. We suspect this because living hunters who use flint tools carry unfinished blanks, or fully prepared spares, with them.

The Tools of Homo Erectus

F o r over half a million years human beings have broken up millions of nodules of flint in an effort to produce tools, and since flint is virtually indestructible, the pieces still remain. Because of their intact survival and because their shape tells us much about their makers and users, archæologists have studied flints intensively. On parts of the earth's surface, erosion has laid them bare, as on the so-called Cherty Plain of the Arabian Peninsula, where it is almost impossible to set one's foot down without treading on broken pieces of flint, many of which are actual implements. In other places where the soil has not been eroded, as in the commercial gravel banks that flank the terraces of the Thames River between London and the sea, they pepper the faces of the banks, like plums in a pudding.

After an archæologist has collected a number of flints from a given site or region, he sorts them. First he separates the flakes from the cores, and then the implements from the pieces discarded in the process of manufacture. If all of the flints represent a single cultural tradition over a continuous time span, then he will find certain regularities among them. For example, one group of people will have made most of their implements of flakes, so that most of the cores left after the last flakes had been struck off them are small and useless. Another people will have concentrated on the cores themselves. In neither case is the use of cores or flakes necessarily exclusive. The distinction is quantitative.

Individual habits of shaping flakes and of retouching them reveal very conservative patterns, as we discovered when, in 1949, our expedition to Iran excavated a small cave at a village called Bisitun in the western part of the country. Out of a few cubic yards of earth we recovered more than eleven hundred finished implements. While our trench was necessarily narrow because of the size of the cave, it was deep. In twelve feet we passed through soil changes that indicated changes in climate and hence a long period of occupation—hundreds if not thousands of years. Yet during this whole time span the types of implements remained much the same throughout. Among the commoner tools were double-edged and single-edged knives.

In digging the cave we established six arbitrary levels, and kept the flints from each level separate. When we made a statistical count of the knives, we found that in each level there were 1.4 double-edged knives to each single-edged knife. I do not know the reason for this figure, but I am certain that its constancy has meaning. The work requirements of these people were specific, and their survival depended on having the right tools ready at the right moment, just as the survival of a soldier when attacked depends on the quality and condition of his weapons.

The Bisitun hunters also made flint spearheads. For this purpose they used several kinds of flakes, trimming them all to the same finished shape. Whatever kind of flake they used, and however they trimmed it, the butt came out the same, as I found by measuring them. Within a very small range of variation the average butt-thickness of all types in all but the lowest level was five sixteenths of an inch. Soon after they began hunting with flint-tipped spears these people must have found that certain heads broke off more easily than others, that some were too thick to penetrate the flesh of their quarry. Still others may have worked loose easily in their hafts. This experience was the standard process of trial and error which governed invention for a long time, and it is the process still used by inventors to iron "bugs" out of experimental devices.

In citing this example I have leaped several hundred thousand years ahead of the known beginning of man's tool-making history, currently dated at about seven hundred thousand years ago, in Africa. We shall now trace in part the chronological order and in part the evolutionary order of the various kinds of ape-men, half-men, and men known or believed to have made tools.

The earliest Australopithecine, from Lake Chad, was found without tools. So were the earliest South African man-apes, but a few crude tools, in dubious association, were recovered in the

same caves as the most recent man-apes of the same region. Crude
tools were also found with the Olduvai child and Zinjanthropus.

The half-brained men of Java were found in the debris of
a flood. No tools have been found in direct association with
them, but many tools of the same geological date have been unearthed on the same island. In Burma and at one place in India
tools have been found. Most of them are chopping tools, crude
cores sharpened on a single edge by rough retouching, and also a
few coarse flakes. In Burma these tools are made of fossil wood.
Archæologists generally assume that Pithecanthropus made and
used these implements.

In the cave near Peking which yielded the bones of Sinanthropus, the debris of his housekeeping was also preserved. With him
were the broken bones of thousands of animals, including deer,
which he had eaten. That the hunting was not always good is suggested by evidence that he ate his own kind. All the Sinanthropus
long bones that have been recovered had been broken like those
of other animals in the deposit. Whoever prepared the cadavers
for a meal had first decapitated the bodies, then poked a stick
through the foramen magnum of each skull, from beneath. In
order to remove the brain, it was easier to pry off the relatively
thin bones at the base of the skull than to crack the vault.

Sinanthropus's tools were made of quartz, quartzite, and many
other materials. Some are crude choppers, others large, coarse
trimmed flakes that could have served as knives. Like the implements of Java and Burma, they failed to follow a specialized tradition of fine craftsmanship comparable to that seen in the earlier
cited knives and points of Bisitun in Iran. Until other evidence
arrives to contradict this statement, we have a right to conclude
that half-brained men could make serviceable tools, good enough
for trimming sticks and cutting up the carcasses of animals, but
that their flint work lacked the æsthetic stamp of the skill of full-
brained men.

From Pebble Tools to Hand Axes

T H E E A R L I E S T - K N O W N tools are those from the Australopithecine levels in Olduvai Gorge, from Algeria, and from Palestine. These tools are mostly water-rounded pebbles, split crosswise, diagonally, or vertically by a single blow and then, in some
cases, retouched along a single edge. Such tools were actually
found with the Olduvai child, with Zinjanthropus, and with the
skull fragments in the Lake Tiberias site in Palestine. Although
the dating of these sites is uncertain, they are probably no older
than seven hundred thousand years. The earliest tools so far discovered in southeastern and eastern Asia are later, but some may
be older than a half million years.

In Africa and Palestine the pebble tools are accompanied by
balls of quartzite so flaked that they are nearly round like base-
balls, while others look more like choppers. The round ones may
have been thrown at animals.[1] These balls appear in archæological deposits of East Africa slightly later than the very earliest
pebble layers. As tool-makers continued to work pebbles, they
came to prefer those split lengthwise to the others, and to chip
the business ends of the longitudinal tools into beaks. Chipped
tools which have a single, horizontal edge, flaked on one side only,
are called choppers. Others flaked by alternate blows from both
sides are called chopping-tools. Choppers and chopping-tools are
characteristic of the earliest sites in southeastern and southern
Asia.

At the beginning of the Middle Pleistocene tool-makers of Africa, Europe, the Near East, and India—but not of the Far East—
graduated from the chopping-tools into a derivative type of implement known as a hand ax, made of either quartzite or flint. This
is a core implement shaped more or less like an almond in that it
has two sides, a point, and a rounded butt, and that it is symmetri-

---

[1] Many explanations of the use of these balls have been offered. Since it was
first thought that they always came in groups of three, they were believed to be
the stones used in bolas, the weapon used by Argentinian Indians in hunting
ostriches, and by gauchos in catching cattle. They do not always come in threes,
and not all are round.

cal in two planes, bilaterally and bifacially. The first ones were crude, but as time went on, the flakes removed from the core to produce this double symmetry were struck off with the greatest skill and most delicate touch. So refined did these implements eventually become that, though many have tried, few modern men

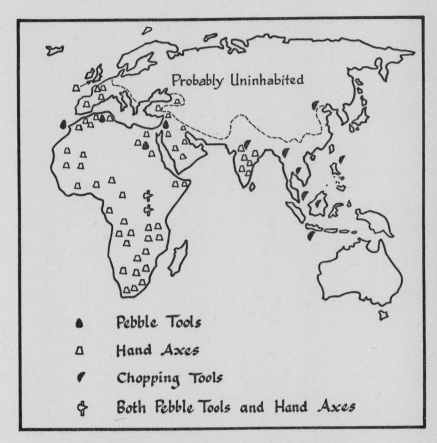

PRINCIPAL FINDS OF EARLY CUTTING TOOLS

have been able to duplicate them. At least one Frenchman makes them by striking the core with a billet of wood. It took him many months to acquire this skill. In all probability the ancient men who made the specimens that we dig up practiced for years, and it is quite possible that some were more skilled than others and made them for their fellows, but we cannot prove this.

These hand axes first appear in Middle Pleistocene times in Africa and during the first interglacial in Europe. During second-interglacial times they reached their peak of perfection. In third-interglacial deposits they are still found, but they were then on the decline. By the end of the third interglacial they were gone from Europe, but they lasted longer elsewhere, particularly in Africa.

All areas occupied by human beings in Middle and Upper Pleistocene times, except eastern and southeastern Asia and Indonesia (including the Philippines), contain hand axes. They have been unearthed over most of Africa, in western and southwestern Europe, on the southern shore of the Black Sea, in western Asia from Lebanon to Iran, and in India. Several have been found in Saudi Arabia, although that country has not yet been dug by professional archæologists. None has been found in Afghanistan. The connection between India and the western region was probably the narrow coastal strip south of the mountains of Baluchistan, now a completely denuded wasteland, where they may be buried in the streambeds. Both Homo erectus and Homo sapiens skulls have been found with hand axes, of different grades of workmanship.

The most striking fact about these hand axes is that wherever they are found they follow the same sequence of forms. During the quarter of a million years when men made these tools, the style changed very little, but what changes were made are to be seen everywhere. Even the most learned specialist in the archæology of the Lower Paleolithic, as the culture of this period is called, can distinguish an English hand ax of a given age from one from Palestine or from South Africa only by variations in material and weathering. This uniformity stimulates certain cultural interpretations.

Today one may find people using monkey wrenches and tire pumps of identical material, form, and size in these three places. The reason is clear: all were made in a single factory or in a number of factories using the same design. Modern methods of transport make it possible for the products of a single plant to be carried over the whole world. But it is highly unlikely that any person in the second interglacial ever visited England, Palestine, and South Africa in his lifetime, or that any system of organized communication or transport existed among these places. Only a cultural tradition of the most conservative nature imaginable could possibly have produced this degree of uniformity.

This means that human beings who lived half a million years ago were able to teach their young the skills that they had learned from their fathers in most minute detail, as living Australians and Bushmen do. Such teaching requires both speech and a firm discipline, and the uniformity of hand-ax styles over wide areas means that members of neighboring groups must have met together at stated intervals to perform together acts that required the use of these objects. In short, human society was already a reality when the hand-ax chippers of the world had begun to turn out a uniform product.

What the use of these objects was we may never know. They vary in length from two inches to two feet. This cannot be said of any standard tool. An industrious archæologist could make a study of the hand axes in the museums of the world, to see how many were chipped by use, how many broken, how many dulled by contact with the soil, and how many polished by repeated rubbing with oily hands. This study might reveal that some of them were not used as tools at all. It is possible that at least the loveliest of them were sacred objects, symbols of the mutual relations of man to man and of man to the landscape on which he lived, with its water and trees and rocks and animals, symbols as necessary for the maintenance of healthy human relations and peace of mind as the cross is to Christians and kachina dolls to Pueblo Indians.[2] The use of such symbols makes it easier for the members of a community to smooth out their differences and work as teams. The most efficient techniques of hunting require teamwork. Hunters who could work together harmoniously through the common belief in a set of sacred symbols could bring home more food than individual spearmen, and with the surplus, boys and their elderly

---

[2] After writing this I saw the same opinion expressed by C. van Riet Lowe in a work written in 1935: *The Pleistocene Geology and Prehistory of Uganda,* Part II, Geological Survey of Uganda Memoir No. 6, Colchester, England, 1952.

teachers could be fed. Thus the superior techniques of hand-ax chipping, and other aspects of early human behavior of which we have no record, could be taught and transmitted. This reason for the continuity of hand-ax types makes sense, but we cannot prove it. Living Australian aborigines, the most primitive surviving human beings, make comparable sacred objects, called churingas, of wood and stone, and use them in the same way, but we do not know how long they have done this.

Wherever hand axes have been found, lighter-weight flake tools have accompanied them. These flake tools were fashioned for specific and self-evident purposes, such as scraping skins or cutting meat, and no mystery surrounds them. The styles of removing flakes from cores and of retouching the flakes vary from place to place and from period to period, while the hand axes change only with time. This suggests that while the hand axes, too heavy to carry around, may have been partly symbolic objects, the flakes were strictly utilitarian. Furthermore, the flake tools are found in more places than the hand axes. It is possible that the hand axes were used only seasonally, when wild food was abundant enough to support hundreds of persons at one place and one time. Then the old men would cut the meat for the assembled multitude with some of these heavy and magnificent ceremonial tools and, like the Australians with their churingas, store them between ceremonies.

Flake Tools

THE FLAKE tools used by the hand-ax makers follow several traditions, depending on the way the core was prepared for striking off flakes, and on the way the flake was retouched for use. The simplest way to obtain flakes is to strike the core at random, turning it around and around between blows to find the likeliest surface for the next one. The percentage of useful flakes so produced is low, and their shape unpredictable. Much retouching is needed to convert them to tools. This technique wastes flint, time, and energy.

If a man can remove a flattish flake from a side of a core, then he can use the new surface for a striking platform, hitting its edge again and again. The flakes so produced are more uniform than before, and less flint, time, and energy are consumed, especially if he carefully prepares an even broader and flatter striking platform by a series of well-placed blows, which leave telltale scars or facets on the glassy surface of the flint. Then he can be surer of his product than before, and even less wasteful. He has spent most of his time in tooling up for production, and that was the secret of success in ancient as in modern industry.

The earliest flakes found in England, France, central Africa, and other hand-ax territory are of the first or random kind, and the same is true of the flakes found in Java, Burma, and China.[3] Faceted platforms go back to third glacial times in Europe, Africa, and western Asia.

Flakes produced by both techniques were retouched either with carefully directed blows, weak but sharp, or with pressure from a piece of wood or bone. Australian aborigines have been seen to pressure-flake the edges of flint implements with their teeth.

These implements were good enough for felling saplings, trimming and scraping wood, cutting up animals, skinning them, and scraping flesh from the insides of skins. Some of them could have been hafted to wooden handles with pitch or gum, to serve as knives or spear points. No special implements had yet been invented for working bone, ivory, or antler, and tools made of these materials are rare.

Recent excavations at Broken Hill indicate, but do not prove, that Rhodesian man was making flake tools, while Saldanha Bay man was found with surface tools of two kinds—very late hand axes and early flake implements. With which of these two industries Saldanha Bay man was associated is uncertain.

With the Solo skulls in Java were found one sting-ray barb, far from the sea, a worked bone point resembling the barb, and

---

[3] Some of Sinanthropus's flakes were also made by setting the core on a stone anvil before striking. Thus flakes were removed from both ends at once.

twenty undescribed stone tools. As these last are said to resemble
Broken Hill man's toolkit, they were probably worked flakes. Because Homo sapiens made, and still makes, such tools, no gap can
be seen between the tool-making techniques of Homo erectus and
those of Homo sapiens. The transition was gradual.

This is also true of Neanderthal man's cultural remains. All
Neanderthalers had a similar assemblage of tools, called Mousterian. Some were made from small cores, others from flakes.
At some sites in western Europe the flakes were struck from
simple cores, but elsewhere faceted cores were made throughout.
The flakes were used as scrapers, knives, and points, so delicately
retouched that their edges and tips could penetrate the hides of
thick-skinned animals. Some Mousterian points could be hafted
to wooden shafts or handles. With a flint-tipped spear, the best
weapon he can have had, Neanderthal hunted such monsters as
the rhinoceros and such elusive crag-jumpers as the mountain
goat. The wealth of animal bones packed into his caves bears
witness to his skill and strength as a hunter.

While all Neanderthal men yet discovered made the same kind
of tools, with reasonable variations in time and space, the tradition that they followed extended beyond their physical range,
particularly into Africa, where either sapiens, Rhodesian, or both
types of men practiced similar techniques. That more than one
kind of man made the same kind of tools is good evidence that
meetings took place between members of different human populations, not only between subspecies and local races of Homo sapiens, but also, quite possibly, between Homo sapiens and surviving bands of Homo erectus.

What the Tools Tell Us

I f we analyze the tools geographically, we obtain a result similar
to the analysis of the physical remains of the tool-makers. Pebble
tools and choppers were very old in Africa. The oldest we have
from southern and eastern Asia are a little later. Crude flakes are

old in Africa too, as old as in southern and eastern Asia or older. The hand-ax tradition of Africa and western Europe extended into western Asia, but it failed to cross the cold mountains of Iran. Instead it reached as far as India, presumably by way of the narrow zone of warm climate stretching along the Persian shore of the Indian Ocean. In India both the chopping-tool and the hand-ax traditions existed side by side in Middle Pleistocene times. Later they met and fused.

This review implies that at the beginning of the Middle Pleistocene man shared the use of crude pebble tools with Australopithecines, and that as time went on he invented more and more efficient implements, some purely utilitarian and others of a partly æsthetic character, until he had nearly exhausted the potential uses of flint.

Prometheus Discovers Fire

O N E great advantage of the primitive hunters of Australia, South Africa, and other parts of the present-day world is that they have fire, which was unknown in the Early Pleistocene. The first sure evidence of fire is the presence of hearths in the Choukoutien caves. Sinanthropus knew how to keep himself warm and thus was able to live in a colder climate than the other members of the human family who were also alive three hundred and sixty thousand years ago. Our next evidence of fire comes from Europe, about two hundred and fifty thousand years ago, at Swanscombe and in Spain.

Yet in Africa there is no sign of it earlier than forty thousand years ago, from a late hand-ax site at Kalambo Falls, Northern Rhodesia. It is not for want of searching that fire has not been found there earlier. One large open-air camp in which human beings lived time and again for long periods has no trace of charcoal or ash. This is the East African site of Olorgesailie excavated by Lewis Leakey. He was looking for traces of fire and could not find them.

None of the surviving Stone Age hunters of the world camp

without fire if they can help it, because even when it is not needed for warmth it protects them during the night from predatory animals. If the hunters of Olorgesailie, a region abounding with lions and other ferocious carnivores, had had fire, they would have used it. The other early sites of the African hand-ax tradition tell the same story. In Indonesia, the home of Pithecanthropus and Solo man, fire has been found, in Borneo, at about the same period as in Rhodesia.

While all modern peoples use fire, some do not know how to make it. This is true of several Australian tribes and of the Negritos of the Andaman Islands in the Bay of Bengal. The first fire was undoubtedly stolen, not made. Wild fire can be obtained from volcanoes and from forest fires. On rare occasions and in a few places a man could pick up a burning piece of wood and carry it away. By nursing it carefully, feeding it punk, and blowing on it when it faltered, he could keep it going indefinitely. One family could get fire from another, and it could spread from camp to camp and even from continent to continent. If the members of a camp should lose it, they could get more if they could reach another camp.

The earliest evidence of fire-making comes not from China but from Europe. In the late third interglacial cave of Krapina, in Yugoslavia, excavators found a charred fire-stick of the kind made by Boy Scouts—material proof that about one hundred thousand years ago Europeans not only had fire, but also knew how to make it.

It seems odd that Prometheus, the Greek god who stole fire from the king of the gods, the culture-bearer and savior of mankind, should turn out to have been a half-brained man in China, while the first fire-maker was a European. This is reminiscent of the later history of gunpowder, which the Chinese used for firecrackers and the Europeans exploded in cannon, with which they conquered the New World and Africa. But the parallel should not be carried too far. So little is known and so much remains to be discovered in the history of fire that generalizations are not in order.

Until he found fire, man was little more than an animal with

tools instead of fangs and claws. When he first had it, he was able
to frighten off beasts of prey with it, beasts that stalked him by
night. He could now keep warm, not only in camp but also on the
trail, by carrying punky, slow-burning torches. Fire let him push
his geographical range a little farther north than before. Other
animals did this by growing fur.

But wholly apart from warmth, fire is vital to the social life of
human beings. After the sun has set, when shadows have faded
and darkness is gathering, the air is still. The earth-smells rise,
and the cries of night-prowlers burst out of the forest. Then there
is nothing like a bright, crackling fire to dispel anxiety and fear.
This is the time when the whole band comes together. Teeth and
the whites of eyeballs gleam. Old hunts are acted out and new
ones planned. In good weather men and women will dance in the
firelight, sometimes until dawn. It is hard to imagine an intimate
group of human beings living without the social cohesion that
firelight gives.

A fourth prime use of fire, after protection, warmth, and serving as a focus for companionship, is cooking. We do not know
when cooking began because charred bones found in living sites
could have been burnt as garbage after a meal of raw meat as
well as in preparing a cooked meal. The Australopithecines had
no fire, but they split the bones of their prey to gnaw out the
marrow, a concentrated food that all hunters prize. Hunters have
been splitting bones for marrow ever since.

If an animal has been roasted, and the bones are still hot,
melted marrow can be sucked out of a bone without splintering
it. But living hunters in Australia often cook their meat where
they kill it and eat it cold in the camp later. Because cold marrow is nearly as hard to get out as raw marrow, the cooked bones
must be splintered. Boiling, however, loosens marrow thoroughly,
and in sites where we know that people boiled meat, the bones
are simply snapped in two. But these sites are late, and they tell
us nothing about when man first cooked.

Cooking does much more to food than to release marrow. It
breaks down the rough fibers of meat and roots, releasing amino

acids and sugars. It gives people softer food to chew and greatly reduces the time spent in eating. Gibbons, as C. R. Carpenter carefully observed in his stop-watch studies in Siam, spend at least half their waking hours eating, and the rest of the time is consumed in travel back and forth between eating places and sleeping places. They eat their food where they find it as soon as they have picked it. Wild gorillas, who specialize on bamboo shoots, which are very coarse fodder, eat during most of the daylight hours. If Australopithecines and early men, no matter how strong their jaws or how large their teeth, munched raw roots and chewed raw meat and gristle, they can have had little time during the average day for hunting and tool-making; but once man began to cook his food, he could cut down his eating time to two hours a day.

With the rest of the hours of dawn and daylight he could go hunting, carry home his game, work on his weapons, talk with his kin, and teach his sons many skills. The introduction of cooking may well have been the decisive factor in leading man from a primarily animal-like material existence into one that was more fully human. Lack of a knowledge of cooking may have given early men too crowded a daily schedule to permit much cultural change. Without the possibility of cultural change, there would have been no biological advantage in evolutionary change. Without fire it is unlikely that Homo erectus could have evolved into Homo sapiens. And, incidentally, it may have been an ignorance of fire that kept early flint-implement styles so conservative over hundreds of millennia.

The use of fire is the only open-and-shut difference between man and all other animals. Fire was the first source of power which man found out how to use which did not come from the conversion of food and air into energy inside his own body. It made man a more efficient animal, and during the last eight thousand years he has found increasing uses for it, and burned ever greater quantities of fuel. Fire has been the key to his rapid rise in mastering the forces of nature, his conquest and partial destruction of the earth, and his current problems.

Œdipus Goes to School

E v e n before the discovery of fire, our ancestors must have learned to live in groups of families who shared food, brought up their children together, and regulated their offspring's marriages by time-honored rules. *The central theme of this book is that man has been converting energy into social structure at an ever increasing pace. As he has drawn more and more energy from the earth's storehouse he has organized himself into institutions of increasing size and complexity.* This progression had to start somewhere. To cap our study of the earliest men we need to discover the kind of social structure in which they could have lived before they mastered fire. Then we will have the base line for the rest of the course of history.

Because no one has yet invented a time machine, we have no way of making stop-watch studies of the social life of man-apes, Pithecanthropus, or Sinanthropus, and even the almost-modern Neanderthals have vanished from the earth. We have only existing primitive forms of Homo sapiens and the living monkeys and apes to work with. The life of our earliest ancestors before the beginning of the Pleistocene can only be deduced from a comparison with these surviving social systems.

All of the groups of primitive food-gathering men discovered by explorers and settlers of the modern world have lived in bands of several related families. Bands of one kind or another are also typical of monkeys. For example, the howler monkeys of South America form households of forty or fifty individuals of both sexes. The females, passing through marked cycles of sexual heat and attraction, are ripe for masculine attention during ovulation. This rut lasts two or three days once every four weeks. When it begins, the female becomes aggressive, presenting herself to male after male; when it is over, she resumes a role of bashful indifference. The cycles of these females are staggered. No more than two or three are sexually receptive at once, and these two or three are mounted by all males in turn.

Baboons, our companions on the ground, live in super-harems.

Four or five powerful males form the nucleus of such a band, each with his private stable of females whom he jealously guards from his fellows. The younger males, excluded from this society, patrol the outskirts for enemies, and have brief sexual encounters with females who later, in full heat, seek out the old kings. Both gorillas and chimpanzees travel in bands of single harems. Besides the active leader one often sees other males, either too young to need driving off or too old to compete. The latter are, in effect, apes that have given up their masculine rights for the palliative of social security.

The gibbon [4] lives in single-family bands, consisting of a male and a female and their pre-pubescent young of both sexes. When a young male grows old enough to make advances toward his mother, or vice versa, his father drives him off. In the same way the mother rids the family of competing daughters. These young apes, sulking in the forest between parental feeding grounds, meet each other, and new families are formed. When, however, a mother is killed and a daughter, nearly old enough to be driven off is present, the father will mate with her instead, and in the same way accidents to the father may produce mother-son unions.

These variations of social structure are based on physiology. Robert M. Yerkes, who has carefully studied the behavior of female chimpanzees, has found that they go through nearly as marked an œstrual cycle as the female howlers. Harem life is clearly a reflection of this condition. The gibbon, who is the only monogamous primate anatomically close to man, differs physiologically from these monkeys. As the female gibbon is always interested in sex, her mate has no need for more than one companion. Being aggressive all the time, she would soon get rid of a rival, or herself be eliminated. The human female most closely resembles the gibbon.

On these grounds it is possible to suppose that the earliest men, at the time when they began to master speech, tools, and fire, lived in single-family groups in which each parent chased away its

[4] Our detailed knowledge of the behavior in the wild of many of these primates is due to the magnificent field work of C. R. Carpenter. See his *Field Study in Siam of the Behavior and Social Relations of the Gibbon*, Comparative Psychology Monographs, Vol. 16, No. 5, Johns Hopkins Press, Baltimore, 1940, as an example.

offspring of the same sex as soon as it began to arouse a gleam in the other parent's eye. A major shift must have come when the need for cultural instruction had become so great that it was bad survival business to be forced to leave home so young, and bad business economically to bring home more meat than a couple and their junior offspring could eat before it spoiled. Then our ancestors began living in bands.

The replacement of Œdipus behavior by an Œdipus complex must have come at some time after human beings had learned to express in words the past and future as well as the present, and to handle abstractions verbally. At the same time, in all but the poorest environments, the need of sharing hundred-pound units of meat to avoid waste must have brought about the consolidation of several families into a band. The easiest way for such bands to take shape was simply for the sons, or the daughters, but not both, to stay on after marriage.

If both were to stay, and were brother and sister or cousin and cousin to marry each other, the band would be a fully self-contained unit. No mechanism would be available for peaceful contact between bands in time of want; neighborly borrowing would be impossible. Furthermore, boys who had been brought up together would quarrel over the girls they had also been reared with, and the peace and unity of the band would be threatened. The wise way, discovered probably less by reason than by trial and error, was to have the boys of one band marry girls from other bands, and vice versa; also the boys would have been taught what categories of women he should avoid in order to prevent destructive rivalries, and how he should treat both men and women of every age.

This teaching must have become the duty of the older men. As before, they would drive out the boys when they arrived at puberty, but not for good. Away from the camp, and with the boys under the psychological influences of fear and partial starvation, the graybeards would impress upon the youthful minds the necessity of obedience to rules which they had no means of understanding, and which we are only beginning to understand today.

Pandora Frees and Joins the Spirits

LIKE the Prometheus story, the Œdipus legend takes us back to the distant time when men were becoming human. A third character in the mythological cast, Pandora, must have entered the stage during the same general epoch. At one time men had no knowledge of death. Then Pandora found a two-handled jar sealed with a lid, and opened it. A host of winged creatures flew out, carrying disease and misfortune. Thus death came to men. This story, like the other two, is an uncannily accurate symbolic portrayal of what must have happened.

No animal knows that death is inevitable. The gazelle lives from day to day, now and then facing death, but each time facing it as a separate event. When finally the lion leaps on his back and claws him to pieces, he dies, and that is the end. There must have been a time when man too lived in this fashion; and then came a time of dawning when he realized that, whatever he might or might not do, he must eventually die. This was a shattering realization, too great a burden to walk about with day by day, particularly in a time and cultural situation in which facing death in one form or another was almost a daily occurrence. Old hunters did not "just fade away," nor did they suffer the numbing haze of arteriosclerosis, bourbon, and television-watching, but were killed young, or died from exhaustion soon after they had passed their prime. Death was not some distant duty or an escape from the intolerable complexity of an over-elaborate civilization, but an ever present and frightening hazard.

One way, and one way only, permitted man to retain his peak efficiency with this problem on his mind—the belief in life after death. Once convinced that he was going to live on, he could people the afterworld with spirits (or discover the spirit world) and place among them the spirits of the classes of animals and plants which formed the non-human context of his daily life. These spirits, floating about, watched him. At times they would come to him, give him messages, and help him over hurdles. If things went wrong, he could blame them. Far from being an opiate of the people, religion became a source of great strength.

When a man fell ill, a belief in spirits focused in a single direction the attention of everyone whom this mischance disturbed. When a girl came to puberty, when a boy was ripe for initiation, when a couple was married, and when a person was born or died, the disturbance that these changes created in the routine of a tiny

RHINOCEROS. FRENCH CAVE ART.

community was allayed by rituals of an emotional nature. The center in man's brain for emotion and hence for religious belief is highly developed. Emotion and belief are essential tools in the building of societies. The highest art and the soundest philosophy are produced by emotional and idealistic men.

When man approached the end of the age-long period of his physical and cultural development (which we have tried to trace from the middle of the Pleistocene to the advance of the fourth ice sheet), human beings, at least in Europe, had long since begun to notice the world about them in a contemplative way and to express their awareness of some principle of world order in terms that have survived. Homo sapiens had long been flaking hand axes æsthetically. Neanderthal man had learned to bury his dead, surrounding their bodies with tools and trophies of the chase to help them in the world beyond.

In terms of religious interpretation, man had acquired a soul. Anthropologically speaking, human beings had become men in the fullest sense, capable not only of using fire and other sources of energy yet to be discovered, but also of understanding themselves.

When the second phase of the Würm glaciation began, men of all races, probably including those that had lagged behind in the far corners of the earth, had become sapiens. Speaking in general, and of European Upper Paleolithic hunters in particular, man had reached an evolutionary level yet to be surpassed. Nature had done all she needed to do for him. He had been toughened on a hard forge, and tested in a ruthless laboratory. He was now on his own, a unique animal ready for the second phase of his history on what may be a unique planet.

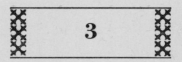

THE SKILLED HUNTER AND HEALER

The Second Phase of History

WHEN, about thirty-five thousand years ago, the first advance of the last ice sheet had reached its southernmost limit and its edge had begun to melt and crawl back north, Homo sapiens had finished his long infancy as a species. As with other infants, the acquisition of food, warmth, and basic experience had monopolized his time and effort, and most of his dealings had been confined to the family circle. So far his life had been more biological than cultural, for, as with other animals, the environment had dictated his place of residence and his numbers.

Yet of all the ground-living primates of the Pleistocene he was the most cultured. He had stimulated his unimpressive muscles with emotion and learned to multiply his strength by co-operative effort, through leadership, teamwork, and the care of the aged and suffering. Strength came to him from weakness when he chanced into rich hunting grounds as the old and the crippled sat by the campfire fashioning weapons and garments for the hunter.

With this task left to others, a hunter could spend more time in his search for game, and the tool-makers and skin-workers could perfect their techniques. Man still had to exert himself physically to nearly the limit to obtain food, but his reward was richer. He was learning to get more with less effort. Not only were his weapons and clothing better, but he had at length found out how to keep alive in the wintertime in the rich hunting grounds formerly closed to him by the cold. By the beginning of phase two of human history, the age of the skilled hunter and healer, his life had become less precarious than before, and in it culture and biology had struck a fine balance.

Man Covers the Face of the Earth and Becomes One Species

F o r the first time, human beings now possessed the technical skills needed to move into the rich hunting grounds that lay just below the edge of the glacial ice which was concentrated, in the Old World, on Scandinavia and the Baltic regions. Men had met the cold before, but not really tamed it. Sinanthropus had survived the winters of North China, but had left Siberia uninhabited. Later, Neanderthals had avoided eastern Europe's biting cold.

The cold that had defeated the European Neanderthals was a wet cold, the bitterest kind. Twice again during the Würm glacial period the cold crept down from the north, but it was dry. Between the crests of the cold, the weather relented a little, so that the zones of treeless arctic desert which skirted the ice moved northward, followed by the forest of spruce and balsam, pressed in turn by oak and ash, which grow in the forests of western Europe today. On the edge of the ice, the melt-water sank into the ground and fostered a narrow strip of rich vegetation, particularly ferns, which attracted reindeer and numerous rodents eager to burrow in the soil loosened by melting and thawing. Bears came to eat both berries and rodents, men to hunt all forms of animal life.

This was splendid summer hunting. The hunter who killed so much meat in season had to stay near by during the winter, for the frost line was too far away for him to reach its shelter when the weather began to turn. Out on the tundra were herds of mammoth, each animal carrying tons of meat. One carcass could feed a whole camp for weeks if only the hunters and their families could keep from freezing. Other herds of wild horses and of reindeer provided equal quantities of meat in smaller packages. The prize was rich food in abundance. The problem was to live through the cold. There was wood for fuel in most places, but the hunter could not carry his fire with him on the hunt. He had to have warm clothing, and in order to make it he needed new tools. These he invented or copied from others—we know not which—and his problem was solved.

During the period that followed, all men were hunters, as before. It began about 35,000 B.C., with the first half-retreat of the ice sheet, and ended about 7000 B.C., with the invention of agriculture. About 8000 B.C. the ice sheet melted for the last time up to the present, and the Pleistocene period ended. The culture of the people who lived between the first successful invasion of the frozen regions and the end of the ice is called Upper Paleolithic, that from the end of the ice to the beginning of agriculture, Mesolithic. In the parts of the world where agriculture was invented, the Mesolithic was brief, but where it took longer for agriculture to reach, the Mesolithic lasted many thousands of years, and in some places is still going on.

In the time span of the Upper Paleolithic culture, and before 6000 B.C. in the Mesolithic, human beings first occupied the vast core of the Eurasiatic continent up to the Arctic Ocean and crossed Bering Strait to Alaska. From there they followed the game trails southward as far as the southernmost tip of South America. The only lands that they failed to reach were the treeless wastes of northeastern Canada and the shores of Greenland, the islands in the middle of the Atlantic and Pacific oceans, and the Antarctic continent. The conquest of these had to await still further inventions.

This rapid expansion carried man into all of the climates of the earth. As zoologists well know, any species of animal which expands into new climate zones must change to meet new conditions, or perish. Man was able to change as needed. One reason may have been that his possibility of variation had been greatly increased, during his expansion, by mixture.

The first kind of man to start these expansions was the advanced race of Caucasoids who had high foreheads and prominent chins. Having evolved in western Asia, they followed the game-trails into Europe, where they replaced the Neanderthals, probably partly by absorption. Twenty thousand years later, similar peoples moved into North Africa and East Africa.

Fully evolved Mongoloids also expanded from their home in

China, moving in two directions. To the north they made their
way along the ice-free stretches of the Pacific coast to Bering
Strait, over which they walked on dry land to America. Before
they reached the strait they apparently met some Caucasoid hunters, who had crossed the mountains from the west and had already penetrated the Amur River country and crossed over to
Sakhalin Island and Hokkaido, where some of them sired the
Ainus. A little of this Ainu-like Caucasoid element entered the racial composition of the American Indians. To the south the
Mongoloids moved into Southeast Asia and Indonesia, mixing
with the indigenous Australoids and pushing them eastward to
New Guinea and Australia.

These Caucasoid and Mongoloid expansions peopled the New
World and brought new populations, with much mixture, into the
Old World lands near and south of the equator. In this fashion
the two northernmost and oldest races of Homo sapiens spread
from their original homes until they, and others whom they had
displaced, had occupied most of the earth's ice-free surface, bar-
ring treeless barrens and ocean-girded islands. These expansions
and migrations caused some peoples to absorb others and broad-
ened the genetic bases of several races, thus offering them a wider
variety of anatomical and physiological possibilities for selection
as man moved into new environments. To this his success as a
world animal may be in part attributed. By its means the first step
in the world unification of man was achieved.

Primary evidence for these statements may be found in numerous archæological reports and in the descriptions of several hundreds of skulls and other bones recovered from caves and outdoor
camps of these periods. The evidence is fuller than that for earlier
periods because there were more people, because they occupied
a wider geographical range, and because they took more pains to
bury their dead. Naturally the bulk of the evidence is from
Europe, because that is where the study of archæology began,
but more and more is coming in every year from Africa, the Middle East, and America.

In Europe itself the bulk of the Upper Paleolithic material
comes from France, and in France the happiest digging ground is

the valley of the Dordogne, in the center of which stands the Upper Paleolithic capital of Europe, the hamlet of Les Éyzies, mecca of archæologists from the whole world. With its wide green canyons spreading out between white limestone cliffs, the Dordogne was a natural paradise for hunters. A lookout perched on a rocky outcrop could see for miles up and down the valley. The moist winds off the Atlantic furnished ample browsing for game, whose herds the lookout could identify as much as five miles away. A whistled signal or manual gesture to his fellows below would let them start their drive in the right direction, and the cliff walls would box in the cornered game. After the hunt, carcasses could be carried to the near-by caves, where bright fires welcomed the victorious hunters. In the walls of the cliffs themselves an abundance of flint awaited the tool-maker. Out in front of the cave ran a stream of cool water. What more could a man want in those, or any other, days?

Within easy walk or a short trip on bicycle or motorbus the visitor to Les Ézyies can reach such world-renowned caves as Cro-Magnon, Le Moustier, Laugerie Haute, Laugerie Basse, and Lascaux. There are to be seen the famous cave paintings, miraculously preserved over a period of at least sixteen millennia by the constant temperature of around 50° F. and humidity of nearly one hundred per cent, which are maintained day and night, summer and winter, year in and year out, in the inner recesses of limestone grottoes.

In the mouths of these caves can also be seen the sections cut through the floor deposits by dozens of archæologists, French, American, British, and German, who have, as a result of the differences in tool types found in the successive layers, worked out a complicated sequence of "cultures" which every schoolboy in Les Éyzies has memorized, and which American college students find difficult to learn.

At the bottom is usually a layer of earth containing the flints and bones left behind by Neanderthal man. Above it may in some sites be a sterile layer, indicating the passage of time during the peak of the first Würm advance. Then comes a series of related Upper Paleolithic cultures, called Perigordian and Aurignacian,[1] which takes us over the peak of the dry cold of Würm II, about twenty-four thousand years ago. This is the time when man was first able to survive such temperatures. Hundreds of awls and needles found in these deposits show that he wore clothing made of warm skins. Tens of thousands of broken bones show that he boiled meat and sucked marrow. Thousands of reindeer antlers, all at the same stage of development and broken off the skull in the same way, show that he used his caves and rock shelters as habitations only during the winter.

If the sequence in our cave is complete, the next layer up will be that of the so-called Solutrean period, when mammoth-hunting was at its peak. In this period France shared the honors with the plains of central Europe, including Czechoslovakia and Russia, prime mammoth country. There whole villages have been excavated, with rows of houses, neat piles of mammoth bones, and graves containing dozens of skeletons. The houses are underground for protection against the winter cold, the roofs held up with logs or mammoth bones. In France, Czechoslovakia, and elsewhere the hallmark of the Solutrean culture is a long, thin, leaf-shaped blade of flint, delicately retouched on both sides and doubly symmetrical like a fine hand ax.

Returning to France, we find the next layer, marking the third peak of dry cold and lasting until the final retreat of the glacier. This is the Magdalenian, a time of reindeer-hunting on barren lands and the borders of the spruce forest. Certain special kinds of bone and antler harpoons are the type specimens of the Magdalenian. When the reindeer retreated northward, some of the Magdalenian hunters followed them, and new folk moved into France with the oak and ash forests, bringing a Mesolithic culture from the southlands and joining the Paleolithic survivors.

The French Upper Paleolithic sequence did not represent any new conquest of energy, nor during its span were any notable inventions made, save perhaps cave art, which were not shared by all of its member cultures. From the point of view of world history

[1] For the entire French sequence see H. L. Movius, Jr., "Radiocarbon Dates and Upper Paleolithic Archæology in Central and Western Europe," *Current Anthropology,* Vol. 1, Nos. 5–6, 1960, pp. 355–91.

the details of this sequence are therefore inconsequential. To the professional archæologist they are of consequence because by means of their variations he can hope to trace the origins of each in the outside world where less digging has been done, and to build up a fourth- or Würm-glacial timetable for the world.

During fourth-glacial times France lay on the fringe of the inhabited world. It is a well-known principle that fringe areas show a complex pattern of the goings and comings of different kinds of living organisms that originated elsewhere, and Upper Paleolithic France was no exception. The earliest Upper Paleolithic human beings of France are represented by a single skeleton, that of Combe Capelle, associated with lower Perigordian implements and dated at the warm interstadial between Würm I and Würm II. Combe Capelle was a man of medium stature and slender build. His limb bones and skull were European in type. His face was long, his nose prominent, and his nasal bones were bent, probably from a break early in life. He could pass for a modern European.

During the rest of the Würm glacial period Europe continued to be inhabited by similar people. We have over fifty skeletons to prove it.[2] Some were tall, others short, and most of the bones give evidence of a vigorous outdoor life. Like members of any population, the skulls vary individually, but despite the changes of tool-style which French archæologists have divided into many "industries," the people remained the same. The best known is the Old Man of Crô-Magnon, near Les Éyzies. He was almost six feet tall and muscular; he had a large head, craggy chin, broad face, and deep-set eyes. He must have looked like a broad-faced Irishman.

We know more about the appearance of these people than the bones tell us, because they created statuettes, bas-reliefs, wall engravings, and wall paintings depicting human beings. Despite the cold they are usually shown in the nude. Women are nearly always obese. Their fat is distributed in the same pattern seen in living fat women of European race. A few are normal, like one engraved on a cave wall at La Magdeleine (see page 102). Men's faces are Caucasoid, with prominent noses, beards, and white skins.

    [2] See C. S. Coon, *The Races of Europe*, The Macmillan Company, New York, 1939.

Three skeletons have been called non-Caucasoid. A mother and child burial of early date at Grimaldi, near Monaco, has been called Negroid, principally because the child's incisor teeth are ridged on their inner surfaces, like those of Negroes. I consider this part of the normal variability of the Upper Paleolithic population. An otherwise ordinary Magdalenian skull from Chancelade has been called Eskimoid, only because it had heavy jaw-muscles.

The Caucasoid invaders of North Africa are represented by an almost equal number of skeletons, twenty-eight of which came from one Algerian cave, Afalou bou Rummel. Number twenty-eight, the oldest, which lay at the bottom, was a thin-faced woman similar to Combe Capelle, who was twenty thousand years older. The others were big, square-faced, craggy people somewhat like Crô-Magnon and like some of the living Berbers.

The origin of these Europeans and North Africans, long a mystery, is beginning to clear up, and the key to it is the flints and skeletons excavated in Palestine, Lebanon, and Syria. During the first Würm period, which was cool, not cold, along the Mediterranean, the population changed. The earliest skull is that of a Neanderthaloid woman found in the cave of al-Tabūn (the Oven) in Mt. Carmel. In the nearby Mugharet al-Skhul (Cave of the Kids) a series of nine skeletons were found imbedded in breccia. Although still Würm I in date, they were ten thousand years younger than the Tabūn woman. These Skhul skeletons were only partly Neanderthaloid. Their skulls were high-vaulted and rounded, their facial features rugged although essentially modern. One of them, Skhul V, on exhibit at Harvard, had heavy brow ridges, a straight forehead, big jaws, and a chin. Some of the ruggedest Upper Paleolithic skulls from Europe and North Africa resembled him, and all of them were later. Another series of seven skulls of the same date found at Jebel Qafza (Jump Mountain) in Palestine has not yet been described, but photographs of one of them look like a more modern and less brutal version of Skhul V, and more like the majority of Upper Paleolithic European skulls.

There can be little doubt that the Upper Paleolithic peoples were descended either from these very Palestinians or from others like them in western Asia, but more to the north. But from

whom were the Palestinians of Würm I descended? Three possibilities have been suggested. They evolved directly from local
Neanderthals of the "progressive" eastern type. They are a mixture between Neanderthals and some other, unknown, Caucasoid.
Their ancestors were Caucasoids similar to Steinheim, Swanscombe, Fontéchevade, and the other early Europeans, people who
lived and evolved in Palestine, a land which was only sporadically
invaded by Neanderthals. We do not know which, if any, of these
explanations is correct.

The Tools Behind His Expansion and Consolidation

U P P E R Paleolithic people were still dependent on flint as a
primary tool-making material. Unlike their predecessors, however, they had refined their control over this medium to its natural
limits. By Early Aurignacian times they were producing tools as
perfect as any flaked by primitive hunters surviving into modern
times. Back at the beginning of the Pleistocene, human beings
had made their basic cutting tools of whatever kind of material
they could find ready at hand: pebbles, quartzite, and fossil wood,
as well as various grades and qualities of flint. As time went on,
they came to use flint more and more. Flint varies in quality, and
the finer varieties were traded far and wide from the few places
in which they were found. Over a period of hundreds of thousands of years the supplies of prime flint in the long-occupied parts
of the earth began to grow scarce. It was not economical to knock
flakes from cores in such a fashion that nine tenths or even half
of the substance of a nodule had to be thrown away, and it made
little sense to carry large lumps from place to place if much was
to be wasted.

The need of a more efficient way of producing tool blanks was
evident to the hunters of early Upper Paleolithic times; it was perhaps even pressing. In the cultural levels of hand-ax times one occasionally finds a piece of flint which was struck off its core in such
a way that its thickness was nearly uniform and its sides were parallel. Such a piece is called by archæologists a blade. Its advantage

over ordinary flakes is that it can be used as a knife without further work, or can be retouched into any one of a dozen special forms for separate purposes. A flick here and a snip there makes an end-scraper suitable for cleaning the tag-ends of flesh from the inside of a skin. A series of flicks blunts one edge so that the blade can be held in the hollow of the index finger as a knife. A concavity in its side gives the woodworker a spokeshave for trimming spear shafts, and if he brings one end to a point he can make a drill.

Now and then, when they struck off a few blades by accident in the process of making flakes, people produced tools like these. This did not happen often because they did not know how to make blades deliberately. Someone, somewhere, sometime discovered that it was possible to prepare a core in a tubular form, and then to remove one blade after another around its perimeter by a series of expertly struck blows, with a horn or bone punch held between the hammer and the face of the flint. A hunter could carry one of these blade cores with him and be assured of ten to twenty good blades to replace those he might break.

The earliest blades that we know of were made in Palestine, Lebanon, and Syria during Würm I. They are found, in a number of sites, with flake tools. Only gradually do the blades come to outnumber the flakes. By the Würm I–II interstadial, a true blade culture had arisen. Also a recent survey of southwestern Iran has discovered a similar evolution from flakes to blades. Blade-making could have been carried from western Asia to the Black Sea shores during the interstadial, either via the Turkish coast and the Bosporus or over the mountains. In southern Russia the European Upper Paleolithic cultures may have evolved out of this Near Eastern prototype. This reconstruction of archæological history is supported by, and lends support to, the theory of a western Asiatic origin of Upper Paleolithic man outlined above.

If economizing in flint and producing an all-purpose tool blank had been all that the invention of blade-making did, it is unlikely that the Upper Paleolithic men would have been able to stay in the colder parts of Europe, to move northeastward into Asia, and to create their wonderful art. It was the perfection of one particular tool that touched off this series of events. That tool was the burin, a special kind of chisel or graving tool which made it possible for him to manufacture secondary implements of bone, antler, and ivory, just as the modern lathe-operator's chisel lets him produce shafts needed for machinery.

The success of the burin lies in the fact that it overcame one of the defects inherent in flint as a tool material. The very property of flint which makes it shatter when it strikes bone also makes it a poor substance from which to make bone-working tools, and the same applies to antler and ivory. That is why the few bone tools that we have found in Lower and Middle Paleolithic sites are large and coarse, and no better than corresponding pieces of wood. The burin is a chisel that cuts on its narrow edge, leaving the broad section of the blade to give it support in depth. It will cut bone, antler, or ivory for a reasonable length of time before it breaks. A chisel made on the broad side of a blade might break at once.

Making a burin is a simple but delicate process. The tool-maker holds a blade in one hand and strikes it a single sharp but weak blow on the end and to one side. This blow removes a tiny blade, leaving a telltale concavity at the head of the scar so produced. The right-angle edge where the blow was struck is sharp and strong, for it has the whole width of the blade to reinforce it. A tool-maker using this blade as a chisel can rout out a groove without breaking his tool. In the case of bone and antler, he can cut through to the marrow cavity or spongy part; in the case of ivory, he can carve it as he pleases.

With this special chisel he can carve out whatever kind of secondary tool he wants from bone, antler, and ivory, which possess special advantages over flint. One advantage is size: a mammoth tusk is big enough to produce an implement several feet long. Another is elasticity: once a hunter has carved a harpoon head out of ivory or staghorn, it will not break easily, while a comparable weapon head of flint would shatter at its first contact with a bone. If there is any question of its penetration, a small flint blade can be set at the tip, and if this breaks, it can be easily replaced. In order to tie thongs to the head, the tool-maker can bore holes in it with a flint drill.

The use of these materials greatly increased man's efficiency in hunting large mammals, not only mammoths, horses, and reindeer, but also such sea mammals as seals and even whales. From the spear he passed on to the harpoon, needed for salt-water hunting. The difference between a spear and a harpoon is that the head of a spear is permanently fixed at the end of its shaft, while the head of a harpoon comes loose from its shaft once its barbs have become lodged in the body of the animal. A thong connects the harpoon head to the hunter's hand. The shaft floats away, to be picked up later. The advantages of the harpoon over the spear

MAGDALENIAN HARPOON HEAD.

are that the shaft is less likely either to break off or to work its head free as the animal thrashes about. In either case the animal would get away.

By Magdalenian times European men were harpooning seals, and in the Mesolithic they were whaling. It was not the seagoing harpoon that made life in the cold possible in the first place, but a much simpler invention, the bone or ivory needle. With it Upper Paleolithic man or Upper Paleolithic woman was able to sew warm skins together into efficient garments that the hunter could wear outdoors in cold weather. Thus he could carry into the cold regions of the earth a few cubic feet of tropical climate in the air space between his skin and his clothing, and thus he came to occupy the previously uninhabited parts of the earth's surface which contained firewood. He did it because of a chain of inventions that began with the burin, which was thus man's first passport to both Russia and America.

It was also the gateway to an even more useful technique that eventually replaced it. When an Ice Age craftsman went about making a weapon of antler or ivory, the burin was not his only tool. All that he could do with the burin was to rough out the

shape that he wanted. In order to finish the surfaces and sharpen
the edges, he ground it smooth with an abrasive, like a piece of
sandstone or a spoonful of emery grit held in a foxskin. Then he
polished it. I have found chisels of staghorn in Belt Cave which
were made in this very fashion, as well as emery.

These chisels are made so that two smoothed and polished surfaces meet at an acute angle, forming a cutting edge. Such
chisels are useful in cutting soft wood, but none of these materials
is hard enough for felling trees or hewing planks. In early post-
glacial times someone was bright enough to think of transferring
this technique of smoothing and polishing the surface of bone,
antler, and ivory to stone.

If you take a very hard and compact stone like jade, and grind
and polish it to produce an implement with a smooth wedge-like
edge, you have a chisel. If you make a larger one and haft it with
a wooden or antler handle so that you can swing it and put some
weight behind it, you have an ax or an adze, depending on the
shape and direction of the bit. A man with a polished-stone ax
can fell trees large enough for house-building, canoe-making, or
sled-making. He can hew planks. He can make in ten minutes
what a man with burins will take several hours to reproduce, if he
can reproduce it at all.

Who made the first polished-stone ax? No one knows. The oldest ones I have so far found come from the Caspian Sea region of
west-central Asia, but only from agricultural periods. Yet the
agriculture of the Caspian shoreline farmers, which had begun by
6000 B.C., chronologically overlapped other peoples' hunting; it
was possible to spread the idea of a polished-stone ax among
hunters, who could see its immediate advantage in making
weapons, boats, tent frames, and fences into which to drive game,
long before it was possible to persuade them to give up hunting
and to live by cultivation. The polished-stone ax was a particular
boon to those living in northern forests beyond the range of agriculture, where canoes, skis or snowshoes, and sleds are essential.
We can see the rationale of this process by witnessing another
step, from polished stone to Pittsburgh steel. In Canada the Indians have been using steel axes for three hundred years; it took

them no time at all to see the advantages of the new ax. In New Guinea there is hardly a tribe left which makes polished-stone axes: during the last twenty years almost all have been given up in favor of the imported product.

The technique of grinding and polishing has reached most of the outermost fringes of human culture. The Andaman Islanders, food-gathering Negritos, have been salvaging scraps of iron from wrecks for several centuries and cold-grinding them into implements. The Fuegian Indians have done the same thing. Even in Australia, that museum of mankind, many of the aborigines had, by the time the first English settlers arrived, begun the manufacture of ground-stone axes. There can be little doubt that this technique was discovered independently in more than one area as a logical culmination to a long period of experimentation in cutting tools under conditions of good hunting and a little leisure.

Burin-making spread from western Europe across Siberia to Bering Strait and into Alaska, where these tools have been found in an ancient deposit beneath a sterile layer of soil which itself underlay an Eskimo site. They were not carried into the southern hemisphere. Being suited for special materials such as horn and ivory, they went only where these substances were useful in hunting and where warm clothing was necessary.

Woodworking is a universal need. That is why the polished-stone ax overtook and passed the burin, which it eliminated, just as later on in history iron overtook and passed bronze. But by the time the polished-stone ax had been invented, human beings had already spread out to the corners of the habitable world. Flint tools, including the burin, had been efficient enough to make this possible.

He Invents the Bow

DURING most of Upper Paleolithic time the wooden spear, with tips of different materials, served as the hunter's principal weapon. In modern times it was still the only weapon used by the Tasmanians and by the desert tribes of west-central Australia. To use it, the hunter has to creep up on his prey until he is within

MESOLITHIC HUNTERS. SPANISH CAVE ART.

accurate casting range. This range can be increased if he uses an additional device, the spear-thrower, which is a piece of wood about two feet long. At one end are holes or notches for his hand, at the other a peg or pit to engage the end of his spear. Serving as an extension of his arm, this gives his arm greater leverage and hence extends the range of the spear. With practice he can achieve the necessary accuracy. Remains of spear-throwers have been found in French Upper Paleolithic sites, and in early post-glacial cave sites in America. The Eskimos still use it for fowling, for it is particularly suited for casting a heavy javelin fitted with bone barbs along the sides, like a hatrack.

It is also in common use for everyday hunting among most of the aborigines of Australia, who are ignorant of the bow and arrow, which appears later archæologically in other parts of the world. In western Europe the bow was introduced in the beginning of Mesolithic times from some other source, presumably Africa, by way of Spain. How old it was in Africa we do not know.

The principle of the bow is that of the spring. You pull the string back slowly and release it all at once. All of the energy that you have put into it bit by bit comes out in a fraction of a second. A man with a good bow can deliver an arrow with an impact velocity of five horsepower into the flank of an unsuspecting elk. If he strikes a boneless part of the animal's body the arrow will come out the other side. Plains Indians using iron-tipped arrows have even shot arrows clean through bison. Earlier Indians could have done the same with arrows tipped with flint points.

The bow also greatly increases both the range of a missile and its accuracy at long distance, particularly when the arrow is feathered. It is a silent weapon; if the hunter misses one shot, he can try another without disturbing the herd. While the spearman can carry at most three spears, the archer may have twenty shafts in his quiver. These he can shoot in rapid succession, as with an automatic weapon. The bow remained man's most efficient hand weapon until the perfection of the Kentucky rifle, and some hunters still prefer it to any firearm. During World War II it was a favorite of the Commandos, for a shaft through the neck would eliminate an enemy sentry without sound. It is hard for a hunter to find a better weapon than a bow, particularly if he also has a well-trained dog. This combination made Mesolithic man a formidable hunter indeed, and gave him time to spare for other kinds of craftsmanship.

Man's Second Source of Energy—the Dog

THE BLADE, the burin, the harpoon head, the needle, the fur garment, the spear-thrower, and the bow were all items of a single category in the history of human invention: mechanical improvements in the techniques by which he used the energy of his muscles to bring food to his mouth and keep the air around his body at an even temperature. This is progress of a certain order. Devices of this kind can be compared to the ball bearings and lubricants of a modern machine: they are energy-savers. The other side of the picture is energy-production. Since his initial discovery of fire hundreds of thousands of years earlier, man had not, until the end of the Ice Age, discovered a second source of energy. This came with the domestication of his first animal, the dog.

By persuading two or three other men to help him, a man can double or treble the amount of muscular energy at his disposal; if it had been nothing more than this that he needed, man could have driven the dog away when it came begging refuse at the edge of the firepit. A dog can run faster than a man, and this is useful in driving game, but men can be posted in advance for driving and beating. What is important about the domestication of the dog is that it gave man an added increment of nervous energy by extending the range of his sensory perceptions. A dog can hear notes too high for the human ear and can pick up traces of scent that no human nose can smell. In the wild state he is a clever hunter. The combination of dog and man thus became a partnership profitable to both.

With the help of man, the dog is more certain of his kill than if he hunted alone, and the bones and entrails are his. At the same time he can increase enormously the efficiency of a party of hunters. He can find and flush birds, surround and drive deer and antelope, run down and kill small game, and guard the body of a large animal until his master reaches it. He can track animals mile after mile over stony or leafy ground where no track remains to catch the hunter's eye, for which his nose is a substitute. At night when the fires are low, his furry body will keep his master warm, and he will warn of approaching danger. In the frozen wastes of the far north he can draw his master's sled, and here his muscular energy is of critical value, for without the dog and sled the hunter could not feed his family.

Those who have traveled in agricultural villages of Africa and the Middle East remark that the people seem to appreciate their dogs little, leaving them to find their own food among ordure, to sleep out on dung heaps for winter warmth, and beating and abusing them when they make advances which we reward with hand-strokes, crooning noises, or crackers. But those who have observed shepherds tell a different tale. Sheep dogs everywhere are well treated, for they protect the flocks against wolves and herd them and make it possible for one boy to do the work of a dozen men. When you reach the desert and meet the proud Arab, Afghan, or Baluchi, with his slender-legged saluki, you will find an even greater change. The greyhound that runs down the swift gazelle by sight is a pampered pet, clothed in a blanket like a race horse. When you go to the desert of central Australia, you will discover that the hunting dog is a member of the family, fulfilling as important a social function as the cocker spaniel in the home of a childless American couple.

We do not know exactly when the dog was first domesticated, but we do not find its bones in archæological sites until the beginning of Mesolithic times. Actually it is difficult to tell the difference between dog bones and wolf bones. The only useful criterion is a general reduction in the size of the jaws, which is not easy to find in the earliest specimens. As not every archæologist who has dug Paleolithic sites during the last hundred years has been aware of this distinction, a number of dog bones may have been missed.

Ancient Methods of Hunting and Fishing

A L T H O U G H we have no direct evidence of the hunting methods of Upper Paleolithic men, we know how living people equipped with the same or inferior weapons hunt, and that should be good enough. Three peoples, separated as far in space as it is possible to separate human beings (though all live in the southern hemisphere, the land connections between them are all north of the equator) and completely different racially, are the Australians, the Bushmen of South Africa, and the Ona of Tierra del Fuego. These three peoples probably represent the hunting techniques of Upper (and earlier) Paleolithic men with considerable fidelity,

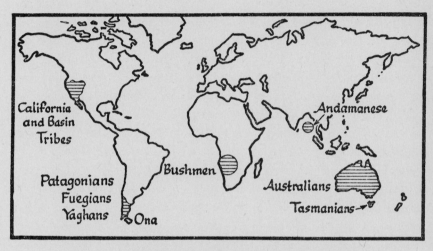

SOME PRIMITIVE HUNTERS IN MODERN TIMES

except that they lack the burin and possess the dog. If we turn to the Tasmanians, who lacked both, we are in effect technologically back in third-interglacial times.

All of these peoples hunt or hunted animals that before dressing weigh in the neighborhood of one hundred and fifty pounds. All of them live in bands of a few related families, making a total of from four to ten adult males of hunting age. These men compose at least one hunting team. The members of the team rise well before dawn and, after eating a hasty snack, pick up their equipment. They go out to a place where they have reason to believe that game will be found. The first task is locating the game, and for this they may have to spread out, keeping in touch with one another by such prearranged signals as imitation birdcalls that will disturb their prey as little as possible. When game is sighted, some members of the team, usually junior, will be sent out to infiltrate from the rear and drive the game toward the killers, or to cut off retreat and kill the animals in their flight.

The killers themselves will either wait in ambush for their prey to approach or walk among them in disguise. In the case of deer, the hunter will wear a mask topped with a pair of antlers, hollowed out to reduce weight. He may carry two sticks to represent front legs, as well as a hidden bow and quiver. By means of this disguise, and approaching upwind, he may come within a few yards of his quarry, and when he is discovered he may have time to discharge a dozen arrows. In the case of a guanaco, the hunter wears a headdress of white fur which resembles the forehead coat of one of the animals. Careful observation and imitation of animal habits enhance the hunter's chances of success.

Stalking, whether or not with animal disguises, is the normal everyday method that most hunting people employ, but it is not their only technique. At times a large group of people will go out together before dawn, and the women and children, as well as some of the men, will form a huge circle, several miles in diameter, with each individual placed within shouting distance of his fellows on either side. They will all begin shouting and beating the bush, driving all the animals inside the circle toward its center. As they reduce the circumference of the circle, they will come closer and closer together, which will prevent animals from bolting out. Finally they are able to hold hands, and eventually to touch shoulders. By this time a milling pound of frightened beasts leaps and darts about in the center, where the hunters dispatch them with clubs, spears, or arrows. This will provide much meat for many people for a short time, but it can only be done once in a long time, for it depletes the animal population of the neighborhood. This method was employed by the Tasmanians, the only modern hunters who had no dogs.

A similar method is to drive animals into a funnel created by making converging fences, and thence into a pound. This was done annually by the men of several Indian villages in California, and it was the only event in which villages had to work together as a unit, a fact reflected in their religious observances, which were so arranged as to make possible the maximum mutual regard and peace among the villages concerned. In the north, the reindeer and caribou make predictable annual migrations. The hunters prepare for this by erecting fences, setting up nooses, and lying in ambush at river crossings. Slaughtering their prey by the hundreds, they preserve the meat by freezing or smoking it, and keep it in tree-houses or underground caches. Judging by the thousands of reindeer antlers found in French caves, and by the art representations of reindeer herds standing in water, we infer that Upper

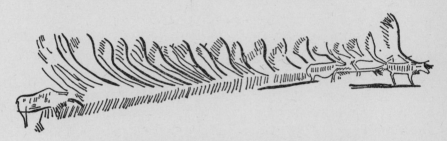

REINDEER HERD. BONE ENGRAVING, FRANCE.

Paleolithic man had already learned these tricks. The antlers, firmly attached to pieces of skull, indicate that the hunting was done in November.

Today hunters in the forests of Canada and Siberia use many traps. The reason is that they make a living by catching fur-bearing animals and trading their skins for goods produced elsewhere by non-hunters. In the days when everyone hunted, there was no such trade, and the inhabitants of the boreal forest killed for food and for the skins needed for their own garments and tents. The marginal hunters of Tierra del Fuego, South Africa, and Australia seldom use traps at all. In fact, the most elaborate traps in the world are made and used by agricultural peoples, such as the Chinese, Malays, and some of the Indians of the Amazon basin. Elaborate traps are made only by people possessing polished-stone axes or metal tools. In Europe traps are lacking in the Mesolithic sites where other wooden objects have been preserved; it is not until after the introduction of the stone ax, after 6000 B.C., that traps appear.

Nor is there evidence of elaborate fishing before post-glacial times. One reason may be that the sea levels have shifted several times as the waters of the earth have been alternately impounded and released by icecaps, and as the earth's crust, shuddering at its release from the weight of ice, has risen. Most marine fisheries of Würm age, if there were any, would now be under water. And, on purely technical grounds, it is hard to postulate their existence at that time. Competent fishing requires seaworthy boats and gear that can only be made with ground tools, and Upper Paleolithic men in Europe had no ground tools.

During late post-glacial times, let us say from 6000 to 3000 or even 2000 B.C., while other people were beginning to farm elsewhere, coastal populations in Denmark and China were learning to catch migratory or shoal-basking fish in great numbers, to dry them, and to put them away as a staple food, much as the farmer stores his grain. With this ample food supply these populations grew, and held their own when farmers began to till the fields behind the coastal villages. The farmers too like smoked and dried fish. A brisk trade with the newcomers made room for more fishermen.

We know little about these fisherfolk except that they built comfortable houses on piles over the tidewater, hewed dugout canoes out of large tree trunks, plaited nets, and made hooks of bone. Their whole technology was dependent on the possession of polished-stone carpenter's tools, which others had invented elsewhere, and which the farmers brought with them. Fisherfolk live in villages, and if they migrate do so only seasonally, the way Americans migrate to the seashore in hot weather. A sedentary life is one of the prerequisites of agriculture, and certain botanists and geographers have postulated that agriculture arose among fishermen, but their argument is purely theoretical. All of the archæological evidence we have indicates that commercial fishing arose only after technical devices such as the polished-stone ax had reached Mesolithic hunters and fishermen following the rise of agriculture elsewhere.

Such a group of fisherfolk who survived into our time were the famous totem-pole Indians of the American northwest coast. They too used carpenter's tools of polished stone, including adzes, chisels, and wedges. With these tools they split planks from cedar logs and produced a magnificent decorative art that flourished even more once they had secured steel tools from the whalers and traders early in the nineteenth century. Food-gathering and food-processing took only a small part of their year. During the rest of the time they were therefore free to devote their attention to human relations. Their chief concerns were amusements and prestige. Amusements were provided by an elaborate cycle of winter dances, representing mythological events and the return of their deceased ancestors for an annual visit from the afterworld over the sea. Prestige was symoblized by elaborate reckoning of rank on the twin bases of birth and wealth, and wealth itself was enhanced by a ceremony called the potlatch, in which rival capitalists competitively destroyed their own property.

From the standpoint of reconstructing the history of our ancestors during the last part of the Pleistocene, the study of these Indians only goes to prove that, given good tools, ample food, and idle seasons, all sorts of social complexities can arise among pre-agricultural peoples, and it is possible that our ancestors of the Aurignacian were living in stratified societies too, as different from the simple existence of the Ona or Tasmanian as that of a member of the Racquet Club is from the life of a Mexican wetback. The professional sculptors and painters of the northwest coast, the Haida, produced masterpieces, but so did the Aurignacian artists, who must also have been able to specialize in order to perfect their techniques.

Of Primitive Arts and Industries

DURING all of these changes brought about by new inventions, one aspect of economic life remained little altered from the days of Pithecanthropus, and that was gathering—the woman's daily task of seeking roots, berries, insects, and other edible objects and substances to supplement the meat brought in by her husband. We believe that it remained unchanged because it is still done today, not only by the wives of primitive hunters, but by the women in peasant communities in Europe and elsewhere, in particular seasons. We still do it ourselves when we go forth armed with pails to pick blueberries.

Picking and gathering requires containers. The most primitive people of whom we know are all expert at weaving baskets and carrying-bags of different kinds of fiber, including roots, bark, and human hair. As this skill requires no implements at all, it may easily go far back in human history. Carrying roots and berries is easy enough, but another even more vital commodity presents transportation problems. That is water. Sub-human primates, like other animals, drink where the water flows. Only man carries it to where he lives. The Tasmanians, technologically the simplest of peoples, had not fully solved this problem when discovered. For the most part, they drank at springs and streams, having no water containers except the hollow portions of certain giant seaweeds, which they used only when near the shore. Luckily, springs and streams are not far apart in Tasmania. In Australia, where sources of water are widely separated, the aborigines carried it about in scooped-out wooden troughs, which probably cost them more trouble to make than any other artifact. A handful of leaves on the surface of the water kept it from splashing out. In South Africa, the Bushmen stored water in ostrich-egg shells at points in the desert where they would need it while hunting. In Tierra del Fuego the Canoe Indians (Yahgans) carried it about in sewn beech-bark buckets, painted red, and the Foot Indians (Ona) used guanaco-skin bags similarly calked.

From what we know of the cooking methods of modern primitives, it seems unlikely that our Late Pleistocene ancestors used any method except roasting. Tasmanians, Australians, Fuegians, and Bushmen all prepare or prepared their food by laying it over the fire; sometimes they clean it, more often not. Tasmanians and most Australians did not bother to skin it. There is no clear evidence of boiling before the beginnings of agriculture. At the same time, the surviving primitives are largely ignorant of food-preservation. All of the peoples mentioned employed the grease stone, a flat piece of stone on which they carried spare fat, just as a housewife saves her bacon drippings in an old coffee can. This grease, useful for many things, could be eaten as an emergency ration. It is highly likely that Upper Paleolithic man in Europe and Asia took advantage of the preservative qualities of cold, and was able to keep meat for weeks or months during the winter, but we have no evidence of other techniques of food-preservation before the rise of wholesale fishing in post-glacial times. This does not mean that it did not exist, but merely that we do not know of it.

Contemporary evidence also gives us a poor picture of early clothing. The Tasmanians habitually went naked, in a damp climate with a mean annual temperature of 54° F., and a July mean of 45° F. Women with babies used a kangaroo skin to tie the baby to the back, and in winter both men and women sometimes covered the back with a robe of one or two kangaroo skins sewn together with fiber strings and tied on by strings around the neck or waist. A sealskin lashed to the back sufficed to warm the Yahgans in the chilly waters of Tierra del Fuego, along with the fires that they kept burning in their canoes on clay hearths. At night they also had fires inside their huts.

On the high plains north of the mountain spine of Tierra del Fuego, where the temperature may average as low as 24° F. in the coldest month, the Ona Indians perfected the simple robe to suit their minimum needs. Sewing together several warm guanaco skins, they made a robe voluminous enough to cover the entire body, and also produced moccasins for their feet. The necessity of holding the robe on immobilized one hand; the hunter habitually dropped his robe when ready to aim with his bow.

Clothing like this is good enough for a climate as cold as, let us say, that of Massachusetts or Michigan, but it could hardly suffice for the bleak plains of Russia during a glacial advance, when some of our ancestors were out hunting mammoths. They must have had garments that not only kept the body warm, but also permitted them unencumbered movement while clothed. On deductive grounds, using as a basis the known history of clothing and the distribution of clothing types among modern cold-climate people, one is reluctant to postulate the invention of the Eskimo suit by that time. Some compromise between that and the Ona's robe, which let a man move his arms actively while clothed, is likely. Warm footgear they must have had. The contemporary cave paintings show men naked and women wearing tailed skirts or aprons. This was probably summer and indoor wear.

Quantities of red ochre have been found in Upper Paleolithic sites, often in the form of lumps of powdered and ground iron oxide. These lumps may have been held together with animal fats. Nearly all living hunters use such a mixture as a cosmetic, smearing it on their bodies in ornamental patterns to indicate affiliation, sex, or status. The fat serves as a protection against cold, and the combination of the grease and the red pigment acts as a protection against the sun. In all probability this trick had been discovered by the beginning of Upper Paleolithic times.

Of Early Transportation

I N the chain of cause and effect which starts with primary tools, speech, and fire, and goes on through secondary tools and such techniques as food-preservation and tailoring, the end product in a technical sense is transport and communication. Moving people and their goods around and letting them talk with one another is what increases the size and complexity of societies. Of the communication of Upper Paleolithic and Mesolithic man we know almost nothing except that Upper Paleolithic hunters apparently kept count of their seasons' kills on notched sticks. These tallies may, however, have been formal invitations to weddings, with the notches indicating the number of days to elapse before the ceremony. Australians make such message sticks.

As far as we can tell, Upper Paleolithic hunters also had no means of transportation other than the power of their own limbs before the last melting of the ice. The same is true of the living food-gatherers of the southern hemisphere, who walk when they travel on land, carrying their goods on their backs or heads. In

Mesolithic times European man invented both the sled and the
ski, which helped him move himself and his possessions in the
winter. In the summer he poled his way along forest streams in a
dugout canoe. Like the sleds and skis, these have been preserved
in bogs.

Even the Australians and Tasmanians, whose tool kits were inferior to those of Upper Paleolithic Europeans, were able to make
boats good enough to carry them across streams. This can be done
by gathering several hundred reeds from the side of the river and
tying them with grass or bark ropes in cigar-shaped bundles.
Three such bundles, when lashed together, with one as a bottom
and two for sides, will carry one or more passengers. The Egyptians used these on the Nile in earliest times, and the Indians of
Bolivia and Peru sail them on Lake Titicaca today. It takes no
tools to build such a boat. Man could have made them at any time
in his history, but when he began to do so is a mystery.

The Social and Intellectual Life of Late Ice Age Hunters

B y the use of all of these new technical devices, Upper Paleolithic man had acquired many advantages over his predecessors
of the Lower and Middle periods. He could hunt more efficiently,
in terms of both time and effort, and he could eat his food more
quickly. The size of his communities was probably larger in most
environments, and the time available for teaching and ceremonies
longer. The archæological record itself gives us some hints about
his social structure, as it did with the earlier periods, but we no
longer have to turn to living apes for ideas about how human
beings may have got along together. Abundant evidence from the
survivors of this ancient cultural level helps us piece out a broad
picture.

The universe in which an individual lived consisted of himself,
other people, the non-human part of the world which he per-
ceived and experienced, and a host of symbols that had meaning
to him in the way of life which he and his fellows led. The individual, having survived the rigors of outdoor life to the age of

twenty-five, would be healthy and in good flesh, as zoo-keepers say: a highly efficient animal in its prime. Granting for a moment that this individual was a male, he undoubtedly had one or more wives and several children. He also had a number of brothers, sisters, and other close kin. Possibly a father or mother survived, but if so, that parent at the age of forty-five or fifty was considered old—in fact, was in the last stages of decrepitude. The total number of persons, mostly kin, whom our man habitually saw and dealt with was under fifty. Everyone whom he was used to seeing he knew; patterns of behavior had been so carefully worked out for thousands of years that he knew exactly what to do when his mother-in-law faced him on the path, or what cut of meat he should give his aging father to masticate between his worn and broken teeth.

If he happened to see a stranger, he would take care. If by some special kind of body paint or other telltale sign he saw that the stranger was a member of a hostile group, he would either kill the stranger or hide from him. The choice of killing or hiding depended to a certain extent on the place of the meeting. If it was on home territory and the stranger seemed to be trespassing, particularly if he was poaching game, then a spear-thrust would be the answer. If our man was himself poaching, he would unquestionably hide rather than take the offensive. If, however, the stranger was painted in some special way—as for example to indicate that he was bent on trade—or carried some sort of message from one group to another, then our man would make himself known to him, and a conversation would ensue, according to polite procedure, either by speech alone, or by sign language if the two had no language in common.

Relations with the non-human world were frequent and important. Animals, being more numerous than men, occupied man's attention. Day after day he hunted them, until by the age of twenty-five he knew their habits intimately and could even identify individual bears or wolves by their tracks. He could tell if they were well or ill, glutted or ravenous, old or young, male or female, pregnant or in milk. He knew when the wolverine would climb a tree or the bear decide to await him in a clump; many of his ancestors and kin had been clawed or bitten to death by animals, and these lessons had not been forgotten. Attention to animals took as much of his time and energy as the work of any man takes today. Hunting kept him away from camp for days at a time and limited him to the companionship of two or three other men, if indeed he did not hunt alone.

To the women the world of plants was almost equally absorbing. From plants came roots and berries and succulent leaves to piece out the menu, providing not only needed nutritional factors, but also sustenance itself when the hunt failed. From them came fuel to cook the meals and keep the family warm. From them came fibers for baskets and bags and cords and mats; from them also mysterious properties for curing sickness and easing pains. These properties were attributed to spiritual beings who either lodged visibly in the plants themselves or worked through their agency. Burned wood became a substance of another kind—charcoal—black paint. From the mineral world came iron oxide to serve as red paint, and kaolin for white pigment. Flint, too, was basic, and flint did not occur naturally in every part of the landscape. Those who had it could trade it, or let members of other tribes come through their territory to mine it. This kind of generosity paid off in that it allowed the members of several groups to meet one another, pass on ideas, and trade in other objects, like iron oxide or special kinds of wood. Only by such meetings could a new technique of flint-flaking be disseminated.

For still another reason it was good policy to carry on periodic relations with one's neighbors over the hill, particularly if the climate was changing or the annual rainfall variable. Suppose that a drought in the territory of band A drove most of the animals over into the land of B; then the A people would starve if they could not move. If they had seen the B people many times and danced and gone through ceremonies with them, perhaps their messenger would return with an invitation: "Come over and share the hunting with us."

Every year there are certain times when food is more abundant than at the other times. During these times of abundance, many people can live off a few square miles of land. That is the time when people can get together, when two or three hundred people, members of from two to a half-dozen bands, can meet. Each meeting of many persons needs an agenda; otherwise it becomes a disorganized mob, and conflict follows. The agendas of such meetings are time-honored and traditional. Older men talk together formally; younger men wrestle; at certain times designated individuals get up and dance, acting out routines derived from the behavior of certain animals, from the actions of hunters pursuing or stalking these animals, and other routines derived from famous deeds of ancestors long dead. At night, fires will glow on painted bodies and painted faces; formal dancing routines shift, and couples make for the shrubbery. Normal sexual rules break down, and only the basic tabus of mother and son, father and daughter, brother and sister, prevent nocturnal unions.

These meetings served a biological as well as a social purpose. Women whose sexual relations with their husbands had been fruitless were given another chance, which enhanced the survival value of all groups concerned. The exchange of genes was just as important as the trading of flint for special kinds of wood which went on under cover of ritual, for it aided the process of variation and selection essential to the perpetuation of all contributing communities. After these meetings formal marriages were also made between groups.

The group itself consisted of a small number of separate families of father, mother, and children; two generations were normally represented, and sometimes three, but few individuals lived past their physiological prime. Generations in themselves were not important. A man forty may have a brother twenty. A woman may have a daughter and a sister of the same age. Age was more important, because persons of the same age and sex did the same things, and did them together.

These age groups were designated by different symbols, in the style of clothing, in manner of using body paint, or in behavior itself. The repertory of symbols used by the members of a band was complete; it represented all of the possible relationships among people and between human beings and the inhuman, or superhuman, world. First of all is the configuration of language.

We do not know what languages the hunters of the Late Pleistocene spoke, but we may be sure they were numerous. Simple
hunters living today have almost as many languages as there are
groups of bands which come together for ceremonies in the fat
seasons. We may be equally sure that they were adequate, in that
every kind of animal hunted had a whole roster of names to indicate its sex, age, and condition; that if snow was important, a
dozen or more words would designate snow, while the list of numbers may have gone from three or six to "many," *i.e.*, infinity.

Other symbols expressed the relationship of man to nature.
Each category of useful beast or herb had its soul, which presented itself from time to time to people, giving men important
messages. Game laws and laws of conservation were rigidly enforced by a system of tabus which automatically protected important species at certain seasons, through the fear of vengeance
from the spirits concerned. These spirits could also be invoked for
success in hunting, by the hunters acting out an event in the
mythological creation of a certain kind of animal. Above all, the
equilibrium of nature in which man participates must not be disturbed; ceremonies symbolically maintain it, making it clear that
for a man to kill a deer is a part of the normal course of natural
events in the environment in which he lives.

The world of the hunter cannot be limited to the part of the far-
stretching landscape on which he pursues his game, to the members of his own group and those of his friends and enemies over
the hills, the animals and plants that sustain his life, and the spirits
of these animals and plants. It must also include the spirits of his
own ancestors, who, though they are dead, are still in a sense
alive. The length of time that the soul of a dead man survives depends on his importance to those who are still alive. If he was a
fine hunter in his prime, the leader of the band, the man who
divided the meat, the arbiter of quarrels, the teacher of boys, and
a good husband, his death will cause a disturbance in the life of
the band which will bring his image often to mind among most of
its members. He is certainly finite and close at hand: he can be
prayed to, invoked, asked for decisions in matters like those which
he was accustomed to settle.

If he was an indifferent hunter, a poor husband, and a quarrelsome person, his soul will be dim, and before many years have passed people will forget about him. His soul will have disappeared. After many years have passed and no one still lives who has actually seen the great man whose soul was large after death, his exploits gradually become merged with those of still greater heroes of the past, whose name his own may supplant. Gradually

ANATOMICAL PERFECTION IN CAVE ART — STAGS IN CALAPATA CAVE, NEAR CRETAS (TERUEL), SPAIN.

the invisible world becomes peopled with a stable cast. These are the men and women who made the landscape, who caused this hill to rise and that brook to flow; some of them symbolize areas of disturbance between men and women, young and old, people and nature. Of the last, of course, the chief ones are the weather; storms may be caused by the anger of some great spirit unwittingly annoyed by human beings who have done something that disturbs the relationships within the group.

One great solace in the face of disturbance is art. Luckily the great art of Upper Paleolithic men has been preserved in the caves of France, Spain, and Italy by a constant temperature and humidity. The cave paintings made with mineral pigments and the outlines engraved with burins stand out among the finest works of art of all time. The perfect treatment of animal bodies indicates that

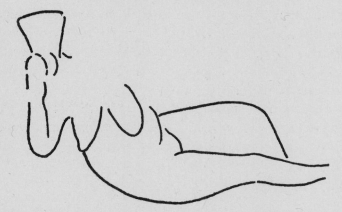

AN UPPER PALEOLITHIC WALL ENGRAVING, LA MAGDELEINE, FRANCE.

the painters, who were consummate draftsmen, knew intimately
the anatomy of the animals they depicted. They must have dissected dozens of such animals in detail before they began to paint
them, just as Leonardo dissected human bodies for his artistry.
According to a noted painter, Percy Leason, many of the Magdalenian cave paintings of animals were meant to look dead. Only
the magnificent frescoes of Lascaux Cave seem to show composition, but in the bone-engravings animals are meaningfully
grouped.

In a Sicilian cave near Palermo is a uniquely composed depic-
tion of a group of masked dancers, surrounding two male victims
who are being strangled with thongs stretched from their heels
to their necks.[3] As often happens when men are being strangled,
having their necks broken, or both, these two victims are depicted
as having erections. The dancers who surround them have their
hands raised. Their masks are hard to identify, and may represent
birds' heads or those of animals. Some look a little like space
helmets.

Many archæologists and other experts have speculated on the
interpretation of this macabre scene, without reaching any definite
conclusions.

---

[3] This and hundreds of other Paleolithic works of art are shown in Paolo
Graziosi's *Paleolithic Art*, McGraw-Hill, New York, 1960.

A well-drawn French cave painting shows a hunter dressed in an antler disguise. Psychologists and critics have read into this work of art all sorts of sinister meanings. To an anthropologist familiar with primitive hunting techniques this is just a man ready to hunt deer. Perhaps he is practicing. Perhaps he is trying to induce the spirit of the forest that controls the deer to make a fat buck walk his way, but to my way of thinking there is nothing more sinister in it than a picture of an American jet pilot putting on his electrically heated stratosphere suit before taking off. Whatever the artist's overt motive in painting it, he did it because he felt a creative urge and liked to express himself, as every artist does, whether he is painting a bison on the wall of a cave or a mural in the main hall of a bank.

Ice Age Institutions

I N place of the word *group,* which has a general meaning, sociologists use the more technical term *institution* in a special sense. The institutions to which a person in any culture may belong are the family, the economic institution, the political institution, the religious institution, the educational institution, and associations. Because the narrative thread of this book is an account of the way in which human beings have unwittingly increased the size and complexity of their institutions through their increasing control of the forces of nature and their growing technical skill, we must make sure that the meaning of the term is understood. If you go to church once in a while and are not a member, you do not belong to a religious institution. That particular religious institution is composed of a number of members who attend regularly and respond in unison to the voice and gestures of the leader. Similarly, the men who work in a factory regularly and obey the orders of their employer belong to an economic institution. If they are union men, they also belong to an association. Unless you are both a bachelor and an orphan, you belong to a family.

Unlike hunting techniques, institutions leave no easily detected archæological remains, but only a few hints here and there. Much deduction, combined with the evidence of the social systems of living hunters, helps us trace them. According to our reconstruction, the Late Ice Age family was a closely knit body, as is nearly always the case. It covered two, and sometimes three, generations, but rarely more. It was in itself an economic institution in that it produced its own food, clothing, implements, and shelter. The band was a sovereign state, informally led by an outstanding hunter, who may also have been a man of good judgment, though the older men as a group probably steered decisions. They themselves acted as a court of law. If a member created so much disturbance that he interfered with the normal functioning of social processes, the old men would get together one night to do away with him. The state also took over economic functions: the best hunter or the older men distributed the meat among families and saw that no one starved.

The educational institution was pooled between the family and the band. A baby's earliest teaching came from its mother, older sisters, and other girls of the older sister's age group; as the child grew older, it played with others of its age, and then the boy began going hunting with his father, the girl continuing to gather with her mother. At puberty the band took over education completely. Boys were isolated in a group, where the older men put them through a series of impressive ordeals, including in many cases mutilation. We know this because silhouettes of hands from which certain fingers had been amputated have been left on the walls of French caves, and in Algeria and Germany skulls of individuals over the age of puberty have had their upper median incisor teeth knocked out. Finger-chopping and tooth-knocking are common puberty-school mutilations among living primitive peoples.

By such jolts to the nervous system and by fasting and keeping vigils, it was not hard for a boy to reach a physiological state where visions are easily seen, particularly if the boy is told to look for them. The appearance of masked men acting out the roles of ancestors or other spirits impressed him deeply. This heavy hazing was accompanied by a series of dramatic lectures on the proper behavior expected of adult men toward women, toward children, toward their elders, and toward the world of animals, plants, and spirits. The curriculum included every contingency likely to occur in the lifetime of the boys going through it. As this school could be held only in times of relative abundance and inactivity, several bands would participate in it at their annual meetings, and the boys who had been through it together would consider themselves classmates in the future. Thus the educational institution sometimes exceeded the bounds of the state, as in our own culture, where students from a dozen countries may attend an American university. For reasons stated in the last chapter, I believe that these bush schools go back to Lower Paleolithic cultures.

The Late Ice Age religious institution likewise exceeded political boundaries, as it should in any healthy society. Ancestral heroes who hovered over the band were shared by other bands that met at ceremonial times. Cult heroes responsible for the landscape and its animal life were likewise shared, as were the combined capacities of the old men teaching the young. Religion is the sum total of behavior concerned with restoring equilibrium to the individual or the group after disturbance. Every person is disturbed at one time or another, either by his own illness or by that of a spouse or child, and this disturbance must be reduced to its lowest possible level for the well-being of the group. Reducing or allaying disturbance requires the utmost human skill. A person possessing such skill is of the greatest value to the group. It can only be acquired by concentration, training, and practice, by an individual gifted from the start.

Healing—the Oldest Profession

THE RELIGIOUS practitioner, the *shaman,* was the first specialist. His profession, not prostitution, is the oldest. There can be little doubt that shamans existed in Late Pleistocene times, for they have been found among all living hunting peoples, even including the recently extinct Tasmanians.

A shaman is usually a man, though sometimes women who have passed the age of childbearing take over these functions. As a boy he is different from his companions. Dreamy, crotchety, ill-adjusted, he may fall ill about the time when he is supposed to show his prowess as a hunter; during these illnesses he has attracted the attention of shamans, who recognize a recruit in him. Instead of, or in addition to, the regular course of higher education which the other boys go through, the novice receives special treatment from the specialists, who hide him out in some retreat

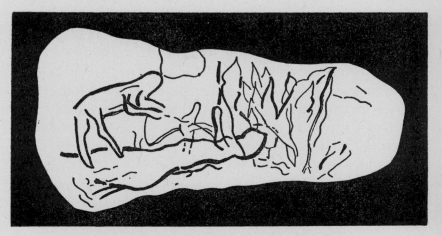

A SHAMAN HEALING A PATIENT. FRENCH CAVE ART.

of their own. Here he does much dreaming, and dreams are taken as seriously by hunters as by Freudian analysts. Something unusual happens. Among the Ona, who are about as legitimate representatives of Upper Paleolithic man as can be found, we are told that the shamans magically eviscerated the novice and replaced his innards with some fluffy soul-stuff like goose down. This formed a comfortable lodging place for spirits when the shaman was possessed. What actually happened will probably never be known.

Of one thing, however, we may be sure. The shaman learned a physiological control of some of his body functions normally considered automatic. Like a youthful Yogi, he was shown ways to produce states of inspiration through controlled-breathing exercises. Whirling dances and repetition of phrases combined to change temperature levels and to produce trance. Professors who lecture for an hour at a time to audiences of three hundred or more students in warm rooms, shouting to make themselves heard, sometimes hyperventilate themselves and say things that they had no intention of revealing. In our eagerness to know everything about the physical world from apes to atoms, we have neglected one aspect of science which requires no laboratory and no instruments, only the human body. Primitive men, lacking laboratories and instruments, studied it exhaustively.

Sober eyewitnesses have given us factual accounts of some of the startling performances of shamans. In his inimitable account of his early life with the Ona, Lucas Bridges [4] describes the actions of a shaman named Houshken. Bridges asked Houshken to demonstrate his powers. "Houshken did not refuse my request, but answered modestly that he was disinclined, the Ona way of saying that he might do it by and by.

"After allowing a quarter of an hour to elapse, Houshken said he was thirsty and went down to the nearby stream for a drink. It was a bright moonlight night and the snow on the ground helped to make the scene of the exhibition we were about to witness as light as day. On his return, Houshken sat down and broke into a monotonous chant, which went on until suddenly he put his hands to his mouth. When he brought them away, they were palms downward and some inches apart. We saw that a strip of guanaco hide, about treble the thickness of a leather bootlace, was now held loosely in his hands. It passed over his thumbs, under the palms of his half closed hands, and was looped over his little fingers so that about three inches of end hung down from each hand. The strip appeared to be not more than eighteen inches long.

"Without pulling the strip tight, Houshken now began to shake his hands violently, gradually bringing them farther apart, until the strip, with the two ends still showing, was about four feet long. He then called his brother, Chashkil, who took the end from his

4 Lucas Bridges, *Uttermost Part of the Earth*, E. P. Dutton & Co., New York, and Hodder & Stoughton, London, 1949. Quotations from pp. 263–4, 284–6, with permission from both publishers.

right hand and stepped back with it. From four feet, the strip now grew out of Houshken's left hand to double that length. Then as Chashkil stepped forward, it disappeared back into Houshken's hand, until he was able to take the other end from his brother. With the continued agitation of his hands, the strip got shorter and shorter. Suddenly, when his hands were almost together, he clapped them to his mouth, uttered a prolonged shriek, then held out his hands to us, palms upward and empty.

"Even an ostrich could not have swallowed those eight feet of hide at one gulp without visible effort. Where else the coil could have gone to I do not profess to know. It could not have gone up Houshken's sleeve, for he had dropped his robe when the performance began. There were between twenty and thirty men present, but only eight or nine were Houshken's people. The rest were far from being friends of the performer and all had been watching intently. Had they detected some simple trick the great medicine man would have lost his influence; they would no longer have believed in any of his magic.

"The demonstration was not yet over. Houshken stood up and resumed his robe. Once again he broke into a chant and seemed to go into a trance, possessed by some spirit not his own. Drawing himself up to his full height, he took a step toward me and let his robe, his only garment, fall to the ground. He put his hands to his mouth with a most impressive gesture and brought them away again with fists clenched and thumbs close together. He held them up to the height of my eyes, and when they were less than two feet from my face, slowly drew them apart. I saw that there was now a small, almost opaque object between them. It was about an inch in diameter in the middle and tapered away into his hands. It might have been a piece of semi-transparent dough or elastic, but whatever it was it seemed to be alive, revolving at great speed, while Houshken, apparently from muscular tension, was trembling violently.

"The moonlight was bright enough to read by as I gazed at this strange object. Houshken brought his hands farther apart and the object grew more and more transparent, until, when some three inches separated his hands, I realized that it was not there any more. It did not break or burst like a bubble; it simply disappeared, having been visible to me for less than five seconds. Houshken made no sudden movement, but slowly opened his hands and turned them over for my inspection. They looked clean and dry. He was stark naked and there was no confederate beside him. I glanced down at the snow, and, in spite of his stoicism, Houshken could not resist a chuckle, for nothing was to be seen there.

"The others had crowded round us and, as the object disappeared, there was a frightened gasp from some of them. Houshken reassured them with the remark:

"'Do not let it trouble you. I shall call it back to myself again.'

"The natives believed this to be an incredibly malignant spirit belonging to, or possibly part of, the [shaman] from whom it emanated. It might take physical form, as we had just witnessed, or be totally invisible. It had the power to introduce insects, tiny mice, mud, sharp flints, or even a jelly fish or baby octopus, into the anatomy of those who had incurred its master's displeasure. I have seen a strong man shudder involuntarily at the thought of this horror and its evil potentialities."

Lucas Bridges was a man of extraordinary detachment, and a splendid reporter. What he saw he could not explain. It is clear that Houshken had to work himself up into some kind of ecstasy to perform these tricks. How he did them is not clear, nor is it important for the purposes of this book. The fact remains that he was able to make the Ona among his audience believe in his supernatural powers. By means of them, in their opinion, he could cause disease among his enemies and cure it among his friends. This reputation made his life both easier and harder. He had to exert himself less in the food quest, for others fed him. He had the satisfaction of being the center of attention. At the same time his life was in constant danger. Illness and ill-fortune might be attributed to him, and he could easily be killed. As Bridges specifically states: "Frequently the chief object of a raiding party, in the perpetual clan warfare of the Ona, was to kill the medicine man of an opposing group."

At one time Bridges let two shamans and the wife of one of

them try to prepare him for initiation into their profession. "My inception took place by a small fire, with the usual shelter of guanaco skins spread on the windward side. After giving me a harangue on the serious nature of my undertaking, Tininisk suggested that I should strip. I did as instructed, and remained half reclining on my clothing and some guanaco skins while he went over my chest with his hands and mouth as intently as any doctor with his stethoscope; moving in the prescribed manner from place to place, pausing to listen here and there. He also gazed intently at my body, as though he saw through it like an X-ray manipulator.

"Then, the two men dropping their robes and Leluwhachin her cape though retaining her [female inner garment], they literally put their heads—and hands—together and produced something that I could see. It might have been the lightest grey down teased out into the shape of a woolly dog about four inches long, with a stout body and prick ears. With the trembling of their hands and possibly their breathing, they gave its movements a semblance of life. I noticed a peculiar scent that seemed to accompany this object as, with three pairs of hands held together, they brought it to my chest with many guttural sounds. I did not feel the pressure of the thing against my body, but without any sudden movement it was no longer in their hands.

"This performance was repeated three times and, though each time a new puppy was supposed to be put in my body, I felt only the touch of the magicians' hands.

"Now came a solemn pause, as if of expectation. Then Tininisk asked me if I felt anything moving in my heart; or if I could see something strange in my mind, something like a dream; or if I felt any inclination to chant. The truthful answer was an unequivocal 'No,' but I put my denial as mildly as possible. . . . No, I would not become a [shaman], to be blamed, maybe, for a fatal heart attack a hundred miles away."

Had Mr. Bridges been an Ona, he might well have believed that these fluffy objects had entered his body. He might have felt something stir within him, and he might have been inclined to chant. He would then have been able to practice as a healer, in the following manner: "Standing or kneeling beside the patient, gazing intently at the spot where the pain was situated, the doctor would allow a look of horror to come over his face. Evidently he could see something invisible to the rest of us. His approach might be slow or he might pounce, as though afraid that the evil thing that had caused the trouble would escape. With his hands he would try to gather the malign presence into one part of the patient's body—generally the chest—where he would then apply his mouth and suck violently. Sometimes this struggle went on for an hour, to be repeated later. At other times the [shaman] would draw away from his patient with the pretense of holding something in his mouth with his hands. Then, always facing away from the encampment, he would take his hands from his mouth gripping them tightly together, and, with a guttural shout difficult to describe and impossible to spell, fling this invisible object to the ground and stamp fiercely upon it. Occasionally a little mud, some flint or even a tiny, very young mouse might be produced as the cause of the patient's indisposition."

Lucas Bridges was the son of Thomas Bridges, missionary to the Indians of Tierra del Fuego. Lucas spent most of his life on the island. While his father had concentrated on the conversion and acculturation of the Yahgans in the waterways to the south of the island, Lucas moved north into Ona territory, where he established a sheep ranch and employed many of the hunters. Had it not been for an epidemic of measles which nearly wiped them out in 1924, he probably would have succeeded in leading several thousands of Upper Paleolithic hunters over a fifteen-thousand-year cultural transition into the Industrial Age. Today a few of them live in shacks near Lake Navarin, and Lucas Bridges has died.

In all of the literature of anthropology I have failed to find a clearer, more circumstantial account of the activities of a Stone Age shaman than his. The shaman, being the first specialist to arise, was an all-purpose expert in human relations. He cured the sick as much as it is possible for human beings to be cured by suggestion, massage, sucking, and phlebotomy. He raised the morale of his own group by his invisible warfare with the enemy. In case of calamity he provided a convenient scapegoat, and above all he furnished entertainment. He believed in his mice and quartz-crystals as much as a Christian priest believes in the wine and wafers that he uses in Communion. From the shaman is descended a long line of specialists, including priests, diagnosticians, surgeons, teachers, and scholars. A good priest, a good doctor, a good teacher, or a good scholar has to be a bit of a showman to do his work properly. At the same time he has to believe in the sanctity of his mission. Those readers who, like myself, are somewhat on the shaman side will understand this.

The Hunter Needs No Hobby

O N E fact about the life of a hunter which all who have lived among such people have noticed is that hunting is fun. Hunters take pleasure in their work. Human beings have been hunters for a long time, and our physiology is adjusted to this kind of life. As E. J. Faris [5] has shown, a man is at his best from the standpoint of fertility if he is away from home a night or two at a time, giving his sperm cells a chance to accumulate. Hunting gives him just these little absences. Hunting exercises the whole body, as few other occupations do. It places a premium on keen eyesight. Farsightedness is an asset. As we grow older, we tend to grow farther-rather than nearer-sighted. Hunting develops the muscles and tissue of his hands properly, instead of deforming and thickening them as farming and unskilled labor may do.

It also places a premium on the capacity to make quick decisions, to act quickly, and to work in teams. Obedience and leadership can be developed in no better school. Courage is also a necessary component, and that peculiarly human thing, the willingness of a man to die in order to save the other members of his group. Man is a creature fashioned around and selected for hunting. Wealthy men who can pick and choose their ways of spending their days like to hunt. The Persians gave us the word *paradise,* which originally meant simply a hunting preserve. A good hunter

[5] E. J. Faris, *Human Fertility and Problems of the Male,* The Author's Press, White Plains, N.Y., 1950.

is always on the alert, always ready to take advantage of unexpected circumstances. He is constantly seeking for new things. In our society, the men who find fun in their work and need no hobbies or vacations are the scientists and research men, including the archæologists and anthropologists, who have carried the hunting spirit into new fields.

4

THE TILLER AND HERDSMAN

The Third Phase of History

B Y 6000 B.C. the Scandinavian ice sheet had melted to a pair of white dots on the map of Europe and had disappeared. Farther south and east, in Turkey, Palestine, and the lands bordering the southern end of the Caspian Sea, the third phase of history had begun as Neolithic men had started to till fields, herd domestic animals, and live in villages. During the Neolithic (New Stone) and the following ages of phase three of history, man invented many new occupations for which the body of a hunter is not primarily suited. His hands became calloused and gnarled with plowing and with handling tools at the craftsman's bench, or soft and stained with the ink of the scribe. His legs weakened as he spent his days working on a stool, and his eyes strained as he focused his vision on small objects of wood, clay, or metal which he fashioned with his hands. Culture now took precedence over biology as the chief guide to man's activities.

The chain of discoveries and inventions which he then made was to increase many times over the population of the earth, his speed of travel, and his range of communication until technology had reached its present global limits. Because his specialized technical work involves the synchronized co-operation and the management of vast numbers of persons, man incidentally and unwittingly converts thermal, mechanical, and electronic energy into social structure. The institutions that he created grew in numbers, size, and complexity of detail, until the world came to be enmeshed in a living framework of interlocking organizations of prodigious complexity. It became an intricate, pulsating pattern held together by modern techniques of communication. As democracy can be enjoyed by the number of persons who can be reached by a single voice, so modern institutions can include the people who can see and hear world personalities by radio, television, and the press. Here too man's expenditure of energy in building and operating communication machinery has been converted into social structure.

Although it lasted only eight thousand years, the third phase of history included eight distinct ages comparable to the Paleolithic and Mesolithic. These were the Neolithic, Bronze, Iron, Gunpowder, Coke, Oil, Hydroelectric, and First Atomic ages. So much more intricate was the third phase than the first two that many times more space is needed to describe it, even in outline. That will take the rest of this book.

The Nature of the Neolithic

SHORTLY before 6000 B.C. the world's climate had reached what is called a post-glacial optimum, a little warmer than at present. In certain parts of the world favored with abundant rainfall and rich animal and vegetable life, men had begun to settle down. Those who lived on the shores of large lakes and broad rivers had an abundance of fish and fowl to eat in season as well as the flesh of animals. By paddling and poling bark or log canoes they could transport heavy loads of foodstuffs, skins, and processed materials. Village life, for at least part of the year, became possible. So did wealth.

In the old days when a man could own only what he could carry on his body as he followed his hunting path from camp to camp, strength, skill, and wisdom had been all that he needed for a successful existence. Some men were leaders, others followers, but the range of variation in material possessions was small. Only qualities of personality and character gave men distinction. Once wealth could be stored from season to season, human life entered a new dimension. Another basis for distinction had arisen. The capitalist will say that this gave the gifted man his chance for progress that could benefit all men in the end; the socialist that it led to exploitation of the masses. In any event, the rise of property stimulated trade, which in turn widened the opportunities of people from different villages and regions to get together.

When nearly all men were Mesolithic hunters, as they still were when the Neolithic was young, human beings differed from the rest of the animal community in which they lived in no conspicuous way that an objective visitor from another planet could have detected at once. They had altered the landscape on which they hunted no more than most other animals had—and far less than beavers, bees, and earthworms. The coincidence of camp-fires with the presence of man might have given the visitor a clue, and the yapping of dogs at his approach could have caused him to remark that here was an example of parasitism, or symbiosis, like that between ants and aphids, and this would have obscured his judgment, for the partnership of man and dog was less material than spiritual. Still, the spears, bows, and knives that men had learned to fashion were really nothing more than demountable substitutes for the fangs, claws, and swift hoofs of the other animals, and to all practical purposes, from a cosmic viewpoint, nature was still in balance. That terrestrial skin-cancer, man, had not yet passed from the latent to the virulent stage. He had not yet felled the earth's forests, caused its soils to wash away, fouled the mouths of its rivers with his cities, or threatened the planet's death with his atomic devices.

Man first began to disturb the earth's surface when he made his third conquest of natural forces, by learning to cultivate plants and to breed animals in captivity. It is reasonable to suppose that for a long time before this Mesolithic hunters, fishermen, and fowlers who lived seasonally in villages had made pets of baby animals and nursed them to maturity, only to eat them or to turn them loose when it came time to move. These same food-gatherers must have observed that food plants grow luxuriantly in refuse heaps where the seeds and pits and tops are thrown, and these unwittingly sown crops must have been eaten.

Neither animal-husbandry nor garden-tilling could have come from these practices and observations until man had devised some means to clear the forest and to build pens and folds. He needed to clear the forest to plant crops in the rich, loose loam between the stumps, and he needed pens to keep his animals from being eaten by wolves and from running away. Both forest-clearing and pen-building require a good woodworking tool. Such a tool was the polished-stone ax. When he got it, he began the life of a tiller and herdsman, a way of life which the majority of mankind still follows, and which forms the basis of our own existence. Wheat, beef, pork, milk, beans, pottery, weaving, wool, beer, and wine came to man as part of this cultural pattern, which is known as the Neolithic stage of human culture.

Just as the burin had been man's first passport to America, so the polished-stone ax was his key to the life of a farmer. Between the two devices, burin and ax, a logical train of invention may be followed. With the burin, Upper Paleolithic man roughed out weapons of antler by gouging and scraping. Then he finished their surfaces by grinding and polishing. Mesolithic man, who was more concerned with woodworking, used the same technique to produce staghorn chisels and wedges. Once he had transferred this method to hard, tough stone, he made an ax, and the Neolithic could, under the right circumstances in a few favored parts of the world, begin. The best of these early axes, which are made of jade, will cut like steel. Pecking, grinding, and polishing them was tedious work. Although it may have taken a month to make one, it would last a long time if carefully handled.

At first man did not need to cut down all of the trees in his plantation, for if he ringed the bark they would die, and he could fell and burn them later. The rich soil, deposited between the trunks by the decay of vegetation, would give him a fine crop, at least for a few years, and then he could clear another patch. When all of the land within easy walking distance of his village had come into use, the community could divide, and some of its members found a new village elsewhere.

The houses of these villages were built, not of logs and planks, but of pole frames with the walls filled in with wattle and daub. Wattling is simply a basketry technique transferred to house-building. You set up a series of poles, an inch or two in thickness, along the line of the wall, planting their butts in the ground and lashing their tops to the framework. Then you use finer rods of some flexible wood like willow cut green in the spring, weaving them in and out horizontally between the uprights to make a basketry surface. When all of these surfaces have been finished, you smear wet clay on the walls, inside and out, and your house is enclosed. The roof frame you make of poles and withes also, and then you thatch it with bundles of straw from your grainfield. Now you have a typical Neolithic house, such as you can find in use in many countries today. The inner shrine of Glastonbury

RECONSTRUCTION OF A NEOLITHIC VILLAGE, FEDERSEE, GERMANY.

Cathedral, preserved for centuries because according to local tradition Christ once lived in it, was such a house.

When the thatch catches fire and the house burns down, the heat will bake some of the clay, turning it hard, leaving it like soft stone. Farmers who have learned the properties of clay from house-building and have seen the baked lumps that are left after a fire, and who need good waterproof and fireproof containers, can go on to the next logical invention: pottery. The heat of an ordinary cooking fire will bake clay hard enough for simple domestic procedures, including the boiling of food. Now his wife could make porridge and soup, economical foods which made it easy to wean children, and which old people with toothless gums could swallow.

As long as old women's fingers remained nimble and their eyes unfogged, they could sit in the sun outside the house in fine weather, or inside when it was cold, spinning wool and weaving it on simple upright looms. Thus the wool of the farmer's sheep, sheared with a flint blade, could be turned into cloth. Squares of cloth were useful not only for garments, but as standard articles of exchange, and hence of wealth. While the man was outside with his ax and his animals, his womenfolk could make pottery and weave between the times of planting and harvesting, when all hands were needed in the fields. Thus Neolithic man extended the hunter's division of labor between the sexes. To the duties of bringing in animal food and of tool-making, the men had added the crafts of hewing wood and carpentry. In place of her daily walkabout, the woman substituted both work in the fields and the skills of the potter and weaver.

The carpenter's task included setting up wattled fences to protect his fields from the inroads of wild animals, and others to keep his animals from straying. As a flock of goats can ruin a crop in a few hours, property lines became even more important than they had been in the hunting days, when hunters would hesitate to chase a wounded animal across a tribal boundary for fear of a retaliatory arrow. In Neolithic times boundaries needed more than marking. They had to be fenced, and fencing requires hard work with ax and stakes and hammer-stones and withes. Robert Frost's immortal line, "Good fences make good neighbors," was just as true in Neolithic times as it has been ever since.

This Neolithic pattern, out of which modern civilization arose, was dependent on the simultaneous exploitation of both animal and vegetable species, each being dependent on the other. Animals provide protein foods, skins, hair or wool for textiles, and milk. They likewise can be loaded with burdens, and their dung fertilizes fields. Vegetable products provide starches, sugars, oils, and some proteins as well, along with fibers and fodder for the animals in the seasons when grazing is poor or impeded by snow. The herding and care of domestic animals and their protection against predatory carnivores continue directly the traditional work of men; from hunter to herder is a natural transition. The cultivation of gardens is an equally direct sequel to the woman's search for wild vegetable foods. Thus in this new pattern each sex was able to make a parallel and separate transition from an old job to a new one, and the relations between men and women remained substantially unchanged. A little later, when men learned to plow with oxen, they took over the heavier work of agriculture, leaving women more time for such home industries as pottery-making and weaving. During the critical stations of the agricultural calendar, such as harvest time, men, women, and children would work in the fields together. Meanwhile, as men took over agricultural tasks, the care of flocks was given to boys or to professional shepherds.

This mixed animal and vegetable economy was not, however, the only agricultural system invented in the world. In some centers, women began to cultivate gardens, while no animals, aside from the dog, were tamed. In North America, for example, the corn-planting Indians from the Gulf of Mexico to the St. Lawrence grew a variety of vegetables, including maize, beans, and squash, which gave them a balanced vegetable diet. Most of the work was done by women. The men for the most part carried on their ancient profession of hunting, going off on long seasonal trips after game; but to them the meat was less important than the need for a well-organized, athletic, and masculine activity. With their particular kind of land-utilization, concentrated on the banks of streams and lakes, overpopulation was a problem, and so was the question of giving the men something to do outside the hunting season. In these societies there arose an elaborate system of games which kept the peace between neighboring villages, and an equally elaborate system of seasonal warfare based on the lifting of scalps; and both games and warfare were highly ceremonial, furnishing a framework for the preservation of order in masculine society. In Melanesia, another Neolithic culture that has persisted until modern times, the same development occurred.

The opposite kind of imbalance arises when a people concentrate on herding without horticulture. The Middle East and central Asia are full of various kinds of nomads who pasture their animals on deserts, mountain valleys, and steppes, but all of these live by trade with farmers, and thus are part of a complex utilization of a varied landscape, one of which we have no record before the ages of metal. All of these adjustments are interesting to the student of history because they show how versatile human beings can be in adapting themselves economically to different environments. While each has contributed something to our modern world civilization, particularly in the form of special species of plants and animals, like the citrus fruits, maize, tobacco, the turkey, and the camel, it was not through them that the main line of history passed.

In the countries in which the Neolithic of the Old World began, progress was rapid. Before the dawn of the earliest age of metal, Neolithic craftsmen equipped with polished-stone tools had learned to adze out large dugout canoes for the transport of goods in bulk on inland waterways, and had probably also invented the plow and the ox-drawn sled. Masons with stone hammers had learned to quarry and move huge stones and to set them up in walls and monuments that remain as engineering marvels to this day. The size of building stones follows the law of least effort: with the inefficient tools available to Neolithic stonecutters, it was easier to move a stone of ten tons' weight than to cut it into ten pieces of one ton each, and to smooth more than twice as much surface area.

From Neolithic times until the present moment, most of the food that men have eaten was the product of fields and flocks; most of his clothing was made of wool, the fibers of domestic plants, and leather tanned from the skins of herd animals. Most houses are still of wood, clay, and stone; most kitchenware is of pottery. Despite the growth of cities and the rise of kingdoms and empires and leagues of nations, most of the people of the world still live in villages and perform tasks invented by Neolithic man.

These tasks are essentially the preparation of fields, planting and harvesting of crops, daily care of animals, and household duties concerned with the preservation and processing of foodstuffs and of animal and vegetable by-products such as wool and flax. In countries where seasons are marked, activities are seasonal. In some of the daily tasks the people of the village work separately as families, but in those which occur seasonally and concern all, the entire community works together, as, for example, in house-building bees, held in slack seasons of field work.

Because the farmer is much concerned about the weather—a storm may ruin a crop—rain priests and wind priests arose beside the healers. Each village was likely to acquire a local spirit or god, which looked after the special interests of its inhabitants in times of crisis. Local, autonomous priests were absorbed into greater hierarchies. A priest provided comfort and strength to the villagers at such critical moments as marriages and deaths, and helped in quarrels between villages.

These quarrels had to be kept at a minimum because of the unequal distribution of natural resources over the landscape. One village might have a good supply of ax stone, another of clay, and another of iron oxide needed for red pigment. The easiest way to distribute these materials was through trade. Trade could go on only when there was peace. Hence villages within an economically unified area would form some kind of alliance, held together by periodic markets, ceremonies, and games, directly derived from the seasonal meetings of hunters.

Such, in brief, is the Neolithic way of life. It has survived not only in the upper reaches of the Amazon basin and the interior mountains of New Guinea, where garden-cultivators still fell trees with stone axes, but over a great part of the so-called civilized world. An airplane passenger flying over the cultivated regions of most of Europe, Asia, and Africa will see the landscape divided up into groups of fields within walking distance of the nucleus of each cluster. This nucleus is a village in which a few hundred human beings who have been born in that very place and brought up together pass their lives in a common effort to make their crops grow and their animals prosper and multiply. The pattern of human relations which arose from these efforts may still be seen in many countries, including France, Italy, Iran, India, Ethiopia, and Mexico, where the rise of cities merely created a division of labor between rural and urban communities.

Only two large nations have seriously upset it. In America, Yankee inventors of the last two centuries manufactured agricultural machinery to use on new land unencumbered by villages. Thus the airplane traveler flying across the continent will see a landscape laid out in a grid of squares so accurately marked that the pilot can set his course by it, and in these squares are individual farms as mechanized as factories. The farmers, by using labor-saving machinery, are able to send their children to high school and college. Because farming requires as much education as business or a profession, and because the modern farmer can commute to work from a town, just as a city worker can, the old distinctions between village rustic and urban sophisticate have been obliterated. Twentieth-century America has lost the Neolithic culture pattern because it never carried it beyond the eastern seaboard, which has become industrial. In Canada, New Zealand, Australia, and Argentina, European peoples have also taken over land not already devoted to mixed village farming. They have followed the American pattern, with improvements of their own.

The other large nation that has tried mechanization is Russia. There, however, the land was already occupied by Neolithic-style villagers, who could not be forced out of their ancient way of life without a severe jolt. Their leaders used the supreme power of the state to uproot them and to cram them into collective farms, on which they are supposed to imitate the American techniques of mass agriculture with machinery. As they own neither their land nor their machinery, and can accumulate little to leave their offspring, these peasants lack even the limited incentives of individual enterprise which they had before. Their synthetic escape from the shackles of Neolithic life has not yet been crowned with success. One wonders how the transition will be made in Europe, India, and China. Although the Neolithic began three thousand years before writing, and five and a half thousand before the birth of Herodotus, the "father of history," Neolithic culture is much more than a subject of inquiry by prehistorians. Moving out of it may be the world's most difficult problem.

The Beginnings of Cultivation

O N E clue to the origin of Neolithic culture, in which farming was so important, is the discovery of the origin of various cultivated plants, particularly through an identification of their wild prototypes. Botanists have gone on many expeditions to central Asia, Ethiopia, and other supposed focal points to look for wild wheats, ryes, beans, and fruit trees, and to see what relationship these have to our common varieties. The object of these searches is not only scientific knowledge, but also plant-improvement through hybridization and selection. Plant-improvement involves not only the size and taste of a fruit or seed, but also the ability of the plant to grow in different conditions of soil and climate, ease of sowing, weeding, harvesting, immunity from insect pests, and suitability for processing and storage.

These very qualities without doubt influenced the choice of the first farmers as to which plants to cultivate and which ones to continue picking wild. All the basic plant species of Neolithic agriculture, such as wheat, barley, flax, and beans, grow best in mid-latitude regions where seasonal change is marked and where everything ripens in a period of a few months. This made storage necessary, and hence the plants chosen for cultivation were those which would keep best when stored. The first farmers were probably people who had begun to collect and store their staples long before they thought of growing them—for instance, the Indians whom the white settlers found living in central California villages. The Indians gathered acorns, piñon nuts, and wild grass seeds in season and put them away in basketry containers to eat through the winter. When the Forty-niners cut down a huge oak tree in the Sacramento valley, the Indians wept, for to them the oak was a sacred symbol of food and prosperity, just as it had been two thousand years earlier in Greece.

Central California has what the geographers call a Mediterranean climate: its pattern of annual temperature and rainfall is similar to that of the lands bordering the Mediterranean Sea. Its wild products are similar to those of ancient, pre-agricultural

Greece, Lebanon, and Palestine, and parts of Iraq, Iran, and Turkestan, lands in which the Neolithic civilization reached far back into antiquity. The Mesolithic inhabitants of these lands must have stored acorns, nuts, and seeds in the same fashion as the Californians, to last them through the winter. Some of them still eat acorns.

In the springtime the womenfolk of these ancient gatherers must have waded along the stream banks gathering watercress and have walked bent-backed through the meadows searching for edible greens, just as Italian women used to comb the suburban lawns of America for dandelions. Through the summer and into the fall they could make excursions to dig up roots and bulbs, particularly those of the onion family, good not only for flavoring but also against worms.

These leaf crops, root crops, and bulb crops could also be cultivated, and many of them were. But they did not, in the times of which we have record, assume the same importance as the crops that could be easily stored and thus preserved in bulk through the hungry winter. The plants that formed the backbone of agriculture in the parts of the Old World from which our own civilization is derived were all of a kind in size, shape, condition, and ways of handling. Wheat and barley, the small grains, furnished predominantly starches. Broad beans, peas, and lentils furnished proteins. Sesame, flax, and hemp furnished oil. Most of them had additional uses: flax and hemp as fibers, wheat and barley as straw for thatching houses and bedding down cattle, and the legumes for adding nitrogen to the soil.

All of them come in the form of grains or seeds that can be dried and stored indefinitely. Thus they can not only provide food to last several years if enough is planted at once, but they can also be used as seed after a number of years, should the crops fail in the meantime. Therefore they are eminently suited for cultivation in regions of fickle rainfall, on the southeastern edge of the westerly storm belt, where rain falls only in the winter months. Being annuals, they all can be sown broadcast, a time- and labor-saving technique. All can be reaped in bulk rather than as individual plants, and the seeds can be removed from the stalks by threshing or flailing. All of them can be made into food either by boiling into porridges or by grinding and baking.

Suitability for reaping is not a feature of wild plants. When a head of wild grain ripens, it opens and the seeds cast themselves on the ground. When a wild pea plant matures, its pods burst open and its seeds scatter. Were this not true, the plants would commit suicide. Human beings gathering such seeds have to work fast,

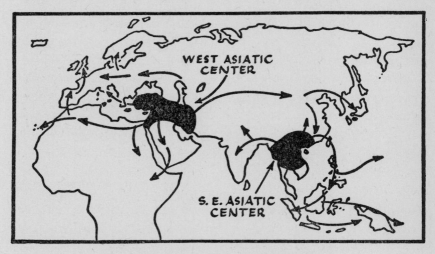

NEOLITHIC ORIGINS AND EXPANSIONS

beating the stems and stalks with sticks at just the right time to make the seeds fall into baskets. The amount of seed that an individual can gather in a season, before it becomes trampled, rots, or has been collected by birds and squirrels, is small.

Now and then a wild plant puts forth a suicidal mutation in which its head or pod lacks the ability to open. Ordinarily such a plant eventually falls and its seed rots. However, if a human being gathers it and opens its head or pod artificially, he can sow the seed next season, and the mutation survives. Its survival permits him to take his time gathering the crop. The grainfield will stand until he has reaped the heads, handful by handful, even if it takes him more than a month. Then he can spend several months more separating the grain from the straw and chaff, and he loses very little.

It is hard to imagine that hunters and gatherers accidentally stumbled at a single time upon both grain and pod plants, each having the same lethal mutation, each requiring similar handling, and providing among them a balanced vegetable diet as well as materials for housing and clothing. The ancestors of our early farmers must have passed through a long period of trial and error during which agriculture was only a part-time occupation, and during which many other botanical species were grown and discarded. Among the discards were probably certain plants that have followed the cultivated species around the world as weeds. Others that started as weeds became cultivated plants.

Of these last the best-known example is rye. Rye began as a weed growing amid soft wheat, and the mutation of non-shattering heads appeared in it as it had in wheat. Owing to the similarity in size and shape of the two grains, farmers had trouble separating them, if indeed they tried. Probably they did not: today conservative farmers in Pakistan and elsewhere habitually sow several kinds of grain together. In regions of mild winters, wheat formed the bulk of the crop. However, during a particularly cold winter the rye would survive while most of the wheat that had been seeded in the late fall would be killed. The next spring's crop would be predominantly rye. When people carried the mixed seed northward and up the slopes of mountains, rye pushed out wheat. That is why you see a line crossing the map of Russia marking off the wheatlands to the south from the ryelands to the north, and why the Riffians of northern Morocco grow rye in the high mountain valleys and wheat on the rolling plains. In the same way, oats started as a weed in emmer, another kind of wheat, and eventually reached the windy headlands of the Scottish Highlands as a separate crop.

For a long time the existence of the rye-wheat boundary dividing his realm bothered Stalin, who liked to homogenize his territory. He ordered Professor Vavilov, then the president of the Russian Academy of Sciences, and the very man who had discovered the origin of rye, to produce a hardy variety of wheat which would grow on the ryelands. Vavilov, the world's most eminent plant geneticist, explained that this would be a difficult if not impossible genetic feat—one which, if it could be done at all, would take many years. Stalin ordered it done in two years. Vavilov, of course, failed and disappeared. As far as his fellow botanists know, he is dead. His place was taken by Lysenko, who has repudiated the gene theory of heredity as a capitalist concoction, and has produced a theory of his own to explain inheritance and evolution, one which satisfies his bosses but no one else.

Were this book being written in Russia, it would be easy—in fact, necessary—to state definitely exactly where agriculture began. As it is being written in America, we can afford to have differences of opinion, and to be vague where exact knowledge is lacking. At the moment we can be reasonably sure that the small grain-legume-oil seed plants were first used in combination somewhere in a broad band of terrain reaching eastward from Anatolia to Pakistan, and southward from the deserts of Turkestan to those of Arabia. We can be reasonably sure because of the early explorations and researches of Vavilov himself.

Within this general zone, human beings also began to cultivate, as part of the same agricultural complex, a number of fruit trees and vines that are still to be seen in our orchards and vineyards. One of these, the rose tribe, has produced rose hips, hawthorne haws, apples, pears, and quinces, all of which are eaten in various places, though hips and haws are seldom seen on Western menus. Wild pears and wild apples still grow as forest trees on the western slopes of the Zagros Mountains in Iran. Another succulent tribe, which reached China before it did Europe, began in Turkestan: that of the almonds, peaches, plums, and apricots. From the same northern portion of the ancient agricultural belt came the walnut and the vine. The latter has been more specifically pinpointed to Transcaucasia, meaning Georgia and Armenia. Olives and figs, native to the Mediterranean countries, were first cultivated in Palestine or Lebanon, and dates are first known from the swampy lands bordering the Persian Gulf.

Most of the anciently cultivated fruits that have been mentioned fit into the pattern of early western Neolithic agriculture in the sense that all of them can be processed and preserved. This is the essential difference between the kind of agriculture that gave rise to our own Western civilization and the old tropical gardening of southeastern Asia and Oceania, in which most foods had to be eaten when ready.

In the Middle East and in Europe, sliced apples can be strung and dried; grapes, split apricots, figs, dates, almonds, and walnuts are dried and kept for winter rations. Olives are pressed, and the oil will keep in jugs. Grapes and apples are pressed, and the fermented products—wine and cider—will keep in skins or pottery containers, to gladden many a dreary winter evening. Pears can also be converted into a beverage, perry.

Many fruit trees have hard wood, and all but the fibrous palm are fine-grained. The reason for this is simple. Each year each tree, if its owner is lucky, gradually adds several hundred pounds to the weight of its superstructure as the fruit swells and ripens. Sometimes the branches break, but the trunk holds. Wood that can bear such a load has to be strong and flexible. It is far better than most forest woods for the fashioning of plows, wagon wheels, rakes, spade handles, and all other agricultural implements, and that is what Neolithic man probably used it for. In a primitive agricultural community, as among mountain Riffians today, every olive tree and every walnut tree is watched carefully; when its production has fallen off to a certain level, it is turned into plow handles, just as old pear trunks, in America, find their way into woodcarvers' studios.

The Animals Enter the Barnyard

NEOLITHIC agriculture, with its balance of starch grains, oil seeds, protein-providing legumes, and oil- and sugar-producing fruits, would never have carried us farther along the path of civilization than the point reached by the Pueblo Indians, had it not been for the other half of the complex, the domestication of animals. Of these, four are basic: the goat, the sheep, the ox, and the pig. Concerning the origins of these animals, experts are as much at odds as they are in the case of cultivated plants. All four are members of the so-called Palearctic or northern fauna, which stretches across the northern temperate zone of the Old World from Britain to China. Within this range, goats, sheep, oxen, and pigs are or have been present in a number of wild forms, and the question arises: which wild form gave rise to which domesticated species?

We archæologists are interested in this question because we know that if we can identify the wild ancestor of each of the domestic animals, we can tell not only where each domestication began, but also whether it started in several places independently, or in one alone. Once we have this information, we can tie it to the evidence for the origins of cultivated plants, and then we can see if the Neolithic economic system started as a whole or resulted from the merging of two separate food-producing techniques, or whether one of them arose out of the other. The origin of our own civilization is what we are therefore seeking.

The likeliest candidate for the title of grandfather of the goats is the so-called bezoar-goat of Turkestan and Afghanistan. The winner of the sheep contest seems to be the argal, a wild sheep of the Elburz Mountains in northern Iran. However, more than one species of wild sheep and more than a single kind of wild goat may have been involved. Sheep and goat coincide geographically with wheat, which is a help in our search, but matters become more complicated when we study the history of the ox.

All humpless breeds are thought to be descended from *Bos primigenius,* the huge, fiery-tempered longhorn depicted alike on Spanish cave walls and in Minoan murals, the animal whose ceremonial death in Spanish bull rings perpetuates an ancient sacrifice. Bos primigenius was a native of the plains from southern Russia to the Altai Mountains, including the Caspian shores and Turkestan. It is a far cry from this majestic beast to the tiny, short-horned Neolithic cattle identified by bones in archæological sites and by survivors in the Orkneys and Shetlands. The early domestic type, *Bos brachyceros,* was a dwarf. If it was descended from Bos primigenius, as we believe, then the question arises: did early farmers catch and tame the huge and powerful full-sized animal and select dwarfs from its descendants, or did they find some dwarfs in the forest and tame them? Berthold

Klatt, who is professor of zoology at Hamburg, and the world's greatest authority on the origins of domestic animals, says that they found dwarfs already formed in the wild state. His reason is convincing. In all domestic animals dwarfed by man, the teeth remain large, as in a bulldog or Pekinese. Wild dwarfs have small teeth to fit their bones.

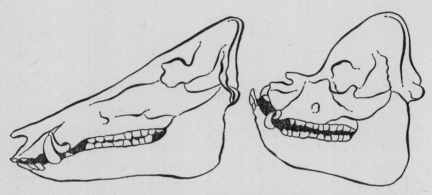

A WILD PIG (*Sus scrofa*), LEFT, AND A MODERN BERKSHIRE (*vittatus* STRAIN). *After Klatt.*

Without reasonable doubt, two wild species sired the domestic pig. One is *Sus scrofa,* the common wild boar that ranges all the way from western Europe and North Africa to central Asia and Siberia; the other is *Sus vittatus,* a wild pig of southeastern Asia. The oldest domestic-pig bones yet known in the world are those which my expedition recovered from the Neolithic levels of Belt and Hotu caves on the Caspian shore of Iran. They are stored on shelves in my office in Philadelphia. They belonged, quite clearly, to the species Sus scrofa. So did the pig bones removed from the mud under Swiss lake dwellings excavated over one hundred years ago.[1] These are also Neolithic, but a good two thousand years later

[1] On page 37 of his *Agricultural Origins and Dispersals,* American Geographical Series No. 2, New York, 1952, Carl O. Sauer states that the Swiss Neolithic pigs were vittatus, on the basis of a statement on page 85 of B. Klatt's *Entstehung der Haustiere,* Berlin, 1927. The original reads: "*Die alten europäischen, jetzt durch Einkreuzung nicht mehr reinen Landschweinrassen stammen von* SUS SCROFA, *die eingeborenen asiatischen Hausschweine, die seit viele Jahrzehnten zu dieser Einkreuzung herangezogen sind, stammen von* SUS VITTATUS." My translation is:

in date. However, the modern pigs of Europe and America, intensively selected for the production of pork and lard, bear little resemblance to wild boars. With their short snouts and rotund bodies they are clearly related to the ancient pigs of southeastern Asia and China. What has happened is that pig-breeders of the western world have substituted the far-eastern species for their own. If we did not know this by other means, we could find it out by a study of pig lice. The lice which infest modern European and American swine are the same as those which live on the hides of both domestic and wild specimens in Siam. The wild-boar lice are different.

This business of tracing relationships between animal species by louse-detection is a new and interesting field of science, based on the discovery that lice are as conservative as they are obnoxious. The environment of a louse consists of a curved patch of skin, in which he crawls about in the shelter of hairs or feathers, at a more or less constant temperature and humidity. During his wanderings he encounters other lice of the opposite sex, and uses his unwitting host's hide as a trysting place. When his host dies, he scrambles out into the cold world to seek a precisely similar environment on the cuticle of another individual. When a mammalian host gives birth to offspring, he finds it possible, in the excitement of parturition, to infest the hapless suckling. In the case of birds, he leaps from the mother's sheltering wing onto the fledgling's plumage. When his host too enjoys the pleasures of mating, the louse can skip from one lover to another, and if the hosts are hybridizing, he can hybridize as well. During all of this activity, over thousands and even millions of years, the environment of a louse may not change at all, though that of his host may be greatly altered. His host may develop long legs, short jaws, and fewer or lesser teeth, while, owing to the constancy of his environment, the louse remains the same. In this way entomologists not long ago solved an ornithological mystery, the origin of the flamingo. Flamingos carry duck lice. A flamingo is a long-legged duck, and not a crane at all.

"The old European domestic pig races, no longer pure because of mixture, are descended from *Sus scrofa;* the native Asiatic domestic pigs, which many decades ago were drawn into this hybridization, are descended from *Sus vittatus.*"

Crane lice are quite different. It is on this basis that the modern breeds of swine have been traced to the pig of southeastern Asia.

No one knows how the first herdsmen caught their first animals, but this has not prevented a host of authors from speculating. Two facts are available which may offer some clues. One is that among living primitive peoples it is a common habit to keep the young of animals after the mother has been killed, to nurse it like a baby, and to fondle and pet it. Another is that some men and women, even today, have the power to make animals come to them. A thorough knowledge of animal habits and animal communication is one of the qualifications of a good hunter. Without doubt many animals, both young and fully grown, had been caught and kept in captivity long before people had the facilities to feed them around the seasons and to protect them when kept in flocks and herds. If, as Klatt has stated, and as my own study of the oldest Neolithic bones tends to confirm, the first domestic animals were dwarfs, then the problem of how the animals were handled becomes simpler.

Wherever they came from, and however they were caught, the goat, the sheep, the pig, and the ox form a working combination as well suited to one another as are grains, legumes, and oil seeds, which they in turn complement. A goat is a hardy animal which can browse off land that will support no other beast besides the camel. It provides meat, milk, and a good strong skin suitable for use as a container for liquids. Its hair is glossy and waterproof, making a good fabric for tents and all-weather capes. The goat, furthermore, serves as a guide and protector of sheep, the shepherds' second aide, after his dog. The sheep itself yields wool, prime material for clothing, as well as milk. Certain varieties of sheep have been perfected for meat, others for their fat tails, still others for the delicate wool of their newborn lambs. The sheep can be fed nearly anywhere, as long as there is grass, either green or dry. As long as there is no serious danger from wolves, lions, and tigers, one man and a dog can take care of a mixed herd of one hundred sheep and goats.

The pig is hard to skin, cannot be milked, and yields nothing but bristles. Yet its tusks can be used for knives as well as for orna-

ments. Its principal virtues are its habit of producing large litters
of offspring at frequent intervals and its capacity for rapid growth.
Thus it is a meat-producer par excellence. Furthermore, it can be
fed on acorns and beech mast in forested glades where it roots for
truffles, leaving the parkland and meadows to support horned
cattle. No one has ever learned how to drive pigs easily or how to
make them respond to calls or other signals; one swineherd can
handle but a few animals.

Unlike his three companions, the domestic ox is large enough to
carry burdens, including tents and household furniture, men,
women, children, puppies, lambs, and kids, on its back. It can
also be hitched to summer sleds like those still in use on the Caspian shore of Iran, in the Caucasus, and in the Basque country,
and to plows, harrows, and wheeled vehicles. It can be milked,
and its milk will separate naturally into cream and skimmed milk.
Cream can be churned, or shaken in a bag, into butter. Cowhide
is strong, and useful for implement straps, thongs, and even
shields and armor. Cowhorn may be carved into spoons, and made
into drinking cups.

Furthermore, the food products obtained from the ox can be
easily processed for storage, along with the grain, beans, and oils.
Butter will keep if it is boiled. Skimmed milk can be converted
into cheese by the addition of rennet, a substance taken from the
stomach of a suckling calf, and cheese can be hung from the
rafters along with flitches of bacon and belly meat, hams and
sausages. Smoking and drying will convert most parts of the
slaughtered animals into food that can be kept through the winter.
The advantage of preserving meat over slaughtering when needed
is clear; the butchering season is the fall, after the animals have
been suitably fattened and before the ordeal of the winter, when
fodder is scarce and when the flocks must be kept as small as possible. Hence it is the young males that are killed off, and the pregnant ewes and nannies that are kept, along with a few particularly
potent rams and billy goats. Following the same principle, date-
farmers in Iraq, Egypt, and Morocco cut down all but a few of the
male trees, which produce no fruit, and fertilize the female trees
by hand with pollen carefully removed from the studs.

Archæologists who have studied the thousands of animal bones dug up in caves in France and elsewhere, bones representing the meals of ancient hunters, have observed that nearly all animals killed were full-grown. Where a Neolithic deposit overlies such a layer, an immediate change is seen. At least half the bones are those of lambs, kids, and other immature animals. Wherever we find such a transition, we know that domestication, from that point on, in that particular place, has begun. To locate this turning point as well as simply to tell what kinds of animals surrounded the bones, we pack the specimens carefully at the site, and after we are home we clean them, harden them in a plastic solution, and number them so that we can shuffle them without fear of losing track of the level in which each specimen was found. Then we sort them by parts of the body, from horn to hoof, and after that by species. In the case of sheep and goats, many bones have to be left in the double category, sheep/goat; but a few, such as the horns and jaws, are distinguishable. By examining the jaws and teeth we can soon discover how many of each species were killed while still carrying their milk teeth, and how many were spared until after the eruption of their permanent dentition. In the case of sheep, goats, and pigs, at least fifty per cent were killed before dental maturity in every domestic series studied. In the case of the ox this is not true because the young animals were preserved into maturity as beasts of burden or traction. In the cases of wild animals such as gazelles and deer, almost all specimens were adult when killed.

Man Toys with the Forces of Nature

W H O L L Y aside from getting new sources of food and more of it, and from building up village life as the characteristic pattern of human society, man started, in the Neolithic, his practice of toying with the forces of nature. First of all, he cut and burned down forests that had been standing for thousands of years, replacing them with scrub growth or fields, and in places where the rainfall was marginal or fickle, starting the whole process of soil erosion which has wasted vast areas of the earth's surface, causing them to resemble scar tissue on the skin of a living body. Playing favorites with some plant and animal species over others, he made them dependent on him for their very survival, for he destroyed their power of procreation or successful living if left on their own. Thus he upset the whole balance of nature by thwarting the forces of natural selection. We have been doing this ever since. Such fruits as apples, pomegranates, pears, and figs are twenty times as big as their wild prototypes. Grains and legumes have lost their capacity to shatter on ripening and have been made completely dependent on man for survival, like many of the domestic animals.

The conversion of the sheep into a walking and bleating woolfactory is one of our ancestors' most dramatic perversions of nature, and so is the selection of cattle for huge udders and great quantities of milk. Both of these alterations involve the ectoderm, which includes the horns and skin as well as the hair and milk glands. If an animal has been selected for wool, milk, or both, it cannot be expected to have the long, sweeping horns of its wild ancestors, for all of this body tissue is fed from a single source. Long horns were no longer needed once the animal came to live in the protection of men and dogs. For the same reason, the domestic pig fails to grow the dangerous tusks of his forest-rooting kin. Changes in the size and form of horns and teeth had already begun in the bones found in archæological remains, though the horns and teeth of these earliest domestic animals were as yet nearer to the wild type than to the modern forms.

Several domestic animals have developed stunted forms, with short, twisted legs and low-slung bodies, like the bulldog, dachshund, the Peruvian (Indian) pug, the short-legged sheep, and many others. In many breeds the tail has grown short, its vertebræ fused. As a rule the bones of all domestic animals are small and spongy, with a high fat content, and we can tell simply by the feel of a bone whether it belonged to a domestic or a wild animal. Domestic animals also have short, thin extremities and abundant body fat. This, of course, is the result of selection for meat, made possible by the fact that under human care rapid motion is no longer necessary for survival. Some human beings also have small hands and feet, and tend to obesity. According to the insurance companies, this is the type of person that dies young. Longevity is of no consequence in herd animals: they are ordinarily slaughtered in a youthful state.

In nearly all species of animals and birds that have been domesticated, both the muzzle and the skull have grown shorter than those of the wild forms. The muzzle is short because man prepares the animal's food for him, reducing the work of teeth and jaws, which then grow small. In this change, the animal copies man himself. The skull grows short because by protecting the animals from natural enemies and bad weather, man has made unnecessary the full development of the animal's senses, and those parts of the brain in which the messages from eyes, ears, and nostrils are received lie fore and aft in the brain. Lack of use prevents the full development of these portions of the gray matter, and thus the brain and the skull that encloses it are both shortened.

These changes can take place in a single generation, as experiments performed in Germany have shown. There a zoologist caught a pair of wild foxes and placed them in a zoo. After the vixen had littered and the young had begun to grow up, he released some of them, and they in turn produced young. Having caught and killed members of all three generations, he weighed their brains. The members of the original wild generation had fifty-gram brains, the generation born and reared in captivity thirty-five, and the second wild generation fifty. This is believed to prove that changes in brain size which reflect a lack of use of the sensory areas are not inherited, at least over a single generation. In the case of animals that have been sheltered and led to pasture and back by man for eight thousand years, one wonders. Reversions have taken place, as with the razorback hogs of the Appalachians and the wild goats of Catalina Island. But how closely do these resemble their distant wild ancestors, and how many of the liberated animals died without offspring in the process?

One of the most conspicuous changes that come over animals once they have been tamed is that their coat-color pattern grows gayer. In the wild form this is rigidly uniform for each species, as a result of natural selection. An albino deer has little chance of living to the age of reproduction in a forest environment in which every move is conspicuous. Yet albino sheep and piebald cattle and goats can live to ripe old ages if their herdsmen so choose. A good instance of deliberate color selection is familiar to all Bible readers, in Genesis 30: 31–43. As part of his payment for his wives Leah and Rachel, Jacob agreed to tend the flocks of his father-in-law, Laban, for a number of years. However, Laban agreed to give Jacob, at the end of his service, all of the black and brown sheep and the striped and spotted goats. The reason for this selection was probably to make it easier for each man to tell his own animals from the other's. Today in Middle Eastern villages where all of the animals are herded together, one man will try to own only brown sheep, others only white ones, and so on, to make separation easier and reduce disputes.

Jacob, however, had another motive. He cut a number of sticks from the side of the stream and peeled them in rings and dots. Having placed these sticks in the water, he brought the goats to that place to drink, in the hope that the quality of being striped and spotted would be transferred from the sticks to the offspring of the goats through the agency of the water. This is, of course, a classic example of contagious magic, like the belief that eating fish will make one brainy because fish and brain tissue look somewhat alike. Jacob was not trying to improve the breed of goats by this ruse, and it is unlikely that Neolithic man, who lived several thousand years before Jacob, knew about selective breeding either.

It is quite possible, however, that features in animals, such as stripes, spots, and white fleeces, for which Neolithic man may have selected his animals on magical grounds or for purposes of identification, were linked hereditarily to others which did actually produce improvements in an economic sense, as, for example, heavier fleeces, more milk, or fatter tails. In the vegetable kingdom, it is quite possible that melons and squashes were first grown as rattles or containers, and then for edible seeds; many wild forms have bitter fruit to keep animals from eating them. Only when sweet-fruited mutations arose did they become edible.

Like non-shattering plants and those that have lost their ability to produce seeds, the domestic animals have become parasites. Their reduction of sensory perception can be compared to the loss of locomotion among certain insects. In the shelter of its host's fires, folds, spears, and bows, they have lost their fear of predators. Lacking man's intelligence, they do not know that inevitable slaughter awaits them. Hence the sheep bleats hopefully, the cow lows at the pressure of full udders, and the goat maas. Begging for food, water, milking, and a return to the fold is more profitable than silence. Yet this alteration of nature did not all come at once, and the Neolithic must have begun without the barnyard noises that had become familiar by the time of the first poets of whom we have record.

The Earliest Farmers—the Archæological Evidence

THESE generalizations about the origins of the Neolithic, in reference to both plant and animal forms, are not being made on the basis of modern distributions or deductions from later sources such as the Bible. They are based on the discovery of actual plant and animal remains in archæological sites, mainly in the Middle East, which, as far as we know today, was the original home of Neolithic agriculture and animal husbandry. They are the product of the excavation of about twenty sites, including both caves and mounds, in Turkey, Lebanon, Palestine, Iraq, Iran, Russian Turkestan, Afghanistan, and Pakistan. From this material we derive our only factual knowledge of the first great step, after the mastery of fire, in our story of man.

Some of these sites, like Byblos in Lebanon, are really city sites in which only the persistence of the excavators led them to reach the Neolithic foundations. Others, like Tepe Hissar in Iran, are primarily Neolithic settlement mounds with Bronze Age and later materials on top. A few, like Jarmo in northern Iraq, excavated by Robert Braidwood, and my Belt Cave, show a continuity from Mesolithic deposits right up into the earliest Neolithic, and on into later sequences. One of them, the upper levels of the same Mount Carmel caves that shed much light on the evolution of

European man, contains a curious mixture of an otherwise pure Mesolithic culture with flint sickle blades.

These flint sickle blades are shiny. All grasses contain silica in their stems. That is why the teeth of grass-eating animals are long, and grow out continuously during the animal's adult life; silica wears teeth down. It also polishes the surfaces of flint sickle blades used to cut it. Shiny sickle blades mean only one thing—the cultivation of non-shattering cereals. Most archæologists, unaware of the botanical fact that wild cereals are never reaped, but are harvested with stick and basket, have taken the combination of Mesolithic implements, wild-animal bones, and shiny sickle blades to mean the reaping of wild cereal. It is highly unlikely that we will find evidence of the first cultivation of shattering cereals, for obvious reasons. We may be sure that wherever we find polished sickle blades, either grain had been grown for some time, or its cultivation had been recently imported from some earlier scene of development.

Why should we have so few Neolithic sites, if the Middle East, long visited by westerners and dug by archæologists, is where the Neolithic began? The answer is simple, if disturbing. The Middle East is the place of origin, not only of the Neolithic, but also of the great literate civilizations of the Bronze Age—those of Egypt, Sumeria, Babylonia, and the Indus Valley. These great literate civilizations produced not only the earliest writing that has survived, but also recognizable works of art, like statues and bas-reliefs and much gold jewelry. Tablets, statues, and gold jewelry are expensive objects for which both private collectors and public museums will pay high prices. They command a thriving black market. Hence the archæologists who have excavated the sites from which such treasures are obtained are art experts rather than anthropologists. Their profession stemmed directly out of the classical archæology of the nineteenth century, which in turn came from the study of classical literature. The attitude that only the best is worth bothering about has been carried over from the classical tradition.

The Egyptologists and Mesopotamian excavators who have dug on the sites from which such treasures are obtained are prepared and equipped to spend large sums, running into hundreds of thousands of dollars, on their excavations. Their job is to bring back what their trustees want. Neolithic objects are unimpressive. Stone axes, flint sickle blades, crumbly potsherds, and broken animal bones do not draw crowds to museums. When an old-fashioned Bronze Age archæologist who works for an art museum gets down to a Neolithic level, he stops. Even if he is personally interested in the origins of the civilizations which he has uncovered, he cannot justify further work to his principals.

Archæologists interested in the more ancient periods, who dig up things less valuable from the art point of view, are rarely supported by art museums. These men represent universities, which have less money to spend on digging, since they are working not for wealthy opera and art-museum patrons, but for the trustees of universities. Such archæologists are more likely to be seen in a cave in New Mexico than in one in Iran or Afghanistan. Only in the last two decades has the situation changed. Now our trustees are beginning to be just as interested in the Neolithic, and in the Paleolithic as well, as in the Bronze Age, and support from the art type of institution is forthcoming for these activities. This is a splendid thing in another sense, as post-war restrictions on the export of ancient art objects from Middle Eastern countries have grown so great that the investment of large sums of money on the excavation of city mounds is no longer justified. If war leaves the Middle East alone for another decade, we may expect to know much more about Neolithic origins than we do at present.

Most of the Neolithic sites that have been excavated consist of mounds. The traveler who has ridden over the road from Baghdad to Tehran has seen thousands of them. Some are still covered by buildings, while others, having grown too tall or too steep, shelter villages in their lee flanks. The presence of a village over thousands of years made such a mound. As adobe walls crumbled, the rubble was smoothed over and new walls were built on top of it. The bottom level of such mounds usually contains pottery and flint sickle blades, as well as the bones of domestic animals. The village was founded by people who were already farmers.

One such site, however, was occupied before its inhabitants

knew the use of either flint sickles or pottery; that is Jarmo, a mound near Kirkuk in northern Iraq, on the edge of the plain flanking the Zagros Mountains. The brilliant work of Robert Braidwood, of Chicago, who excavated it, shows a transition from Mesolithic to Neolithic habits of life. The earliest material in it, represented by a sample of snail shells, was given a carbon-14 date of 4758 B.C., ± 320 years. This date is pre-ceramic. Although the people who lived there at that time had no pottery, they had begun to cultivate cereals and to breed sheep, goats, pigs, and cattle.

Braidwood's good fortune or good judgment cannot often be repeated. In my opinion the best place to look for the beginnings of agriculture is not at the bottom of mounds, but in caves. The earliest agriculturalists, particularly before they had begun to raise cereals, probably practiced slash-and-burn agriculture. After ringing the trees of a few acres of forest and allowing the wood to dry out, they would burn them and plant in the soil around the stumps. After a few years the underbrush would have become so dense that it would be easier to move on to a new spot. Even if the underbrush was kept under control with stone tools, at the cost of immense labor, the soil would soon be impoverished. Early farmers moved about from place to place, rarely remaining long enough at one site to produce a mound.

The earliest agriculturalists were, after all, basically Mesolithic people, and Mesolithic people were cave-users where caves were available. Caves are fine places to shelter sheep during the winter, and the dung creates warmth. They are also good places in which to bury the dead. Once a fairly sedentary life has been adopted, and the population has increased from a few families to a hundred or more persons, the number of deaths increases and the disposal of bodies becomes a problem. In some Neolithic sites in Europe they were buried under the floor. In France, Malta, and the Canary Islands they were stacked in caves. Because Neolithic peoples usually place objects with the dead to aid them in the afterworld, one finds in caves some splendid stone axes, flint tools, digging stick weights, and ornaments, still associated with the bodies with which they were placed. One also may find actual seeds and grains. Furthermore, potsherds and the bones of domestic animals pack the soil. Everything that one needs to study Neolithic life is here, except for the houses in which the people themselves lived.

In 1949 and 1951 our expedition dug a site in northern Iran called Belt Cave, which contained a sequence of cultures; at the bottom, dated at 9530 ± 550 B.C., was a Mesolithic level with many seal bones and every evidence of a wet climate. Next came a dry Mesolithic culture, dated at 6620 ± 380 B.C., in which the gazelle was the dominant animal. After this came the beginning of the Neolithic, with domestic goats and sheep, but no pottery; date, 5840 ± 330 B.C. Whether the people who inhabited the cave at that time cultivated wheat or barley, I do not know. At any rate, they kept sheep and goats, and killed off some of the lambs and kids every year; for twenty-five per cent of the bones of the animals are those of babies. Somewhat later, at a date established at 5330 B.C. ± 260 years (between 5070 B.C. and 5590 B.C.) by carbon-14 analysis, they had begun to make pottery and to reap grain as well as to keep pigs and, a little later, cows.

Since these excavations earlier Neolithic finds have been made farther west. The city of Jericho, lying in a warm oasis below sea-level, has been continuously occupied since 7865 ± 160 B.C., when it was a Mesolithic settlement. By 6480 ± 160 B.C. its inhabitants had adopted the Neolithic way of life, although without pottery.

Between 1952 and 1961 James Mellaert found a sequence of Neolithic cultures in two central Anatolian villages. The first to be discovered was Hacular, which acquired pottery about 5500 B.C., the same time that it appeared in Belt Cave. Under this was a level without pottery. In 1961 Mellaert found an earlier village, Catalhuyuk, as old as Jericho.

Both Jericho and the Turkish sites consist of rooms of masonry connected by passageways. In the Turkish sites whole houses are preserved well enough to let us know that the earliest structures were built around courtyards, with separate storage rooms entered by ladders from the roofs. In each living room was a hearth, oven, grain-bins, and a sleeping platform under which were deposited the bones of ancestors. Some of the skulls had been restored with plaster and given eyes of shell, as in modern New Guinea. Similarly decorated skulls were found in Jericho.

Carbon–14 Dating [2]

T H E E X A C T dating of archæological sites only began in 1948, when Willard F. Libby, with the assistance of E. C. Anderson and J. R. Arnold, set up their laboratory in the University of Chicago as a part-time avocation. Specimens from Belt Cave, consisting of charred bone, were among the first that Dr. Libby studied. Since then he has dated hundreds of specimens sent him from all parts of the world, and other laboratories have been set up in many universities and government agencies in the United States, western Europe, New Zealand, and Japan. One of the first institutions to follow Chicago was the University of Pennsylvania. Also at least one oil company and one commercial organization make carbon-14 tests. Dr. Libby has held the post of head of the United States Atomic Energy Commission and has received a Nobel Prize for having invented a peaceful use of the world's most destructive (to date) force.

Carbon-14 dating is one of the benefits derived from research on atomic energy. It is based on the knowledge that "carbon dioxide is rendered radioactive by cosmic radiation. Since plants live off the carbon dioxide, all plants will be radioactive. Thus we conclude that all living things will be rendered radioactive by the cosmic radiation." As long as an organism lives, its carbon retains the same amount of radioactivity; gains make up for losses. Once it has died, only disintegration takes place. The disintegration of the carbon-14 atoms in the dead organism proceeds at a fixed rate, which is "independent of the nature of the chemical compound in which the radioactive body resides and of the temperature, pressure and other physical characteristics of its environment." To make a long story short, atomic physicists can date a piece of organic or organically formed material by measuring with Geiger

² W. F. Libby, *Radiocarbon Dating*, University of Chicago Press, Chicago, 1952. Quotations are from pp. 5–6.

counters the state of disintegration of its carbon-14 atoms. Up until 1952 they could go back to twenty thousand years before the present; with improved apparatus they can now reach forty thousand years. The best material for dating is charcoal; wood, basketry, ancient bread, seeds, and peat are equally good, but are less frequently preserved. The same is true of skin, horn, and other forms of animal epidermis. Bone can be used if it has been charred, and shells are datable. Unburned bone and horn cores are useless so far. Since archæologists began collecting bottles full of these datable materials the laboratories of the free world have been so swamped with orders that they have had to set up schedules of priorities, and some of them specialize in different geographical regions and archæological horizons. Each new date is put on a punch card, sets of which are distributed among subscribing organizations. Each date published has a code letter (P for the University of Pennsylvania, L for the Lamont Laboratory of Columbia University, etc.) and a serial number: for example, P–39 for 11, 860 ± 840 B.P. at Hotu Cave, Iran.

Operating difficulties have grown also, slowing the process down. The medical use of carbon-14 makes the neighborhood of some hospitals unsuitable for dating tests, for every time the wind blows from the hospital's smokestack toward the laboratory, it throws the Geiger counter off. Several times during the summer and fall of 1952 our laboratory had to stop operating, wait a week or two, and begin over again. The cause was free C-14 in the atmosphere, blown over from Nevada. Atomic debris shot into the air by bomb tests in North America and Eurasia generally follows the westerly winds in a path around the northern hemisphere, the very path in which most laboratories are located. That is why the laboratory in New Zealand has been relatively little disturbed. But many of our archæological sites, including those of the Old World Neolithic, also lie in the westerly storm belt. Nowadays when we expose charcoal in the ground during a dig, we collect it immediately, sealing it in thick polyethylene tubes, to be removed only in the laboratory. But if many more atom bombs are set off, in play or in earnest, Dr. Libby's method of dating may itself become outdated.

Neolithic Migrations in the Old World

IN Hotu Cave and in Turkey, the oldest pottery is a soft, thick-walled burnished red ware. The next oldest is a thinner, harder ware, painted in two colors. But in Iraq, Iran, Afghanistan, and Pakistan painted pottery is the earliest. It comes in two styles, red on buff and black on red. The buff ware is centered in Iraq, and the red in Turkestan and the Iranian plateau, while the Pakistan sites have both. Of little importance in themselves, these types of pottery, decorated in some cases with attractive representations of the ibex, serve as tracers of early agricultural movements. But the results are not yet fully worked out to the satisfaction of everyone, it being a habit of archæologists for each to think that his site is the earliest.

In any event, these painted pottery wares had developed and spread throughout the Middle East before the beginning of the age of metal—that is, before 3000 B.C. This was not, however, the only diffusion of Neolithic culture. Farmers who grew the conventional grains and bred the conventional animals crossed the Egyptian Delta to settle the fertile plains and valleys of North Africa, where an expedition of which I was a member dug their remains from caves in 1947. These caves are located in the territory of Tangier, near the Strait of Gibraltar, directly under a Spanish bar, and overlooking one of the finest bathing beaches in the world. Seldom has an expedition worked under such conditions.

The Neolithic people of North Africa concentrated on pig-breeding, which is not surprising in view of the heavy forests of oak which once covered the landscape. Their pottery was of the familiar soft type; their flints were the conventional blades, their axes made of basalt. They arrived at the Strait of Gibraltar before 3000 B.C., exactly when we are not certain. Personally I would favor a date at least six hundred years earlier. Some of them crossed the strait to Spain and eventually settled France and the British Isles, while others, moving in parallel fashion along the opposite Mediterranean shore, settled in Greece, Crete, and Italy. In the meanwhile other pioneers had moved across the Hellespont and along the western shore of the Black Sea to the mouth of the Danube. Following the banks of this river and its tributaries, they eventually reached Germany, where they met the vanguard of the southerly migration. The Danubians, as the northern branch is called, also made soft pottery and blackstone axes and adzes. Some of the Neolithic villages of Europe have been carefully excavated. As a rule they are located on low hills and surrounded by walls of logs set vertically in the ground. The houses were small and single-storied, made of wattled sticks smeared with clay, and the floors were of beaten clay. Apparently the people went out to their fields in the morning and returned at night within the protection of their ramparts, just as their descendants have been doing ever since.

Probably a thousand years elapsed before painted pottery was carried into Europe over the Danubian corridor, and imitated. If software goes back to 5400 B.C. in Neolithic Turkey, and painted wares to between 5000 and 4000, then the rate of movement into western Europe was exceedingly slow. Compared with the Middle East, the Western world presented many barriers and challenges, of cold and snow, of wide rivers, and chilly mountains. It was a world of incomparably greater natural resources than the Middle East, harder to tame, but bearing greater promise for the future, a promise not evident even as late as the times of the Greeks and Romans.

The eastern route out of the Caspian basin was even harder. Neolithic farmers, with the usual plants and animals, are believed to have entered China at a date slightly later than that of their arrival in Europe, for they had to cultivate, on the way, not river valleys filled with loess (a fine, wind-deposited, easily worked soil), but desert oases, and a lofty continental divide had to be crossed. As the road to China was harder, fewer people can have passed over it. Furthermore, to the east of the mountains they found a different climate. Early Neolithic agricultural plants are those which thrive on a cycle of winter rain and summer drought. In Europe, these conditions obtain along the Mediterranean, while elsewhere the even distribution of the rainfall throughout the year offered no barrier. But in northern China the winter is dry and winds off the Pacific bring summer rains. The imported plants could be grown only with difficulty. The answer was, of course, the domestication of local plants suited to local climatic conditions.

Actually China is the world's greatest center of plant domestication. Two of its economically most important species are rice and the soybean. Rice, which produces twenty times as much grain per acre as wheat, requires more hand labor, but less use of animals. However, it will feed large agricultural populations, so that in rice country, village follows village almost without interruption. There is no room between villages for shepherds to pasture their flocks. So many economic uses are there for rice straw, such as for building and clothing material, for mats, and for fuel, that where rice is the staple there is hardly enough fodder for draft oxen, let alone for animals kept for milk or meat. An excellent vegetable substitute for milk and meat is provided by the soybean, rich in both fats and proteins. In the form of curd cakes, this is extensively eaten with rice. The Chinese long ago gave up milking animals, if they ever began, which is highly doubtful. The only animal that they breed especially for eating is the pig, a scavenger. Not only does it clean the village walks, but it also converts human excrement into meat. Pottery models from the Han dynasty, 100 B.C. to A.D. 100, show privies built over pigpens.

Water, which is good for rice, is also good for travel and transport. The Chinese long ago learned to carry their goods and their persons along rivers and to build canals; the abundance of these natural waterways and their artificial supplements has made the use of domestic animals for transport unimportant. To what extent this substitution of water transport for animal transport had begun in the Neolithic is hard to discover, for the Neolithic sites in China which have been scientifically excavated number less than the fingers of a human hand. As in the Middle East, the abundance of art objects from later periods has obscured scientific inquiry. It would be extremely interesting to know just how the shift-over from a Caspian type of Neolithic to the Chinese type of agricultural life took place. Perhaps someday our children will be able to find this out.

It will be particularly interesting to know whether the cultivation of plants in central and southern China and in Indo-China really was introduced by Neolithic travelers arriving over the oases and mountains of central Asia, or began independently in local domestications, as some eminent botanists believe. Unfortunately almost all the early archæological sites of China are located in the north. It is possible that a local Neolithic, with polished-stone axes, black and mat-marked pottery, and with local food plants, as well as with the vittatus species of domestic pig, and the dog, existed in southern China before the date of 2400 B.C., the conventional starting point of the North Chinese Neolithic. Unfortunately there is no way of proving or disproving this theory. The best argument for it, aside from botanical reconstruction, is the carbon-14 date of 1530 ± 200 B.C. recently obtained from an early site on the island of Saipan in Micronesia. If agricultural people had reached the Marianas by that time, they must have left the Philippines somewhat earlier; and if they had come to the Philippines from South China, as we presume, the nine hundred years that intervened between 2400 and 1500 B.C. is hardly enough time to account for all of the activities and events of their journey.

Neolithic techniques of making polished-stone axes had to be diffused to South China, along with the domestic pig. Taro, yams, citrus fruits, and the mulberry had to be domesticated, along with the pandanus, a close relative of the litchi nut. Breadfruit, the banana, and the coconut had to be domesticated either on the Asiatic mainland or on the islands. The domestic fowl had to be tamed. People had to migrate in two main jumps: to Indonesia and thence to Micronesia. The evidence for a separate and indigenous South Chinese Neolithic is purely circumstantial, but it cannot be dismissed with a wave of the hand.

A new complication has been added to the problem of Neolithic origins in the Far East by the determination of a carbon-14 date of 7500 ± 400 B.C. for the beginning of the Jomon pottery in Japan. This pottery is a crude nipple-bottomed ware, apparently indigenous. As far as we know the Early Jomon was a food-gathering culture. The Late Jomon, which was agricultural, is dated at about 2550 B.C. Sometime between these two dates, agriculture began in Japan.

The question of Neolithic continuity will eventually be clarified when we have found enough Neolithic skeletons to trace the physical movements of that period. The oldest yet known in western Asia were European in type. A group of skulls recently found in the pre-pottery layer of Jericho, in Palestine, confirms this. Faces had been modeled on these skulls in plaster, and the features painted on. These and other Neolithic skulls from central Europe, western Europe, and the Mediterranean countries are all similar. A single type of human being familiar today among Nordics and Mediterraneans carried the earliest Neolithic culture westward from central Asia over various routes. But in the East? The Jomon skulls, one early and others late, are all Mongoloid.

What we still need to know about the Neolithic, physically and culturally, vastly exceeds our present knowledge. Neolithic sites, or Neolithic levels in composite sites, are not as exciting as the remains of Pleistocene man, or as rewarding to the treasure-hunter as those of the Bronze and Iron ages. But from the standpoint of the history of civilization, the Neolithic is very important.

During the first phase of human history man became a hunter, and during the second he carried this skill to perfection, acquiring surpluses of food, a rudimentary division of labor, and some degree of settled life. Hundreds of generations of hunting selected him biologically into a special physiological pattern reflected in his behavior toward other persons. However much cultural needs may have modified human behavior, it is still an extension of physiology. When, some eight thousand years ago, the first farmers and herdsmen abandoned hunting, they retained these inherited patterns. Their problem was to fit them into the new requirements of village life, and that is a problem that most of the world still faces today.

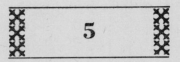

5

THE COLD AND THE SEA

NEOLITHIC habits of living have survived in modern Europe, India, China, South America, and other regions of high civilization. This does not mean that their inhabitants still cut wood with polished-stone tools, but that their village life retains a Neolithic pattern in its frame of mind. To find whole Neolithic cultures surviving into recent times we must trace the early migrations of food-producers to their final goals and see how Neolithic man filled in the gaps on the map unoccupied by earlier hunters. So efficient was Neolithic technology that by its means men conquered the treeless cold and sailed to new islands across distant seas. At the ends of the ancient earth we find them living in communities and kingdoms ranging in social complexity from that of the simplest band of hunters to that of the English of King Alfred's day. From the start the third phase of human history gave man the means to become a universal as well as a primarily cultural animal.

After the first three thousand years of Neolithic history, Neolithic culture-bearers finally reached the borders of cultivable land. In the northern forests of Europe and Asia they taught their techniques of tool-making to hunters, who could now build cabins, sleds, and elaborate traps. In place of cattle the forest people domesticated the reindeer for meat, skins, milk, and traction. Reindeer-breeding spread all the way from Lapland to Bering Strait, where the earliest Russian explorers found villages of people who lived by hunting sea mammals and by trading blubber, ivory, and seal and walrus skins to the reindeer-breeders in return for reindeer skins. The people in the interior needed sea-mammal hides for thongs and boots, and ivory for tools. The people who caught the sea mammals needed reindeer skins for clothing. Of the sea-shore villages, some seven were occupied by Eskimos, a people who had arisen on both sides of the Bering Sea, and who had spread eastward along the barren arctic shore of Alaska and Canada to Labrador and Greenland by the time that modern white men had come to explore those territories. On the American side they hunted both sea mammals and caribou and hence obtained the two kinds of material that they needed.

The Eskimos Occupy the Treeless Arctic

E s k i m o culture, with its variations from Alaska to Greenland, is without doubt the best known to Americans of all the "primitive" ways of life. The Eskimos live near the North Pole, build snow houses, wear warm clothing, hunt animals that look like reindeer, and drive fuzzy dogs attached to sleds. The Eskimos are closely identified with the Santa Claus myth. Because much of Eskimo culture is ingenious, mechanical, and healthy, it is a suitable subject of kindergarten study and furnishes out-of-door patterns for children's play. To the children of America the Eskimos have come to symbolize winter, fun in the snow, Christmas trees, and the stamping of reindeer hoofs on the roof.

Besides furnishing a subject of infant-indoctrination, the Eskimos are important in world history because they were the first people, as far as we know, to find a way to live in an extremely cold environment without firewood, and thus to occupy a previously uninhabited part of the earth's surface.[1] On the Asiatic side of the Arctic the forests come close to the shore, but on the American side the tree line is too far inland to be within reach of sea-mammal hunters. They were able to survive because with Neolithic tools they carved lamps out of soapstone or made them of pottery, and boiled their food over lamps in kettles of the same materials, using blubber as fuel.

Stone-carving, pottery-making, and boiling are Neolithic tech-

---

[1] The discovery of implements of earlier type in parts of the Eskimo country may reflect the presence of men in an earlier and warmer period.

niques. The burning of blubber may have been original with the
Eskimo, or borrowed. Olive oil was used as fuel in the Middle East
three thousand years before our earliest evidence of the existence
of Eskimos, and the Turks and Mongols of central Asia have long

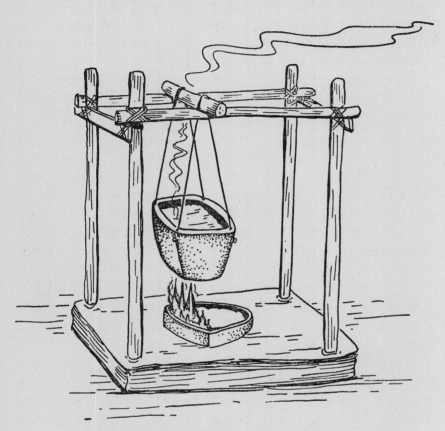

ESKIMO BLUBBER LAMP AND KETTLE.

burned butter; this practice was carried to the Arctic shore of
Siberia by the Turkish peoples. The Chinese have long burned the
oil of various seeds in their lamps, and both the Ainu and the
Japanese use fish oil.

Whether or not the Eskimos invented the use of blubber for
cooking, heating, and illumination is academic; the important
thing is that they did use it. But a source of fuel was not enough;

good transport was essential for survival in their environment. Here again inventions that had been made in the Neolithic served them. Ground-stone knives and adzes made it possible for them to make the most of their slender supply of wood and to produce the frames of sleds and boats. Both sleds and frame-built boats were Neolithic devices elsewhere. So was the use of a team of animals for traction. Whether or not the Eskimos invented their sleds and boats and the idea of dragging both by means of dog teams is just as immaterial as the question of blubber-burning. Functionally, the point is that these were Neolithic inventions made possible by the use of Neolithic tools.

These inventions, however, and that of the blubber lamp, would not have availed the Eskimos had they not been able to make for each person, young and old, male and female, at least one perfectly tailored double-fur suit. This garment consists of twelve principal pieces: a parka complete with hood, a pair of trousers, and a pair each of mittens and boots, each in duplicate, so that the inner set covers the body with the hair in, the outer with the hair out. This is even more important for survival than the blubber lamp; in these suits the Caribou Indians of the barren lands, who suffer from a scarcity of fuel in winter, can survive without heat in their snow houses if they eat enough fat.

The essential feature of such a suit is skilled tailoring. The tailors are the women. In order to cut the furs in the exact patterns needed for each individual, the woman must have a good knife. This knife is the *ulu*, a semi-lunar ground-slate implement nearly identical with our saddler's knife, which every skilled leather-worker in the western world uses. This knife is the second key to the Eskimos' ability to live in the barren Arctic, as important as the blubber lamp.

The Eskimos were able to live happy and successful lives in the treeless Arctic not only because they knew how to make Neolithic tools, blubber lamps, kettles, and warm clothing, but because they were bright people who exercised the utmost economy, inventiveness, and skill in the use of the few natural materials and trade objects available to them. In Alaska a little iron came across from Siberia in trade. In Greenland they cold-ground

ESKIMO CLOTHING.

hunks chipped off a huge lump of native iron, and in the Coronation Gulf country of northwestern Canada they treated native copper similarly. These metals were useful for tool-making, but the Eskimos were not dependent on them. When they had no metal, they fashioned flints into knives and harpoon points, slate into ulus and adzes, and soapstone into lamps and kettles. Their meager supply of driftwood served them for piecing out and patching the frames of boats and sleds, and for the shafts of weapons. Skin became clothing, tents, and boat-covers. Sinew was converted into sewing thread and cordage and the springy backing of bows; intestines were worn in the form of raincoats and rainhats; bone and ivory were carved into sled runners and the joints, toggles, and sockets of harpoons. Even snow was used for housebuilding, ice for windows.

The mechanical principles that distinguished Eskimo culture were also known in the world's centers of civilization at the time the Eskimos are known to have first used them. Therefore we cannot be sure how many were invented on the spot and how many borrowed. One of these is the spring. An Eskimo hunter shapes a strip of baleen (the whalebone of commerce, formerly used in corsets) into a flat, double-ended skewer, then rolls it tightly and secures the roll. He freezes this into the center of a lump of fat and throws the fat out where it will be available to marauding wolves. The wolf sniffs it, swallows it, and departs. The fat melts, the baleen uncoils, and the wolf dies.

Another is the toggle, used together with the ball-and-socket joint in harpooning. The Eskimos mount their harpoon heads on a bone or ivory foreshaft lashed into a socket fixed to the end of a wooden shaft. When the head has penetrated hide and blubber of seal or walrus, the impact of the strike frees the foreshaft in its ball-and-socket joint, and at the same time the head is pulled from the end of the foreshaft, remaining in the wound. When the line tightens, the head is turned at right angles to it, becoming an embedded toggle that will hold against any strain that the line will bear. The shaft floats free of breakage by the thrashing animal (a great advantage in the Central Arctic, where wood is scarce), while the hunter draws the dead or exhausted animal to him on ice or shore.

The combination of the toggle and the ball-and-socket facilitated seal-hunting, but a further invention was needed to make it possible to bring whales and large walruses ashore. That was the

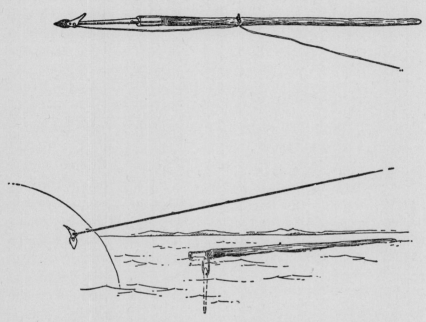

ESKIMO HARPOON, BEFORE A STRIKE AND JUST AFTER.

pulley. To the line coming out of the harpooned sea monster an adventurous hunter in a boat would tie an ivory pulley-block. At the shore end the thongs would be passed through slots carved in the solid ice. A team of men, hauling on the thong, could warp the carcass ashore.

Probably the best-known Eskimo invention is the snow dome, used as a regular house-building device only on the central Canadian coast. Elsewhere igloos are emergency houses only. Many youthful Americans who have failed in their attempts to build such houses may not have known that the Eskimo dome is made by setting tapered blocks in a spiral. Each block is supported by the one to its lower side as well as those beneath it. When a small enough aperture has been produced at the top, it is capped by a single piece. This differs entirely in principle from the brick or stone dome of Iran, the other world center of domes, in that the Persian dome is based on a series of four arches covering the lip of a circular opening; when the four have covered the periphery, four others are built between them, and so on until the top has been reached. Both the Eskimo and the Persian types can be built without temporary support.

Even with the help of all of his ingenious devices, the Eskimo hunter is limited as to the number of seals he can harpoon and the number of fish he can catch. Food is scarce, and in most of the Eskimo country lying between Alaska and Greenland the number of people who can live in one village or camp must be limited to between fifty and eighty. In the winter two or three families, totaling about twenty-five persons, live in one house. In the summer each family lives in its own skin tent. Individual families are free to leave the community and join another. There is no formal chieftainship, though people are more likely to listen to a good hunter than to a poor one. Too much has been said about wife-swapping among the Eskimos. Like many other peoples in the world, an Eskimo host will offer the services of a wife to a male guest, out of courtesy and often against the woman's wishes. Members of the same household or camp do not frequently commit adultery with one another's wives, for this would arouse the same kind of feelings there as elsewhere. Eskimo men kill one another for this.

In the whaling days, ship's masters used to set a cook ashore in an Eskimo village at the beginning of the season, with a stove and a barrel of molasses, to make rum. The reason was that a still will not work in a constantly moving vessel. At the end of the season, before the freeze-up, cook, stove, and rum would be taken back on board. At Point Hope in the 1930's the Eskimo population was 250. Of these, some 22 or nine per cent of the whole, were frizzly-haired, the result of one Negro cook's activities while making rum.

Eskimo society is as simple as any in the world, simpler than that of many flint-using food-gatherers. Its simplicity is a function of the number of persons who see one another, and of their strug-

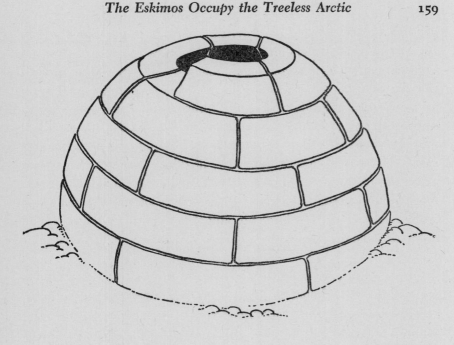

ESKIMO AND PERSIAN DOMES.

gle to keep alive. There is no division of labor other than that between the sexes, no elaborate kinship, no age grading, no formal
political organization, and shamans are only part-time practitioners; they too have to hunt to live. It is practically certain on
archæological grounds that at one time or another the ancestors
of these people had more to eat, and hence lived in larger communities, and that the requirements of living together made a
more elaborate structure, remnants of which are still to be seen
among the Eskimos of southern Alaska, where food and wood are
more abundant than elsewhere. If any of us survive the next war
and adjust ourselves to hardship and the simple life as well as the
Eskimos have done, our social structure will have become simpler
also.

On theoretical grounds, it is of interest to examine the religious
and cosmological beliefs of the Eskimos. Here is a people able to
employ some of the most advanced mechanical principles invented
by man. An Eskimo can take apart an outboard motor and put it
together again without trouble; nothing in our mechanical civilization seems to lie beyond his immediate mental capacity. Yet his
explanation of the natural phenomena with which he is immediately concerned is of a simple order. Once upon a time a father
was out fishing with two daughters. The girls fell overboard. As
they reached for the gunwales, he cut off their fingers and dropped
them into the sea; from the joints came seals. The souls of the
seals are controlled by an old woman named Sedna, who lives
under the sea. When she chooses, she releases the souls of seals,
which rise to the surface to be harpooned. When food is scarce,
the members of the village or household believe that someone has
done something to anger Sedna and to make her hold back the
supply of seals. Much soul-searching takes place, with confession,
until the cause of Sedna's wrath has been determined and expia-
tion made.

The belief in Sedna is a mechanism that helps to restore equilibrium in a group of people after a disturbance. As such it is a
life-saving device as necessary as the very techniques of hunting
and keeping warm which the Eskimos employ. Its lack of sophistication is not remarkable; most pre-literate and some literate peo-

ples of the world place their faith in equal naïvetés. What is important is that it makes no differentiation between kinds of people. The Eskimos have other gods and spirits, but all of them symbolize, like Sedna, some aspect of the weather or of hunting, affecting all persons alike. This set of beliefs and the practices that go with it are as simple as the society they serve. The simplicity or complexity of a religious system has nothing to do with intelligence, but is dependent on the relative complexity of societies, as another example will presently show us.

The Neolithic Island Paradise of Hawaii

DESPITE the possession of Neolithic tools, sled dogs, and boats with sails, the Eskimos lived within the confines of a social system as simple as any known, because food was scarce, communities were small, distances between settlements were great, and most of their energy was needed to keep warm. In contrast the Polynesians, who also had Neolithic tools, dogs, and sailboats, developed a social system as complex as many of those of medieval Europe because food was abundant, island communities were large and close together, and the climate was warm.

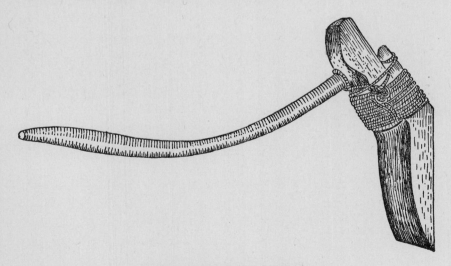

STONE ADZE FROM HAWAII.

At some time in the not-so-distant past the ancestors of the Polynesians sailed out to their islands in large double-ships hewn from logs with Neolithic tools. These ships were manned by huge crews. With square and crabclaw-shaped sails they rode before the wind, and when it was necessary to move upwind they paddled. Lacking the single outrigger ships with asymmetrical hulls in which modern Micronesians sail close to the wind, they got where the wanted to go by sheer muscular effort.

HAWAIIAN DOUBLE SHIP.

Dogs howled, pigs grunted, and cocks crowed on these seagoing barnyards laden with coconuts to supply life-sustaining fluid. On them the wives of mariners clutched sweet-potato tubers under their breasts, to keep the delicate plants warm so that they would sprout in gardens yet to be made on islands still undiscovered. On low-lying islands, where no hard stone could be found to replace the imported tools that had been broken, Polynesian craftsmen ground axes and adzes out of the shell of the tridacna, a giant clam. In ignorance of pottery, which could have been made on some islands but not on others, they made fine containers of gourds, wood, and coconut shells. In place of weaving they hammered tapa cloth out of the tender bark of mulberry and pandanus, trees that they had brought with them. With the same ingenuity as shown by the Eskimo, they worked out a way of life eminently suited to their new environment.

The route or routes that the ancestors of the Polynesians took to sail to their islands is/are unknown. Many eminent scientists

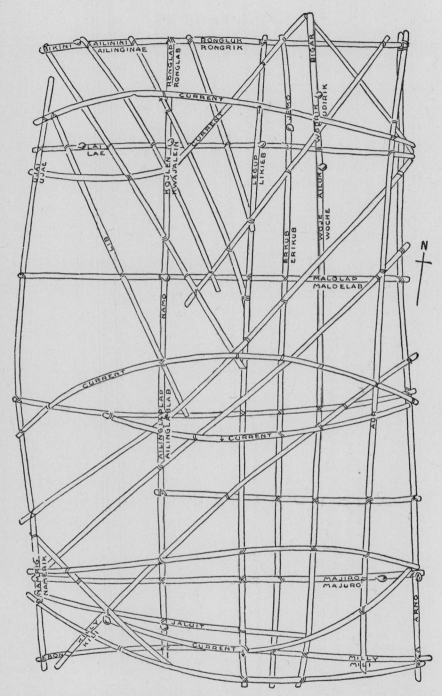

NATIVE CHART OF THE MARSHALL ISLANDS, COLLECTED BY ROBERT
LOUIS STEVENSON. THE UNIVERSITY MUSEUM.

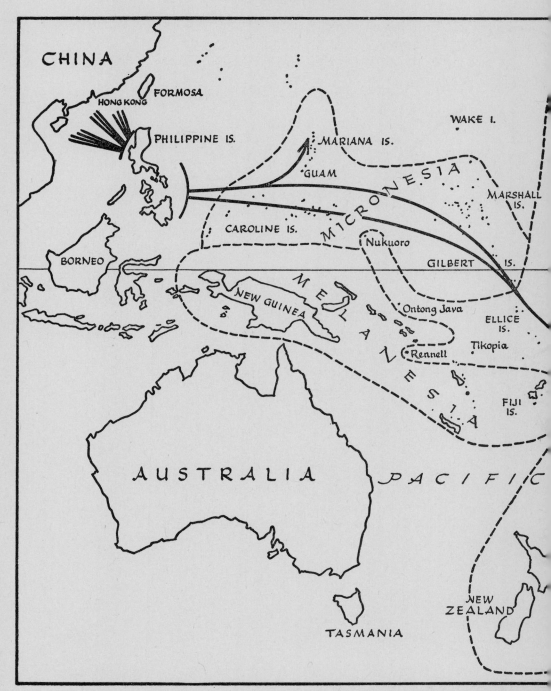

POLYNESIA AND MICRONESIA:

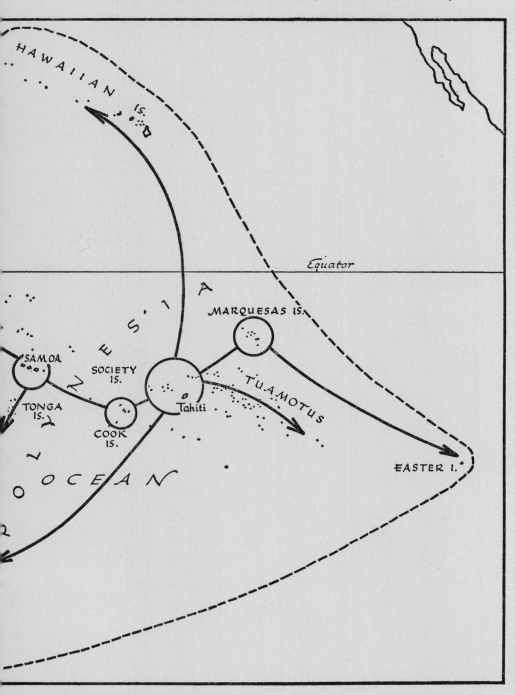

MIGRATION ROUTES

have speculated on this problem and come up with different theoretical reconstructions. The conventional and older opinion is that they sailed out of Indonesia, by way of Micronesia, to a rallying point in central Polynesia, which means Samoa, Tahiti, and Tonga; thence they dispersed northward to the Hawaiian Islands, eastward to the Marquesas and Easter Island, and southwestward to New Zealand. A more recent opinion, which has not yet had time for critical evaluation, is that they came out of the coast of South China, from the region of Canton and Hainan Island, sailing to the Philippines and thence to Micronesia, and from there eventually to Polynesia as previously stated. A carbon-14 date of 1530 ± 200 B.C. from Saipan brings the seafarers to Micronesia at a time when the Chinese people were beginning to expand from their home in North China into central and southern China, and when the non-Chinese Neolithic inhabitants of these regions were beginning to feel the push. Some went later to Siam as Thais. Others invaded Indonesia. The current opinion is that the invasion of Indonesia took place via Hainan and the Philippines, and thence southward around the island chain to Sumatra, rather than via the Malay Peninsula as previously postulated. This hypothesis, based mainly on linguistics, makes better archæological sense than the others, as the Malay Peninsula is essentially a refuge area. In any case, the settling of the outer Polynesian islands was not old. The oldest archæological level in Hawaii is dated at A.D. 1004 ± 180 years.

A third opinion, dramatized by the voyage of the *Kon-Tiki* in 1947, and sponsored by Thor Heyerdahl, is that the Polynesians came, in several waves, from America. This we will deal with later, when we come to discuss the origins of American Indian civilization. For present purposes Polynesian origins are less important than the fact that the Polynesians maintained a highly organized Neolithic culture up until modern times, late enough so that anthropologists have been able to study it in detail. This culture was naturally most complex in the larger islands or groups of islands where tropical plants could be readily cultivated. Such a group was that of Hawaii.

On the 17th of January, 1779, when General Washington was

waiting out the winter at Morristown, New Jersey, a British sub-ject named James Cook, who had been skirting around the smaller islands of the Hawaiian group, dropped anchor in Karakakooa Bay in the largest island, Hawaii. Having visited Tahiti, New Zealand, and other parts of Polynesia previously, and indeed having several Polynesian members in his crew, the famous mariner was sur-prised only at the size of the island and the numbers of persons who came out to his three ships in their canoes. Theirs was the greater surprise. Never before had the people of Hawaii seen Euro-pean vessels or European faces.

It happened that the time of Captain Cook's arrival fell at the climax of an annual four-month period of feasting, sports, and re-ligious worship, and was sacred to the high god Kane. At this time the king's emissaries circumambulated the island, collecting taxes. With them they carried a large rectangular sheet of white tapa cloth suspended from a cross bar at the head of a pole, in turn surmounted by a small wooden idol. Seeing the ships from afar, the Hawaiians remarked the close resemblance between their sails and the Makahiki god, as this idol and its emblem were called. Captain Cook's arrival fitted a prophecy. When he went ashore, people fell on their faces before him as he walked to the royal enclosure for an audience with the high king of the island. Al-though he did not know it then, later accounts explain that he was mistaken for a returning deity.

Despite this identification, the Hawaiians felt no compunction against stealing from the ships all objects of metal on which they could lay their hands, and their thievery was matched only by their generosity in furnishing pigs, taro, and other foods to the ships' crews. On the morning of February 14th it was found that during the night they had made off with the cutter of the *Dis-covery*, and Captain Cook himself went in pursuit. In the rather complex sequence of events which followed, the king lost control of the huge mob of people who had assembled, and Captain Cook was killed by means of an iron dagger that he himself had brought to the islands for trade. Twenty-four days later, on March 10, 1779, Benjamin Franklin, American Ambassador to France, issued from his residence at Passy an open letter to all American shipmasters, bidding them spare and aid Captain Cook and his fleet, despite their nationality, calling Captain Cook's mission "an undertaking truly laudable in itself, as the increase of geographical knowledge facilitates the communication between distant nations, in the exchange of useful products and manufactures, and the extension of arts, whereby the common enjoyments of human life are multiplied and augmented, and science of other kinds increased, to the benefit of mankind in general. . . ." When this letter of Dr. Franklin's reached Congress, the orders contained in it were instantly reversed. By then Captain Cook, in the form of a few dismembered bones, was safely under the sea a few miles off the island of Hawaii.

Despite the enormous distances that separated them, the islands of Polynesia supported a culture which was more or less the same everywhere, except that in New Zealand certain modifications had taken place to allow for the chilliness of the climate, and except that on the smaller, more isolated islands, the cultural pattern was perforce simpler than on the larger ones, such as the Hawaiian and Marquesan and New Zealand groups, or the closely packed archipelagoes in which individual islands could be visited by short voyages in canoes. Among such archipelagoes the Society Islands (Tahiti), Samoa, and Tonga, each with its dependencies, were most notable.

In each of the larger islands or island clusters, the people lived in family groups of from twenty to forty persons, in hamlets set in the midst of extensive gardens, where a minimum of work produced a maximum of food. Sweet potatoes, taro, yams, breadfruit, pandanus, bananas, and coconuts were staples, with the paper mulberry providing the finest bark for tapa cloth. Pigs, dogs, and hens provided food for feasts and sacrifices, while a more abundant source of proteins was found in the fish that the islanders caught, by hooks or nets, in the lagoons and the open sea, as well as in turtles, dolphins, and stranded whales. While there was enough food to provide a surplus and to support a large body of specialists, the number of persons whom each island could support was limited. The population was kept down by techniques of birth control, including abortion; by warfare, by human sacrifice, and, in certain but not in all islands, by cannibalism. In earlier times, during the period of exploration and settlement, emigration was of course an obvious means.

When white men discovered them, each island of moderate size was a separate kingdom. Some of the larger islands, such as Upolo in Samoa, supported three self-governing districts, in this case loosely united under the authority of the paramount king of all Samoa. Kingdoms were small because each district produced most of the products its people needed and because Neolithic techniques of transport, communication, and warfare are not efficient enough to permit wide conquest. No matter how skillful his sailors and how brave his warriors, no king could administer a territory larger than a New England county when his equipment was limited to canoes and wooden spears.

When Captain Cook arrived at the island of Hawaii he found that the ring of villages that encircled the central volcano had been united into a single kingdom, as large as any in Polynesia. After the Hawaiians had taken over the ships and firearms of the white man, Kamehameha I was able, in 1795, to unite them under a single rule. We know the details of the social structure of his kingdom,[2] both before and after his conquest. It was probably the most complicated Neolithic society to survive into the period when modern educated men were able to see and describe it. As no better account of an intricate Neolithic social system can be found anywhere, it deserves our study. From the details of its institutions we can see how complex Neolithic societies could have been five thousand years ago, and how efficiently men using Neolithic technology in a favorable environment could convert energy into social structure.

The early European observers, rank-conscious because of the social structure of their own countries, observed that the Hawaiians were divided into classes of nobles, commoners, and slaves, each with its special duties, privileges, and insignia. The nobles could also be distinguished by their physique, for they tended to be larger and fairer-skinned than the others, no doubt

[2] This picture of Hawaiian culture is based on David Malo, *Hawaiian Antiquities*, B. P. Bishop Museum Special Publications No. 2, Honolulu, 1903.

as a result of differences in diet and shelter from the sun. This is true of nobles everywhere, including Europe and Arabia.

As in other rank-conscious countries, genealogy was of utmost importance to the Hawaiians. Every person of any consequence could trace his descent on one or the other side, if not both sides, to the time when the islands were settled, twenty-four generations before, and beyond that to the gods. A typical genealogy would go back through the father's line for several generations, then switch to the mother of a certain ancestor whose father had been of lower rank than his spouse. The king was a person whose ancestors all had been of utmost importance. In order to perpetuate this distinction, the youthful monarch married his sister. After an heir had been produced, he and his queen could take other mates, and usually did.

Some of the nobles were deputy rulers of outlying districts, others soldiers, priests, and courtiers, all resident in or near the royal compound. One courtier was keeper of the royal wardrobe, another the steward in charge of the king's food, another the keeper of the royal chamber-pot. Others were poets and professional dancers. One of the most important offices was that of genealogist. He and other long-memoried courtiers attended the king at official meetings of the council of nobles. On these occasions two guards were posted outside the throne house. When a person presented himself for admission, a guard called out his name. Then the company inside challenged him, demanding: "From whom are you descended?" After the newcomer had traced his descent through the male line for ten generations and the genealogist had verified his statement, he was admitted. The next man would have to trace his descent for ten generations in the female line, and so on until all had been seated.

The courtiers were fed from the royal larder, which was filled by gifts and taxes rendered in the form of foodstuffs and clothing. In addition the king owned all sea mammals that drifted ashore and all of the iron washed in on wreckage, particularly the hoops of barrels. Before Captain Cook's arrival, the Hawaiians had been using this metal for some time, cold-hammering and grinding it into chisels and weapons.

The courtiers, much given to sports, games, music, and the dance, had a reputation for licentious living, including homosexuality, and for arrogance and rapacity in their dealing with commoners. The nobles who were destined to hold high government posts, however, were secluded as youths and assigned to tutors of ripe age and wisdom.

Among the commoners the men followed special occupations, which were to some extent hereditary. While the majority were farmers or fishermen, a minority were craftsmen. Probably not more than a few hundred followed any one skilled craft. At the base of the industrial pyramid were the axmakers, a highly esteemed group. The carpenters who bought their axes were divided into the categories of shipwrights, house-builders, and tapa-log makers. There were also workers in fibers, including net-makers. These craftsmen exchanged their products with farmers and fishermen on a simple barter basis. Because each island was large and varied enough to produce everything its people needed, there was no inter-island trade.

Little is known about the lowest class, perhaps inaccurately described as "slave." Its members, few in number, were specially tattooed on the forehead or about the eyes. Like the outcastes of India and the Etas of Japan, they were not allowed to enter the houses of the higher classes.

Each family compound contained five houses of a single room. They were the connubial chamber, the man's eating house, the woman's eating house, the woman's tapa-beating shed, and the house in which the husband kept his idols. Outdoors were two separate cooking places for the husband's and wife's food. The wife could not enter her husband's eating house or shrine, on pain of death. While menstruating, the wife occupied a sixth structure, a special hut, the only habitation in which her privacy was assured, for the penalty for male intrusion was death.

The roster of Hawaiian gods, goddesses, and minor spirits reflects the areas of disturbance in the people's life. Kane, the creator or over-all god, symbolized the relationships of all the people to one another and hence was the special god of kings. Ku, the god of war, represented the relationship between kingdoms;

Longo, the god of agriculture, the source of food and hence of the crises that might arise if it were cut off by drought, hurricane, or war. A fourth god, Kanaloa, symbolized the ancestor cult and the ceremony of kava-drinking, comparable to the tea ritual of China. As ancestor-worship and kava-drinking were noble activities, the nobles worshipped Kanaloa.

Carpenters worshipped eight male gods and one goddess, representing specializations within the woodworking profession. Fishermen had one major deity and many minor ones devoted to different aspects of their work. In all the special trades and occupations the same principle was applied. If one were to list these gods, one would have an outline of the division of labor in Hawaiian society, a highly complex system.

In his private shrine each commoner kept his personal idols, which he believed to be the perches of his gods, or at least sensitive spots through which his prayers could be transmitted to the home of the gods in the sky. He worshipped them privately, praying aloud and making sacrifices of food. The nobles and king worshipped in temples, where their prayers were said for them by priests. The priests also performed public ceremonies, including human sacrifice, on holy altars in the sacred enclosure near the palace grounds. The proximity of temple and palace symbolized the twin forces of government and ritual in maintaining order in island society.

The Neolithic priests, as exemplified by the Hawaiian hierarchy, had gone a long way from the simple shaman of hunting cultures. They were specialized for service to the four great gods, and within each of the four divisions some were specialists at praying and others at sacrificing, while still others, in the role of oracles, interpreted the will of the gods from tapa-covered perches high on poles. Special clergy of another category recited on occasion the long and complicated legends, carrying their ancestors back to the days of creation, which served the same purpose as holy books in literate cultures, recounting the deeds of the gods, of early kings, and of priests who had led the people in worship long before.

The chief privilege of the king, and indeed his principal vehicle of authority, was his right of privacy. So powerful was his person believed to be that if he should venture out of his palace all commoners would be forced to fall on their faces, or risk instant death. No one could sit in a higher position than he, and only special persons could eat in his presence. As a rule, to avoid disturbance, he went out only at night; and night was the time when the court was held, first by the light of kukui-nut candles, then by coconut-oil lamps after the evening meal was finished, and finally by torches until dawn. The right of privacy took the form of the issuing of tabus, a word that has found its way into our common language.

When the king placed a tabu on an object, class of objects, period of time, or action or class of actions, that meant that no one but himself could have the object, or do the act, or that during the designated time span all normal activities were to be suspended. The punishment for breaking a tabu was death. While execution was in the hands of the king's guard, so firmly did most people believe in the efficacy of tabus that fear could provide its own punishment. By the same token the king's own health was in mortal peril at all times lest some subject break a tabu, and his every illness and indisposition was a source of constant search for culprits, an easy source of victims for human sacrifice. This was, however, a relatively merciful death, for the victim had no advance warning of his designation, but was clubbed from behind into unconsciousness.

All in all, Polynesian culture as exemplified by the Hawaiian suited its rich tropical environment. The possession of good polished-stone tools, a wide range of cultivated plants, three meat animals, good sailing ships, and an abundance of fish permitted the Hawaiian people to live well and to be numerous. In a land where little effort was required to obtain food, an extreme development of specialization not only kept everyone busy, but also allowed the rise of excellent art. In times of national crisis the tabu system, which in ordinary times may have seemed burdensome and unnecessary, kept order and prevented panic. If a hurricane destroyed all the coconuts but a few, the king could say who would eat and who would die. If warriors from another island invaded, the king would command his men, in strict discipline, clad in his brilliant cape of red and yellow feathers. The tabu system served to keep order in any crisis foreseeable to Polynesians. With the arrival of white men out of the sea in huge ships with square sails, cannon, and muskets, order broke down, just as ours might were flying saucers real. The vivid modern accounts of Polynesian culture as it functioned in Captain Cook's time serve to let us know how rich a Neolithic civilization could become.

Western Neolithic Culture Survives in the Atlantic [3]

JUST as an eastern form of Neolithic culture lasted in the islands of the Pacific until the age of discovery, so did the western Neolithic form, from which our own civilization is derived, survive in remote islands of the Atlantic. The place was the seven islands of the Canary archipelago, isolated in the stormy seas off the coast of the Spanish West African colony of Rio de Oro. The inhabitants of these islands, whom the Spaniards conquered in the fifteenth century, were Berbers, related to the Riffians, Shluh, and Kabyles of Morocco and Algeria, who themselves had been Neolithic farmers until Roman times. At one time their mainland ancestors must have made boats, for otherwise they could not have transported themselves and their animals to the steep shores of these mountainous islands. At the time of discovery they had no ships and no way to communicate between islands. The reason was that the islands contain no stone suitable for making polished-stone axes. The few that have been found by archæologists were made of imported stone and probably dated from the arrival of the inhabitants. The lack of axes limited their carpenter work, but not their capacity for a rather elaborate social organization, for they still had Neolithic food plants and animals.

Although the details differed from island to island, these people were growing wheat, barley and beans, as well as figs. Their domestic animals were the dog, sheep, goat, and pig. The lack of

[3] See E. A. Hooton, *Ancient Inhabitants of the Canary Islands*, Harvard African Studies, Vol. 7, Cambridge, Mass., 1925.

cattle of course meant that they cultivated cereals by hoe rather than by plow. They milked their horned animals and made cheese.

On all the islands they made coarse pottery, but on the largest island, Gran Canaria, they had advanced to painted pottery, which is also still made by mainland Berbers. Weaving either had not reached them or had been abandoned. Their garments were made of curried goatskins partly tanned with some red vegetable material. The needles with which they stitched their capes were of bone, as were many of their other implements. For houses they erected windowless single-storied edifices of mortarless rough stone masonry. One house, that of a king, was paneled inside with wood. In view of the lack of axes, this was a great luxury.

On the smaller islands, life was uncomplicated, and social structure simple, as is true today on such isolated dots on the ocean as Corvo in the Azores and Tristan da Cunha in the South Atlantic. The way of life was insular as well as Neolithic. On the larger islands, notably on Gran Canaria and Teneriffe, however, the land surface was large enough and the rainfall heavy enough to support several thousand people. Distances were great enough and mountains steep enough to isolate individual villages inhabited by people whose only means of transportation was on foot. Two ingenious devices helped reduce the effect of these distances. The men pole-vaulted over the mountain streams and meadows, and had worked out a whistling language for communication between distant hills. Each of these islands was divided into villages, and these villages were grouped into independent kingdoms. The kingdoms varied in number from island to island and from time to time, but there were never less than two per island.

In each kingdom two social classes existed: commoners and nobles. The commoners, who wore short hair, tilled the fields and herded the animals, milked them, and made the cheese. The nobles were not permitted to perform any economically useful task; their business was administrative and military. Despite the crudity of their tool kit, they made excellent spears, with tips notched to break off in the wound. They also made shields and used skins wrapped around the forearm, like the Homeric gods, to ward off blows. At slinging stones they were most expert. Limited to these

weapons, they stood off the Spaniards for many years, the relief
of the nobles from work having given them the time for martial
exercises, and particularly for military organization and discipline.
It should be noted that the division of labor in this Neolithic community was not primarily between men and women, as with the
garden-tillers of Melanesia and aboriginals of North America, but
between nobles of both sexes and commoners of both sexes. Not
all men were warriors, only noble men. The king himself stood at
the head of the noble group, their leader in war and peace, but
he could take action only after full consultation with his council
of nobles, who convened for this purpose at a special place. One
special privilege of the king was the right to sleep with his host's
women wherever he went, and the children so produced were en-
nobled when they came of age, providing that they had behaved
well in the meanwhile.

In Gran Canaria there were two kings, each fully independent;
but both recognized the judicial primacy of a religious leader who,
by his knowledge of tradition, by supernatural activities, or by
both, passed on the legality of administrative matters. On the hill-
tops were shrines to which people repaired in time of stress to
sacrifice milk and butter to the spirits of their ancestors, and a
special white building housed a company of priestesses clad in
white goatskin robes and ruled by an abbess. This building was
sanctuary. Any man fleeing an enemy could take refuge there, and
no one dared harm him. In times of crisis, as during a drought, the
priestesses would lead the people in a procession to some rocks
by the shore, where they would make sacrifices, beat the waves
with sticks, and wail. The island also contained a special shrine
housing two statues, male and female, and a number of sacred
rocks to which pilgrims repaired.

There can be little question that in its basic principles the social
structure of the Canary Islanders reflected Neolithic life in the
Middle East and Europe, the cultural basis from which Bronze
Age civilization, and hence our own modern culture, has evolved.
Mixed agriculture, with cereal culture and herding, provided balanced work for both men and women, and enough of a surplus to
support an elite whose primary occupation was human relations

rather than technology. Specialists in government, law, and ritual, standing at the head of political and religious institutions, held this society together internally by their ministrations in time of crisis, while the body of the elite, acting as a military force, took care of international troubles. Pilgrim shrines, colleges of sacred women, oracles, and temples of refuge are ritual phenomena that we shall see over and over again in the history of the civilizations derived from this Neolithic culture, in the Middle East, in Europe, in China, and in India. The oft-repeated statement that our ancestors went through an early agricultural period of woman rule, female inheritance, and the worship of a supreme fertility goddess is completely unsupported by known facts or logical deductions. The main line of cultural evolution that has culminated in our modern western civilization has followed a path in which the relationship between the sexes has been constant from hunting days to the present.

Sex and Magic in the Neolithic

A N O T H E R belief commonly expressed by social theorists is that Neolithic farmers, once they had become aware of the role of sex in the reproduction of plants and animals, invented orgiastic rituals to help nature along in its task of procreation. In New Guinea, for example, we know that Neolithic cultivators have a habit of copulating in their gardens as an agricultural ritual. At first glance it would seem that they were evoking human fertility in order to promote that of plants, but this explanation is based on modern thinking and is not a product of the Neolithic mentality. In order to understand this rite, a brief review is necessary.

Among hunters who make their living by killing animals, sex has little to do with their attitude toward work. Only when women are menstruating or in childbirth must they be excluded from masculine company. These are critical situations in which the food-winner must not be implicated, for he must be disturbed as little as possible. Among garden-cultivators, however, whose women do most of the agricultural work, the men have little to do.

Seasonal expeditions into the forests after game keep them busy, and provide them with a framework of organization, as a large hunt that takes several weeks must have a leader who can enforce discipline. Sometimes instead of hunting they go on the warpath to lift heads or scalps from their neighbors. This requires even more discipline than a hunt and produces even more excitement. Both hunting and fighting give the men a feeling of superiority over their women which they need to compensate for the woman's superior role in food-production.

In preparation for such an expedition the men exclude themselves rigorously from the women, remaining celibate and practicing for the tasks ahead, just as soldiers drill and shoot on the rifle range. Full concentration being needed as well as a feeling of superiority, any attention paid to women would be not only a distraction, but bad luck as well. Once the men have killed their game or slain their enemies, they return, resplendent in paint and feathers, and bearing meat or heads. Now the women, properly impressed, flock out to meet them with high enthusiasm, and sexual activities will be resumed with the abandon traditionally tendered to conquering heroes.

The orgies that ensue on such occasions are no more vigorous or promiscuous than the reunions of several bands of primitive food-gatherers when they meet once a year to conduct ceremonies in common while feasting on some ephemerally abundant bounty of nature, like a crop of wild cactus or the corpse of a stranded whale. The difference between the attitudes toward sex held by hunters and planters is simply this: hunters notice that the time when it is easiest to kill is the time when the animals are preoccupied with sex, and that this is also the time of year when meat and skins are prime. In the Andaman Islands, turtle harpooners rejoice when their disk-shaped quarries copulate. Hence, in hunting magic, means are employed to induce this preoccupation so that the animals will dull their warning senses and let themselves be killed. If the hunter abstains from sex at all, it is to remain more alert than his prey. When the senses of animals are befuddled, his must be keen and clear. Since the connection between sexual intercourse and procreation is not manifest, hunters do not worry about reproduction. All female animals reproduce anyhow; this is not important to him. All women are married, most women have relations with a number of men at one time or another, and women, as a rule, have babies. The father of a child is the husband of the woman who bears and rears it. Some of the world's most aboriginal peoples have, in modern times, shown an ignorance of the basic cause-and-effect relationship between sex and procreation, though there are anthropologists who will deny this. The point is that while the people in question are quite bright enough to understand this matter, it is not important to them.

To the farmer who lives on the product of his wife's gardens, no cleavage appears between sex and agriculture; in fact, women work the gardens, women are sexual creatures, and therefore copulation and cultivation are equivalent and linked. The most important thing you do with women makes the garden grow. This is a much more reasonable explanation of the magic of primitive cultivators than the idea that they understand the sex life of plants or very much about their own. However, the farmer who keeps herd animals and who kills off most of the male offspring in his preoccupation with the supply of milk is much more concerned with sex, as the comparison of animal and human behavior is much more obvious and his interference more patently useful. Agricultural rituals, such as those of the ancient Greeks, which include sex, emphasize the animal world by using goat horns, cloven hoofs, and tails as symbols.

In most human societies mechanisms exist to ensure the sexual satisfaction of nearly everyone. Our society, or the society from which we are emerging, is unusual in that so many persons in it are frustrated. That is why we project our own anxieties onto the lives of others to whom sex is a constant, and hence nothing to worry about, a matter far less important than the question of whence the next meal will come.

The principal preoccupation of a primitive herdsman is not the sex life of his animals, which under normal circumstances will, like his own amorous activities, take care of itself, but their proper care, safety, and health. This is reflected in the common folklore of every European people, and in our own familiar nursery rhymes.

"This little pig went to market, this little pig stayed at home."
"Little Boy Blue, come blow your horn, the sheep's in the meadow,
the cow's in the corn." Barnyard animals and flock animals which
are herded into folds or sheltered through the winter in caves live
under unnatural conditions of crowding and uncleanliness. They
are prone to attacks by contagious diseases. These diseases are
dreaded. In ignorance of the true cause, the Neolithic herdsman,
as indeed his descendant the Pennsylvania Dutch farmer, turns
to the supernatural world for an explanation. Some evil-doer has
hexed his herd. Some vampire is secretly sucking the life's blood
from the veins of his withering cows.

Who is that evil-doer? Probably some person whose very presence is a cause of disequilibrium in the community. Perhaps it is
some ancient widow living on charity and cackling between her
toothless gums as she waddles bent-backed along the path. Perhaps it is that loudmouthed fellow on the other side of the village
who annoys everyone by his avarice and evil temper. He was seen
spitting blood a few days back; he must be the one who has been
sucking the cows. Kill him. Kill the old woman.

Hire a magician to make up a potent charm of unusual substances, along with scraps of cloth or hair from the evil-doer; slip
this under his pallet. It will fix him. Or hang some shiny beads of
bear's claws around the cow's neck; they will scratch him. Magic,
magic, magic. It cannot cure, it cannot heal, but it can restore the
husbandman's peace of mind. It can provide an excuse for the
community to rid itself of persons who trouble their fellow villagers, though the villagers cannot explain exactly why—they have
not studied anthropolgy. With the witch dead, the vampire staked
through the heart, the community can face its troubles with re-
newed vigor.

When, in the ages of metal, cities arose, the villages were left
behind, virtually unchanged. The new division of labor between
kinds of communities did nothing to alter the daily activities of
villagers, or their relations with one another, that could affect
their way of thinking. The Neolithic mentality is still with us in
most of the world, a social cœlacanth on the beach of time and an
impediment to global peace and unity.

6

THE POWER OF THE SUN

The Barrier of Race

As we stand today on the threshold of the fourth phase of history, the human species, unified in phase two, faces several threats, behind which lies a single source of trouble—cultural lag, as exemplified by the survival of Neolithic-style villages and of Neolithic mentality. Some peoples have advanced more rapidly than others in energy-consumption, technical skills, social complexity, political power, and an understanding of the nature of the universe, including human nature.

Now that global means of communication have showed the inhabitants of straw villages in distant valleys and on remote islands the wonders of Hollywood and the benefits of modern education, the so-called underprivileged peoples of the world will not rest content until they have come to participate in an Atomic Age standard of living. In Asia and Africa social revolt is already under way. That the peoples of these continents should make orderly cultural transitions is to our interest also, for our own safety. Overpopulation can be reduced and epidemics controlled only when the peoples of all nations have reached a satisfactory level of modern culture without reduction of our own. One such reduction, austerity, is a mechanism of survival rather than of progress.

If the world standard of living is to be raised peacefully, we must overcome a number of emotional barriers that, like the tail of a distant ancestor, were once useful but now no longer are. Among the greatest of these barriers is race, greater even than differences in language and religion, because, while a man can learn a new language or change his faith, he cannot change the color of his skin.

There is nothing more shameful about belonging to a given race than there is in being a man or a woman, a child or an adult, because no one selects his own race, sex, or age. Whether or not the average mental capacity of one race exceeds that of another is interesting to know but hard to do anything about now that the major human subspecies all have independent nations. Each race includes bright, average, and dull people, no two of whom are exactly alike. We have yet to discover a society in which whole classes of persons are discriminated against because of their inability to pass intelligence tests. If such a society existed and the population included several races, each class would be racially variable.

Racial discrimination is a holdover from a time when it served a purpose, when a racial division of labor carried with it a certain material and social efficiency. This purpose no longer exists, and now race is a nuisance. It can cease to be one only if we can make people understand it. That is the reason for this chapter.

I have placed it in the middle of the book, between the chapters on the Neolithic and Bronze ages, because by 3000 B.C., which was the dawn of written history, most of the races of the world had already come into existence. Those yet to be formed, such as the Polynesian, if it is a real race, are merely combinations of old races. By setting the time threshold of our study at the dawn of history, whenever it came in each part of the world, we give ourselves the advantage of historical and technical simplicity. America was still inhabited by Indians, and Africans had not yet been shipped over oceans and driven across deserts to serve peoples of other races in cooler climates, and to mix with their masters. Australia was still the land of the boomerang and the kangaroo.

While simpler than the present period, the dawn of history was also more clearly documented than the ages that had gone before, our knowledge of which is based wholly on archæological records and cultural survivals. From this point on we have the fuller but less objective evidence of contemporary texts written or inscribed on stone, clay, papyrus, and skins, to supplement the familiar mute testimony of flint, polished stones, and sherds. What is even more important from the point of view of race, we now have access to accurate representations in the art forms of ancient Egypt, Mesopotamia, India, China, and other regions of the bodies and faces of human beings, many of which are shown in color. These look very much like individuals living today.

The races of man have failed to change since the beginning of written history because no further changes were needed. All of the presently habitable regions of the world had by then been occupied for some time. In each place enough generations had come and gone to provide material for the biological forces of mutation and selection, which are the only proved mechanisms of evolutionary change. The isolation, in the far corners of the land areas of the earth, of small local populations exposed to climatic extremes, is believed to have speeded up the pace. Thus racial differentiation arose not by chance alone, but by a natural Procrustean process in which the environment shaped the man to the heat or cold, to the drought or damp, and to the light or shade of the landscape he inhabited.

Naturally at the dawn of history relatively few parts of the world were visited by Bronze Age writers and artists. However, so great has been the cultural lag in the far corners of the earth that many if not all of the races which existed at that time have survived into the modern age of scientific measurement and photography. A few racially distinct peoples like the Tasmanians are extinct except in tenuous mixture. Others, like the Andamanese and Fuegians, are nearly extinct.

These survivors of the hunting stage of man's history die off after contact with Europeans and Asiatics for two reasons. They often lack resistance to our diseases. Measles killed off most of the Ona in 1925. Also, peoples unused to crowding are genetically unprepared to be huddled onto reservations, to suffer loss of privacy, and to have to live in a highly organized society. Like many other animals man has been selected, over thousands of generations, for this very capacity. The peoples who are the most numerous today are those whose ancestors were most rigorously selected for an ability to tolerate crowding and regimentation.

To anthropologists the tag-ends of humanity, the few thousands of hunters scattered on deserts and marooned on islands hemmed by southern oceans, are just as important as the hundreds of millions of China, India, and Europe. So widely do these survivors differ from each other physically that their bodies show us how great was the plasticity of man when he had nothing but a fire and a few animal skins to protect him from the elements. Thus they help physical anthropologists solve the problem of man's differentiation into races.

Scientific Procedure and Racial Systems

S U C H a solution requires a strict adherence to scientific procedure, which in turn demands that before a phenomenon can be explained it must be accurately described. This applies as firmly to race as to the expansion of steam under compression. Descriptions involve the study of variations, which need classification if they occur regularly. In the case of man, variations in such features as size, shape, and surface color are particularly important because man is the most variable of animals. Throughout the scale of living organisms, variability increases with complexity. The viruses and single-celled organisms are little more variable than inorganic chemical compounds, and even among the cœlenterates, such as corals and jellyfish, and among worms, one animal is much like another. In man, no two individuals are absolutely identical, and variations of body chemistry and personality are at least as great as those of visible anatomical features.

Although unable to agree on a single method of classifying this most variable animal, physical anthropologists are beginning to borrow a concept widely used in the broader fields of botany and zoology. This is the *Rassenkreis*,[1] which can be translated by the term *racial system*. Take, for example, the titmouse, a bird familiar to nearly everyone who lives in the suburbs or country. In the Old World a certain species of titmouse (*Parus major*) inhabits a

[1] See Berthold Rensch, "Some Problems of Geographical Variation and Species Formation," *Proceedings of the Linnean Society*, London, 149th Session, 1937, pp. 275–85, and Ernst Mayr, *Systematics and the Origin of Species*, Columbia University Press, New York, 1941.

continuous band of terrain all the way from England to China. Although all English titmice are by no means identical, any knowledgeable bird-lover can tell one from a Chinese titmouse. An ornithologist faced with the body of one of these birds can even tell with a fair degree of accuracy where, between England and China, the specimen was collected.

The species of titmouse with which we are concerned constitutes a racial system of which all members are similar in general, but in which a gradual change in such characteristics as size, shape, and color can be plotted from one end of the bird's geographical range to the other. If the country in between were all flat and if changes in rainfall, temperature, and brightness of light were all very gradual, then only gradual changes in the size, shape, and color of the birds could be expected. However, its range crosses mountains and seas, and passes abrupt transition lines between forests and grasslands which divide the land of the titmice into a number of distinct provinces. In each of these provinces the titmice are visibly and racially different from those inhabiting the next ornithological duchy, because mating across barriers is less frequent than unions within them.

Now and then the territory of a racial system is discontinuous, particularly when part of it is formed by islands. Birds, mammals, and other forms of life that are blown or washed out to sea and that survive on some insular shore have little or no chance to mate with their kin left behind them. If conditions of climate, soil, and terrain are new to them, changes may take place rapidly, with extinction as the alternative. That is why naturalists find so many new or unique species on islands, where processes of differentiation may pass the bounds of races.

As man can neither swim far nor fly, he was unable to reach such isolated places before the Neolithic, and since then culture has made species-differentiation unnecessary. Only exceptionally in historic times have human populations been completely isolated, and then for but a few generations. The period of species-formation in man fell much earlier, while racial differentiation was aided by the invention of warm clothing, snowshoes, sleds, boats, and other devices that let him move into extreme climates in phase two of history. Since then man has formed a human racial system of global spread; in this system major races have developed in climatically extreme geographical provinces, and intermediate forms have developed in between them. Two subspecies, the African Negro and the Australoid, include both full-sized populations and dwarfs—Pygmies and Negritos—which evolved independently.

Popular Attitudes toward Race

THE ORNITHOLOGIST, interested in titmice in particular or birds in general, runs into little trouble with the public, because the birds have nothing to say about whether or not they are to be studied. The field worker in physical anthropology runs into all sorts of trouble because each time he measures a human being he has to tell him why, and obtain his consent. In many countries he first must convince the government of the purity and objectivity of his intentions. During World War II race was used as a national symbol, and even before that in colonial areas natives were made to feel sensitive about color. It is no wonder that persuasion is sometimes difficult.

Even before race had become unpopular in America and Europe, and before the pigmented peoples of much of the world had been given political independence and hence the choice of whether or not they should submit to anthropometry, the field worker encountered barriers of still another variety. Many of the less educated of the world's peoples believe that the touch of shiny metal instruments on their skins will somehow injure their souls, and that the camera is an evil eye devised to trap their spirits and to enslave them. Blood-letting for blood-group analysis falls into the class of blood-letting in general, and evokes the whole ideology of blood-brotherhood, the fear of injury by contagious magic, and that of ritual condemnation based on the analogy of menstruation.

Once in a while magic helps, but not often. One wintry day in a small mountain village of northern Albania I set up my stand outside the house of the *bairaktar*, or clan chief, while my wife seated herself on a case-oil box with her book of measurement blanks and her battery of pencils, struggling to write down the numbers and descriptive words I called off, despite the double hazard of speed and cold fingers. "Slow down," she said. "My hands are stiff." My vocal pattern shifted in an effort at accommodation, and while measuring a few more subjects I held it at this lowered stroke. To my surprise I soon found that men were forming in line to be measured. They looked up at me with happy faces. Then, between subjects, I asked our interpreter his explanation for this change of attitude, and he answered: "Now that you are talking more slowly they think that you are praying. All of them want to receive your blessing."

When it comes to collecting skeletons, there is no such chance of competing with the clergy. In fact, men of whatever cloth in the local fashion frequently show up at excavations to make sure that their honored dead shall not be disturbed. More than once have I raised my eyes to see a row of bearded and turbaned mullahs squatting on the edge of my trench, asking about each bone as it rose from the ground: "Is it human?" Mullahs are not the only ones who object to disinterment. A physical anthropologist was once jailed in a Cape Cod town for removing the skeletons of a few American Indians from some small mounds in a Portuguese farmer's field, mounds which the owner wanted leveled for agricultural reasons. The anthropologist was jailed not just for digging up Indians, but because these particular Indians, it was claimed, had been converted to Christianity.

Once the facts are in, further hazards must be faced at the time of publication. Fundamentalists of several religious persuasions still erroneously believe that the study of race among fully evolved men somehow pertains to evolution, and they are against it on general principles. While dying out, their objections are not yet feeble enough to be disregarded. More serious are the activities of the academic debunkers and soft-pedalers who operate inside anthropology itself. Basing their ideas on the concept of the brotherhood of man, certain writers, who are mostly social anthropologists, consider it immoral to study race, and produce book after book exposing it as a "myth." Their argument is that because the study of race once gave ammunition to racial fascists, who misused it, we should pretend that races do not exist. Their prudery about race is equaled only by their horror of Victorian prudery about sex. These writers are not physical anthropologists, but the public does not know the difference.

At the other extreme stand the geneticists who are eager to see race studied and have given us some valuable concepts and techniques. In combination with taxonomists they have shown that no race is "pure," in the sense that no group of animals or persons living together as a breeding population is completely homogenous in all inheritable features. Even in Finland, where most people are blond, some have brown hair. In nearly every population yet studied, except for a few groups of American Indians, more than one blood group is to be found. What characterizes a race is a given proportion of each known set of features. All desert Arabs are not narrow-nosed, but most of them are, and a narrow nose is one of their distinctive traits.

Geneticists who work with such rapidly breeding and easily studied species as fruit flies and Indian corn usually refrain from classifying their specimens into races until they have worked out the whole genetic pattern of each chromosome. For obvious reasons this is impossible with man. Were we to await the day when the genetics of skin color, eye color, hair form, and hair quantity, to cite but a few variable human features, should be as well known as the inheritance of blood groups and hemophilia, we would be unable to speak of race for decades to come.

We do not need to wait for the simple reason that before the inheritance of a character can be determined it must be described, and all of its variations plotted geographically. The biologist who studies race among birds and mammals is less concerned with laboratory genetics, which he can seldom arrange, than with observable variations in size, shape, and color, many if not all of which can be attributed to environmental adaptation. He knows that, whether adaptive or not, they are all inherited, though he can rarely trace the exact channel of transmission. He also knows that some characters, like the blood groups in man, are inherited without margin. There are no borderline cases. What you see is exactly what the genes have ordered. Another example is the shape of the teeth. They can be worn down, broken, or ulcerated, but they never grow once they have been formed.

Other features are less closely controlled. A man's stature depends on a number of genetic factors, and can be influenced by nutrition. A woman's skin may be white or dark brown, depending on how much time she spends on the beach or under a sun lamp. What she has inherited is the capacity of her skin at a certain time of her life to be a certain color if unexposed, and its further capacity to respond to the power of the sun with a change of color. A Negro's skin generally lacks the latter capacity, as does that of an albino. One is black without the sun, and the other cannot darken with it. An American Indian or an Arab has the greatest range of possible skin colors, all of which may be seen on different parts of his body, depending on the duration of exposure and the strength of the sun's rays in the region in which each lives. Still, one must say that the skin colors of both Negro and Arab are inherited, but in a more devious fashion than the mechanism which governs the shapes of their teeth.

My view of race is that as all characteristics are inherited, one is as interesting as another.[2] Some are merely easier to trace than others. As the primary, visible criteria of race are adaptive features, we must regard the division of mankind into races as the total product of his adaptation to various environments at various times in the past. That members of different races should look as unlike as a squat Eskimo and a long-legged Watusi noble is not surprising. No other animal except man's oldest domestic companion, the dog, has been able to live in so many environments, and he has succeeded only with his master's help. No other animal except the dog is as variable.

[2] See C. S. Coon, *The Origin of Races*, Alfred A. Knopf, New York, 1962, for an extensive discussion of the forces molding the formation of races.

Man's Five Geographical Ranges

THE MAJOR racial variations of mankind, as they were seen at the dawn of history (according to the adaptive view), occupied five major geographical ranges, each of which appears to have constituted a racial system. By this it is not meant to imply that man is more than a single species. So numerous and so widespread is he, however, that finer distinctions can be made than with most other animals. The proof that only one species is involved is that each of the sub-systems dissolves along its boundaries by blending with its neighbor.

Athwart the equator in Africa lived, at the time of our first accurate knowledge, a population of black-skinned people, most of whom had woolly hair. Non-anthropologists, who do not have to worry about scientific proof, will tell you that these people also have the gift of laughter, a keen sense of rhythm, and a love of dancing. Similar but probably unrelated peoples were to be found in a discontinuous band across the Indian Ocean as far as New Guinea, with outposts as far afield as Tasmania, the Fiji Islands, and the Philippines. Some of these black-skinned peoples are extremely tall, others short enough to be called dwarfs, some thick-set, others skinny. All of them can be called Negroid, just as a simple means of classification, without implying which is desended from whom, or even that all tribes and groups so designated are genetically related to one another.

North of the African Negroes and Pygmies, in North Africa, nearly all of Europe, and much of western Asia, live the Caucasoids or Whites. Their territory occupies the center of the land mass of the Old World. With a long ocean coast line and many seas, its area is climatically tempered by the proximity of water. Straight to ringlet-curly hair form, full beard development, and relatively narrow noses characterize most Caucasoids, while the unexposed skin color of their bodies ranges from pinkish white to deep brown. This range is extreme.

At one end, in northwestern Europe, live many individuals whose skin is so fair that it cannot tan, but peels and burns again

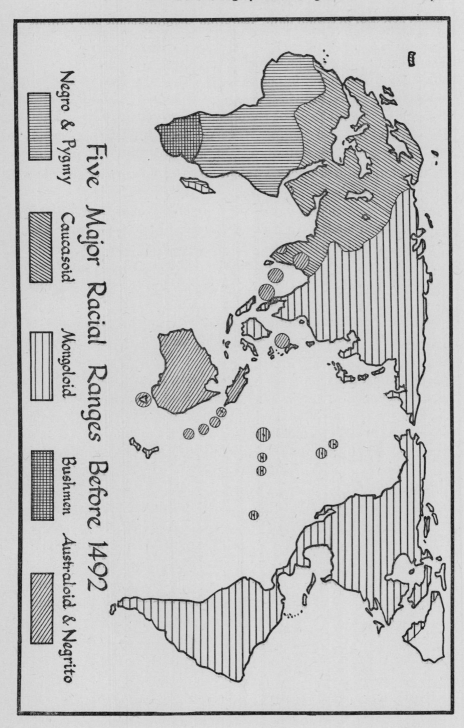

Five Major Racial Ranges Before 1492

Negro & Pygmy

Caucasoid

Mongoloid

Bushman

Australoid & Negrito

when exposed to strong light. Seafaring Scandinavians and Britons, and American oilmen in Arabia sometimes develop raw and puffy facial skin that looks like uncooked meat. For sunny environments their skins were never intended. At the other end of the range, in India and Ceylon, individuals whose facial features and hair form are identical with those of Europeans may have unexposed skins as black as those of Negroes. Like the Negroids, the Caucasoids also vary greatly in stature, weight, and body form. Some adult male whites who are not corpulent are more than twice as heavy and bulky as others.

In all of eastern and northern Asia a third major racial sub-system is to be found, the Mongoloid. Mongoloid peoples have skins varying from brunet white, with a slight yellowish or coppery tinge, to dark brown; straight, coarse, black hair; scanty beard growth, flattish faces, and eyes that may be embedded in thick fat, with a fold of skin, in extreme cases, stretched across the upper and inner corner of each eye. In this sub-system also, great variations of body size are seen, along with moderate variations in form.

The racial domain of these Mongoloids, centered in the chilly land mass of central to northeastern Asia, extends seaward to China and Japan, along the mountains of southern China and eastern Tibet to southeastern Asia, and thence out to sea, via Malaya, to the islands of Indonesia, including Formosa. Although this statement is subject to much controversy, the American Indians of all tribes and nations from Alaska to Tierra del Fuego may be said to show some Mongoloid characters in facial features, skin color and texture, hair form, and shape and size of the extremities. Those who are least Mongoloid deviate in a Caucasoid direction. This tendency probably reflects the fact that, back in the time when the ancestors of the American Indians crossed Bering Strait, some Ainu-like Caucasoids joined their Mongoloid ancestors.

Negroids, Caucasoids, and Mongoloids occupy most of the earth's land surface north of the equator, which is the land hemisphere and that half of the earth where most of the middle and later stages of human evolution probably took place. South of the main

Old World land masses, in the sea hemisphere, in the portions of the earth's land surface that project from its central land masses, tag-ends of ancient humanity remain, culturally as well as physically archaic. Similar to Negroids, Caucasoids, and Mongoloids in some respects while unique in others, they are much harder for the classifier to fit into categories, let alone explain.

In South Africa, for example, at the time it first became known to the literate world, the grassy plains, deserts, and scrub forests of this vast peninsula were occupied by a number of peoples who together formed a distinct racial sub-system, soon to be decimated and absorbed by a pincers movement. From the northeast and overland the Bantu tribesmen invaded, converging on the northward trek of the Dutch, who had landed at Cape Town. After the inevitable collision of these two invading columns, all that is left of the members of the indigenous sub-system which got in the way of this clash is about fifty-five thousand Kalahari Bushmen and a few thousand mixed descendants of the Hottentots, submerged in the Cape colored population.

The South African racial sub-system once included peoples of different sizes, as we know from a fair number of skeletons of various ages from the later Pleistocene to the present. Now all that we have to work with are the undersized and probably atypical Bushmen, some of whose ancestors had heads as large as Thomas Edison's. Yellow skins, ranging to brown, flat faces, low orbits, Mongoloid-looking eye folds, and peppercorn hair so tightly curled that it leaves bare scalp between clusters, characterize the modern Bushmen, and may have also characterized the other tribes and nations of their racial sub-system. Other peculiar features are a local deposit of fat on the buttocks, comparable to the hump of a camel, and a forward stance of the penis when at rest. These two anatomical peculiarities alone set the Bushmen and their kin far apart from the rest of mankind, as befits the inhabitants of a geographically marginal area.

In Australia, even more isolated and also more marginal, a fifth major sub-system existed, and lucky we are that its various components lasted long enough to be studied. Most of the living aborigines are slender, long-limbed people with brown skins, little body hair, and wavy to curly head hair and beards. Their teeth are large and strong, their nostrils wide, and their eyes set far apart. Some of them, bearing heavy brow ridges and projecting jaws reminiscent of Solo man, look, and probably are, the most archaic of mankind. They are concentrated in the fringes of Australia, particularly in the northern islands, including Melville and Bathurst. Some of them still use choppers as their principal tools.

The people of the central Australian desert are less reminiscent of Homo erectus, with steeper foreheads and more prominent noses. Some women and children are blond. These aborigines, who have a very elaborate system of kinship, intertribal relations, and ceremonial life, are the most highly evolved in Australia.

In the cool and fertile Murray River basin, and in the climatic paradise of Gippsland, once dwelt a much denser population of aborigines who differed from the desert folk as much as a Bavarian differs from an Arab of the Rub'a al-Khali. These people were thick-set and heavy, with long trunks and short extremities. Their bodies were hairy in the extreme and their beards luxuriant, while their scalps were subject to balding. Since theirs were the lands that the Englishmen found most suitable for settlement and cultivation, few aborigines of this category are left. The survivors live on reservations. There they wear white men's clothing, which makes the color of their unexposed skin easy to observe. It is usually light brown. Their eyes are in some cases greenish or bluish, their hair sometimes red.

The native Tasmanians, now extinct except in mixture, resembled the Melville Islanders in brow ridges and blackness, but they also had woolly hair. Short and stocky, they lived in a temperate climate and wore little or no clothing.

Of all the aborigines, the heavy-set people from the Murray River country and Gippsland look most familiar to persons of European descent. At Harvard I used to show a slide every year in Anthropology 1, casting on the screen the facial features of one of these aborigines, a portly old person with white hair and a mustache. Without fail, this exhibit always brought howls of laughter. Not until the third time I had shown it did I discover what the class found so funny. I finally found out that, in their opinion, the man in the picture looked exactly like me, particularly in September after a heavy sunburn. Another picture that pleased the nine-o'clock customers was that of a hairy Ainu from the northern island of Japan, who closely resembled Tolstoi or Darwin, depending on the individual student's choice of a literary or scientific field of concentration. Obviously, Tolstoi, Darwin, and I, if I may be permitted to join such distinguished company on a purely anatomical basis, represent (or represented) individual survivals of genetic recombinations of an ancient and marginal European population, and these Australians and Ainus are, if not European, certainly marginal. Geographically speaking, Europe too is a fringe area. European, Australian, and Ainu marginals are relatively undifferentiated varieties of mankind, left over from man's wide wanderings through Late Pleistocene time.

Even more agreeable to the students, however, was a slide of a Samoan princess tastefully clothed in a tapa skirt, a necklace, and a headdress. Although she had died long before these students were born, her generous figure, back in style in the 1940's, aroused the somnolent, and even persuaded the sophomores in the back row to glance up from their hidden newspapers. The princess looked like a generalized human being, with features that might be attributed to some midway point between the major races of mankind. If this were the result of mixture, as the students were told, then mixture seemed like a splendid idea. The princess belonged to the Polynesian-Micronesian division of the Mongoloids, which today includes many American citizens, mainly in Hawaii.

An Outline of Racial History

L I K E any other descriptive framework, a classification of races is meaningless unless seen in the dimension of time. Our information about race throughout time is based on written records, artistic descriptions, and skeletal material. Only rarely are the soft parts of ancient peoples preserved. In Egypt it was the dry climate, rather than embalming, that kept the bodies of the Pharaohs and their subjects, as well as their furniture and their loaves of bread, intact. The same is true of the cliff-dwellers of the American southwest, of their sandals, and of their ears of corn. On the coast of Peru archæologists and looters have disinterred thousands of mummy bundles consisting of desiccated Indians swathed in hundreds of yards of fine textiles. Desiccation has thus saved for us the hair, skin, and some of the internal organs of these widely separated and racially diverse peoples. Immersion has also saved a few fair-haired Scandinavian corpses dredged out of Danish bogs, and a squadron of Bronze Age riders and their horses buried under a stream in the Altai Mountains. Freezing has given us Eskimo mummies from the Greenland permafrost. Most of our information about early peoples in the times and places with which we are now concerned comes, however, from dry bones. Dry bones yield much information, but they are still little more than the props that held up the man.

Because most of the digging has been done by Europeans in their own countries and in the Asiatic lands from which some of their ancestors came, most of the bones we have are those of early white men. In Upper Paleolithic and Mesolithic times most of the skeletons recovered from Europe, North Africa, western Asia, and the Upper Cave of Choukoutien were those of bulky, thick-set, muscular people with large heads, broad faces, and prominent chins, like the famous Cro-Magnon skeleton. These were forest people, built like such forest animals as the wild bull and the boar.

In both Europe and North Africa the very earliest Upper Paleolithic skeletons were slender, and had narrower heads and faces than those that followed them. Resembling rather the greyhound and the gazelle, they patently had moved northward off the rich grasslands of the Sahara and Arabian desert, which received abundant rainfall during Würm-glacial times when the storm tracks moving eastward from the Atlantic passed over them, far south of their present route. Few skeletons have been found in the Sahara, and these are hard to date because of soil erosion. In Arabia prehistoric archæology has barely been started. Yet we can be reasonably confident, until other evidence upsets the theory, that these deserts were the home of the slender variety of

Caucasoid man. In East Africa this type has survived among the slender, narrow-faced Watusi and other cattle people.

In Upper Paleolithic or Mesolithic times some of these hunters crossed the mountains of western Asia to enter the grasslands and deserts of Turkestan. After the glacial icecap had melted, and during the post-glacial climatic optimum, men of this same type began tilling fields and taming animals. The few skeletons that we have from this time and region confirm this identification. From their center in western Asia these Neolithic people spread out in all available directions, around the Black Sea to the Danube Valley and up it to central and western Europe; along the northern shore of the Mediterranean, to Iraq, Syria, and Palestine, to Egypt, North Africa, and Spain, and thence to western France and the British Isles; to Afghanistan and the Indus Valley; across the oases of the two Turkestans to the Upper Yellow River Valley, across Korea and eventually to Japan.

Along all of these Neolithic routes we can find traces of this gracile (fine-boned and slender) branch of the white race today. In Europe it is the predominant element in the genetic composition of many countries, in either its blond (Nordic) or brunet (Mediterranean) form, and the same is true in North Africa. In the Middle Eastern lands it is much stronger. In China one can see traces of it in individuals, particularly in the north and west, and in Japan it appears in the linear build and narrow, prominent noses of the nobility. In the north of India it is also the principal racial element. However, the agriculture that went from China to southeastern Asia and thence to the Ganges was carried by other hands. The shift from plants that need winter rain to those that must be watered in summer was made by a new group of farmers in whose physical appearance the genetic characters of the original bearers of the art of cultivation could scarcely be detected.

Our knowledge of the early movements of Negroids is as poor as our knowledge of Caucasoids is rich. One skull from Olduvai Gorge is probably from an erectus Negro ancestor, and the Kanjera skulls may be sapiens ones. Another is a woman drowned in a former glacial time. Its Negroid features are not very pronounced. No one is known to have found a single skeleton of a pygmy, which is not surprising, as they cling to the forest, where leaching would soon dispose of their fragile bones. Nevertheless there is every evidence that people of one Negroid type or another —that is, having broad noses, black skins, and woolly hair—are exceedingly ancient in the lands forming the southern fringe of the Indian Ocean, and this is particularly true of the pygmies, or jungle dwarfs. These are found in small sylvan bands in southern India, in the Andaman Islands, in the Malay Peninsula, in some of the Philippines, and throughout Melanesia, where they grade into larger forms. The early history of these tiny people is unknown, but dwarfs occur in other species of animals, and even in plants, as a response to confinement in environmental areas too small to maintain breeding populations of full-sized individuals. In animals dwarfing comes from a reduction of certain pituitary cells. The same must be true of man.

The history of the full-sized African Negro is equally obscure. If the forest was the home of pygmies, and East Africa of narrow-faced and narrow-nosed people, while all of the southern part of the continent was Bushman territory, all that was left to him is the western Sudan, and that is probably where he developed. Since our first knowledge of Africa, the Negroes have expanded greatly. In the sixteenth century Ethiopia was invaded by hordes of Galla, non-Negro cattle people who had come from somewhere to the west and south. Someone or something must have pushed them. The Bantu occupation of East Africa coincided with this movement, and the subsequent southward march of the Zulu, Matabele, and other Bantu warriors toward the Cape took place at about the same time that the Dutch were settling there. By then Negroes were also being carried to the New World, and it is safe to say that the number of Negroes in the world today is hundreds, if not thousands, of times as great as it was in the year A.D. 1000, less than forty generations ago.

Recent discoveries in China have shown that the Mongoloids evolved directly out of Sinanthropus. A series of seven consecutive skulls and skeletons make this clear. Like Sinanthropus, they have flattish faces, projecting eyeballs, and distinctive teeth in which the incisors (front teeth) are curved into the form of shovels and the back teeth are relatively small. With small hands and feet, straight, coarse hair, and a reduction of beard in the male, the Mongoloids are our most distinctive subspecies. Their center of differentiation was China, whence they spread along the Arctic shore to Bering Strait and the White Sea. Such is the mountainous structure of Asia that it was easier for such people to migrate to the east and south than to the west. By the time the bearers of agriculture arrived from the west, a hunting population of Mongoloid type covered China, while on the outer margin of Japan a fringe of European-like hunters, the Ainu, remained.

With the expansion of Chinese civilization other Mongoloids, who had also learned about agriculture, moved southward and invaded what is now Burma, Siam, and Indo-China. This movement reached out into the islands, so that by the time of Christ, Sumatra, Java, Bali, Borneo, and the Philippines, to name but a few, had become populated by an essentially Mongoloid people. Others, having mixed with the predominantly Australoid aborigines of these islands, continued on out to the Pacific and sired the Micronesians and Polynesians. Meanwhile America had been entered by predominantly Mongoloid people walking over Bering Strait. Australia and New Guinea are one unit because when the first people arrived, during late Würm times, the shallow seas between these land masses were dry. Whether through multiple invasions or by geographical selection, curly-haired elements came to occupy the fringes—New Guinea and Tasmania—and a straight-haired element the center. Other Australoids invaded central India, where they remain as aboriginal tribes. In South Africa the yellow-skinned peppercorn-haired people were reduced by invasion and competition to about fifty-five thousand Bushmen and a few thousand Hottentots. They are also part-ancestors of the Cape colored people.

And that, in a nutshell, is the racial history of man up to the great periods of migration and expansion which are commonly called history. During that time all of the major races of mankind had developed. We are the remains.

Ecological Rules Governing Size, Shape, and Color

O N C E man's prehistoric movements have been traced, the historic distribution of races begins to take on meaning. The true significance of race appears, however, only when we have studied its function. First of all, we know that nature is not wasteful. The arctic fox does not put on a white coat in winter simply by chance, or through any choice of his own. Wild animals of a given species vary from one end of their geographical range to another, and their variations follow definite ecological rules, of which zoologists have long been aware.[3]

One is Gloger's rule: that animals living in wet forests tend to have black or red coats. Another is Bergmann's: that animals of a given species are larger in colder regions and smaller in warmer ones. A third, Allen's rule, states that animals living in deserts and arid grasslands have longer extremities than those of the same, or closely related, species living in forests or on mountains. Rensch, the latest of the rule-makers, has showed that within a species or group of species those animals which live in the colder regions of the earth have longer hair than those whose homes are hot. He has further demonstrated that while arctic animals store fat all over their bodies beneath the skin, fat-storers who live in deserts, particularly warm deserts, carry it in lumps, as with the camel and fat-tailed sheep.

These rules serve to describe uniformities in the adaptations of different species of warm-blooded animals to geographical variations in heat, light, and ultra-violet radiation. The solar spectrum, of which these are but three contiguous segments, ranges from a wave length of about 24,000 angstroms (an angstrom is what physicists call one one-hundred-millionth of a centimeter) to 2,900. Wave lengths between 24,000 and 7,700 angstroms, called infra-red, produce heat alone. Between 7,700 and 3,900 angstroms lies the visible part of the spectrum, by means of which we see. From 3,900 to 2,900 is ultra-violet, a range of invisible short-wave

[3] For an extensive bibliography on this subject, see my "Climate and Race" in Harlow Shapley, ed., *Climatic Change,* Harvard University Press, Cambridge, 1953.

White race, Mediterranean variety.
The Venus of Benghazi, third century B.C., Greek.

PLATE IX

White race, Upper Paleolithic type. The Emperor Caracalla. Princeton Art Museum.

PLATE X

Mongoloid race, Chinese type. A Lohan, or original disciple of Buddha, in a heroic-sized porcelain from the Tang Dynasty, A.D. 618–906.

PLATE XI

Negro race, West African type. A Benin bronze
from the sixteenth or seventeenth century A.D.

PLATE XII

Australoid race, desert adaptation. Two views of a bronze figurine of a dancer, probably from Harappa, Indus Valley, third millennium B.C.

PLATE XIII

Pacific Negroid race, New Guinea variety. Two Melanesian skulls embellished with plaster and cowrie shells.

PLATE XIV

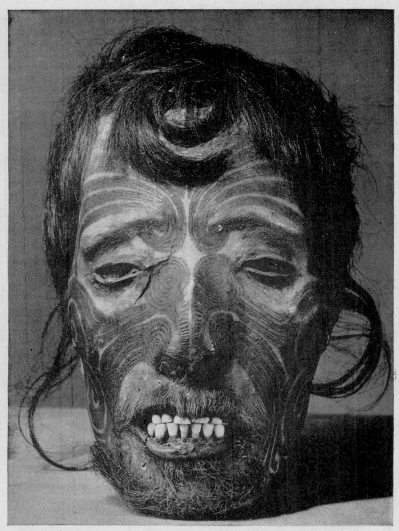

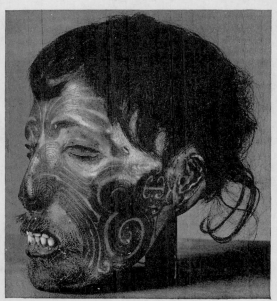

Polynesian race, Maori type.
Two views of a Maori face,
carved and tattooed during
its lifetime.

PLATE XV

Mongoloid race, American Indian variety. BELOW: a Peruvian Mochica pot, about the time of Christ. RIGHT: a Maya stucco head from Piedras Negras.

PLATE XVI

radiation which burns the human skin, tans it, and creates Vitamin D by irradiating ergosterol, a component of the body's subcutaneous fat.[4]

Geographical variations in temperature are the result of the amounts of infra-red and visible energy which reach various parts of the earth's surface after having been modified by other factors in their journey through the atmosphere. Both latitude and altitude affect their strength. Ozone, carbon dioxide, and water in the atmosphere reduce them. Seas, deserts, and snowfields reflect them outward, while clouds and the blue ozone of the outer sky bounce them back earthward. Vegetation absorbs them. Large bodies of water create winds which blow masses of cool air into warm regions and warm air into cool ones. All of these factors create irregularities in the pattern to be expected if temperature varied by latitude alone. Where land masses are large, extreme temperatures are the rule. Where they are small, the bordering oceans reduce the annual variation. The land masses of the earth are so distributed that all of the regions of great seasonal contrast lie north of the equator.

Even subtler and harder to trace than temperature variations are those of ultra-violet radiation. In all parts of the earth's surface, the U–V waves that strike the outer atmosphere are of equal strength. The difference lies in the amount that gets through. All else equal, this depends on the angle of the sun to any particular point on the earth's surface. When the sun stands directly overhead, the U–V rays have a minimum of atmosphere to penetrate, and hence a maximum of penetration. When it stands at an angle of 45° to the earth's tangent, by striking diagonally they have half as much atmosphere again to go through, and at an angle of 22° they have more than three times as much. Owing to the tilt in the earth's axis, the vertical radius of the sun moves seasonally over a 44° path, from Capricorn in December to Cancer in June and back again, crossing the equator at the vernal and autumnal equinoxes.

New York City, at a latitude of 41° N. Lat., is capable of receiv-

[4] See Matthew Luckeish, *Applications of Germicidal, Erythemal, and Infrared Energy,* D. Van Nostrand Company, New York, 1946.

ing, at noon on Midsummer's Day, slightly more U–V radiation than cities situated at sea level on the equator. However, because clouds and vegetation reflect and absorb U–V as effectively as they do other segments of the radiant-energy spectrum, all of the tropical lands are not equally bombarded. During the current geological sub-period a girdle of forest covers most of the world's equatorial regions. To north and south this is flanked by grasslands, which in turn are bordered, at the latitudes of the tropics of Capricorn and Cancer, by deserts. Only in Africa is there today a large area of open country near the equator. This is the world's greatest concentration point of U–V penetration.

On the basis of these regional variations in heat, light, and U–V penetration it may eventually be possible to explain all of the ecological rules known, particularly those concerning color, size, and form. Gloger's rule—that animals living in moist forests tend to have black or red hair and birds black or red plumage—probably has to do in part with the balance between sunlight and Vitamin D. Animals and birds obtain Vitamin D by licking fur and preening feathers. Vitamin D is produced in body oils by U–V irradiation, which may be more efficient in dim light with black and red coats than with buff and gray ones. Some species of animals occupy both forests and open country. The forest-dwellers have dark coats, and the others buff or gray ones. Buffs and grays afford camouflage that is not needed in the dim light of the forest. When individual animals are taken from the open into the forest, their coats tend to darken.

Bergmann's rule—that animals living in colder regions are larger than members of the same species inhabiting warmer regions—depends on the need of all warm-blooded animals to maintain a constant internal temperature. Volume is a cubic measurement, and surface area is two-dimensional. The larger the animal, all else equal, the more volume it has per unit of surface area, and the greater its efficiency in preventing heat from escaping through the skin. In climates where the air temperature exceeds that of the body, survival depends on the organism's ability to lose heat by radiation, convection, and evaporation. Therefore the smaller of two bodies, all else equal, is more efficient than the

BERGMANN'S RULE. *a*. A POLAR AND A BROWN BEAR; *b*. A PYGMY AND A EUROPEAN.

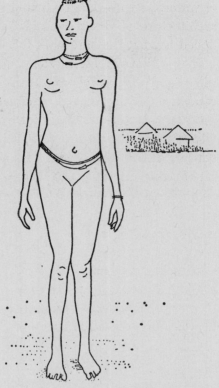

ALLEN'S RULE. *a.* A CEN-
TRAL ASIATIC AND AN ARA-
BIAN GAZELLE; *b.* AN AUS-
TRALIAN ABORIGINE FROM
GIPPSLAND; *c.* A NILOTIC
NEGRO.

larger because its surface area is greater proportionately to its volume.

Not so simple is Allen's rule regarding the length of extremities, in which at least two principles are involved. As Allen discovered, a jack rabbit caught on the desert of Arizona has long ears, but a member of the same species shot in British Columbia will have much shorter ears. The ears are the rabbit's radiators, its chief vehicle for body temperature regulation. Where the normal air temperature is above body level, the body needs to lose much heat, and the ears are long. In colder regions, where the need for heat loss is less and the ears are in danger of freezing, they are short. Long legs are also characteristic of large animals living in deserts. Although these animals do not lose much heat through their limbs, long legs hold their bodies as high as possible above the superheated ground and let them travel swiftly, at a minimum of effort, between grazing grounds or from grass to distant sources of water. As with the greyhound and the gazelle, the whole body architecture of desert animals is long, compressed, and rangy. Speed is what they are built for.

In addition to these three major uniformities a number of other rules have been discovered. Rensch's rule regarding length of hair concerns heat-regulation: witness the contrast between the Tibetan yak, with its long coat trailing the ground like a Russian winter uniform, and the short-haired cattle of India. His rule regarding distribution of fat also concerns heat-regulation: while the fat of arctic animals keeps them warm, so that a polar bear can sit on a cake of ice without discomfort, it has to be evenly distributed over the body to be effective. In other climates fat can be also used for food storage if it is concentrated on small areas of the body so that it will not interfere with total heat loss. The fleshy knapsack of the camel and the fat-tailed sheep's flapping appendage thus provide these animals with spare rations of energy on long trips in fodderless country without interfering with either heat loss or locomotion.

Their Application to Man

T H E S E ecological rules would have little bearing on the subject of this book were they not just as applicable to man as to yaks, polar bears, and fat-tailed sheep. Thanks largely to the efforts of the U.S. Quartermaster Corps during and since World War II,[5] to the research branches of the U.S., Canadian, and British air forces, and to a number of civilian agencies in many countries, such as the Fels Research Institute of Antioch College in Yellow Springs, Ohio, we are beginning to unlock the secrets of human racial variation. In man as in animals and birds, races seem to exist for the principal purpose of accommodating the organism to differences in heat, visible light, and U–V radiation.

We know, for example, that really black Negroes do not sunburn as severely as white people, nor are they as liable to skin

[5] See particularly L. H. Newburgh and others, *Physiology of Heat Regulation*, W. B. Saunders Company, Philadelphia, 1949.

RENSCH'S DESERT FAT RULE. IN BOTH THE CAMEL AND THE BUSHMAN (SOUTH AFRICAN CAVE ART) FAT NEEDED FOR SURVIVAL IN THE DESERT IS DEPOSITED IN LUMPS WHERE IT WILL NOT INTERFERE WITH BODY-HEAT LOSS OR LOCOMOTION.

cancer. Their skins contain massed granules of melanin, or pigment, a chemical substance deposited in the deepest layers of the epidermis. Persons with unpigmented skins suffer sunburn, peeling, blistering, and even fever and prostration, because of the pentration of a very narrow band of U–V radiation concentrated at a peak of 2,967 angstroms. Melanin absorbs these rays before they can reach the sensitive layers of the skin and converts them into radiant heat, which is expelled along with that produced inside the body by work and food metabolism.

Negroes and other black-skinned peoples inherit dark skin pigment, while brunet whites and members of other races of intermediate skin color inherit the ability to acquire it by seasonal tanning. In regions of high latitude and seasonal cloudiness a white skin is advantageous, at least in winter, for it permits a maximum of Vitamin-D irradiation, which would be partly impeded by more pigment granules. In man, as in other hairless animals, Vitamin D is absorbed directly into the blood stream because it is produced inside the skin instead of on the hair cover.

Negro skin also has a thick superficial horny layer. This resists scratching and impedes the penetration of germs, which need ten times as much U–V to kill them in a hot, damp atmosphere as in dry air. Negroes infect less than white men in the tropics. For all these reasons the distribution of black-skinned peoples around the equatorial belt of the Old World makes sense, as does the concentration of pale-skinned peoples in the cloudy regions of northwest Europe.

The human eye is also concerned with U–V regulation. The lens, while transparent to visible light, in all races completely absorbs atmospheric U–V, thus removing a potential source of blindness. The eye also regulates the amount of light which it lets in by means of an automatic diaphragm, the iris. Except in the eyes of albinos, defective in this sense, the back of the iris is rendered opaque by a layer of melanin comparable to the dull black paint on the inside of the diaphragm of a camera, and serving the same purpose: to keep light from entering the chamber of the eye or camera except through the hole provided for it. In all races this peculiar layer of pigment is present in the eye of the embryo. Like the pigment of a Negro's skin, the organism produces it unaided by the sun.

This is the only pigment that we see in a blue eye. Although its real color is chocolate brown, the tissue in front of it changes its appearance. The same thing happens to venous blood seen through the skin of the forearm in a light-skinned person. In dim to moderate light, one layer of pigment is enough to keep the iris from letting in light. An additional layer, deposited on the outer surface of the diaphragm, prevents even extremely bright diffuse light from leaking into the chamber. Eyes provided with this extra protection appear brown. If the superficial layer is particularly dense, the eye appears to be chocolate brown, or black. Brown and black eyes possess a further advantage, a deposit of melanin granules among the rods and cones of the retina which absorbs diffuse light and helps prevent glare. The black eyelids of the Negro and the fat lids and narrow eye slits of the Mongoloid help to do this also.

The gene, or combination of genes, which produces light eyes appears commonly among mankind, as among some nocturnal animals. Blue, gray, and green iris patterns are found among Australian aborigines, Ainu, some American Indians, Arabs, inhabitants of India, Siberian natives, and many other non-European peoples. However, only those European populations long established in dimly lighted country like the British Isles and the lands around the Baltic, and recently established overseas extensions of these populations, possess light-colored eyes in the majority.

Blond hair is also shared by Europeans with other peoples. Some Australian aborigines living in the desert are blond in childhood, and a few remain blond until their hair turns white. Blondism also turns up among monkeys and chimpanzees. It is but one of many possible genetic variants in a very variable stock. Like that of light eyes, its frequency in a population can increase through genetic mechanisms. If it has a selective value, this remains unknown.

While U–V and visible light influence the color scheme of animals and men, extremes of climate set limits to their size and form. One extreme is damp heat, found in the tropical forests where tall trees form a leafy canopy overhead. The evaporation from their foliage keeps the temperature of the dimly lit, damp, and motionless air underneath at about 83° F., a critical limit in a saturated atmosphere. On deserts situated near the tropics of Capricorn and Cancer, during the times of year when the sun is directly overhead, the temperature often rises to 120° F. in the shade during the middle of the day, while on the stony or sandy surface of the ground it can rise perilously close to 200° F.

In middle and high latitudes, the lowest temperatures are found in regions of high altitude far from the tempering presence of oceans. Northern Asia fulfills these requirements. Verkhoyansk, Siberia, the cold capital of the inhabited world, has yielded records of —87° F. The whole belt of northern Asia, with an extension into northeastern Europe and southward to the Tibetan plateau, forms a block of cold country unequaled elsewhere in size and frigidity except by the uninhabited icecaps of Greenland and Antarctica. In the New World the mountains run north and south instead of east and west, as in Asia. Because of this simple fact, the comparable cold zone of North America is not similarly boxed in, and without question this difference has had something to do with the comparative lack of differentiation of species and races, in both animals and men, in this hemisphere.

As everyone knows, the internal organs of human beings operate efficiently only at a temperature close to 98.6° F., with a very small margin of safety. These organs are grouped in two places, the trunk and the head. Neither the viscera nor the brain can be allowed to grow much hotter or cooler than the norm without serious loss of efficiency. At 77° F. and 110° F. death intervenes. On the other hand, the skin surface of the entire body and the inner tissues of the limbs can and do vary considerably in temperature without danger. Now the heat that the body produces in order to maintain this constant temperature comes from one source only, the food eaten. This food is converted into energy, which heats the body through the regular cell chemistry of the body and through muscular work. Each person must eat and everyone must lose a certain amount of heat if the organism is to keep on functioning.

When the temperature of the atmosphere is below 83° F., the normal healthy white human being at rest loses his heat by radiation from the surface of his body. At 83° he begins to sweat. If the atmosphere is saturated and there is no wind, his perspiration fails to evaporate, and heat loss by this means is prevented. If the humidity is low, the perspiration evaporates satisfactorily up to a temperature of 104° F. Beyond these thresholds perspiration fails to evaporate rapidly enough to cool the skin. The heat load becomes great, and if work is done at such temperatures, it increases more. A man working under such conditions is obliged to drink large quantities of water. In eight hours he may drink as much as his entire blood supply. Under these conditions the heart of a normal white American is greatly overworked pumping blood through his extremities in order to provide his sweat glands with water. Little blood gets to the brain, which may be why it is difficult for some white men to do creative work in hot weather.

Although the human skin has sweat glands all over, the principal channels of heat loss are the limbs, particularly the hands and arms. In a normal person under normal circumstances of sweating, twenty per cent of the entire heat loss of the body comes through the forearms and hands, and particularly the fingers. This is because of the relatively narrow form of these extremities, and the special richness of blood vessels in them, useful also to supply energy for manual work. When the temperature of the outside atmosphere is moderate, the blood that flows to the hands through the arteries returns along a network of veins that weave around the arteries. Thus the chilled blood returning from the hand cools the arterial blood on its way out, preventing much heat loss, and at the same time the returning blood is warmed before it gets to the heart. However, when the external temperature rises above the danger point, which is 83° F., the venous blood returns through an alternate or emergency network that lies close to the surface of the skin, and the quantity of blood moving through the forearm and hand increases. The emergency network supplies the sweat glands copiously, and thus the blood moving to the internal organs is cooled. This emergency network is again activated at a lower threshold, 41° F. When the external temperature drops to this second danger point, the blood that has been flowing through the inner venous system again shifts to the surface and increases in volume. Thus the hands and arms are kept from freezing.

Racial differences in both the length and the skin-surface area of the forearm and hand, and the pattern of veins directly underlying the skin have much to do with the ability of individual human beings to withstand extremes of heat and cold. One experiment to test this is to hold a person's hand submerged in icy water over a given length of time, and to measure the blood-flow and heat-loss. Physiologists applying this test find that Fuegian Indians, Alaskan Indians, Eskimos, and Siberian tribesmen keep their hands warm by excessive blood flow. All are Mongoloids. No Caucasoids tested, including Lapps and Norwegian fishermen of the Arctic, responded to the same degree.

Mongoloids alone have been shown to be able to resist moderate cold when naked by burning more calories than other people do. This has been found particularly among the Alakaluf Indians of southern Chile who, until well into the twentieth century, went naked in snow and sleet. Only Mongoloids, in the Andes and Tibet, are able to work and breed successfully at high altitudes.

But other peoples have other adaptations. Australian aborigines can sleep naked on the desert at near-freezing temperature. They are able to do this by a heat-exchange between the outgoing arterial and incoming venous blood in their arms and legs. While the Alakalufs burn off calories the Australians conserve them. Oddly enough, the Reindeer Lapps of Scandinavia keep from shivering in their tents at night by the Australian system. Negroes are particularly noted for their ability to keep cool in wet heat, exactly how we do not yet know, but hope to soon. One reason is that young, active Negroes have less fat than most whites of the same age, nutritional history, and work habits.

Fat, however, is not a racial monopoly. Human beings of all races who overeat, live indoors, and exercise too little can become obese after the fashion of barnyard animals. Having made it impossible for themselves to fight or flee, they have become dependent on the protection of more active human beings and have thus domesticated themselves. Under the steam-heated, air-conditioned, and labor-saving conditions of modern life, all kinds of people can live nearly anywhere that they can carry their equipment.

The Meaning of Race

S o m e of the differences between human populations can be acquired in a single generation or a few generations. Americans born of Sicilian parents who immigrated in their twenties stand head and shoulders taller than their fathers. Americans of British ancestry who have attended Harvard are taller each generation. Some Americans born in Minnesota of Italian parents and others born there of Finnish parents are equal in size, though old-country Finns are much bigger than old-country Italians. Sabras, the new generation of Jews born in Palestine, are larger and more robust than their ghetto-born parents.

Many of the changes cited have as much to do with nutrition and outdoor versus indoor living as with changes in climate. The human organism is so plastic in size and shape that we can shift sizes and shapes in a few generations in response to new environmental stimuli, and shift back again as these stimuli are reversed. Other differences are more closely controlled by our genes, and these are ancient racial differences in skin color, hair form, face form, and tooth size. Such characteristics, when they are possessed by entire populations, can be altered only by mixture with other stocks and selection.

While Negroids and the northern Mongoloids became adapted for living in physiologically trying environments, the Caucasoids or whites remained unadapted because they continued to live in parts of the world where climatic conditions were optimum in terms of heat and light, where the ultra-violet radiation was not too strong for a skin with a capacity for seasonal tanning, and where, during most seasons of the year, a man's vascular system was not overtaxed in keeping his body cool or warm. The whites arose in the Old World's best land; it was they who carried the main line of civilization to the threshold of the ages of metal, and beyond.

This does not necessarily mean that only the whites have or had the capacity for creating cultural change. The Mongoloid peoples have produced high civilizations, as have the American Indians. In Africa, under climatic disadvantages, Negroes have developed social systems of considerable complexity and a high art, the quality of which the white world is just beginning to appreciate. Among the whites themselves one can see much lag; the hairy Ainu of Japan is an aborigine pushed onto reservations by Mongoloids; and the aborigines of Australia, particularly the few that remain of the tribes that were living on the cooler and more fertile lands when the English arrived, were still flint-chipping hunters within the memory of living men.

Because race was once necessary, it fulfilled its role in the development of man. It made possible the opening up of all areas of the earth not covered by ice, the domestication of many kinds of plants and animals, the invention of many categories of devices of transport and communication. Our modern civilization would have been impossible without the pooled contributions of many races.

But during certain stages of cultural development, race served as a symbol of social and economic status, useful in maintaining order in a world in which many contrasts in wealth, technical skills, and levels of education had been preserved. This use of race as a symbol made a deep and lasting impression on the peoples of the world adapted for extremes of solar radiation. After the conquest of terrestrial space had progressed farther, and education had spread more widely, people who had been called black and yellow, and who had been kept out of the best clubs in their own countries, reacted violently, and the fruits of this reaction are still with us. Modern technical advance has created a situation in which people of all races will achieve some measure of cultural unity, just as Homo sapiens became a single species in Late Pleistocene time. The question is, how to achieve unity peacefully without loss of the variability necessary for further progress.

During the first phase of history, race could hardly have been a serious social problem. Man occupied a single zoological realm, adaptation meant physical rather than social survival, and inter-race competition was overshadowed by competition between genera and species. In the second phase, when Homo sapiens expanded into the cold parts of the Old World and into the Americas, life was still too simply organized for the rise of classes based on racial differences. We know this from our study of surviving hunters. During phase three of history, human ingenuity devised the means to provide comfort for a few and an increasingly elaborate division of labor. It was possible for kings and employers to move whole populations from one environmental realm to another. Then race became a symbol of rank and status. We know this because the Egyptian government established an immigration station at the southern border of its domain to control the northward movement of Negroes. This was done during the third millennium B.C., near the dawn of written history, to which we now return in our survey of the story of man.

7

WHEELS, METAL, AND WRITING

The Significance of the Bronze Age

ABOUT 3000 B.C. a celestial observer, after scanning the face of the earth for tens of thousands of years and watching the movements of the glacial icecaps and the shifts in the edges of forests and deserts, could at length have seen, in certain mutilated places, numerous scars and bare spots on the planet's skin where the hand of man had been at work. A number of straight lines and crisscrosses, recalling the canals on Mars vaguely and in a minor way, indicated the presence of irrigation ditches and their dependent fields. Dots on the glassy surfaces of great rivers, moving independently of the direction and force of each stream, gave evidence of inland navigation, and rows of smaller dots crawling over the yellow hills revealed the continuation of this organized transport overland on the backs of animals. Here and there a protuberance, rising like an anthill, honeycombed like a wasp's nest, threw up streamers of smoke from the many fires of brick kilns and bakery ovens, smelteries and foundries, baths and altars, of a small city or large town. In a few parts of the world the Bronze Age had begun.

During the Neolithic the material base of modern life was laid down. People had learned to till the soil and to herd animals. The foodstuffs that they grew are still the principal ones that we eat. Farmers with no better means of transport than the backs of oxen and small boats had found that living in villages is the easiest and most economical way to exist. In late Neolithic times large communities had arisen in the more favored parts of the world where transport was easiest, and where food could be accumulated and stored.

It had already been found that quarrels between villages were unprofitable. Some central authority that kept the peace between villages more than earned its keep. Such authority, centered in the new large communities, must have arisen here and there before the end of Neolithic times because it was already functioning by the beginning of the Bronze Age. Some writers have said that the need of regulating irrigation created government, but in my opinion this was but one of many factors. More important, I believe, was the ability of soldiers and police to move up stream and down by boat in the great river valleys of the Old World.

The Early Bronze Age king was nothing more than an exalted version of the Bushman band chief who sits under a sacred tree, takes in all the animals killed, divides the meat, and distributes fire on which to cook it. The king took in all valuable commodities, kept a good share for himself, and distributed services in return—famine insurance, maintenance of irrigation ditches, armed protection for travelers, an opportunity to trade with standard weights and measures, and, above all, peace and order under the sanction of law and religion.

Transportation was facilitated by the domestication of the donkey and the invention of the wheeled vehicle and the sail; communication by the invention of writing. A leader could now reach a much wider audience than before, even persons unknown to him or to one another. When social institutions ceased to be simple face-to-face groups of companions and acquaintances, they grew formal, as organizations always do when they include strangers.

The quintessence of formality now surrounded the person of the king, which at the same time became holy. All of the de luxe products of the craftsmen became his private possessions—gold, stone vessels, metal weapons, statuary, jewelry, rare woods, and perfumes. There was no public distribution of luxury objects, except as gifts of the king. As the Bronze Age wore on and metal became commoner, this monopoly was gradually loosened. When horses and chariots were introduced into the river-valley civilizations, kings could send out military expeditions to conquer and plunder

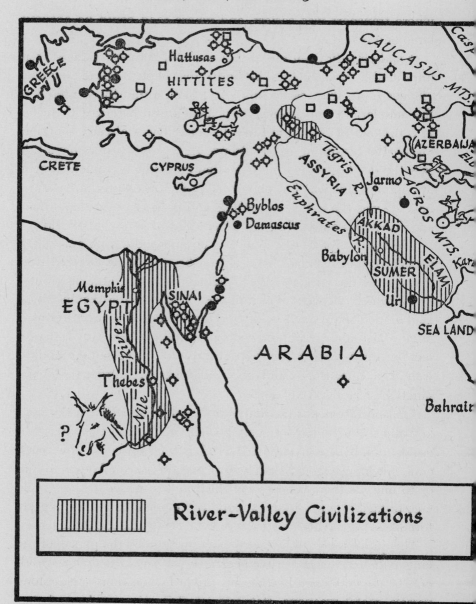

River-Valley Civilizations

their neighbors; international trade and cultural borrowing increased, and so did the size of the territory inhabited by Bronze
Age peoples. However, the high civilizations of the Old World

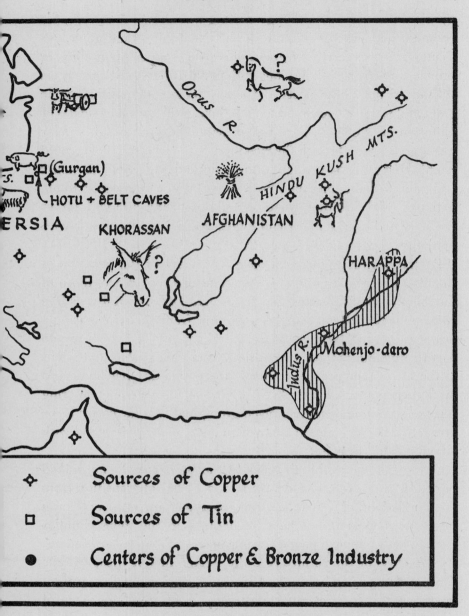

- ⟡   Sources of Copper
- ▫   Sources of Tin
- ●   Centers of Copper & Bronze Industry

THE BRONZE AGE WORLD

which arose at the beginning of the Bronze Age covered but a
tiny fraction of the habitable surface of the earth.

In the elite civilizations which developed writing, the social pyramid was narrow. Although writing was known to scribes, the common man was as illiterate as his Neolithic grandfather. Although warriors carried weapons of copper, copper-silver alloy, or bronze, and covered their vitals with metal armor, most carpenters still adzed out house posts and ship's keels with polished-stone tools, and farmers continued to reap their grain with flint sickles or imitation ones of very hard-baked clay. The farmer, laboriously goading his oxen through the rich mud of the riverside field, could see his king glide by in a fancy barge decked with precious stones and gold. When a king died he was buried in a sumptuous tomb, with oxen and furniture, weapons and ornaments, and with either the slain bodies of soldiers and handsome young women, or with miniature clay replicas of such ghostly servitors.

By the beginning of the Bronze Age many of the peasants of the three river valleys in which these events took place, those of the Nile, Tigris-Euphrates, and Indus, had lost their status as free citizens, and had come to be separated from their increasingly powerful masters by as great a cultural gap as that which was to part the fellahin of these very valleys from their pashas and rajahs at the turn of the present century. The population had increased until each man no longer knew everyone he met; encountering strangers became a commonplace event, and it is far easier to be brutal to strangers than to men whom one sees every day and with whom one has to live.

While it is impossible to speak of the Bronze Age as a unified period, it is possible to conceive it as a period of transition from the simple kind of human relations obtaining among people on a single level of laborious hand technology to the more complex system found among peoples using mass-production techniques. By the close of the Bronze Age the inhabitants of these Middle Eastern valleys had achieved a kind of culture which no further inventions or world events could really shake until the dawn of the modern age of power machinery. In the meanwhile, details of the culture that these riverine peoples had acquired were disseminated in various directions by land and by sea. Their basic technological inventions, codes of law, scientific discoveries, and religious concepts were carried to nations situated in potentially richer areas, nations which, while they had arisen from the same Neolithic base, had failed to advance with equal speed.

Bronze Age civilization depended on the use of three basic discoveries or inventions: the forced-draft charcoal-fed furnace, the rotating shaft, and writing. A fire that can generate inside an enclosed chamber a temperature of between 1100° and 1200° C. can be used to bake, in a single operation, a whole ovenful of loaves of raised bread. These loaves can be issued as standard rations to a large number of men engaged on a single work project too far away from home to have their food brought by wives or children. This heat can also fire a kiln full of pottery. The lower temperatures of wood-burning open hearths during the Early Neolithic produced thick-walled pottery, soft inside and easily broken, as well as thin pottery hard all the way through but too fragile for rough use. Bronze Age pottery is both thick and evenly fired, hard enough to be bounced about on the back of a donkey and unloaded on the ground without especial care. The same fire and the same furnace can also be used to smelt ores, including copper, tin, gold, silver, and lead, all of which were in use during the Bronze Age. Once smelted, the metals can be cast, in pure or alloyed form, into a wide variety of shapes impossible or impractical with stone. While no harder than jade or basalt, copper and bronze can be cast into such convenient weapons as battle axes with hafting holes, socketed lanceheads, and tanged swords.

The time it takes to make a metal weapon is but a fraction of that needed to produce a comparable one from stone or flint, and it is much less likely to break. Even if it does break, it can be remelted and recast, and nothing is lost. Sheets of metal can be beaten into armor much tougher than hide or fiber, and much more terrifying to look at. Metal rivets and nails and metal tires make possible the production of light, fast chariots; though bumpy for ordinary travel, these revolutionized warfare in Late Bronze Age times by their speed of approach and quick getaway. The prototype of the wagon was probably the summer sled, in use by both the Sumerians and the Egyptians, and still to be seen in out-of-the-way parts of western Asia and Europe. Such a sled found in the royal cemetery of Ur contained no metal parts; it could have been made in Neolithic times. In Egypt, heavier sleds, with rollers under the runners, were used to transport monumental stone.

Whether or not wagons had been invented before the Bronze Age we do not know. It is more likely that the wheel was first used

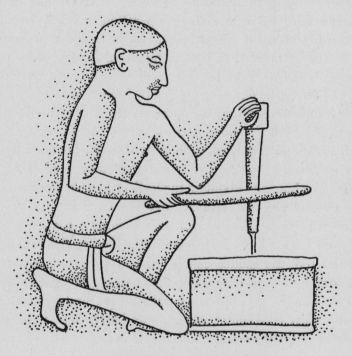

EGYPTIAN BOW DRILL.

for manufacturing pottery, a speed-up technique that fed the furnaces of the kiln-operators and helped provide an abundance of large, strong containers for grains, wines, beer, and oils. The potter's wheel was in turn probably suggested by the bow drill, of use to carpenters and jewelers alike, which was derived from the simple fire-shaft used by all of these peoples nearly to modern times and is now employed in ceremonies by Boy Scouts and Indians. Further application of the principle of the rotating shaft and wheel, on which our modern industry depends, was not made in the Bronze Age but had to await the discovery of cheaper metals, more abundant sources of power, and a number of subsidiary inventions, such as the toothed wheel.

In each of these riverine societies the increasing complexity of government, religious affairs, and economic processes taxed the human capacity for memory to the point where writing was necessary, and writing was therefore invented. When the royal sculptors chiseled the statue of a king in hard stone, it was convenient to have them carve his name on the product so that there could be no doubt in the future as to which king had been meant. Royal treasurers needed stock lists, which Egyptian scribes indited with reed pens on sheets of papyrus, an invention that George Sarton, the renowned historian of science, hails as one of the greatest of all made by the ancients.[1] In Mesopotamia, where stone was an import and papyrus was not made, other scribes impressed their records with styluses into tablets of clay shaped like Shredded Wheat biscuits, baking them to ensure the permanence of their record. In both Egypt and Sumeria the metal that royal craftsmen fashioned into swords and diadems had to come from afar, and the finished products of the jewelers' art, and that of the smiths, were as eagerly sought after in distant places as Captain Cook's iron nails were in Hawaii. Royal expeditions to obtain ores and precious stones had to be protected. Traders whose business kept them away from home for months or years at a time needed the assurance that their property at home would not be molested. Written contracts were safer than the oral assurances of witnesses, who might in the meanwhile die or be bought off. In Egypt the seasonal rise and fall of the Nile, on which agriculture depended, had to be predicted.

The agricultural cycle, the setting of days for markets, the prediction of wind and weather for those planning travel by land or by water, all produced the need for a calendar. Standards of length, volume, and weight were also needed for the evaluation of both staples and precious commodities. From the effort of producing standards of time and space, and from the mathematical techniques of measuring and relating them, science arose.

[1] George Sarton, *A History of Science*, Harvard University Press, Cambridge, Mass., 1952, p. 24.

Early science was chiefly concerned with the study of the causes of variations in the climate, such as frosts and droughts, floods and rainfall, which affected agriculture. In Egypt farmers needed to know exactly when the Nile would rise in order to be able to plant their crops at the right moment, just as in a tropical forest, where no change in seasons is apparent, rice-planters must know when to expect the arrival of the rains. Because the events that became the subject matter of early science were also the causes of disturbances to people, and because priests exist principally to allay such disturbances, the pursuit of science became an attribute of the priests. Their ability to predict natural events made it appear to the uneducated that they could also control these awesome happenings, and this enhanced their power.

Because disturbances to people and communities are the chief causes of lawless acts, the maintenance of the priesthood is the most efficient and least expensive agency for law-enforcement within a society in which all persons participate in a single culture, and whose beliefs are all more or less the same. But a secular authority is needed to deal with other peoples whose cultures are different in detail and who worship different gods. The efficiency of this authority, which used armed force to keep peace, was mightily increased in the Bronze Age over Neolithic standards by the possession of metal weapons and metal armor. Such twin hierarchies of church and state arose in Egypt and Sumeria, with the king supreme over both establishments.

Egyptian Civilization of the Early Bronze Age [2]

O F the two valleys in which these civilizations arose, that of the Nile is the simpler in structure because it contains but a single river. Its civilization likewise was less complicated by the proximity of other peoples than that of Mesopotamia. I shall therefore deal with Egypt first.

[2] My principal source is Adolph Erman's *Life in Ancient Egypt*, Macmillan & Co., London, 1894, supplemented by conversations with the members of the Egyptology Department of the University Museum, Philadelphia.

The Nile is what geographers call an exotic stream; it rises far south of Egypt in central Africa, where it is fed by the summer monsoon rains from the Indian Ocean. Crossing the entire width of the Sahara, it flows between flanking deserts all the way from the Sudan to its delta. At various points in its desert passage it has hewn its way through outcrops of ancient stone, the northernmost of which, known as the First Cataract, formed a barrier

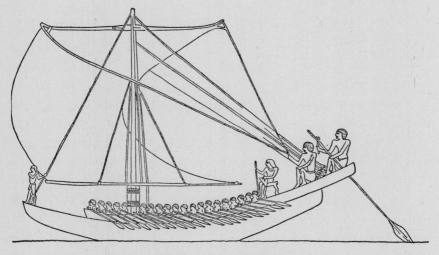

EGYPTIAN SAILING-SHIP.

to ancient riverine navigation and thus marked the southern boundary of Egypt.

Between the Cataract and the apex of the Delta, the river formed an easy highroad for anyone with a boat. So common was river travel in ancient Egypt that the language contains a special word meaning "to be without a boat," as if that were an unusual condition. Between Delta and Cataract, where rain rarely falls, the winds blow constantly from north to south, so that a boatman can sail upstream and then, lowering his sail, float back down again with the current. This made the valley of Egypt a cultural unit. It was also a linguistic unit from the earliest known time. Ancient Egyptian is a Hamitic language, like many others in East and North Africa.

The cultivable land of Upper Egypt covered some five thousand square miles, and that of the Delta seven. Each of the two kingdoms of Upper and Lower Egypt was divided into about twenty districts called nomes. Those of Upper Egypt were strung out serially along the banks of the river, easily accessible to anyone traveling upstream or down, for in but few places is the valley more than ten miles wide. The nomes of the Delta (Lower Egypt) were located radially along the banks of the many mouths of the river, and were therefore more difficult to reach, particularly as the channels were constantly silting and shifting. The relative backwardness of the Delta people, who were mostly cattle-herders pasturing animals driven down from the valley, is easy to understand on geographical grounds. Only the eastern half of the Delta was inhabited by Egyptians at this period, for the western half was the home of a Berber people, the Libyans.

The typical valley nome covered about two hundred and thirty square miles and supported about one hundred thousand persons, out of the six millions estimated as the population of all Egypt in Old Kingdom times. Agriculturally speaking, the nome rather than the Neolithic-style village formed the unit of Egyptian civilization, because the control of river water, which was the deciding factor, involved a number of villages united into just such an area. Every year the river begins to rise about the nineteenth of July, and the flood reaches its peak about the first of September. At Cairo the normal rise is twenty-three feet; a few feet more or less can cause drought or dangerous flooding. A normal rise flooded the fields lying nearest the banks, but those farther inland had to be watered by irrigation. The muddy water was carried in local canals, partly by direct flow, and partly by the use of a hand-operated water-lifting leverage device, the *shaduf*, which is still employed. The area that possessed a single set of such canals was a nome. Each nome was ruled by a governor sent there by the crown. He also officiated as high priest. His court and the local temple served as the nuclei of the nome, around which the lives of the villagers revolved.

Technologically speaking, these lives were simple in the extreme. When the river fell, the farmers plowed the sticky mud of the fields and broke up the clods with hoes. Having sown grain by hand, they later reaped it, threshed it, and stored it in their masters' granaries. Plowing required oxen, while threshing and burden-carrying needed donkeys. Other barnyard animals were sheep, goats, pigs, and geese. The cereals, legumes, and other plants grown were those inherited from the Neolithic: wheat, barley, broad beans, lentils, onions, sesame, and flax in particular.

As far as one can determine, not a single tool that the Egyptian peasants used contained metal. The plow and hoe were both of wood, while the sickle was of wood with flint teeth. Mills for grinding grain were the familiar flat metates, or stones for grinding meal, of the Neolithic. Obviously, governors and landlords must have employed carpenters to make these implements for their dependents, but to what extent the carpenters worked with metal tools, and to what extent, in the earliest dynastic times, they persisted in using polished stone, is not easy to find out.

The period which concerns us here is that of the Old Kingdom, from about 3000 B.C. to 2530 B.C. During the preceding millennium the northern and southern kingdoms each had become internally united. Then, under Menes, the fabled founder of the First Dynasty, and thus of the Old Kingdom, all of Egypt became one, with its capital at Memphis, near the modern Cairo. Despite the union, the two kingdoms were considered equal, and the crown worn by the Pharaoh was a double one.

Useful information about the life of the people of this period is hard to come by. Aside from the inscriptions on stone, few contemporary documents remain. Most of the texts believed to be derived from the Old Kingdom are copies and recopies written down in later times when the subject matter meant nearly as little to the descendants of the original writers as it does to us. Greek accounts of Egyptian life, on which historians draw heavily, represent a much later and different situation, that of the Iron Age. Our best source of evidence is the corpus of statuary and bas-reliefs carved and painted by Old Kingdom sculptors and artists.

These represent not only the best work ever done in Egypt, but also the model for a whole artistic tradition that was followed with little technical change down to the time of the Greeks. During all of this time the government of Egypt grew alternately strong and weak, while invaders came and went. The key to this æsthetic continuity lay in temples that continued to function and to harbor artists as well as priests during fair times and foul, for the people always needed the assurance of their religion, with all its symbols. Each of the four major temples was situated at the head of a road leading to the quarries of fine stone, or at the quarries themselves if they lay near enough the riverbank. Their priests controlled the supply of limestone of which the pyramids were built, of alabaster, needed at all periods for sculptural trimmings and for lamps, of diorite and porphyry, which are hard dark stones used for statuary, and of red granite, from which Egypt's finest monuments were built.

Just as the Chinese love the feel of jade, and the French the taste of fine wine, so did the ancient Egyptian cherish a deep æsthetic feeling for hard, heavily polished stone. Stone, which was permanent, gave them a sense of continuity with the past, an æsthetic experience of a religious nature, which was best guarded in their most permanent institution, the temple. The temple was also the stronghold of the art of writing and of the religious and scientific lore of ancient times. In it scribes copied documents that became less and less easy to understand as the vernacular grew away from the holy language of their ancestors.

While Egypt contained at all periods a number of functioning temples, each large enough to house a college of priestly scribes, in the third millennium the nation needed only one city, because the only activity then highly enough developed to warrant the growth of such a community was that of the royal government. Memphis, the Old Kingdom capital, no longer stands, and we do not even know its size. But judging from all available sources of evidence, we believe that it, like Thebes and later cities, was centered around a palace and a temple. Palace and temple were in turn surrounded by large compounds in which lived and worked the administrative officers and priests, and the artisans who produced the fine objects of metal, stone, and wood which today grace museums all over the world.

From what little we know, it seems that the craftsmen who produced these works of art were attached to the palaces and temples as regular staff members. Not enough of them worked independently for the public to warrant the construction of a bazaar, or to form a guild. The basic condition under which great art can be produced is the mutual association, in a condition of security, of a number of artists who can compare notes, learn from one another, and compete with one another for the favors of the consumer. This condition can be brought about in a number of ways, one of which is to have a group of artists attached to a great household, and that was the Egyptian system.

The members of each craft who worked in the palace fell under the supervision of a special officer of the court. The goldsmiths, for example, were graded into three ranks: the supervisor of goldsmiths, chief goldsmiths, and ordinary goldsmiths. Carpenters were similarly organized. Their tools, made of copper in Old Kingdom times, included saws, adzes, axes, chisels, and drills. The wood that they worked for ordinary purposes was acacia, felled each year by the carpenters themselves on the edge of cultivation just after the retreat of the flood water. For royal and other de luxe consumption they used cedar brought by sea from Lebanon and hard woods from other parts of Africa. Owing to the scarcity of these imported lumbers, they painted imitation grain on common wood, and built coffins out of linen and glue. In late times, old papyrus manuscripts replaced the more expensive linen.

Carpenters, sculptors, jewelers, and soldiers all needed metal— not only copper, but also gold. These were the two metals first used in Egypt, and probably elsewhere, because both occur in their native form in surface deposits and may be easily seen. Five thousand years ago they were undoubtedly easier to find than today, when most of the world's native deposits have been exhausted. The first copperwork was confined to hammering off pieces of the native metal and then pounding them into shape. This has been determined by spectroscopic analysis of the earliest specimens. However, unless copper is heated first, it breaks

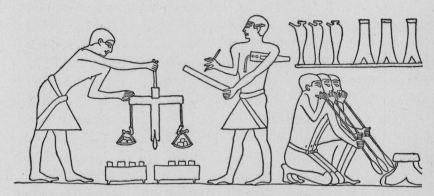

EGYPTIAN METAL-WORKING SCENE: WEIGHING METAL, MELTING AND

when pounded, and so the second process, known as annealing, soon developed. When copper was heated in a furnace built for bread or pottery, it melted, and thus the use of the open mold was discovered. When a lump of copper attached to a piece of ore is put into a furnace to melt, the visible volume of the metal increases as the ore succumbs to the heat, and the amount of usable copper is greatly increased. This, in general, is the early history of pre-bronze and pre-ferrous metallurgy as deduced, in Egypt and elsewhere, by expert metallurgists.[3] The old theory of the accidental melting of ore in a campfire can be discarded as technically impossible.

Most of the copper that the Egyptians used in Old Kingdom times came from the Sinai Peninsula, outside the confines of the settled agricultural country. To get it the kings sent royal expeditions, consisting of technical supervisors who were army officers as well as engineers, porters and miners who were also soldiers, and scribes who were not. Although mining and portering were their main duties, these men were also prepared to repel attacks. These cannot have been numerous or serious, as the local nomads were probably nothing more than shepherds traveling on foot or mounted on asses, and armed only with wooden and

[3] H. H. Coughlan, *Notes on the Prehistoric Metallurgy of Copper and Bronze in the Old World,* Pitt Rivers Museum, Oxford, Occasional Papers on Technology, No. 4, 1951.

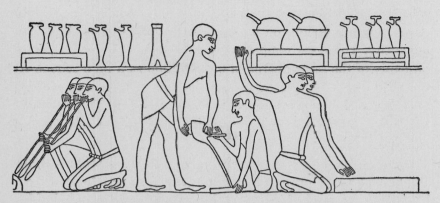

CASTING COPPER, AND BEATING GOLD INTO THIN SHEETS.

flint weapons. These expeditions were the principal reason for the army's existence.

In the history of metallurgy, it would appear that once men had begun to smelt copper, they could also recognize the potential value of other ores, which resemble copper ore in being noticeably heavier than ordinary stone. By experimenting with these, they produced other metals. One of these, rare in nature and never occurring in a conspicuous form, is tin. Somewhere far from Egypt, by 3000 B.C. metallurgists learned that if they smelted tin ore and copper ore together, they could produce bronze, harder and more useful than copper and easier to cast. Except for one isolated piece of earlier date,[4] bronze was not brought into Egypt before Middle Kingdom times (1990–1880 B.C.), when it probably came through the agency of sea traders from the north or land traders from Palestine and Syria. From then on, bronze was a common import, particularly in Late Kingdom (Empire) times, after 1560 B.C.

In Old Kingdom times Egypt was still an isolated country, and copper weapons were good enough for the defense of the realm and for the maintenance of internal order and security. The political framework which had arisen for these purposes was the most

[4] A razor from the Fourth Dynasty, with 8.5 per cent tin, is the only proved exception. See A. Lucas, *Ancient Egyptian Materials and Industries*, 4th ed., Edward Arnold & Company, London, 1950, p. 253. There may, of course, be others which it has been impossible to certify.

complex institution that the world had yet seen, but in modern terms it was probably no more complex than a small American university. The great temples, of which there were several, were probably of the same degree of organization as a high school. At the head of both hierarchies stood the king, a person considered to be a god in his own lifetime, one who at his death went away to join the numerous company of other gods in the distant land of Osiris.

In theory the king was omnipotent and his rule absolute. Actually he had a staff of ministers and advisers, some inherited from his father's reign who had known him as a boy. The symbol of his authority was a double crown representing the two kingdoms. That of Upper Egypt was a lofty, attenuated bulb made of some white material; that of Lower Egypt a rim of red material, pointed to the rear. The white one fitted into the red one. In front, over his brow, no matter what else he wore or failed to wear, was fixed the uræus snake, the symbol of royalty. Wigs and false beards were worn on special occasions.

The care of these properties and of his clothing needed a corps of valets, including at least ten classes of specialists, such as wig-makers and sandal-makers, and a secretarial staff to keep track of all these accouterments. The superintendent of valets was also a priest, for everything that touched the body of the living god was thus rendered too holy for handling without ritual. An entirely separate palace corps, similarly organized and subdivided, had charge of the production and maintenance of the royal jewels, including objects of gold and precious stones. One of their tasks was to make and keep up the royal throne, an ornate chair of modern appearance set on a platform and sheltered by a canopy.

For trips of any distance the king was conveyed by boat, like Antony and Cleopatra in later times, but for short journeys he was carried on a twelve-man litter, flanked by two fan-wavers and escorted by a walking nobleman who carried a small fan, the symbol of his rank, in one hand, and who squirted perfume into the royal atmosphere from a vessel held in the other. Such a procession might be seen each year on the anniversary of a coronation. No matter when the former king had died, the coronation was held at the beginning of the harvest, to coincide with a first-fruits ceremony.

Across a field of newly ripened grain two litters approached each other. In one rode the king, in the other the hidden statue or relic of Min, the god of agricultural fertility. When the two met, priests released four wild geese to carry to the gods of the four corners of the earth the splendid tidings that the king had

EGYPTIAN LITTER.

received the red and white crowns from his father, the god. Now the king dismounted. Taking in his hand a golden sickle, he cut a sheaf of ripe grain. This he strewed on the ground in front of a pure white bull.

No ceremony could be easier to interpret than this one. The king represents the over-all power of the nation, and that of the sun, which provides warmth and fruitfulness. The litter was the swiftest and most spectacular means of land travel then known. Wild geese, flying swiftly on pulsating wings and honking their message, represent the flight of the soul. Gold is a sacred and precious substance, sparkling like the sun. Grain is the food of the people. The ox is their source of traction, food of the mighty, and symbol of strength. The color white, in animals, being un-usual, is sacred. Harvest time is a critical moment, when hungry people might begin reaping and eating before the grain is ripe, and might trample it in their haste. Little can go wrong if everyone agrees to wait until the reaping has been officially started by the king, who himself partakes of godhead.

His daily life was formal, simple, and secluded. When he appeared in public, everyone had to fall on his face before him. Actually he spent little time outside the grounds of the palace. At dawn he arose, read his correspondence, and wrote letters with the help of scribes. Although he was literate himself, he dictated to save time. Then he was bathed and dressed. Going to the temple, he heard the high priest pray for his welfare. Woven into this prayer were comments on the monarch's recent deeds and suggestions for future action. Now the king himself offered sacrifice, and the priests read from holy books tales of other kings of the distant past. During the rest of the day the king walked in his palace grounds, past the offices of clerks and officials, the courts of justice, the royal workshops, the council chamber, and throne room. He visited his family and harem, and sat in audience. His doctors watched him carefully and regulated his diet, which consisted basically of beef, gooseflesh, and wine.

The sons that his wife and concubines bore him were educated in the palace school, also open to the sons of high officials, in many cases royal cousins. Here a class of boys, possibly as numerous as those who are sent annually to Groton or Eton, grew up together as equals under conditions of strict discipline, and formed friendships that could last throughout life. Here they learned reading, writing, arithmetic, and geometry. They memorized holy texts, and copied out homilies that consisted of pieces of advice from some sage but dreary father of the past to his obedient son. The boys also learned gymnastics and swimming, but the most important subject was good manners, with special emphasis on protocol. On the whole, the Egyptian youth received the rough equivalent of a junior-high-school education, minus history and foreign languages, and plus a finishing-school polish. Higher learning, if any, was confined to the temples.

From the graduates of this school were recruited the officials of the government. Among these were the nomarchs, or governors of nomes. Such an officer had the use of crown estates, from which he derived cattle and grain and the services of resident farmers and artisans. In addition he drew a share of income from the property of the local temple, for he was technically high priest, just as the king theoretically headed the priestly college of the temple serving his capital. Although he collected taxes for the king, he had the power of discretion, in time of famine, to open the royal granaries. Being the ruler of a miniature state, he had a miniature government, staffed by the usual stewards and artisans, a treasurer, and a speaker, who served as special inspector and intelligence officer.

Next to the king in rank was the chief justice, a man of noble birth and princely rank, who was chief of the nomarchs and of the deputy judges seated in the nomes, head of the civil service, and a lawmaker.

A second departmental chief was the head of the treasury, whose office was symbolized by two hieroglyphs representing a bee—which stores honey in its comb—and a sealed bag. Among his subordinates was a sub-treasurer who was also minister of shipping and of war, being in charge of the military expeditions beyond Egypt's borders to obtain precious woods, incense gums, and other exotic materials, as well as of the quarrying and mining enterprises in the desert.

The third branch of the political institution was the royal secretariat, symbolized by a roll of papyrus. Under its chief was a superintendent of scribes, who controlled the ordinary secretaries. This arrangement was not unique, for each branch of the government, including the palace itself, had its own secretariat, probably but not certainly trained by the priesthood rather than in the royal school.

The Old Kingdom political institution therefore consisted of an elaborate palace staff to care for the needs of the king, and two departments, each headed by an official of cabinet rank and containing at least three steps of hierarchical complexity, with sub-departments and a staff of secretaries and clerks. When the United States government was first organized, its departments were not much more complex than these, and the Neolithic government of Hawaii approached it in complexity. Compared to most modern governments, it was an example of utter simplicity. But in 3000 B.C. it was undoubtedly the most elaborate government in the world, and it had become so because advances in technical processes, particularly metallurgy, writing, and water transport, had brought several hundreds of thousands of persons into a mesh of mutual relationships which required this kind of structure.

The task of government was facilitated by the popular belief that the king was at least partially divine. A religious institution

EGYPTIAN SCRIBE WITH HIS WRITING KIT.

that mirrored the state in its complexity fostered this conviction, and provided other ritual means for maintaining order. A professional priesthood, with as many as a hundred priests in the largest temples and from five to ten in the small ones, was divided into three specialist categories. In each the novice had the chance to move up through three intermediate stages to the high priesthood. First in rank were priests who conducted public ceremonies. Next were the reciters, who reeled off from memory passages from the holy books, no doubt as a carry-over from preliterate times when the sacred literature had to be learned by heart, as in Hawaii. The third were meat inspectors, who also

poured liquid sacrifices in the temples. In addition to these full-
time professionals, companies of laymen known as "hour priests"
volunteered their services, one of them serving each month in the
local temple. On feast days the members of this brotherhood
marched in holy procession, accompanying the litter-borne and
shrouded image or relic of their deity.

The religious system that these priests maintained was based
on the worship of a vast number of gods, totaling at least two
hundred in the earliest dynastic times and later increasing. These
gods represented areas of disturbance in human relations brought
about by both natural events and the divisions of labor based on
age, sex, and occupation. Some of these objects of symbolization
were: the sky and rain; night, darkness, north, and evil; the sun
in a multitude of daily and seasonal aspects, and royal power; the
moon; the Nile; wind, air, and the perfume of flowers; fire; agriculture; sexual attraction; writing; metallurgy; and justice. These
twelve subjects can be multiplied by the number of nomes, and
reduced by the number of those which merged as Egyptian culture became increasingly homogeneous.

Like their hunting ancestors whose lives had been spent observing the habits of animals and birds, the Egyptians symbolized their gods with animal attributes, making Ra, the sun god,
an eagle, and Isis a crane. Thoth, the god of writing and learning,
was a baboon, an animal that gives an appearance of scholarly
persistence by turning over stone after stone in search of vermin,
and of counting when he grooms his fellows. Set, the god of the
underworld, was depicted as a mysterious animal with a long
snout and tail and square ears, somewhat like the aardvark, which
digs itself out of sight, presumably in the direction of the underworld, in a matter of seconds when disturbed.[5]

Each of these gods had not one but a number of myths, which
were as familiar to the ordinary Egyptians as the story of Jonah
and the Whale is to Christians. The best-known and most influen-
tial of these was the Osiris story. It contains certain episodes that
may have to do with the origin of the Neolithic element in Egyp-

---

[5] The explanation of Thoth's identification, and the comparison of Set to the
aardvark, are my own. My Egyptological colleagues do not accept them.

tian culture. Osiris introduced agriculture, animal-husbandry, and arts and crafts to Egypt. After his death he returned to his original home, from which he had presumably brought the plants and animals that the Egyptians raised. There he received the souls of dead Egyptians who had memorized the text of the sacred guide-book known as the *Book of Coming Forth by Day* (*Book of the Dead*) and knew the way.

Osiris's home was not in the west, as is usual with such happy hunting grounds, but in the north. The land was foggy and bor-dered with high mountains, some of which were volcanic. On the side away from the mountains stood a huge lake, and in between lay a network of rivers and irrigation ditches. Toward the moun-tains rose a dense forest, while away from them and away from the tillage stretched a desert. Many of the trees were conifers, sacred to Osiris. In a hall built of reeds lived the lord of the afterworld.

Nothing in this description resembles Egypt, nor was it thought to. Among various places which it brings to mind is that part of west-central Asia that lies north of the Elburz and Hindu Kush mountains, over to the shore of the Caspian Sea, and which in-cludes the Amu Darya region, even down to the fog, volcanoes, and trees. Judging by present evidence, this Transcaspian region was a seat of early Neolithic culture, how early we are not yet sure, though a date of 5400 B.C. seems reasonable at the moment. Whether this or some other place, such as the lake region of cen-tral Africa, was the land from which the culture-bearers of Egypt, personified by Osiris, came, remains to be seen.

The Sumerians Trade by Land and Sea [6]

A S I M I L A R mystery surrounds the origin of the Sumerians, the only other people known to have had writing as early as the

[6] This section is based largely on the voluminous work of Sir Leonard Woolley, particularly his *Royal Cemetery at Ur*, Oxford Press, Philadelphia and London, 2 Vols., 1934; *The Sumerians*, Clarendon Press, London, 1928; *Ur of the Chaldees*, Charles Scribner's Sons, New York, 1930; on correspondence with Sir Leonard, and on conversations with Dr. Samuel N. Kramer of the University Museum.

Egyptians. Linguistically they were as exotic as the Egyptians were indigenous. They brought their language, which has not yet been related to any other, into the swamplands of Lower Mesopotamia, previously occupied by people who were probably of Semitic speech, after a flood of the twin rivers had wiped out some of the more vulnerable settlements of the earlier inhabitants, Late Neolithic or Copper Age people. The date of this flood is estimated as about 3000 B.C.

The Sumerians maintained a tradition of having left a home in mountainous country where navigation was possible. They arrived in their new home fully equipped with metal, including not merely copper and gold, but also real bronze. Somewhere their ancestors had learned to smelt copper and tin together, for there is nothing but mud in Sumeria.[7]

Tin is a rare metal, which they could have obtained from Turkey, Syria, or three places in Iran—Azerbaijan, Gurgan, and Khorassan. Syria can be eliminated because, had this been the Sumerian source, the Egyptians of the Old Kingdom, who went there for cedar, would also have had it. Turkey, Armenia, and Azerbaijan are geographically a single mountain area; Gurgan is located on the Caspian shore of northern Iran; Khorassan is the northeastern province of Iran facing Afghanistan. All three could have been sources of tin because the Sumerians obtained obsidian from Armenia and lapis lazuli from Afghanistan. Trade routes for these stones would have led through Gurgan and Khorassan. The Sumerians also brought wheeled vehicles with them, and wheeled vehicles are characteristic of central Asia, where open steppes make roads unnecessary.

The earliest wheeled vehicles yet found are two four-wheeled carts and a two-wheeled chariot that Sir Leonard Woolley found in 1927 in the royal tombs of Ur, dating from the earliest Sumerian times, between 3000 and 2700 B.C. In both carts and chariot the wheels were made fast to their axles, so that when the vehicle turned, both wheels of a pair had to revolve at the same speed and

[7] For this discussion of the earliest Sumerian bronze, see R. J. Forbes, *Metallurgy in Antiquity*, E. J. Brill, Leiden, 1950, and H. H. Coughlan, *Notes on the Prehistoric Metallurgy of Copper and Bronze in the Old World*, Pitt Rivers Museum, Oxford, Occasional Papers on Technology, No. 4, 1951.

one had to drag or slice itself into the ground. A wagon of this kind is good only for slow, coarse farm work in soft terrain, and a chariot built on this principle is unsuited for serious combat. With these vehicles Sir Leonard found a delicate land-sled of a kind still used in the Caspian provinces, Georgia, the Basque country, and Portugal.

Oxen drew Woolley's wagons. The animals hitched to his sled and chariot have not been positively identified. They were small

CHARIOT FROM THE SUMERIAN ROYAL STANDARD OF UR.

members of the horse family, either tarpans—the wild horse of eastern Europe and west-central Asia—or domestic asses, or domesticated forms of the onager, a Persian wild ass that is now only wild. Owing to their poor state of preservation, the bones were not saved. A silver statuette of such an animal, forming part of the rein guide of the chariot, and representations on a lapiz and ivory plaque found in the same site, only add to the mystery. Neither representation is definitive.

If they were asses or onagers, this find reveals a premature and unsuccessful attempt on the part of the Sumerians to use an animal unsuited for warfare for this special purpose. If they were tarpans, it means that the horse had already been domesticated in Iran or central Asia and that chariot fighting had already begun there. For over a thousand years after these mysterious animals had been sacrificed to escort the soul of a queen, no horse bones, horse trappings, or representations of horses were left in sites yet excavated. Possibly the horse itself disappeared from Sumeria. Tin also disappeared, leaving the Sumerians to work copper, like the Egyptians, in place of bronze. Bronze, horses, and chariots

HORSE OR ASS? REIN-RING ORNAMENT FROM ROYAL TOMBS AT UR.

all came in at once from the north about a thousand years later. When they did, they revolutionized transport and warfare, and kingdoms expanded to the threshold of empire.

Unlike the Egyptians, the Sumerians had no ready source of hard and beautiful stone to use in monumental construction, but were forced to erect temples, palaces, and most tombs of the same dreary adobe with which they constructed common walls. Hard black stone turns up in excavations, in the form of inscribed door-post sockets, used over and over again, of cylinders on which laws or other public documents of great importance were inscribed, and of seals. A few statues are made of this stone, which must have been carried a great distance from the mountains. Most statues are of limestone, which could be obtained in the Arabian desert some thirty miles away or in the Zagros foothills an equal distance on the other side. Slabs of Arabian limestone covered the burials in Sir Leonard's tombs at Ur.

The Sumerians differed from the Egyptians in several vital re-

BABYLONIAN PLOWING SCENE, FOURTEENTH CENTURY B.C., FROM A SEAL IMPRESSION.

spects that influenced the later history of these two regions and their relative impact on the rest of the world. Instead of one river, they had two, between which, with great industry, they dug a network of canals so perfectly planned in terms of space and slope that the Iraq government's greatest hope at the present day is to restore them to their former condition. No modern engineer could plan a better system. The construction of these canals greatly widened the area of tillage, while permitting inland navigation, not merely upstream and downstream, as in Egypt, but crosswise as well. Thus the realm of Sumer achieved two dimensions to Egypt's one. Like the maintenance of the canals, this spatial factor had its political repercussions. As in Egypt, a central authority was needed to keep all canals in good working order. In Egypt, however, no rebel could hope to hold out long, for the king's soldiers had only to police the stream and the arable land within sight of the riverbanks. In Sumeria the labyrinth of canals made distances shorter, but evasion easier. Thus Sumeria was never unified in the Egyptian sense. One city state after another conquered its fellows, and those that had been conquered before sometimes staged comebacks. Shifts in power were frequent. In Egypt the comparable shifts were in degree of centralization rather than in the place of power.

At the same time the Sumerians were far less isolated than the Egyptians. To the east the Elamites occupied the alluvial plain of the lower Karun River, which the Sumerians could reach by water. To the north a Semitic-speaking people, the Akkadians, shared with the Sumerians the flatlands between the Tigris and Euphrates south of the point where these two streams approach each other most closely, like the knees of a knock-kneed man. Being partners spatially, they became political partners as well, taking turns in ruling the irrigated tillage that they shared. Eventually the Sumerian language ceased to be spoken as a household language, but the Akkadians and later the Babylonians continued to use it as a language of high culture and of religion, just as Church Latin was used for centuries in Europe after it had ceased to be spoken by laymen, and as Jesuits still use it. Not only was Sumerian itself borrowed, but also the cuneiform system of writing, which, before the spread of the alphabet, was adapted to many different languages. Egyptian hieroglyphs, in contrast, were used by Egyptians alone.

The western neighbors of the Sumerians were the shepherds of the Arabian desert, which must have appeared less barren before the introduction of the leather-lipped camel, than it has since become. To the south the Sumerians, themselves navigators, met other sailor folk whose bones remain in thousands of as yet unexcavated burial mounds on Bahrain Island. At the head of the Euphrates Valley various Bronze Age peoples occupied what are now Syria and, over the mountains, Lebanon. Out in the Mediterranean both the Cypriots and the Cretans used metal, and the Cretans had invented an as yet mostly undeciphered system of hieroglyphs of their own. With most or all of these peoples, as with the Metal Age villagers of the bleak Iranian plateau, the Sumerians had trade connections.

From the beginning, trade meant foreign relations. Hence the structure of the state had a dual purpose: internal security and protection from without. As a result, of the three classes into which the population was divided, a military aristocracy stood at the top, followed by a middle class whose men could be called into the militia as needed, and then Old Testament style slaves. From the military aristocracy were drawn the king and his kin, government officials, and priests, as well as professional soldiers. These latter were given grants of land in perpetuity as long as the fields were tilled. Both palace and temple owned estates.

However, members of the second class could also own land. They were farmers, artisans, shopkeepers, schoolmasters, and merchants. As in Egypt, much of the metal work was done in the royal ateliers, and the temples contained loom sheds, but some of the work was private. Schoolmasters were not attached to the temples, and their pupils of both sexes went into every kind of activity, for all transactions were written, and literacy was high. Merchants, trading far and wide, set up branch offices in strategically located towns as distant as the southern shore of Asia Minor.

As far as we can tell, neither companies of artisans nor trade associations existed. The most complicated economic institutions were the trading houses, with their branches and foreign connections. For speed and ease in trading they had to have ready mediums of exchange. For simple and local transactions, barley was the standard. For big business and foreign trade, it was the silver shekel, a unit of weight, or gold at the rate of one to eight against silver. As credit was recognized, merchants could go out with tablets authorizing specific accounts to be drawn. They could also borrow at interest, up to a ceiling of 33.3 per cent per annum for barley, and 20 per cent for silver. In addition to these limits, the government set commodity ceilings from time to time. The commercial atmosphere of Sumerian civilization, as contrasted to the governmental monopoly exercised by Egypt in the same period, is striking, and is of course a function of the relative isolation of the two peoples. The Egyptians needed to go abroad only for luxury objects. The Sumerians had to trade to live. Their emphasis on commerce and craftsmanship and on the importance of the middle class placed the Sumerians squarely on the highroad leading to modern civilization, with the Egyptians slightly to one side.

As in Egypt, the king served both as temporal ruler and high priest. The government had five ministries: harem, war, agriculture, transport, and finance. The priests, divided by functions, included two types of specialist recalling Neolithic antecedents, the diagnosticians and the healers. The former discovered the cause of an individual ailment or a public calamity by watching the flights of birds and by comparing the livers of sacrificed animals with specially marked clay models. Once the evil spirits had been identified, the healers exorcised them. However, all medicine was not magic. Members of a third profession, the surgeons, actually performed operations and prescribed medicine, probably largely magical in nature.

Sumerians built pyramids, not for Egyptian-style royal tombs (theirs were underground), but to serve as platforms for temples. Their deities, which symbolized forces of nature and human skills, assumed human rather than animal form. Each city had a temple in honor of its local patron-god, a temple that included special shrines to other gods for the convenience of strangers. Sumerian religion, like Sumerian society, was built for trade.

Although the Sumerians and Egyptians were not the only two literate metal-using peoples of the Old World during the third millennium B.C., they are the only ones whose writing we have been able to read and whose manner of life and system of organization we have been able to reconstruct in detail. They both represent a stage in the history of social evolution in which both the political and religious institutions had become internally complex, with special departments and a chain of command. In Sumeria independent economic institutions, on which modern society is based, had already come into existence in a simple form.

The Egyptian evidence points to an early contact with a region of high culture somewhere in west-central Asia. The Sumerian evidence points to a later and more highly evolved form of the same or a similar culture. What that culture was and where it was are questions many archæologists would like to be able to answer.

The Hittites Drive Chariots over the Mountains

D u r i n g succeeding centuries the civilization of Mesopotamia gradually passed through several hands as its center shifted northward to Assyria. As in Egypt and other literate countries, the consumption of metal increased, and so did trade, while the various nations of the ancient Middle East came into closer contact with one another. This gradual cultural growth was greatly accelerated, however, by the reintroduction of bronze and of the chariot, now with genuine horses, by invaders from somewhere to the north about 1700 B.C. At this time the Hyksos invaded Egypt and took over the government, the Aryans invaded India and destroyed the Indus Valley civilization, about which we shall speak later, and the Kassites, who were Indo-European-speakers, invaded Mesopotamia.

Something was going on in the north, either in the region of Georgia and Azerbaijan, or more widely on the steppes of southern Russia and central Asia. Whatever was happening also occurred in the highlands of Anatolia, the home of the Hittites, who deserve special attention because they apparently pioneered in iron metallurgy. Their country was central Anatolia, the land enclosed by the bend of the Halys River, and the plain south of the salt lake. It had no coast. Their capital was Hattusas, a large, heavily fortified ruin near the modern village of Boghazkoy. Hattusas strategically commanded the valley and lay at the crossroads of the main north-south and east-west trade routes. The Hittites themselves, judging by the results of linguistic researches, were an aristocracy of Indo-European-speaking invaders superimposed on an older Caucasic-speaking Neolithic or Early Bronze Age population. Several such related aristocracies dotted the map of Anatolia.

Hittite history is divided into two parts: that of the Old Kingdom, from 1740 to 1460 B.C., and that of the Empire, from 1460

HITTITE CHARIOT.

to about 1220 B.C. During the former period the inhabitants of Hattusas expanded their realm by raiding over the mountains and drew a number of neighboring regions into an integrated kingdom. During the empire the Hittites crossed the Taurus to rule Syria and parts of Mesopotamia. Their power was brought to an abrupt end on their native plateau by the invasion of the Phrygians from Europe. In Syria, fragmented Hittite kingdoms persisted for centuries until finally destroyed by the Assyrians,

who were smashed in turn by the Persians, the founders of the
first true empire.

Technologically speaking, two things distinguished the Hittite
empire from the kingdom: the introduction of the horse-drawn
chariot and the inception of ironworking. The chariots that appeared at this time were light and mobile, with free-moving
wheels of six spokes each. A few well-armed and well-armored
warriors, dashing out in front of the ranks in chariots of this type
driven by specialists in horse-handling, could leap to the ground,
fight furiously where least expected, jump back aboard, and dash
to safety. A few such special warriors could cut through hundreds
of men on foot and win the battle. When this maneuver was systematically conducted by members of literate city states, strategically located, it meant the first stage in the rise of empire. There
is also evidence of riding astride during this period, not for military operations, but as a means of bearing messages, thus greatly
speeding up communication.

The second item is iron. For a Bronze Age nation the Hittites
were well situated, for they produced quantities of copper for
export, and also of silver, which passed for currency. Their trade
balance was good. They had, however, no tin. The existing Anatolian mines either were exhausted or had not yet been worked.
This metal they obtained from the Assyrians, who in turn got it
from some source farther east. Sometime during the period of the
empire they learned how to smelt and to forge iron, which they
exported to the Assyrians, but in small quantity. A letter from
King Hattusilis III (1275–1250 B.C.) to an unidentified monarch
excuses himself for not having filled an order, on the grounds that
it is a bad time for iron-production. He promises, as soon as his
workmen shall have finished the order, to send it to his brother
king. Meanwhile he keeps him happy with the dispatch of a
single iron dagger blade.[8] This does not make it appear that the
Iron Age was in full swing. Such as it was, the Hittite empire had
risen and fallen before iron had become a common article of trade.

In the days of the Kingdom, the Hittites occupied the neighbor-

[8] O. R. Gurney, *The Hittites,* Penguin Books Inc., Baltimore, 1952, p. 83.

hood of Hattusas and a few other towns with their surrounding villages. Each of these areas was distinguished by one of separate languages, most of which were closely related to one another. Each town had its special deity worshipped in the local language, and cuneiform tablets detailing these special formulæ have been preserved. The population was divided into three classes: nobles, commoners, and slaves. Some of the land was in the hands of fiefs granted by the king to noble warriors, some belonged to temples, some directly to the king. The rest of the land was privately owned by commoners living in free villages. The situation was thus almost exactly the same as in Iraq and Iran today and in Turkey until within the memory of living men.

During the summer the Hittite kings crossed the mountains that rimmed their domain and went to war. Usually they marched southward, for the lands to the north and northeast were occupied by tribes too tough for them. The flatlands of Syria and northern Iraq were their prey. During various campaigns they conquered Aleppo and Babylon. The Hittites of whom one reads in the Old Testament as hostile northern neighbors of the Israelites were the broken-down, post-empire Hittites of northern Syria.

If the enemy's king refused to surrender early in the campaign and to become a vassal, the Hittites fought his armies in the field and, having defeated them there, laid siege to his city, using covered hoods and battering rams to approach and smash down gates and walls. Then the Hittites looted and slaughtered, burning the city to the ground and carrying off the surviving human and animal inhabitants to be distributed among the officers and officials of the realm. When a land was incorporated into the Hittite empire, it was allowed to keep its own god, and the Hittite king made a special round each year to lead the worship in each religious center. The god of Hattusas was a storm god, symbolized by the bull, the chariot, the battle ax, and lightning, and pictured as riding over the crests of mountains. He had much in common with Zeus, Jupiter, and Thor, as one would expect in the mythology of an Indo-European-speaking people. Although the Hittites are extinct, they serve the anthropologist and the historian well, as they formed a bridge from bronze to iron, from kingdom to the beginnings of empire, and from Middle Eastern to Western civilization.

Gods and Heroes of Homer's Greece [9]

I T would be a wonderful thing if we could cross one of the bridges, to find a firsthand eyewitness literary account of an Indo-European civilization of the Late Bronze Age somewhere on the grasslands of west-central Asia or eastern Europe. Without doubt, much of interest was going on there at that time. But such a windfall is next to impossible. Except for the Hittites, the Bronze Age Indo-European-speaking peoples seem to have been illiterate. We have in the poetry of Homer, however, a priceless document of such a civilization transplanted to the Mediterranean region. Whatever classical scholars and historians may have to say about the dates of the period depicted, the date of the composition of the epics, or of Homer himself, there can be no doubt about two points: the culture depicted is a whole culture and a real one because it makes sense internally. No man could invent a civilization out of whole cloth and have it fail to strike a false note. The Homeric civilization is essentially that of an Indo-European-speaking people transplanted into a Mediterranean setting, and not that of an urban, literate [1] eastern Mediterranean Early Bronze Age people. We know now that Homer's kings had scribes who kept tally of the stores on clay tablets, and in Greek, but either Homer did not know this, or if he did, living later in an illiterate age, bookkeeping details seemed unimportant to him. Otherwise the poems are truthful in a general if not in a specific sense.

The landscape was without question Greece, but a Greece far richer in forests and meadows than that of today, or even that of

[9] In making this reconstruction of Homeric civilization I have used the compilation of T. D. Seymour, *Life in the Homeric Age*, The Macmillan Company, New York, 1907, as well as the texts.

[1] J. Ventris and J. Chadwick, "Evidence for Greek Dialect in the Mycenean Archives," *Journal of Hellenic Studies*, Vol. 73, 1953, pp. 84–103.

the famous fourth century B.C. Lofty stands of pine clothed the mountainsides, forests of beech and oak blanketed the lower slopes and flatlands, and perennial springs supplied water to men and to animals. Lions, leopards, and wild boar roamed the woods, along with bear, deer, and fox. Clouds of wild ducks and wild geese alighted on ponds and inlets, quacking and honking, and grouse darted out of the underbrush. Only a small part of the

HOMERIC CHARIOT, FROM A GRECIAN VASE.

land was under cultivation, and much more was given over to pasture. The forest trails between settlements were more hazardous than the sea.

In the barnyard of a Homeric hero's farm could be seen, smelled, and heard a flock of cattle, driven to high pasture in summer and grazed on stubble in winter. Never milked, they gave the farmer a mobile source of energy and wealth with which he plowed his fields, bought brides for his sons, appeased the gods, and supplied his table with beef. Only goats and sheep were milked, and their curds turned to cheese. Ordinary sacrifices were of pigs, fed cheaply on beech mast and acorns in the near-by forest. Donkeys carried ordinary burdens, horses drew chariots, and mules hauled non-military wagons. These various vehicles were parked around the inner edges of the courtyard, their poles raised against the walls. Geese waddled in and out among the animals, flapping the feathers for which they were bred—prime fletching-material for war arrows. The typical Homeric meal consisted of beef broiled on skewers shish-kebab style, bread, a few onions, and an occasional apple. Butter was not made, and olive oil was used as a cosmetic only. Marrow, suet, and lard were the only fats eaten. Fish, shellfish, and eggs were considered unfit for human consumption. The domestic fowl had not yet appeared in Greece.

Behind the courtyard stood a porch, on which boys and male guests often slept. Inside, the house consisted of a single large hall, in which the family and guests ate at small movable tables set beside large, fixed chairs. Movable beds, stacked during the daytime, accommodated married couples at night, when the fire from the central hearth had burned down to a bed of coals. When more light than that of the fireplace was needed, Homer's heroes burned slivers of pitch pine on metal wall-brackets. No one ever made fire in the poems, but people borrowed it from one another when their hearths had grown cold. Behind the hall was a smaller room in which the unmarried girls slept, and their mothers also when the men were away. Outdoors was a small bathhouse in which members of the family and guests were scrubbed down by the women of the household.

Nothing could have been simpler than the basic garment of Homer's characters. Both sexes wore the same thing, one or more squares of woolen cloth. One cloth draped over his shoulders was the usual garb of a man, who took it off when fighting, working, or entering a house. Women wore two, one in front and the other aft, pinned at the sides with brooches and belted at the waist. Nudity bothered no one.

Weaving these standard squares of woolen goods was the work of the women, and by it they amassed wealth, for the pieces were interchangeable and hence served as a form of currency, as among the American Indians of the northwest coast three millennia later. While herding and farming took up most of the time of the men, a few were specialists, carpenters and smiths. Often one man practiced both professions. The carpenter built houses, ships, and chariots, while the smith made weapons, tools, and armor. Although he could cast as well as hammer and rivet, the smith did no smelting and no mixing of tin and copper. All of the metal was bartered from the Phœnicians, who wanted slaves, cattle, hides, and wine.

The carpenter-smith was a man of good standing, and a skillful one could travel from kingdom to kingdom, working for the high-

HOMERIC SHIP, FROM A GRECIAN VASE.

est bidder. However, the ordinary householder knew something of these crafts, for among the Greeks of Homer's time, as among the old Norse and the Saxons, there was no concept of a strict division of labor. The tradition was—and we still retain the bones of it despite the labor unions—that any man is entitled to do as much of any kind of work as he wishes to and can, particularly for himself.

The chariots that Homeric carpenters built differed in no essential way from those of the Hittites. Owing to the terrain, few people traveled by land when the seas were calm enough for navigation. The typical Homeric ship, on which the heroes sailed to Troy, carrying with them their horses and chariots, was forty feet long, with an eight-foot beam. The keel was of oak, the planks of pine. Bow and stern were decked over for a few feet, affording stations for the captain and helmsman on the afterdeck, and for a lookout in the bow. Stepped in a hole in the keel, the mast

rested on a notched thwart. Two forestays were meant to keep it
from falling backward and killing the helmsman, but in one instance this accident took place. When not under sail, the crew
lowered the mast and made it fast to a crotch. The sail, of woolen
cloth, was square, lashed to a yard. The halyard was a thong of
oxhide, which also served as backstay. Two braces from the yard
and two sheets held the sail in position. Tacking was not attempted. Unless the wind was fair, the crew of twenty oarsmen
rowed, directed by the captain, while the helmsman steered with
an oar. Sailing close to shore and navigating by landfalls, they
beached their craft each night. As a rule they hugged the coast.
To sail from Lesbos straight across the Ægean was considered a
great feat, one to be attempted only in the finest summer weather.
In winter they put their ships up out of reach of the waves.

As with most Indo-European-speaking peoples of later times,
the Homeric Greeks recognized four social classes: royalty, nobles,
commoners, and slaves. The king and his family were supported
by the produce of a royal domain and by voluntary contributions
of food and cattle brought in by his subjects on special occasions.
There was no formal taxation. In addition, the king received a
special share of war booty, and more if he fought in person. Although he took in much wealth, the king handed out nearly an
equal amount in presents, prizes, and hospitality. He was a clear-
ing house for property, a leveler of rich and poor, an intermediary
between the different classes in his realm. His chief gift to his
people was leadership, and their chief gift to him loyalty.

When a commoner distinguished himself by outstanding deeds
of bravery, the king would give him an estate and confer on him
an inheritable title of nobility. Some of the commoners, including
as a rule the carpenters and smiths, were landowners, others hire-
lings. Slaves were captured, bought, or bred. Some had been kings
and princesses in their own countries. Only female slaves were
kept by their captors in the role of concubines. Their children,
nothoi, were second-class offspring. A bastard so produced might
serve his nobler half-brother as charioteer. Male slaves, bought or
home-born, worked outdoors on the estate.

As in Neolithic society, the countryside was divided into small kingdoms. Nobles and commoners assembled outdoors in council meetings at the king's pleasure, and ruled during his absence. One special officer, the herald, regulated the protocol of debate, handing a special staff to the next to speak. This staff was the herald's badge of office, and possession of it permitted him to walk unscathed from kingdom to kingdom delivering messages. The king himself had but a single badge, his scepter, with which, in one instance, he struck an unruly council member over the head. Generally speaking, he was the eldest son of an earlier king, but exceptions were common. Sometimes the office went to the king's brother, sometimes to the widowed queen's new consort, and sometimes to the royal daughter's husband. As elsewhere in Indo-European oral literature, it was a common event in the Homeric poems for a wandering hero to slay a monster, marry the princess, and take over the kingdom. Only the favor of a special god could give a man power to fill the role of king, who by this token served as priest to his people, leading them in prayer and conducting public sacrifices at critical moments.

Visiting was the winter sport of kings. Having sent his herald ahead, a monarch would be met at the border by his royal neighbor, who would escort his guest to his hall. Feasts and games were held in the visitor's honor. As a result of such visits, betrothals and alliances were made. As most kings thus came to know one another, when they combined forces in war they were prepared to choose a commander in chief—as, in the epic, Agamemnon was elected. These alliances were loose. Whenever he wished, any king could quit fighting and take his men home.

Probably not more than five thousand Greeks sailed to Troy. Not one was a professional soldier. In Greece every freeman was trained to fight. Each king knew his men personally and could call them all by name. Mustering the troops took but a single hour. The elite were the heavily armored heroes, either nobles or candidates for that position, who dashed out in chariots to do single combat. These were few in number. Next came the spearmen, protected only by sheets of stiff rawhide hanging from their necks. They formed the front battle line, where they engaged the enemy in combat and helped the heroes out of tight spots if near enough. Slingers and archers, who formed the rear, wore wolf-skins or bearskins, with paws dangling, after the style of Herakles, one imitated by professional strong men of later times.

The organization of such an army was of the simplest possible character. There were no ranks but those of kings, heroes, and men, with the herald acting as adjutant. There was no commissariat: what food and drink the men could not take by plunder they bought from traders in exchange for captured armor. In battle, kings and heroes fought kings and heroes, footmen fought footmen, and archers and slingers peppered all impartially with their shafts and stones. One or two heroes could turn the tide of battle, and two heavily armored men could hold a rear. Few lines could stand against the hoofs of galloping horses. The critical part of any battle was the single combat between the champion heroes of both sides. Such a hero dashed out in a chariot driven by a trusted friend, such as a bastard brother; on the loyalty and bravery of the charioteer depended his chance of getting back behind his own lines alive if he should survive the combat. Dismounting from the tailboard, he took his stand behind his huge, metal-rimmed shield. Being made of as many as seven oxhides, this weighed up to two hundred pounds. If he fell backward and the shield covered him, he would be unable to rise without help. First the heroes cast spears at each other; then if both were still active, they closed with swords. Some fought with maces as well, and all carried knives for slitting the throats of fallen foes. During the fight the two men taunted each other, like wrestlers, and the spearmen could hear this. Often the deciding blow fell when one hero, bereft of his weapons, lifted a large stone off the ground and threw it at his opponent with deadly aim. Once a hero was down, there was a scramble for his armor. His own men tried to save it, while the objective of the winner and his charioteer was either to strip it and run, or to hitch the corpse to the tail of the chariot and drag it behind the lines, where the armor could be removed at leisure. Being valued at an average of nine head of cattle, and a maximum of one hundred, the prize was worth the risk.

These combats were spectacular events. Anthropological literature contains few descriptions of battles like those that took place in the *Iliad*. Most American Indians, Melanesians, and other peoples living in the Neolithic or in peripheral Metal Age cultures have been content to ambush one another or to raid one another's villages in surprise attacks at dawn. Few stood up in broad daylight like Homer's heroes to trade lethal blows. The Homeric viewpoint was that a man who would risk his life in such a combat was a man of quality, deserving the fruits of his bravery, including women and power. Being expendable was an honor. As the Homeric poems were to later Greeks what the Bible is to us, this point of view was carried down to the civilization of Athens in the famous fifth century, when a learned man like Socrates went out to fight alongside his students.

As a result of the gory wounds that bronze weapons produced, Homer knew much about the anatomy of the skeleton and of the muscular and circulatory systems. There was no knowledge of the nervous system, and the function of the brain was not even suspected. Two surgeons in the Greek camp cut out arrowheads and stemmed blood with powdered roots. They also applied bandages. Wounds are visible and their cause is clear. There was no magic in diagnosis or cure. Illnesses of a more subtle nature were differently explained.

This is brought out in the most familiar passage in all of Homer, Book One, page one of the *Iliad*. When the tale opens, the Greeks are encamped before Troy, living among their ships, which are drawn up on the beach. Some are camping in tents. They have been there for ten years. As any modern person would expect, in view of the utter lack of sanitation, an epidemic has struck the camp. Many men have died. Dogs and kites have eaten their bodies lying about on the bare ground. Typhus, typhoid, amœbic dysentery, any form of vermin-borne plague may have been responsible. To the Greeks this mass affliction was so mysterious that they believed it to have been a divine punishment for some offense against a god.

Obviously, the way to relieve it was to discover both the identity of the god, and the nature of the offense. From their ranks they brought a seer, the Hellenic counterpart of a shaman. He found the god to be Apollo, who had shot magically invisible arrows from a silver bow into the camp. The offense was as follows. A local priest named Chryses cared for a shrine to Apollo. Chryses had a daughter named Chryseis. Agamemnon had seized her as part of his booty, and was living with her in his tent. Achilles had similarly annexed a young lady named Bryseis. Chryses had begged Agamemnon to return his daughter. Agamemnon had refused. Chryses then (as the Greeks believed) had prayed to Apollo for revenge. Apollo had answered by bringing the plague on the camp.

Once this diagnosis had been made and accepted, the Greeks brought pressure on Agamemnon to give up his concubine. This he did, but at the same time he took Bryseis away from Achilles. Achilles, as one might have expected, resented this behavior, and when the story opens, he is sulking alone in his tent. However, Chryses was satisfied, and Apollo lifted the plague. This is all, of course, pure magic, of the same kind that one can find in New Guinea or among the tribes of the Upper Amazon. The Greeks were human beings.

The gods in whom the Greeks, at least in Homer's time, believed, symbolized, as is the habit of gods, areas of disturbance in human relations. Zeus, father, leader, and king, also represented stormy weather, including thunder and lightning. In Dodona, a mountain shrine of Epirus, he had a sacred grove. In it lounged a company of unwashed priests who cared for the sacred oak trees and slept on the ground. The oak was sacred for an obvious reason; it supplied food in time of famine. Before agriculture had begun, it was the source of a Mediterranean staple, the acorn. At any rate, these priests, upon demand, asked questions of Zeus, who replied by rustling the oak leaves with his breath. The priests translated these messages, in language as ambiguous as that of a professor who is not sure of his ground.

Hera, Zeus's wife, was jealous of the numerous infidelities by means of which he begat numerous minor gods and outstanding mortals. It was easy to believe that a man of great bravery or a woman of great charm was indeed the offspring of the father of gods. Hera was responsible for the mists and fogs, which she sent to prevent actions of which she disapproved. She also sent minor gods to earth upon occasion to interfere in the affairs of men. Being on the side of the Greeks, on the second day of battle she kept her husband busy with her sexual attentions to prevent him from helping the Trojans. Here is our old hunter's concept of using a preoccupation with sex as a means of distracting the game or one's opponent.

Hephaistos, crippled son of Zeus and Hera, was the god of smiths and carpenters, while his sister Athene was goddess of all the unspecialized crafts, such as spinning and weaving, which were performed by women. Apollo was the lord of mysterious diseases, his sister Artemis mistress of the hunt, still an important source of food. Aphrodite symbolized sexual charm in women, whom she rendered irresistible by lending them her belt. Hermes was the divine herald. Ares, a ferocious and destructive giant, was the prototype of Finn McCool, Gargantua, and Paul Bunyan. Only in post-Homeric times did he become the special god of war. In the time about which Homer sang, all gods, like all men, were interested in warfare.

All the Greek gods, including many not mentioned here, were believed to concern themselves with people, just as Apollo ran in front of Hector in the heat of battle, knocking down all opposition. It was believed that the gods could be influenced to a certain extent by prayer and sacrifice, but many things happened which seemed patently beyond the reach of human intervention. As the tragedians later showed, some calamities were simply acts of the gods, and as such should be accepted with fortitude. This philosophical approach to life has been carried to an extreme in orthodox Islam, in which God's will is monotonously invoked as an explanation of all phenomena, great or trivial. Among the Greeks who believed in Homer's gods, man still had a chance to succeed in his ambitions by his own enterprise if he conducted himself in such a way as not to anger the gods, which means, in anthropological language, if he took care not to disturb beyond the tolerance of their cultural situation the equilibrium of the members of the society in which he lived. This respect for honest enterprise, plus an occupational versatility, had much to do with the later success of the inhabitants of the Grecian peninsula, and with the development of our own modern Western civilization.

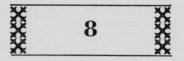

IRON AND EMPIRE

T HE THIRD millennium before Christ opened with bronze, the first millennium with iron. Now the ordinary man whose grandfather had still used stone tools in the Bronze Age wielded a cheap, sharp ax. With it he leveled forests to make charcoal with which smiths smelted and forged the new metal, and as trees disappeared the pace of waste and erosion quickened. As two new animals, the large riding-horse and the camel, were added to his stable, the speed, volume, and range of man's travel increased enormously. The invention of a twenty-six-letter phonetic alphabet and the elimination of hundreds of cumbersome syllabic signs and determinants took the monopoly of reading and writing out of the hands of scribes and made the common man, in several favored countries, literate. Coins, stamped with the symbol of a state to guarantee the purity of their metal, speeded up commerce.

The price of these improvements in transport, communication, and exchange was an increase in man's use of the earth's supply of expendable energy. The result was a growth in the size and complexity of social institutions as kings became emperors, small nations became ethnic minorities, and craftsmen organized themselves into guilds and corporations. Wise men, freed from labor by the toil of slaves, conceived the idea of order and unity in the universe, and philosophers disassociated science from religion. A civilization that some still think higher than our own arose in Greece, and in Palestine a man was crucified for preaching the brotherhood of man. Before the Iron Age was over, millions had come to worship Him, and Christians had crossed the Atlantic to visit the New World.

Compared to earlier periods, Iron Age history is well known. Many people today have already explained its principal events to their own satisfaction and have identified themselves emotionally with peoples and systems of belief which were formed in the Iron Age. This book presents a different explanation. I have already interpreted earlier history in terms of the conversion of energy into social structure, and I shall interpret the key events of the more complicated and better documented Iron Age in the same terms.

Ironworking began in the same general area as copper and bronze metallurgy. The Anatolian highlands, Transcaucasia, and northeastern Iran were particularly suited for the birth of this industry because they were rich in both ore and hardwoods suitable for the manufacture of charcoal, and because the inhabitants of these highlands had a tradition of mining and skilled metallurgy. It began later than copper and bronze because iron requires a different kind of furnace and is a more difficult material to handle and to master than the non-ferrous metals previously worked. Four per cent of the earth's surface is iron. It is a cheap metal, available to the ordinary farmer, herdsman, and carpenter. As such it became the poor man's friend in its day, just as the Model-T Ford did in our own. The little fellow had a chance. All kinds of production increased, and trade boomed, not primarily in military and luxury materials and products, but in such staples as grain and hides, things that everyone could eat or use. Domestic hens were added to the barnyard, and eggs to the menu.

Early in the Iron Age the breed of horses was improved, and men learned to ride instead of being drawn in chariots. Horsemen could move about faster, and over any kind of terrain which provided grazing and water. Where grazing and water were scarce or lacking, other men could travel long distances on an entirely new mount, the camel, whose origin as a domestic animal is an unsolved mystery. During the Iron Age the post-road system was invented. A Persian emperor could send a letter across mountains and plains, and along the fringes of deserts, from his throne behind the battlefield in such distant spots as Egypt or Asia Minor to his capital; it traveled at the constant rate of a horse's gallop, by night and day, as one rider leaped from saddle to saddle in successive posts and as fresh rider relieved exhausted rider. Traders perched on camels could cross the wastes of Baluchistan, Arabia, and the Sahara to do business in India and in different parts of Africa. Now that shipwrights were able to build more vessels more quickly and more cheaply than before, trade by sea increased also, bringing the western Mediterranean into the orbit of contemporary civilization.

Two more inventions speeded trade: the alphabet and money. In the eastern Mediterranean the Phœnicians converted the basic consonants of Egyptian hieratic script into an alphabet suited to Semitic languages, while the Persians similarly adapted cuneiform to their needs. In Asia Minor, the ancient world's chief source of silver, the Lydians invented money. Now a trader could pay for his goods in silver or gold coinage and sell them for the same. There was no need to weigh the precious metals as long as the coins looked intact and unclipped. The Phœnician alphabet could be adapted to other languages, particularly after the Greeks had inserted vowels. Reading and writing became easier and literacy higher. The free citizen could now vote by scratching on a potsherd the name of his favorite candidate for office or for exile.

Free voting citizens also made further inventions, such as the rotary grain-mill and the screw, which speeded up the production of such staples as flour, wine, and oil. Power transmission from shaft to shaft and from one direction to another was made possible by a third invention: the toothed wheel, or gear. With it began the use of water power as a further improvement on the technique of milling. The Greeks who created these inventions also produced jet steam-engines and taximeters. These devices, however, remained toys throughout the Iron Age, the materials and conditions needed for their use not yet being available. More important than the inventions themselves was the advance that the Greeks made in theoretical science, upon which our own technical civilization is based. And the Greeks invented the technique of writing history. Thanks to them, most of the period covered in this chapter is well known to the reader in advance. In it I cannot hide behind the curtain of special anthropological or archæological knowledge to cover mistakes of fact or judgment, nor do I need to spell out in detail things that are common knowledge.

For example, it is common knowledge that the Iron Age was an age of empire. Following the expansion of the Egyptians in the last centuries of the Bronze Age, the Hittites, who lived in the home of iron, rose to power in Asia Minor. After them, as one empire succeeded another, came the Assyrians, then the Persians, then the Greeks under Alexander, then the Romans, and the Byzantines, the Arabs, the Mongols, and the Turks.

What does this mean in terms of the history of civilization? Structurally speaking, it means an increase in the complexity of institutions Craftsmen multiply until they cease to be tame purveyors to kings and priests, and work primarily for the people. Their standards of excellence and their price ceilings are set not by royal overseers, but by their own guild chiefs, whom they themselves have elected. Thus during the Iron Age did a middle class grow, big enough to produce its own institutions. At the same time the weapons that the craftsmen forged permitted kings to outfit large armies, which they could lead to distant conquests by horse, sea, and overland marches. Politically, another new idea arose. Instead of massacring conquered peoples, one could govern them. The state came to include many kinds of people, all with equal or adequate rights to live, to work, and to move about within the confines of empire. Certain peoples began to specialize in local skills, and colonies of these specialists arose in cities and towns throughout the realm.

While the political institution became universal, the concept of god initially remained local, confined at first to regions, then to special peoples wherever they might find themselves. With Greek philosophy and the Hebrew prophets the concept of a universal good, a system of equilibrium for all mankind, took root and grew until it reached its culmination in the life and message of Jesus. At first rejected, then incorporated into the state, Christianity gradually spread; but meanwhile, in Arabia, Islam, a religion much more easily understood and much more immediately suited to a specific time and place, arose. Its rapid spread over the old centers of Bronze Age civilization divided the Western world once

Ancient Egyptian river boat. From a model. Travel on inland waterways was crucial in the early Bronze Age civilizations in the Nile, Tigris-Euphrates, and Indus valleys. Metropolitan Museum picture.

PLATE XVII

Persian vision of Paradise. Emperor Khosrau II
attending a hunt. Bas-relief of Taq-i-Bostan, Iran.

PLATE XX

Outpost of empire.
A Byzantine fort at
Majmar, Jordan, pro-
tecting a water tank
on the edge of the
Arabian Desert.

PLATE XXI

Arab astrolabe. First one star, then another is sighted through two holes in the ends of movable arm to measure the angle. Two of many detachable supplementary disks are shown.

PLATE XXII

Chinese Bronze Age
ceremonial vessels.
Shang Dynasty bronze-
casting is generally con-
sidered the world's
finest.

PLATE XXIII

Chinese silk square. Worn by a civil official of the
fourth grade during the late eighteenth century.

PLATE XXIV

more, and very clearly, into its two original components: the well-watered north and west, and the arid east and south. At the same time it opened up contact with India and China. Certain inventions from these places, taken over and improved by the Christians, ushered in the next period of history, which Europe dominated.

Iron Age Technology

O N E of the principal reasons why the center of civilization shifted to the west during the course of the Iron Age was the relative richness of Europe both in ore and in forests, and forests meant charcoal. However, around 1400 B.C. the Armenian highlands and neighboring portions of Georgia and Azerbaijan (including what are now Russian and Iranian provinces) were rich enough in both ore and fuel to serve as a center of invention and of initial world production in what has come to be called heavy industry. This production could not have taken place without a previous period of experience with copper and its alloys, produced in great quantity in this very region. The materials were at hand, and so were the skilled technicians capable of going a step forward.

Experts in early metallurgy such as Forbes and Coughlan [1] recognize four progressive stages in metal craft: the use of heavy lumps of metal as hammers; the hammering, cutting, and shaping of native metals, with or without heating them in a low fire; the ore stage, in which the composition of the metal itself is the primary factor with which the smiths are concerned; and the iron stage, in which processing the metal, rather than its composition, is the craftsman's principal area of skill and applied learning. Hammering, tempering, quenching, and annealing are the techniques of the blacksmith, with which he can turn a piece of soft metal into a sword capable of decapitating a man at a single stroke.

Like copper and gold, iron occurs as a native metal, and was

[1] R. J. Forbes, *Metallurgy in Antiquity*, E. J. Brill, Leiden, 1950; H. H. Coughlan, *Notes on the Prehistoric Metallurgy of Copper and Bronze in the Old World*, Pitt Rivers Museum, Oxford, 1951.

worked in the early metal age by hammering and grinding. Most
of the world's native iron is meteoric, and contains from 5 per cent
to 26 per cent of nickel, and from 3 per cent to 5 per cent of cobalt.
Owing to these impurities, it is both very hard and very rust-
resisting. Hence the few iron objects found in Bronze Age archæological sites in Egypt and Mesopotamia are in a better state of
preservation than the younger Iron Age objects, made of purer
metal, found in the same sites. The latter are often too badly rusted
for easy identification. The meteoric iron of the early Bronze Age
was actually a better metal than any that was manufactured anywhere in the world before A.D. 1890. It was probably a lump of this
material which Achilles offered as a prize at the funeral games of
Patroclus (*Iliad*, Book 23).

Iron ore comes in many forms, some of which are easily recognized, while others fool all but experienced prospectors. Among
the most noticeable is hematite, so called for its blood-red color.
This is used as a pigment by primitive hunters all over the world.
Powdered and mixed with fat, it formed the crayons with which
Cro-Magnon men made the cave paintings of France. Australian
aborigines smear it on their bodies today, as did American Indians
in colonial times, whence the name Red Indians. This same hematite was smeared on the surfaces of pottery in Neolithic times to
form a colored slip (a surface layer produced by washing with
fine clay before firing); it is the red of the black-on-red painted
pottery beloved by Near Eastern archæologists as a tracer of cultural movements.

Copper metallurgy was a natural extension of bread-baking and
pottery-firing in a two-chambered oven. Underneath glowed the
charcoal fire, fed air by a forced draft. Above, in a sealed chamber
where smoke could not foul them, sat the pots or the loaves. Put
copper ore in place of the bread and ceramics, and it smelts out.
Put the smelted copper in a crucible over a similar fire, and it
melts, becoming ready to cast. Iron cannot be worked in this fashion. While it can be smelted at from 600° to 700° C., the bloom, as
the iron that oozes out of the ore is called, is messy-looking and
fouled with its own slag. It cannot be remelted for casting because
its melting point is 1530° C., too high for the Bronze Age furnace.

Even if, by a freak, this temperature is reached, and the iron is cast, what good is it? It is too brittle for use as a tool or weapon. To work over the bloom, heating and reheating, pounding and re-pounding, in order to remove the slag, takes strength, endurance, and skill. That, however, is exactly what the early blacksmiths did and had. Eventually they discovered that iron can be smelted more easily in a special one-chamber bloomery, where the ore is inserted directly over the fire, along with charcoal. They also found that if crushed limestone is added to the mixture, it will melt, fuse with the silica of which the slag is composed, and draw the slag away with it.

Once these skills had been learned, it was possible to obtain iron with temperatures no higher than 700° C., much easier to produce than those needed for copper and bronze. Another dis-covery was that if hot iron is placed in contact with charcoal on a forge at a temperature of 1170° C., then taken off and ham-mered, then quenched, then heated on charcoal, hammered, and quenched again, the smith can produce an edge of steel. The char-coal and iron in combination form a brittle, crystalline structure, which is lost if the metal is cooled slowly. Quenching reduces the temperature so rapidly that the structure is retained. By repeated forging, the smith could put a hard edge, capable of being sharp-ened, on a chisel, an ax, or a sword.

This is hard work. It is also hazardous work; sparks fly about, hot metal may drop on someone's foot, and hammer heads may fly off and strike someone. In our tradition, glorified by Long-fellow, "The smith a mighty man is he." He is a respected citizen of the community, a person of stamina and prowess, whose shop is a meeting place for other respectable citizens. In the Philadel-phia suburban telephone directory, 2,353 families named Smith are listed. The second commonest trade name is Miller, with 1,364, with others like Taylor, Cooper, Chandler, and the like trailing. The Smiths are solid people, to be found in every profession and social level. In the old western European civilization from which we came, their ancestor's job was an essential one, treated with due honor.

In the Middle East, however, this is not true. Blacksmiths are

definitely in the lower social brackets. This I found out very clearly
once when conversing with a Persian friend always eager to learn
about America. I confided to him the fact that my great-grand-
father, John Coon, who had moved to America from his native
Cornwall in the 1830's, was a blacksmith. My friend, blushing,
said quickly: "I won't tell anybody."

GREEK SMITHY, IRON AGE, FROM A GRECIAN VASE.

In the Middle East, blacksmiths are likely to be members of an
unfashionable race or religion. Why Muslims should hold such a
prejudice against the men who provide them with their most essential tool material is not easy to explain, and many theories, mostly
of a historical nature, have been offered by numerous authors.
These fall into two classes; that iron was introduced by persons
who were discriminated against, and that at the time of its introduction the bronzesmiths were so firmly entrenched that they
reacted with jealousy. Neither holds an ounce of water. A much
simpler explanation is that in Europe iron and charcoal are abundant, wherefore iron is easily obtained locally. In the Middle East
both are rare, and iron has to be imported from other, better-
favored countries. Because iron must be imported, the men who

carry it from place to place and work it into tools and weapons must be absolutely immune from molestation, so that this critical material will get through. One way to secure this immunity is to have the government send armies out to protect them wherever they go. That would be very expensive—in fact, impractical. Another way is to have the smiths so despised that no armed man will deign to touch them. In his humility the smith is free. He can go and come as he pleases, and work for the master of his choice in the desert or mountains or the city bazaar. He can carry his precious substance alone on the desert and at night, and no one will rob him. A cheaper system could never be devised, short of giving internal security to an entire nation or group of nations.

There was in the Middle East a certain amount of internal security in Egypt, in Sumeria, and in Babylonia during the Bronze Age, but it did not, as far as we know, extend very far. This security could be maintained because the government controlled both the arsenal and the best means of transportation. During the Iron Age every peasant could arm himself with a billhook, as useful in cutting jugulars as in lopping the limbs from trees. And the superior means of transportation also became more commonly available, making it possible for whole tribes on the outskirts of urban centers to live in freedom and to take toll of passing caravans in return for protection. During the Iron Age much wider regions came under the rule of a single government, but that rule did not give equal security to all corners of its empire.

This was particularly true of deserts. During the Bronze Age we hear little about people living on the desert, but after 1100 B.C. they are increasingly mentioned. At that time Babylonian documents also mention a new animal, the camel, called the Beast of the Sealands. Sealands meant the Persian Gulf coast of Arabia. Arabs possessing camels built a succession of kingdoms in southern Arabia, including Hadhramaut, Kataban, Saba, and Ma'an. These kingdoms fringed the southern and western edges of the Rub' al-Khali, or Empty Quarter. From one kingdom to another passed camel caravans, carrying incense gums from the Dhofar coast, and imported spices, ivory, and other luxury materials from India and Africa which had been discharged from vessels on the Hadhramaut coast. These caravans made it possible for mariners to avoid the stormy weather that has always impeded navigation on the Red Sea at a point just north of Jidda; here the prevailing winds that blow over the water from the north meet those from the south.

Other caravans crossed Arabia from the Persian Gulf to the Red Sea and from the Persian Gulf to Damascus over the route now traveled nightly by the Pullman buses of the Nairn Brothers. Camel caravans also passed from Persia to India across Baluchistan and from Khorassan across the oases of Turkestan to China. It was the Persians who brought camels to Egypt in the fifth century B.C., whence they were quickly taken up by the Berbers, who moved out onto the Sahara to form the nation known as the Tuareg. These Tuareg guided caravans across the desert to Negro Africa, carrying ivory, gold, slaves, metal, textiles, and other commodities back and forth to such emporia as Sijilmasa, Fez, Taroudant, and Timbuktu. Meanwhile, immigrants from southern Arabia occupied the Ethiopian highlands, and the camel was carried over to Somaliland, where it was quickly taken over by the Somalis and Dankalis.

The introduction of the camel at the beginning of the Iron Age permitted merchants to cross previously impassable deserts with large caravans. These caravans stimulated international trade between moist regions separated by deserts; they also created a new kind of institution in themselves, with their tight organization under a leader, their camel-drivers, guides, passengers, and supercargoes. Besides, the possession of camels made it possible for people who had been tending sheep on the edges of the desert or trying to farm increasingly arid fields to take advantage of the wealth of desert plant life following the spring rains. A second result was the rise of pastoral tribes, mobile, warlike, and chivalrous, who took over command of the deserts at about this time and kept it until the introduction of the automobile and airplane. A third result was the increasing soil erosion of all the countries where the camel went, for it not only removes bushes, but also peels the bark off trees, killing them. Its power of destroying vegetation is rivaled only by that of the goat. It is interesting to note that in spots in Arabia where oil installations are fenced in for protection against grazing animals, the original desert cover, with sage and other brush, has come back in as few as five years.

Another improvement in transportation came when horses were ridden. In the earliest Sumerian times people rode asses, and cattle

MOUNTED GREEK.

were probably mounted during the Bronze Age. It is possible that even camels were ridden before horses. No one knows exactly why it took people so long to begin riding horses after having driven them for at least one thousand years. It could not have been the lack of a saddle, for the Greeks of the fifth century, as anyone can see on the Parthenon frieze, rode bareback. It need not have been bits, for these can be cast of bronze; nor stirrups, which were not invented until the Middle Ages. It could only have been the size and durability of the horse. Bronze Age chariot horses were really ponies. As far as we know, large, saddle-sized horses like the ones we ride today were first bred by the Medes in the cool, grassy country of western Iran, near Hamadan. This country looks like Montana. From it were exported the famous Nisean horses of antiquity, which even the Chinese sent emissaries to purchase in Han times, the second century B.C. It may be no coincidence that our 1949 expedition found the teeth and toe bones of such horses in the Bisitun cave, not far from Hamadan, in two levels. Near the bottom of the deposit, in what was probably early Würm glacial times, these remains were common. The horses were wild. Near the top, dating from the time of Darius, they appeared again as domestic animals. Teeth and bones are the same for both levels.

It is very likely that horses were domesticated more than once, in more than one place, and from more than one breed. Taming horses is no easy matter. It means capturing mares in heat and letting them breed with wild stallions. Mother and foal must be sheltered and fed through the winter, and the colt broken for riding at just the right age. As anyone who keeps riding-horses knows, it is an expensive and time-consuming business, beyond the reach of simple farmers. During the Bronze Age, horses belonged to kings and nobles, who alone were equipped to handle them, and in the Iron Age they were the symbol of knighthood. It was not until medieval times that horses became common draft animals hitched to plows and wagons.

The only place where horses were bred for meat and milk like other herd animals was central Asia, and we do not know that was done before the seventh century B.C., when riding is known to have begun in Iran. Shortly after this, they were ridden in central and western Europe and introduced into Greece and Italy. Then the Arabs produced a special breed, hand-nurtured on the desert, to be led into battle behind camels and mounted only for the last vital hand-to-hand duel. These Arab horses, though jealously guarded for centuries, now form part of our modern thorough-bred stock, and pure herds are raised in California.

What the camel had done for the desert, the horse did for the grasslands. Nomads who could ride on horses, shoot arrows from short bows at full gallop, eat horseflesh, and drink mares' milk were well equipped to defy the mightiest armies. In agricultural regions the man on a horse held a great advantage over people on foot. He could reach down to smite and quickly escape. The horse became the symbol and aide of the landlord and his retainers. For military purposes in fertile, reasonably open country, nothing before cannon could equal cavalry, and only tanks have rendered it obsolete in most countries.

In the mountains of the Middle East, where nomads drive their sheep and cattle to alpine pastures in the spring, leading them back to the warm lowlands in the fall, the saddle horse is a virtual necessity. The migrations must be perfectly timed so that exactly the right number of each kind of animal moves over the right trail and crosses the proper pass at the right moment, or else they will leave too late and suffer from thirst, arrive too soon and be bogged in the snow, or foul one another up and get in fights on the way. Furthermore, the tribesmen who are herding the animals must be protected from the sedentary people through whose territory they pass, and vice versa. Timing, command, and protection require the firm authority of a chief, and if he is to get around quickly and to make the migration a success, he must be on a horse. Anyone who has seen the migrations of the Kurds, the Bakhtiaris, or the Qashqais in Iran, or of the Middle Atlas Berbers in Morocco, will quickly recognize this. The horse also gives these tribesmen military power, making it possible for them both to resist the attempts of lowland governments to relieve them of their animals and to raid the lowlanders in hungry years. We hear much about the warlike mountaineers in the *Anabasis* of Xenophon, to whom the Kurds gave a hard time in his march across Anatolia, but before the Iron Age they do not seem to have been troublesome. Like the other nomads of desert and steppe, they may not have existed as such before the introduction of horses and of iron.

With the riding-horse, the Persians invented the postal system, which was to facilitate the growth of empire. But to the Romans this was not enough: they wanted fast transport of goods as well as of information and orders. Hence the invention of the Roman road. This worked on the principle of the railroad, in that the stability of the carriage depended more on the smoothness of the road surface than on the presence of springs between axles and box in the vehicle. These roads were of the old turnpike variety, taking the shortest possible distances between points, and rising

ROMAN ROAD.

over grades too steep for modern motor vehicles. However, they were suited for the horse-drawn wagons and chariots of their epoch. The foundations, forty inches deep, were made of squared and fitted blocks of stone, more solid than our modern roadbeds, which go to a maximum of thirty-six inches. At current rates, it would cost over a half-million dollars a mile to reproduce a narrow two-lane Roman road.

Over these roads infantry could march, and their baggage trains follow closely behind, drawn by horses; it was the hard surfaces of these roads that forced the Romans to invent a detachable horseshoe. The government built the road and the resthouses situated a day's march apart. Owing to its heavy construction and the light weight of the traffic over it, such a road needed little maintenance, only guarding. As long as the government kept the surface smooth and the passes clear of bandits, it could maintain its power in such distant places as Yorkshire and Syria with a minimum of expense. When for some other reason military power failed, the road could be broken at strategic spots, but it could not be torn up without great effort. Travelers can still see long pieces of these roads crossing the open heaths of northern England, and in the 1930's they were the principal highways in northern Albania, as they may well still be. They are not suited for motor traffic, because they are too narrow and because the lanes are rutted by wagon wheels.

The principle of the rotating shaft, first applied in the Early Bronze Age to jeweler's drills, potter's wheels, and wagon wheels, was extended by the Alexandrian Greeks to several new inventions that found immediate use.[2] That of the screw, which Archimedes invented, was soon applied to two practical devices: the water pump and the press. The second of these revolutionized the olive-oil industry when combined with another Greek invention, the rotary millstone. After the olives have been picked, the workmen dump them from their baskets onto a masonry table, the top of which is circular and slightly convex. Through the center of the table rises a pole. At right angles is attached a second pole, which serves as spindle for a large circular millstone standing on edge. The outer portion of this spindle is a handle. Men, or donkeys driven by men, walk around and around rotating this stone, which crushes the olives. Scooping the mash into shallow baskets, the workmen set them on the press one above another, until it is full. Then they turn the screw down until the plate at its end engages the top basket, and continue screwing it until the oil has been pressed. This seems like a simple enough device, but it did not come into common use until the time of the Roman empire, after which it spread throughout the olive-growing world.

The principal use of the rotary millstone was the hand quern, or simple pivoted grain mill. Installed in the home, this could be used to grind the family's quota of flour in a fraction of the time needed on the old-fashioned saddle quern of the Neolithic and

[2] R. J. Forbes, *Man the Maker*, Henry Schuman, New York, 1950.

Bronze Age, a piece of machinery still used in Ethiopia and parts of Central America. The Romans, who needed vast quantities of flour every day to feed their citizens in the public bread line, built large, hourglass-shaped commercial hand mills to be turned by slaves. These mills were set up in long rows in dreary factories.

Another invention, the toothed wheel, was made at about the same time. Although it has formed the basis of our modern machinery, it failed to revolutionize industry for over one thousand years. As the Greeks and Romans knew, the toothed wheel made it possible to use water power instead of manpower for grinding grain. The water turns a wheel, which rotates a horizontal shaft. Gears transform the movement to a vertical shaft, which turns one millstone upon the other. Practically speaking, this invention was not well adapted for use in the lands of high civilization during the centuries just before and after the time of Christ. In Mediterranean and Middle Eastern countries the rain falls only in winter and runs off rapidly, often in torrents. The smaller streams are dry during much of the year. Even the Tiber fluctuates so much that the Romans were forced to use undershot wheels set in floating mills to allow for the shifts in level. Gear-fed water mills became useful as year-round devices only in the countries where the water supply is constant and abundant—in Roman times barbarous territory.

Another reason for the failure of the classical peoples to use shafts and gears in general is the expense and difficulty of making them. Only bronze could be cast in the form of serviceable gears, and bronze was expensive. It was too much work to forge them out of iron and to temper them. Furthermore, the only known source of smelting and forging fuel was still charcoal, which was becoming scarce as the countryside was increasingly deforested. Even Plato, writing in the fourth century B.C., mentioned with concern the change in the landscape and climate of Attica, from a land of meadows and permanent springs and forest glades to the bare skeleton of white limestone filled with a little earth in the hollows, which it has been ever since. In Egypt, Iraq, and Arabia, where all metal had to be imported and charcoal was at a premium, such a development was impossible. It was much cheaper

to buy or capture slaves and force them to grind grain by hand
than to attempt to make such machinery.

Sometime during the late Iron Age, probably in Byzantine
times, a new invention was introduced into the classical world
which circumvented some of these difficulties. It was the vertical

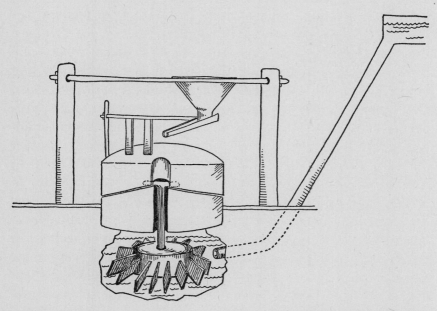

TURBINE WATER MILL, STILL IN USE IN THE MIDDLE EAST AND THE
BALKANS.

shaft, or turbine, water mill, which could utilize the flow of irrigation ditches or small streams in mountainous regions. Having no
gears at all, it could work with maximum efficiency. Today one
finds these mills all over Iran, northern Iraq, Turkey, the Balkans,
and North Africa. They are so simple that a village carpenter and
mason together can set one up, and so easy to operate that a housewife can bring her grain to one of them and grind it without help,
just as a modern housewife carries her family's wash to a laundro-
mat. In eastern Iran and Afghanistan this principle has been
applied to windmills since about the seventh century. Where the
wind blows steadily from a single direction, vaned paddle-wheels

are set up on vertical shafts. A mud-brick wall keeps the wind off one side of the wheel, and the grain is ground.

These inventions influenced in varying degrees the institutions of Iron Age society. During the Bronze Age, the Neolithic craft of pottery-making was taken out of the hands of women, at least

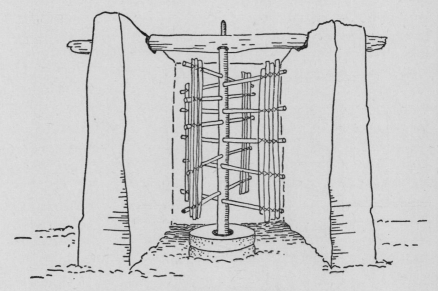

VERTICAL-SHAFT WINDMILL, MODERN IRAN.

in the cities, and given to male specialists. So was some of the bread-baking and the finer weaving. Still the onerous task of grinding grain remained. A housewife was lucky if she had a slave, or her husband a concubine, to take over this drudgery. In a household too poor for slaves or concubines, several brothers and their wives could live together with the brother's parents. The younger women would do the grinding, as well as fetching water and washing clothing, while the old lady dominated the household. Hence the household was a busy place, and the optimum size of a family ranged from six to ten persons.

Once grain-grinding had been taken out of the house, there was less work for the women to do, and less need for a large family, particularly when, as in Athens, Rome, or Pompeii, water brought to the city by aqueducts was piped into the lower floors of the richer houses and to neighborhood fountains. In Greece, women were secluded. In Rome they apparently found ways to amuse themselves in their spare moments, judging from the dire pronouncements of Latin authors of the late republic and early empire. In Arabia where nearly all economically useful activities were men's work, and men spent weeks and months at a time away from home on business, the seclusion of women is easily understood.

One result of the new Iron Age technology was a reduction in the amount of processing done in the house by the members of the family and thus in the need for a large family institution. The new technology was concerned more with the regimentation of human beings than with the uses of new sources of energy in industry. Improvements in transport and communication had made it possible for the citizens of ruling nations to conquer, buy, and impound human muscular power plants. Because energy is energy, whatever its source, the growth of slavery produced a corresponding growth in the complexity of political and economic institutions along with a reduction in the complexity of the family.

On Slaves and Special Peoples

N o t everyone who thinks about the golden days of Athens and pictures in his mind's eye a company of handsome young men strolling around the agora in flowing linen sheets or reclining gracefully on marble benches while listening to a lecture by Socrates or Plato realizes that these people were simply an upper crust of 43,000 citizens out of a total population of 315,000, or one out of every seven. They were able to spend their time in the pursuit of beauty and learning because a number of other people, at the other end of the town, were doing their work for them. Several hundred potters were pumping their wheels to mass-produce Grecian urns, not to put them on museum shelves, but to contain wine. The more attractive the bottle, the likelier its sale when filled and sealed. Several hundred other men were banging away

on forges, producing cutlery, while rope-makers, bending far
forward, moved slowly back and forth in their ropewalks. Few
of these men were voting citizens; in fact few of them were even
Greeks. Most were slaves. The civilization that is usually cited
as a model of democracy was founded on an economic basis of
slave labor.

In Roman times, as the empire expanded and its soldiers and
other officials came into contact with more and more kinds of
people, the slave market grew. It was possible for a rich man, the
proprietor of an estate in Italy, to own as many as one thousand
slaves. In government copper mines in Spain, hundreds of boys
could be kept underground indefinitely like coal-pit mules, seldom seeing the light of day. The educated Greeks themselves
were sometimes taken to Italy as slaves, to serve as physicians to
their masters and tutors to their masters' children.

The practice of slavery dominated the growth of Iron Age economic institutions. In fourth-century Greece a citizen such as
Pericles might own a sword-making factory in which the actual
work was done by slaves. Pericles, Inc., was thus a processing
institution in which a capitalist owned both equipment and labor,
including the source of energy. The mines of Laurium, which
furnished Athens with silver, were worked by slaves let out under
contracts drawn up between the city and their masters. In
Roman times the government operated factories for grinding
grain by slave labor, and much of the processing of agricultural
materials was done by slaves on family estates comparable to our
Southern plantations before the Civil War.

In Athens a few craftsmen were free men and citizens; more
were metics, or free foreigners without civil rights. In Rome, as
citizenship was extended to the lands from which skilled laborers
came, a class of independent artisans began to replace the slaves.
While the empire was expanding, it was easy for the Romans to
take captives along the way, but once it had reached its natural
limits in terms of space and technology, it had already encompassed most of the lands from which skilled workmen came.
Slavs, Germans, and Picts were all right to chain to millstones, for
they were strong and durable, but they didn't have the special

skills of the Syrians and Jews, whom one could no longer buy on the open market.

Slaves, furthermore, had a habit of buying their freedom through industrious parsimony, and masters had a habit of liberating slaves with whom they had established warm personal relationships. When master and slave are all of one race, it is hard to tell them apart physically, especially after they have lived in the same place for a generation or two. When master and slave have both become Christians, as was the case in the Byzantine empire, such a separation creates more disturbance than it is worth, and a class of free artisans can rise.

While artisans were acquiring a semblance of freedom in the east, and thus finding it possible to organize themselves into guilds, traders were moving as free men in both parts of the Roman empire. It is possible to oversee a slave if he is sitting at home making some product, but one cannot set him loose to travel and trade and expect him to remain in servitude. Furthermore, Roman citizenship was gradually extended to parts of Asia in which particularly able traders were at home, notably Palestine. Large numbers of Jews followed the Roman armies into Spain, Gaul, the Rhinelands, and North Africa, as well as into the Crimea and the Danubian countries. Just as some of their descendants set up trading posts in the Wild West two or three generations ago, so enterprising Israelites established trading centers at Cologne and Worms, in London, Granada, Tangier, and Carthage, as well as in the East. It may be said that the Jews whom Hitler ousted had been living in the Rhineland as long as the German tribes themselves, and that in Spain the Jews whom Ferdinand and Isabella expelled in 1492 had lived in that peninsula since before the Spanish language developed out of Latin. In Morocco it was the Jews of the Roman empire who ushered the Berbers from the Neolithic to the Iron Age.

The Jews were only one of the special peoples who moved about the Roman empire. Armenians and Syrians went to France in large numbers. During the Arab empire, Persians went to Spain to make wines, tiles, music, and poetry. When Mulai Idris, the founder of Fez, pitched his tent by the side of the stream from which the city takes its name, he found the banks occupied by Jews, Christians, and "fire worshippers." Zoroastrian Persians had apparently reached Fez ahead of the Arabs.

Under the various states that the Arabs founded, the system of utilizing the special skills of special peoples reached its zenith. Without much question, this was something they had learned from the Greeks of Alexandria and from the Syrians, both of whom had belonged to the Byzantine empire; but, wherever it came from, the Arabs developed it to its natural limits. Their concept was that civilized people who were more or less monotheistic were human beings with whom one could deal, if from a slight elevation. Christians, Jews, and Zoroastrians could be incorporated into the political system if they would pay a poll tax, which of course those within easy reach of provincial capitals did. As these alien "People of the Book" were not inhibited by the prohibitions that bound the Muslims, such as those against the castration of eunuchs (learned from the Byzantines), the manufacture and sale of wine, and lending money at interest, they might suitably be employed for these purposes, either overtly or under cover. In the same way the Jews, as I observed when living in a Jewish house in San'a, Yemen, before the migration to Israel, used to bring Muslim boys into their houses to light the lamps and blow them out on the Sabbath eve, which is Friday night.

Persia: the First Empire

THE SIXTH century B.C. was the time in which the first true, full-fledged empire appeared. In the region of Hamadan, then called Ecbatana, six tribes of a people called Medes had formed a confederation under an elected king, Deioces (708–655 B.C.), and had consolidated the western plateau of Iran. These were the very people who bred large riding-horses on the lush grass of a cool open highland ideal for the purpose. They were conquered by their kinsmen to the south, the Persians, whose land, though lower in latitude, was higher in altitude, and hence equally good horse country. Instead of slaughtering or subjugating the Medes, the Persians assimilated them. Cyrus II, "the Great," who was enthroned in 559 B.C., claimed Median descent. It was he who started the Persian empire by conquering the lowlands to the west, long the seat of an ancient literate Bronze Age civilization. He and his immediate followers also took over Asia Minor, Syria, Palestine, Egypt, Yemen, and Ethiopia, as well as Afghanistan and parts of the central Asiatic lowlands.

They did this by means of an efficient military organization run by an elite of noblemen specially trained from boyhood for this purpose in the cool highlands of the Persepolis country. These noblemen formed a royal guard of 10,000 horsemen armed with javelins and short cavalry bows. From their ranks were recruited the officers of the six corps of 60,000 each, making an army of 360,000 men. Each corps had six divisions of 10,000. Regional troops were allowed to wear their own national costumes and carry their own kinds of weapons. Some marched, others rode horses and camels. As they came from a variety of terrain and of climate, the troops were versatile, and the great mass of the army made it invincible against smaller forces occupying open landscapes.

The empire was divided into provinces, called satrapies, which numbered a maximum of thirty-one. Special roads linked their capitals. Garrisons guarded these highways, on which both the postal riders and other travelers equipped with official documents could make use of the post-horse services. In each province a civil and a military governor shared the power. Neither was superior to the other, and each reported independently to the capital, which moved with the seasons between Susa, Babylon, Ecbatana, and Persepolis. At the same time, special inspectors whom neither of the two governors could impede came and went, reporting privately to the emperor. A strict code of law, handed down from the Medes, was rigidly enforced, and Persian justice was proverbial. Regional peoples, and special peoples in all regions, were permitted to carry on their private ways of living without hindrance as long as they remained loyal. Each province was taxed in money, in special products, or in both.

Information is not available on the details of the organization

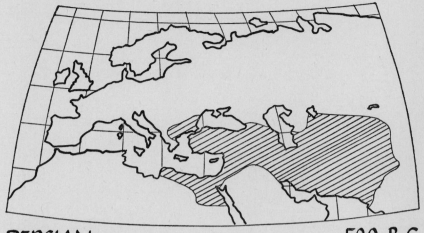

PERSIAN   500 B.C.

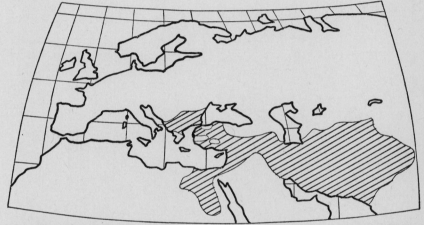

ALEXANDER'S   323 B.C.

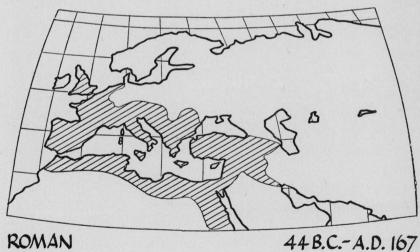

ROMAN   44 B.C.- A.D. 167

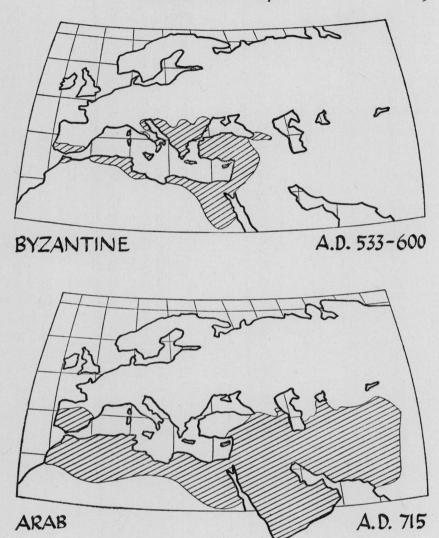

IRON AGE EMPIRES: MAXIMUM EXTENT

of the Persian political institution. The court itself, in which the emperor led a life of seclusion, must have been at least as complex as that of ancient Egypt. The royal treasury at Persepolis employed a large staff, and an army of a third of a million men required a hierarchy of at least five grades of officers. Keeping these men fed, armed, and equipped must have required a specialist corps, as well as a clerical staff. Maintenance of roads and post stations, the collection of taxes, the inspection services, and the courts required a number of government offices, all of which filed their records in the archives at the capital. These documents were written in Syriac alphabetic script, distinct from the cuneiform alphabet devised for monumental inscriptions. It is unlikely that any other political institution in the world had reached the complexity of the Persian empire by 500 B.C.

The term *empire* is commonly applied to the Late Bronze Age governments of the Egyptians, Assyrians, and Hittites in a popular sense, in the same way that the word *institution* has a loose popular meaning. Technically speaking, an empire is a complex political institution in which one people rules a number of others, permitting each to retain its own language, laws, and customs. This association of nations is to the economic advantage of the whole. It is made possible by improvements in the techniques of transport and communication above those needed for a kingdom, and such improvements depend in turn upon an increase in the rate of energy consumption. Ironworking raised the per-capita consumption of energy greatly over the Bronze Age level.

Democracy in Athens

THE GREEKS, who halted the Persian expansion into Europe, never, during the Iron Age, became consolidated into a nation. However, individual city states formed leagues, and the leading cities within leagues established colonies of traders and artisans in touch with the homeland by sea. The so-called Athenian empire was a network of such trading posts linked to Athens. During the fifth and fourth centuries B.C. the government of Athens was a democracy riding on the backs of one third of a million drones. Only forty-three thousand persons had political franchise. These were free farmers from the country districts of Attica, and members of the original tribes of the city. Some of the city men were rich; others had to work for their living. The metics, or free foreigners, and slaves had nothing whatever to say about the government.

The system itself was an amazingly primitive survival of a village type of government in which the entire community met in a single outdoor marketplace to debate and to vote. Offices that did not require special skills or capacities were filled by lot, as we select jurors. Generals were elected, and obnoxious persons exiled, by a majority vote. By scratching a name on a potsherd and dropping it in an urn, the Athenian citizen exercised the secret ballot. Every citizen was required to do military service, and in time of national crisis no office or trade prevented any man from going to battle.

The Athenians were able to keep up this form of government because they were rich. The state income from the silver mines of Laurium amounted to one hundred talents, worth about six hundred and thirty thousand dollars, per year, enough to pay for the marble buildings and statuary that made Athens the architectural wonder of the world. Trade was good. The Athenians built ships, sailed them, brought in raw materials, processed them, and exported processed goods. Following an old tradition that a warrior must always be fit, the citizens took regular exercise and baths, and tried to keep themselves in good shape. The average citizen was able to spend as much time in the details of government as he wished, interlarding debates in the agora with visits to the theater, participation in religious processions, and attendance at the schools operated by philosophers.

Whereas the Persian government could be described as an orderly hierarchy in depth, focused at the office of emperor at the top, that of Athens was a shallow maze of interlocking channels of authority in which each citizen could rise in turn, by lot or election. It worked nicely because the group was small and intercommunication easy. It could not be extended to wider areas and larger populations without the discovery of new means of transport and communication. With existing means of transport and communication, the political institution had to grow more rigid as it expanded. This type of change was seen in the rise of the Roman empire from a democratic city-state base somewhat similar in principle to that of Athens, to an enlarged version of the Persian system, with the addition of the concept of citizenship.

The Roman Empire

A s the Roman empire expanded, it came to include all of those lands within reach of the Mediterranean shores by overland travel in which the winters are mild—that is, with a mean January temperature of 32° F. or over, excepting deserts. This meant that the Romans could travel by a combination of ship and military road to any climatic region where their own kind of mild-weather material culture could be imposed. Roman roads were not practical in countries of heavy winter snow because they could not be kept open, nor where heavy frosts would heave up and shatter the roadbeds. Roman villas, intended for keeping cool in summer rather than warm in winter, were unsuited to severe winter climates. No cities large enough to need aqueducts for water could be built in places where the water would freeze. Roman clothing was not warm enough for cold winters. The Roman armies, which moved on foot and carried heavy armor, could not defeat spear-holding desert nomads mounted on camels. The geographical limits of the empire make sense when seen in this light. The "barbarians" were safe behind their barriers of cold and drought. In such regions they could assimilate at their own pace the elements of Roman culture most useful to them.

Much has been written about the decay of the Roman empire of the west, and many causes suggested for it. One reason was the failure of the Romans to mechanize their industry. The retention of slave labor was one of many aspects of this. Another was that with hand labor it was possible for the citizens of a colonial town in Portugal, Gaul, or Spain to produce locally all of the products that they needed. As each part of the empire enjoyed nearly the same climate as each other part, there was no important regional specialization, and hence no necessary exchange of processed goods. When Roman civilization was copied in the colonies, with increasing fidelity to the model of Rome itself, the difference in level between mother and daughter cities was reduced. It was just as much fun to live in Marseille, where the baths and circus were just as amusing, as in Rome. The reason for centralization had disappeared. These self-sufficient colonies broke off into their natural geographic and ethnic components, and eventually became nations, as in the cases of Portugal, Spain, France, and Italy. Right up until the present century it was more efficient for these countries to be independent than to be parts of a single empire. Like the British in India, the Romans had spread their own culture too widely and too competently for the perpetuation of their political control.

Meanwhile the peoples of northern Europe, who had invented such non-Roman devices as soap, barrels, boots, and trousers, had been gradually moving southward with their herds of cattle, in search of year-round pasture. During the fifth century b.c., when the first raids of Celts and Teutons on the Mediterranean lands took place, the climate of Scandinavia and the shores of the North Sea had suddenly turned colder and wetter. Whereas before this shift in the weather the Germanic tribes had been able to let their cattle browse in the forests and meadows during the winter, after it they were forced to stall-feed them on hay, stripped bark, and leafy twigs, all of which required much time and effort to lay in.

By the time that Roman rule had become fragmented for other reasons, whole tribes and nations of Franks and Goths and Visigoths and other Germanic peoples were moving southward. As the ruling classes of countries like France and Spain came to be composed of acculturated northerners, the justification ceased for them to feed the population of a central Italian city, no matter how famous. I see nothing mysterious about the fall of Rome, but rather a complex picture, parts of which are clear; nor do I see in it the calamity depicted by historians, whose viewpoint is local rather than global.

Rome did not, after all, disappear as an empire, but rather shifted its political center to Byzantium. From the capital on the Bosporus, Roman ships and Roman armies could reach a variety of climatic regions, including the steppes of the Ukraine, the highlands of Anatolia and the Balkans, and the old provinces of Egypt, Palestine, and Syria. As the last three fell under the power of the Arabs in the sixth and seventh centuries, the focus of the empire shifted more to the north, where Slavic tribes were crossing the Danube. These the Byzantines civilized as the western Romans did the Germans. Hence the schism included not only a breach between Italian and Greek, but between German and Slav as well. This division is still with us.

Although thousands of books have been written about Rome, not one contains a workmanlike table of organization of the imperial government. The reader, having been exposed to the same sources as the author, knows as well as I do that it was a bureaucracy of a complexity equal to that of any country in the world up to the time of the Industrial Revolution, in which a class of people known as Roman citizens could move freely inside what to them seemed an entire universe. We know much more about the workings of the Byzantine system, a direct continuation and outgrowth of the Roman.

The Byzantine Bureaucracy [3]

THE POLITICAL institution of the Byzantine empire was never frozen. Changes took place in it from time to time to meet new conditions. What I shall describe represents basically the situation at the time of Constantine, after Christianity had become the state religion. The military and civil command had been separated, and the size of provinces reduced to prevent revolt. Whereas in the western empire the Catholic Church had arisen to replace the imperial power with a religious rule, holding the former provinces together in a cultural union, in the eastern empire the state never relinquished its authority. This empire was divided into four prefectures, each under a prætorian prefect. Each prefecture was split into dioceses under vicars, and

[3] See N. H. Baynes, *The Byzantine Empire,* Henry Holt & Company, New York, 1926.

each diocese into provinces under governors. All these officers down to the level of vicar were appointed personally by the emperor, to whom they could report directly, as well as through channels. Like his Persian predecessor, the emperor could send out special inspectors. The only military duties of the prefect were raising troops and supplying rations. From prefect to governor, the civil officers were matched by military counterparts.

In the capital the Master of Offices served as prime minister, controlling the palace guard and the arsenals. All communications from the provincial administrators passed through his hands, for he was the postmaster general. He was also the minister of foreign affairs in that he introduced the ambassadors to the emperor, and the head of the civil service, which was divided into four great bureaus. These employed several thousand people working under a rigid system of tenure and seniority, with a regular ladder of promotions.

The imperial treasury was divided into two offices, that of the Count of the Sacred Largesses, responsible for the principal financial obligations of the empire, and that of the Count of Private Estates, who managed estates that earlier emperors had confiscated. A third kind of treasury was that belonging to each prefecture, from which the financial needs of the army were met. Items on the military budget included not only the army itself, so supported when away from the capital, but also the navy, forts, weapons, and the pay of mercenaries. This was the largest single budget, as the unity of the empire depended on it. Another heavy budget was that of the court, to provide for its elaborate ceremonies, including processions and state journeys, gifts to high officials of church and state, and alms to the poor of the city. Earthquakes, then as now, sometimes rocked the neighborhood of the Bosporus. Such calamities were met by special items on the court budget, plus a remission of taxes to the inhabitants of the areas affected.

Public buildings were separately scheduled, as was the fund for the distribution of free food to the populace; bread, meat, oil, and wine. A fifth budget took care of the maintenance of roads, bridges, aqueducts, cisterns, and the city walls, while a sixth provided for religious foundations: hospitals, homes for the aged, for orphans, for expectant mothers, and for retired prostitutes. These foundations were supported not only by the treasury, but also by private gifts, which were tax-free.

The money that the treasury budgeted came from a number of sources. If a man died intestate without heirs, the state took all. Sometimes subjects made voluntary gifts. Officials were supposed to pay richly for their appointments. Certain domains in Anatolia paid tribute directly to the treasury, and the rest of the budget was made up by taxation. While the taxes varied from time to time, they usually included a land tax, a five-per-cent inheritance tax, an income tax on all crafts and trades, and a special tax to pay for special ceremonies celebrating coronations, anniversaries, and military victories. Market taxes, court fines, harbor dues, and customs brought in more money. At Abydos, the old Egyptian frontier post on the edge of the Sudan, customs officers taxed imports of spice, cotton, skins, ivory, precious stones, dyes, slaves, pages, and eunuchs.

The land tax placed the local bigwigs directly inside the fiscal framework of the empire, as contrasted with the system that grew up in the west, where landlords owed the state military services instead of money. In the east, the military service was taken out of the hands of the landlords and given exclusively to the army. However, services were also required in the east in the sense that traveling officials had the right to demand entertainment, as well as the use of post horses, everywhere.

Justice was centralized under the emperor, who had the right to make laws, to interpret them, and to serve as a last court of appeal, though when he needed to settle difficult legal questions he himself turned to a high court of twelve judges. In the city the prætorian prefect, who acted as mayor, also had charge of justice with the help of a quæstor. In the provinces, local courts heard local cases. Ecclesiastical courts tried clergymen and any civil case that both parties wanted given to them. All matters concerning marriage and religious foundations went to the ecclesiastical courts.

The army, which had started out as infantry, shifted to cavalry after a force of mounted Goths had defeated the imperial forces in A.D. 378. The prætorian guard of Cæsar's time was abolished and two new corps were organized. One was a mobile imperial guard that could be sent anywhere, a frontier force whose officers were given hereditary land grants. The other was a palace guard made up of two old army corps. The commander in chief of the whole army was called the *Exarch.* Under him were two masters (*Magister*), one of horse and one of foot, and under each of them a general (*Dux*) in command of the frontier force in each border province.

In the seventh century the empire was redivided into seven so-called themes, each commanded by a military governor who outranked the civil governor. The military governor had the rank of general (*strategos*) and commanded a corps of 10,000 men divided into two brigades of 5,000 each, under brigadiers. Each brigade was split into five regiments under colonels, each regiment into five companies of 200 under captains, and each company into twenty squads of ten each, under corporals.

Heavy cavalry was equipped with steel caps, long mail shirts, gauntlets, steel shoes, broadswords, daggers, lances, and short bows. The horses in the front rank wore steel breast-protectors and frontlets. Light cavalry wore mail and carried bows. Heavy infantry wore mail shirts, steel helmets, and carried swords, lances, and axes. The light infantry carried bows with forty arrows each, or else a bundle of javelins. A medical corps had bearers on horseback who carried the wounded to doctors in the rear; and a corps of engineers carried sections of pontoons on the backs of animals, ready to lay a bridge across a stream, and they also fortified the camps with walls and ditches. The generals and the officers of the specialist corps were able to instruct themselves from many handbooks on strategy and tactics. Throughout the so-called dark ages of Europe, the Byzantine empire had a standing army of over 160,000 men in constant service, plus a navy of about 40,000. It was the only continuously organized and functioning empire in the world during the entire millennium of its existence.

However, the so-called barbarians from whom most of us are

descended were not the utter louts many historians have made of them. Tacitus greatly admired the Germans, whose virtues he extolled in order to chide what he considered a decaying Roman society; but he did not have much to say about how they were organized. It stands to reason, however, that hundreds of thousands of persons cannot march across a countryside with oxcarts, tents, livestock, women, children, and horsemen, without some kind of political structure. For the pagan Saxons, Scandinavians, and Celts of Ireland, the outlines of this structure are known.

The Golden Age of Pagan Ireland

IRELAND, which the Romans never conquered, was divided into four kingdoms: Ulster, Munster, Connaught, and Leinster. Where the four met, each kingdom had a special ceremonial ground where games, rituals, and commerce could take place. In A.D. 130, when the O'Neills united Ireland, these four corners were made into a fifth province, Meath, with its capital at Tara, the ancient meeting place of Leinster. Meath, the richest land in Ireland, was able to support the court.

Each province was divided into basic units known as *tuath,* or people. Originally designating a tribe, tuath came in time to mean a unit of land. One tuath equaled thirty *ballys* or townships, one bally equaled twelve *sesreachs* or plowlands, and one plowland equaled one hundred and twenty Irish acres. A bally was the land needed to pasture three hundred cows, a plowland all that a single plowman could cultivate in a year. All in all, there were one hundred and eighty-four tuaths in Ireland.

The *Ari-Ri,* or high king, ruled at Tara. Under him were five provincial kings (Munster was divided into an east and a west kingdom), and under each of them a number of county kings, a county being called a *mor tuath,* or great tuath. Below the county king in the administrative hierarchy was the head of the tuath, called the "king of the hills and peaks." Besides this four-step administrative organization, the Irish recognized five social classes, starting with the kings listed above. Class number two consisted of nobles, who owned all of the land aside from the estates of the various grades of kings. They were subdivided into four grades on the basis of the size of their estates and the numbers of tenants employed on them, and the members of each grade were entitled to a fixed number of armed guards, horsemen, poets, bagpipers, and other dependents who could go with them when they rode about the countryside on formal occasions.

Class number three consisted of *bo-aires,* or cattle chiefs, who owned their farm buildings and animals, but rented tillage from the nobles. Class four consisted of freemen without property, who rented from nobles or sub-rented from bo-aires, and could rise to the third class if they became rich enough. Craftsmen were also freemen. Master craftsmen and all who worked in metal belonged to class three, while the journeymen and apprentices of the non-metal trades were fitted into class four. Class five was again composite, under the name *bond classes.* Its members could not make contracts or use land independently. Some were tribal members who had no rights other than to live on tribal territory, and worked as herdsmen, laborers, and house servants. Others were slaves, mostly of English origin, who were again divided into those who served the nobles and those who belonged to untitled freemen. It was easy to tell a man's rank because each was entitled to wear a different number of colors in his clothing. Slaves could wear but one, the fourth class two, and so on up to the king and queen, who wore six.

Succession was not by primogeniture, but by election from within the royal clan. The candidate had to be without physical blemish. One king, Cormac, abdicated after he had lost an eye in a battle. The new king was chosen before the old one died, and was maintained on public lands as the second-highest-ranking person until the old king's death. Special families had the hereditary right to inaugurate each king; the O'Hagans and O'Cahans performed the ceremony for the O'Neills of Tara. After his inauguration, the high king toured his land, traveling clockwise around the island, with the sea on his left hand, visiting all the sub-kings of different ranks, who entertained him with great ceremony. These minor kings paid him tribute in food and country products, while in return he made them presents of de luxe objects, such as weapons, armor, and ceremonial drinking-horns. The exact list of all tributes and presents expected of this exchange was recited on occasion, and the refusal to accept a present was a symbol of rebellion. In each district, public buildings known as hostels were situated within walking distance of one another. Here travelers were entertained at public expense according to rank, by a staff headed by a brewy, or hospitaler. It was here that the king stayed on his circumambulation of the kingdom.

At home on the hill of Tara he had a royal hall seven hundred feet long by about seventy wide, with six or seven doors on each side, and one main entrance at the north end. This was divided lengthwise into five strips. In the middle were the hearths and caldrons in which the meat for feasts was boiled. To either side ran a row of ground-level booths, equipped with benches, while against the walls raised booths stood. Here on formal occasions persons of all ranks and occupations met and ate together. The list of booths and seating arrangements constitute as elaborate a piece of protocol as ever faced a hostess or majordomo, and give a perfect key to the hierarchical complexity of the political and dependent institutions within the kingdom.

The king himself was accompanied at all times by a retinue of ten persons, a noble, a judge, a druid (later a bishop), a doctor of laws, a poet, a historian, a musician, and three servants, besides an armed guard of at least four soldiers, including at times the king's champion. This last was a big, powerful, and belligerent man whose duty it was to fight anyone who challenged the king. In the Hall of Tara he was seated in booth number eleven along with fourth-grade poets, not because he belonged with them in rank, but to be near the door in case of trouble.

Most of the terms used in the list accompanying the seating plan are self-explanatory, but a few may require elaboration. The historians and poets were part of the religious hierarchy under the chief druid, and so were the judges. The historians were specialists among the poets of the first of ten grades, ranked according to the number of poems they had memorized, from seven

SEATING-PLAN OF THE HALL OF TARA.

N

42	41	40	39	38	37	36	35	34	33	32	31
30		29	28	27	26	25	24	23	22		

H CS C H H H

21		20	19	18	17	16	15	14	13		
12	11	10	9	8	7	6	5	4	3	2	1

S

1. Charioteers and Stewards
2. Deer-stalkers
3. Nobles of the First Rank
4. King and Queen
5. Third-Grade Nobles and Third-Grade Poets
6. Second-Grade Nobles and Historians (no grade mentioned)
7. Fourth-Grade Nobles and Fifth-Grade Poets
8. Sixth-Grade Poets
9. Cooks
10. Fort-Builders
11. King's Champions and Fourth-Grade Poets
12. Sappers
13. Chess-Players
14. Spencers (keepers of larders)
15. Braziers (Bronzesmiths)
16. Physicians
17. Pilots
18. Merchants
19. Jesters
20. Buffoons
21. King's Fools
22. Flute-Players
23. Schoolteachers
24. Goldsmiths
25. Blacksmiths
26. Shield-Makers
27. Chariot-Builders
28. Conjurors
29. Satirists
30. Doorkeepers
31. Horsemen
32. Harpers and Drummers
33. Judges (Druids)
34. Chief Druids (Doctors of Letters) and their Understudies
35. Chief Poets and Second-Grade Poets
36. Hospitalers (men who have charge of public hostels)
37. Master Wrights and their Understudies
38. Soothsayers and Ordinary Druids
39. Builders and Wrights
40. Horners and Pipers
41. Engravers (men who decorate metal objects)
42. Cordwainers (Leatherworkers)

at the bottom, to three hundred and fifty at the top. Like their Polynesian counterparts, these poets remembered the laws of the nation and recited them at trials, just as our jurists consult law-books. Their repertoire included historical events that gave the contexts of the laws. They also composed original poems on specific occasions. Like all druids, all poets were noblemen. Bards and soothsayers, who were country practitioners, were commoners.

A clear idea of the relative position of the persons fed in the booths can be obtained by co-ordinating the graded cuts of meat with the listed ranks and occupations. MacAlister,[4] our authority on this subject, lists fifteen cuts of meat, forty-two seating positions, and fifty-three classes or occupations, not including tenant farmers or slaves, who, if they ate in the hall, must have been in the open space near the main entrance. A co-ordination of cuts, ranks, and seats reveals six over-all classes or ranks, from king to fools and leather-workers, with numerous subdivisions and specialties on three parallel axes; political, ritual, and economic.

An analysis of these data shows that the side seats were better than the center aisles, the back better than the front, the middle better than either end, north better than south, west than east, right than left. Champions and merchants have incongruous seating positions because of their special functions in the meetings. Hunting was nobler than farming; economic pursuits were on the whole ranked low, with metalworking at the top and leather-working at the bottom of the trades; religion and education were highly honored; harpists were esteemed above other musicians; and fun-makers were deemed the lowest of all persons entitled to seats in the king's presence. When one considers that this seating plan, revealing as it is, did not include the different ranks and corps of the army, one realizes that the old Celtic civilization was as elaborate as a culture can possibly become in pre-literate circumstances. That of the Gauls whom Cæsar conquered was much the same as that of the Irish; and the Germanic system, while more flexible, was far from simple. The northern peoples who invaded

[4] R. A. S. MacAlister, *Tara, A Pagan Sanctuary of Ancient Ireland,* Charles Scribner's Sons, London, 1931.

Roman territories and set up the feudal system were barbarians only in the eyes of those whose lands they conquered. The main stream of cultural development from which our own is derived draws equally from both sources.

Iron Age Religious Institutions

S o complex had human society become in the empires of the Iron Age that much effort was needed to keep the peace between social classes, ethnic groups, practitioners of different crafts, trades, and professions, and different provinces. One of the two functions of the state is to regulate the order of events in the human relations of its subjects, the other being to protect them from the aggressions of the outside world. As we saw in Egypt, peace can be kept more efficiently and more cheaply by the development of a central religious system than by the police. In a complex society like that of Rome a complex religious hierarchy becomes a necessity.

As long as Rome remained a republic, the cults of the gods were served by small numbers of priests and priestesses, simply organized, and by associations of laymen. Once Rome had become an empire, godhead, Egyptian style, was attributed to the emperor. The purpose of this change was not so much to impress the Romans themselves as to provide the other members of the commonwealth with a powerful symbol to unite them. As the political institution in the western empire became fragmented, its former complexity of organization was taken over by the Christian church, the single power able to hold the former provinces together.

Next to the Byzantine state, the Catholic Church of the Middle Ages was the most complex institution in the western world, with graded ranks from Pontiff to worshippers, and a multiplicity of orders with special duties. In the eastern empire the Orthodox Church closely paralleled it, and produced branch organizations in Egypt and Syria which, under Muslim rule, became independent. Orthodox evangelists converted the Russians, Serbs, and Bulgars and gave them an alphabet, based on the Greek, especially suited to their jaw-breaking sounds. From it is derived the Russian alphabet of today.

That the Christian churches should have become structurally complex was to be expected because of their function. The first step in the formation of empire in the Iron Age was the concept of tolerance toward subject peoples, in which each was allowed to follow its own customs, including its religion. This was a contribution of the Persians. The next step was a realization of the universality of human needs, and hence of ethical principles. This was a contribution of the Jews, through the succession of prophets who tried to level out differences of wealth and rank which were causing disturbances in the Middle East as the population grew, as the land deteriorated, and as people became more and more specialized. It was the prophets of Israel who changed the concept of Yahweh from that of a tribal war god, helping the Children of Israel to conquer Canaan, to the concept of a principle of equilibrium in human affairs, which is the God of Jesus.

Whatever else may be said about Jesus Christ, He preached the principles of the equality of mankind and of the universality of the laws that govern human relations. It is no wonder that these ideas ran counter to the concept of a stratified society which then obtained in the Roman world, but they fitted the concept of a universal empire, and as such were finally adopted as the basis of the state religion. Once adopted, they could be spread to peoples outside the political boundaries of empire, being simple and sweeping enough to be capable of universal application. No matter how much theologians haggled over details or how complex church hierarchies grew, these principles were never completely lost from view.

The Rise of Associations

O N E of the most characteristic features of modern civilization is the large number of associations to which people belong, like the Red Men, the Elks, the Book and Thimble Club, and the Society for the Preservation of the Hawkins House. The average American belongs to at least a dozen. They bring together persons of different occupations who belong to a more or less clearly defined level of the total population, and also help to tie these levels together. As they are not needed until a society becomes extremely complicated, they were historically late in putting in an appearance. While virtually lacking in the Bronze Age, and rare in the early days of Iron, they grew common during the later part of the Iron Age.

In the economic sphere, the guild was the first kind of association to arise. In Athens, for example, sculptors and artists, being free men, belonged to guilds. In Rome the various categories of traders and artisans organized themselves into separate corporations, and this system was carried to a high point in Byzantium. In the tenth century a book was issued detailing the guild regulations. The prefect of the city controlled them, and under him were the presidents of guilds, elected by the members with his approval. His regulations set wage floors and price ceilings, and specified that no man could belong to more than one guild at a time. Each guild purchased its raw materials as a unit and distributed them among members. Middlemen were discouraged. Purchasers were supposed to come to the special bazaars and guild streets. This system is still in effect throughout the Middle East.

Probably the oldest type of association known to man is the religious cult. Among the Australian aborigines, for example, when several bands meet in the ceremonial season, a special group of men who hold the kangaroo sacred join, in costume, to act out the ageless myth of the first kangaroo men. Such ancient rites survived in many places into the culture of the Iron Age, as they continued to satisfy a basic human need of ritual at the change of seasons. In the countries of the Mediterranean, then the center of world civilization, several rival cults gave strength to the social fabric as members of different social classes and occupations joined each of them.

In Athens of the great period these cult associations were called mysteries. As time went on, the processions to the various gods became increasingly complex, like our Mummers and Mardi

gras, until certain aspects of them developed into the theater.
Comedy began as a phallic procession. The men who led it carried a phallic image, while others, dressed as satyrs, wore false
penises of red leather. In Sicily, about 560 B.C., this rite developed
into a play, which traveling companies carried to the Greek
mainland. In 465 B.C. its performance was made official at
Athens. Tragedy developed out of a procession of worshippers
of Dionysus dressed as goats. Until the time of Euripides, every
tragedian had to add a satyr dance to each trilogy of short plays
which he wrote. The goat dance always ended with a death scene
in which a drunken goat-god was hacked to pieces. In this cult,
as in that of Orpheus, many resemblances to the old Egyptian
Osiris cult can be seen.

The theater was a holy place, and performances held in it were
rituals. The theater of Dionysus at Athens, built in the open air,
seated fifteen thousand persons, who sat through five plays a day
for three days in a row, once a year, at what is now Eastertime.
Each year the playwrights submitted their manuscripts to the
archon of the city, who picked fifteen. Originally the chorus was
everything. In it there were two lines of dancers, who sang alternately. Then an actor named Thespis, from whom we derive the
adjective *thespian,* gave himself the role of reciting lines antiph-
onally to the chorus, and shortly afterward a second actor was
added. Sophocles added another, Eurypides a fourth, and then the
chorus disappeared. The actors, who were all males, formed a
powerful guild. Being international performers, they were allowed
to go unharmed through the lines of battle.

Another set of international associations was that of the Pan-
hellenic games, including the Pythian at Delphi, the Isthmian at
Corinth, and the Olympic at Elis. These fulfilled the same function as pilgrimages did later in Christianity and Islam, bringing
together a large number of people from many separate states in
peace for a common purpose. The Romans, who used games for
another purpose, carried their spectacles at the hippodrome and
circus to the limit, which is human sacrifice. These gory displays
served to engage the attention of a large urban population with
little else to keep it busy. At a time when the world was at peace

and most of the work was done by slaves, the excitement of glad-
iatorial fights and horse races was worth its cost to the emperors.
In Byzantium, once Christianity had become the state religion,
the emphasis shifted to horse-racing alone. The whole city was
divided into two factions, greens and blues, as ardent in their
partisanship as the fans of Dodgers and Giants. Within the closed
world of the eastern empire this interplay of matched rivals
served to focus the attention of the citizens inward. While
strengthening their social structure, it tended to blind them to
the stormclouds rising in the east and an impending change of
masters.

The Emergence and Growth of Educational Institutions

EDUCATIONAL institutions also grew mightily during the
Iron Age. It was, in fact, the efflorescence of this kind of institution which brought this age to a close. Like the mysteries, educational institutions were rooted in the distant past of man's life
as a hunter, when the old men of several bands used to bring
together an age class of frightened boys, to teach them the secrets
of survival and the ancient rules of behavior toward persons of
different sexes and ages. By the beginning of the Bronze Age the
Egyptians had established schools in the royal court to train an
elite governing class, adding to the curriculum rules of behavior
toward persons of different social levels. In Sumeria independent
schools were open to the public.

The Greeks, who bought paper from the Egyptians and borrowed their alphabet from the Phœnicians, further liberated education from the political and religious institutions. Professional
schoolmasters ran one-man classrooms to which boys were sent
at the age of six. There were no boarding schools. Each day a
special slave called a *pedagogue* (boy-leader) took the boy to
school and brought him home again. It was he who punished the
boy when necessary. The teacher taught all subjects, which he
divided into three disciplines: writing, music, and gymnastics.
Writing encompassed reading and arithmetic; music included

poetry as well as lyre-playing. No foreign languages were taught. This school kept the boys busy until the age of fourteen to sixteen.

In the fourth century, young men could continue as postgraduates with individual teachers, such as Socrates, as long as they wished; but after 336 B.C. a law was passed obliging all young men to do their military service from the ages of eighteen to twenty-one. In 383 B.C. Plato had opened his endowed school of higher education, the Academy, in an olive grove a mile out of Athens. This site, which included gardens and fountains, had begun as the ceremonial grounds of a religious association dedicated to the worship of the Muses. Tuition was technically free. If parents were wealthy, they made gifts, and Dionysius II of Syracuse gave it the equivalent of half a million dollars (eighty talents). The students wore caps and gowns and carried canes. Mathematics was an entrance condition. Plato himself taught advanced geometry, astronomy, music, literature, history, law, politics, and ethics. If he had a staff, they helped him in a general way only; there was no division of labor among teachers according to subjects. Aristotle, who studied under Plato for twenty years, went to Athens in 334 B.C., after having tutored Alexander for four years, to open his own school, the Lyceum, which had a zoo. His interest was primarily in science, while Plato's was in mathematics. Isocrates, who had founded a school even earlier than Plato, favored grammar and oratory. In 323 Ptolemy I founded, along with the library at Alexandria, a school that he called the Museum, a word which meant simply that it was dedicated to the Muses. It contained no collection.

In Rome, Greek-style schools were established by imported professors, but in 161 B.C. their curriculum was cut when the Senate banned instruction in philosophy—meaning physics, metaphysics, politics, and history—on the grounds that these subjects were somehow subversive. The Byzantines, whose tradition was more Greek than Roman, let them continue, and set up another school at Constantinople to rival the schools of Athens and Alexandria. Meanwhile a law school arose in Beirut. By legal decree, its professors were state-supported.

In Athens the Academy remained open until A.D. 529, when it was closed as a result of monkish objections. Until that time the Academy had been the most popular center of learning. The state paid one philosopher, while the city, using the Academy endowment, paid two philosophers and one grammarian. Students, coming from everywhere, went to one man's classes only. Professors were deadly rivals. Incoming freshmen were caught at the docks by rival gangs of students and forced to enroll with the professor of the winning group. Each new man was ducked in the baths and made to treat the others to a banquet. One professor still continued to teach everything, using textbooks written by Plato, Aristotle, and many others, to which exhaustive commentaries had been added. But there was little if anything new in the commentaries. As time went on and Christianity became increasingly monastic, the study of the physical sciences clashed with the statements of Genesis, and the monks won a temporary victory. However, though the Athenian Academy closed in A.D. 529, philosophy was still being taught in Alexandria in A.D. 640, when the Arabs conquered Egypt. There is no reason to believe that philosophy ceased to be taught in Alexandria, in the Greek language, before A.D. 972, when al-Azhar University opened in Cairo, and Greek learning was taught in Arabic. A hundred years earlier a Byzantine emperor had sent a library of Greek books to the Caliph of Baghdad, who had had them translated into Arabic by Syrian Christians.

In Spain the University of Cordova opened twenty-two years before al-Azhar. Bologna opened in A.D. 1000 as a law school, and soon became a university. Fez, Paris, Oxford, and Cambridge followed. These universities of the tenth, eleventh, and twelfth centuries differed from those of the Byzantine period in one important respect. At last men admitted that the field of human knowledge was too vast for one brain. A division of labor arose among professors. A student could take geography from one man and law from another, while attending lectures on mathematics from a third. Real universities now existed. For this, unless I am mistaken, we can thank the Arabs, who were extremely division-of-labor conscious. In my opinion, this, aside from monotheism, which does not really conflict with education, for all learning leads ultimately to a single principle, was the really great contribution of the Iron Age to human advancement.

Each time a new division of labor appears in history, man becomes a correspondingly more efficient animal, able to utilize increasingly greater amounts of the earth's supply of energy, and to approach with gathering speed the threshold of phase four of history. At each such time new kinds of institutions are born as the web of mutual dependence between individual men, classes, and nations grows larger and more complicated.

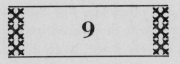

9

GUNPOWDER[1]

F I V E hundred years ago a new age began. Because Byzantine power in the east was broken by the Turks, it fell to western Europeans to take the lead in this new episode of phase three of history. Italians, Spaniards, Portuguese, Englishmen, Frenchmen, Dutchmen, and Germans began to use three basic improvements in transport, communication, and the exchange of property, as revolutionary as the riding-horse, alphabet, and money had been at the dawn of the Iron Age. These were ocean-sailing ships, printing, and banking. These inventions carried western Europeans around the world and brought into a single cultural orbit all the ancient civilizations that had grown up independently or in tenuous knowledge of one another.

An increase in the consumption of energy through improvements in furnaces, through the harnessing of water power and wind power, and through the discovery of the explosive force of gunpowder, made these inventions possible. This chain of events was touched off in turn by the appearance of a new division of labor. Occupational differences based on sex and age had sufficed for simple hunters. Among later hunters, healers and weather shamans had emerged as specialists. In the Neolithic and Bronze ages, craftsmen, merchants, soldiers, and priests had arisen; in the Iron Age free educational institutions and political bureaucracies arose. Shortly before the dawn of the Age of Gunpowder a division of labor arose among professors who taught different branches of science. Inside the universities founded in the Mid-

[1] In this and the next chapter I have drawn heavily on two splendid books: Boies Penrose's *Travel and Discovery in the Renaissance,* Harvard University Press, Cambridge, Mass., 1952; and R. J. Forbes's *Man the Maker,* Henry Schuman, New York, 1950. I heartily recommend both to the general reader.

dle Ages, scholars, no longer able to encompass all knowledge individually, specialized. Now they found time to conduct experiments, which paid off richly. For the first time in history a new source of energy was discovered by pure, objective, scientific inquiry, as all sources found since that date have been discovered.

In 1241 Roger Bacon of Oxford issued the correct formula for gunpowder, and stated that it would really explode, instead of merely fizzling like medieval Chinese rockets and firecrackers, because he had added *pure* saltpeter to sulphur and charcoal, in the correct proportions. By 1450 the use of this new chemical, developed by Rhineland manufacturers, had reached the point where 4,000 Frenchmen utterly defeated 7,000 Englishmen at Formigny, near Caen, in Normandy. After the English had formed their battle line, with horse in the center and archers on the wings, the French wheeled up two culverins, one at each end, and mowed the English soldiers down with enfilade fire. Twelve Frenchmen fell to 5,600 Englishmen. Cannon had come to stay.

Two years later the Turks, using cannon that threw one-ton rocks, took Constantinople, effectively blocking the trade routes from Europe to India and the Far East. Princes and merchants in Italy, Spain, and Portugal now turned their eyes to the open Atlantic in search of new routes. Their marine architects soon improved the hull designs of ships so that they could not only stand the buffets of Atlantic storms, but also "tumble home" after the impact of a broadside of cannon lashed to the deck. At the invitation of Prince Henry the Navigator, a company of scholars assembled at Sagres, near Cape St. Vincent, Portugal, to tabulate and co-ordinate all of the existing knowledge on the science of navigation. Shortly after this Vasco da Gama reached India around the Cape of Good Hope, Columbus discovered America, and Magellan circumnavigated the world.

As gunpowder stimulated new achievements in marine transport, so printing marked the greatest advance in communication since the invention of writing. About 1454 both Gutenberg and Coster were operating presses. The tedious work of copying manuscripts by hand was ended, within a few years of the invention of spectacles designed to relieve eyestrain by a gentleman of Florence, Italy. The invention of printing with movable type, and that of spectacles, would have been of minor value had not the Arabs, in the meanwhile, brought the craft of paper-making from China to Europe by way of Samarkand and Baghdad. Paper became a cheap and abundant substitute for expensive parchment made of sheepskin. New books were printed by the thousands, their price fell, and reading ceased to be a privilege of the wealthy and of churchmen. Ordinary merchants and artisans in

EARLY CANNON.

the guild towns learned to read and write. Authors were encouraged to write new books on a great variety of subjects, in the everyday languages of western Europe as well as in Latin. Executives could now communicate with their members, clients, and employees by issuing large editions of notices, pamphlets, and books, as institutions of many kinds now came to include hundreds of thousands of persons who never saw one another face to face.

So limited had been the facilities of transport and communication during the Iron Age that they had been nearly monopolized by the state and church, the two institutions needed for preserving order and social equilibrium. Now that they were available also for the use of economic institutions and commercial associations, the Europeans who lived along the Atlantic seaboard sailed with cannon and Bibles to all the salt-water ports of the world, establishing trading beachheads in densely populated but poorly armed countries like India and China and settling colonists in potentially rich but isolated lands that until then had supported only the survivors of the hunting era and slash-and-burn farmers. For the first time the world had become, in a sense, a single piece.

From some of the new lands, such as Mexico and Peru, the westerners looted fabulous treasures in gold and silver; from others, such as India and China, they obtained their treasures in trade. While treasures were transitory, the new plants and animals that had been painstakingly reared in these newly found lands greatly enriched Europe. Potatoes, maize, tobacco, beans, squashes, rice, citrus fruits, chocolate, bananas, tomatoes, turkeys, cotton, silk, coffee, tea, and sugar were only some of the best known of these products. Among the principal exports from Europe were metal goods in the form of containers, cutlery, and firearms. The art of making spring steel, invented in India, had passed through Arab hands to Damascus and Toledo, and thence to England. Now such steel was carried back to India to be traded for cashmere shawls.

Out of all this activity, the like of which had never been seen before, grew up new institutions. Traders and manufacturers needed capital, and banks were formed to accommodate them. Kings issued charters to mammoth corporations like the British East India Company which eventually brought about political conquest in some countries and trade monopolies in others. In the New World, Spain, Portugal, France, and England established colonial governments the purpose of which was to enrich the homelands. With new needs, some of these governments took on forms of organization new in the world. Although these overseas enterprises raised the standard of living and of knowledge in the countries of Europe, these activities did nothing to bring the nations together. To the contrary, their rivalries abroad accentuated the differences among them at home, so that they came to repeat, on a vast scale, the earlier schisms among the states on that smaller peninsula, Greece, at a time when the Mediterranean and Black seas constituted the waterways of the world. These very rivalries made possible the almost unnoticed rise of the British colonies of North America in an even more richly endowed part of the world.

Wind, Water, and Steel

W H A T made these great advances possible was the gradual development of new ways of exploiting wind- and water-power, and a closely related improvement in metallurgical techniques. By A.D. 400 pious Buddhist pilgrims were turning vertical-shaft prayer wheels, and within three centuries the Persians were grinding grain in similarly rigged windmills. These mills would work only in barren regions where the wind blew from a single direction. To make them more generally useful, someone, either the Crusaders who brought them to Europe or the Arabs from whom they may have got them, invented the horizontal-shaft windmill with triangular vanes. As the functional head of such a mill, or the whole structure itself, can be wheeled around to face any direction from which the wind may blow, it is useful along gusty seacoasts as well as on deserts. These are the mills that Don Quixote charged with his lance, the mills that can be seen today busily converting grain, with the help of the Atlantic breezes, into flour on the island of Fayal in the Azores. Using them to pump water, the Dutch drained the land below sea level which they now cultivate. The earliest recorded operation of these mills was in Normandy by A.D. 1180.

The undershot Roman waterwheel was also taken over by the Arabs, who used it on barges anchored or moored in the Tigris to grind grain and to make paper, no matter what the level of the water. These mills had wooden cogwheels, as did the earlier overshot mills built in Europe around the eleventh and twelfth centuries. By the thirteenth century, water power had begun to mechanize the textile industry in Europe. Fulling, the process by which woolen cloth was cleaned of oil, shrunk, and tightened, and its fibers felted together, as with worsteds, flannels, and Harris tweeds, was a laborious and messy process. The fuller trampled and beat the cloths consigned to him in a smelly pit outside the town, in a mixture of sheep's urine and fuller's earth. The first step in mechanization was to build tread-hammers on pivots, operated by foot. The second was to have these hammers tripped by cogs on a shaft from a waterwheel. The stream could supply both water and power. These mills, common in Europe in the thirteenth century, are still used in the mountains of Albania. In the thirteenth century, Europeans began to build semi-automatic spinning wheels, hand-powered, in which the winding process was mechanical, while the twisting was still done by hand. In the sixteenth century, power was shifted to the foot treadle.

All of this machinery, including the tools for woodworking, required an increase in iron production and a method of casting iron to replace forging as a means of making cogwheels and other machine parts. The very waterwheels that ground grain and fulled cloth provided the answer. By A.D. 1300 the smelters along the Rhine were using water power to move large bellows and thus to build up the temperature in their blast furnaces to a level at which iron could be made to flow from the bottom of the furnace into molds. At the same time and place, water-powered triphammers, based on the principle of the fulling machine, were used to forge wrought iron and steel. Meanwhile, steel-making itself had improved.

During the Iron Age, steel had been produced accidentally when smelters had come upon deposits of manganese-bearing ores, free of phosphorus, arsenic, and sulphur. A bloom from such ore, if quenched to prevent loss of carbon, would be steel. The Celtic smiths of Noricum, a Roman province coinciding more or less with what is now Lower Austria, made good steel as early as 500 B.C. and traded it to Italy. Several other peoples during the Iron Age made steel by holding wrought iron in the charcoal of the forge until it reached white heat, and then quenching it, but this was not as good as the Celtic product, and neither could compare with the so-called Damascus steel, the only true spring-steel known before the Age of Gunpowder.

Damascus was not the home of this steel, but a processing station from which it was distributed. It was produced by smiths of the Hyderabad district of India as early as the fifth or sixth century B.C., by a fusion process known as *wootz*. One takes black magnetite ore, bamboo charcoal, and the leaves of certain plants, and seals them in a clay crucible. A forced draft melts this combination, which turns into a button of metal. Such buttons, alternately melted and cooled four or five times, are fused together into cakes five inches in diameter, a half-inch thick, and weighing about two pounds. In Roman times these cakes were exported to Adulis, a seaport on the Eritrean coast of Africa, where the merchants who supplied Rome obtained them, in ignorance of their origin. When the Arabs conquered India, they carried these cakes to Damascus, where a lively industry in converting this unique material into weapons and armor arose. They also took it to Toledo, in Spain, for the same purpose.

Unlike the Romans, the Arabs visited the Indian smelteries and saw how wootz steel was made. They carried this knowledge as far west as Toledo, whence it eventually spread northward. However, from melting two pounds of steel in a small crucible to casting it on an industrial scale was a technical advance that medieval metallurgists were not prepared to make. When cast steel finally appeared in the world in 1722, it ushered in still another age. In the meanwhile the hand production of spring steel made possible improvements in cutting weapons and armor, and the invention of the crossbow, which rendered most armor useless. Steel in small quantities was used in making needles for compasses, which have to be of steel because iron quickly loses its magnetism, and in or about 1500 Heinlein of Nuremburg made the first spring-driven watch. Probably the greatest immediate utility of fine steel, however, was in tool-making, the key to all metallurgical advances.

Better tools helped harness, in a literal sense, another source of energy previously inadequately utilized, that of the horse. Metal horseshoes and stirrups came in at this time. So did the horsecollar, which made it possible to use more of the horse's strength in pulling than was possible with the old yoke-and-strap system, which, though suitable for oxen, tended to choke horses, whose necks differ anatomically from those of cattle. Now horses could be used for plowing, at which they are speedier than oxen, and for drawing farm wagons. In northwestern Europe farming improved greatly, especially after New World crops, such as potatoes and maize, had been introduced. Coach riding began, though it was some time before either roads or springs were good enough to make this a pleasure. And horses could draw cannon and munitions wagons onto the field of battle.

With Cannon and Bibles He Sailed the Seven Seas

A N D the cannon could be fired only because of the invention of iron-casting, which made possible the manufacture of cannon balls and of cannons on a useful scale. The first cast-iron firearms were mortars, used in 1340 in Italy. They were the invention of Merklin Gast, of Augsburg, who also made the first successful matchlocks. In 1540 the principle of rifling the barrel was invented, making the shoulder gun a really accurate weapon. Most firearms were muzzle-loaders until the middle of the last century. Loading and firing cannon required a specialist corps, the bombardiers, who had to be able to fit the cannon balls into the muzzles of their weapons. To do this, both cannons and balls had to be made of standard sizes, such as twenty-pound balls and ten-pound balls, and the same was true of rifle ammunition. The need for accuracy of fit in firearms thus produced a concept of standardization in production which was essential for the whole industrial development that followed, as important a step in its time as the standardization of coinage had been in the Early Iron Age.

While the Germans led in the production of firearms for use in land warfare, the Venetians, Genoese, Spaniards, and Portuguese were interested in adapting them to warfare by sea. How to mount cannon on ships was a problem that taxed the best scientific minds of the fifteenth century. These ships had to depend on sails, for a single ball could rake off a whole row of oars. Mounting a cannon or a brace of cannon on the forecastle deck would not work, for they would have to be fired when the attacking vessel was dead on its target, and no fifteenth-century ship could come about fast enough in a brisk, fair wind to avoid the risk of ramming its target immediately after the salvo, particularly without oars. If the wind were light, the recoil might

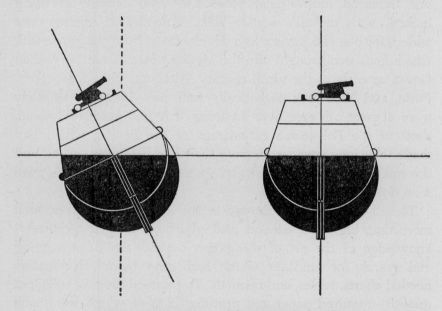

THE PRINCIPLE OF THE TUMBLE-HOME.

cause the sail to luff and throw the ship out of control at a critical moment.

The answer was to mount the cannon amidships, in rows along each side, and to fire broadsides. The advantages of this procedure were many, including greater firepower, less interference with navigation, holding the victim on the target long enough to reload and fire a second salvo, greater accuracy of timing the command to fire to a roll rather than to a pitch, and the choice between a clean getaway and the chance to grapple and board without injury to one's own ship. There was only one objection to the broadside: it might capsize the ship. This bug was soon ironed out, in Italy and elsewhere, by educated marine designers, who took over the broad-hull design of the Frisian cockboats, in which the Dutch traded from the Mediterranean to the Baltic, and made it bell-bottomed, with sides converging upward. Now the ship could roll after a broadside, and "tumble home" again. Meanwhile the hinged rudder had come into general use, and the displacement of ships increased to between five hundred and one thousand tons. Frisian ships had been capable of being tacked, with movable square sails. Fore-and-aft rigging was added, for jibs and jiggers, as a development from the lateen sail, which had been brought into the Mediterranean from the Indian Ocean as early as the ninth century. Although the *Santa Maria*, *Pinta*, and *Niña* look pathetically frail and clumsy to us, they were a great advance over anything that had antedated them, short of the Polynesian catamarans of the Pacific, which had made their long voyages no more than four centuries earlier, and the smaller replicas of which the Spaniards and Portuguese were soon destined to encounter.

To sail from western Europe to the Far East, however, took more than big ships, cannon, and adjustable sails. It required a knowledge of the art of navigation beyond the coast-hugging and search for landfalls which had gone before. Navigators needed charts, tables, and manuals. To produce these in sufficient quantity required paper and printing, both of which were soon available. After 1454, printers began issuing not only Bibles, but also treatises on such scientific subjects as alchemy and medicine as well as technical manuals on artillery and navigation. Although the marine observatory at Sagres, Portugal, had been founded in 1419, without printing the products of its research could not have been disseminated by the time of Columbus and da Gama.

The Academy at Sagres

THE ACADEMY at Sagres was headed by a Jew from Majorca, and included Muslims and Christians as well. These scholars of three faiths worked as a team on mathematics, astronomy, medicine, cartography, and marine architecture. After each discovery their maps were brought up to date. At the academy itself were trained the captains and pilots whom Prince Henry put in charge of his ships. The caravels designed at Sagres were conceded to be the best ships afloat. To sail them on deep water, a navigator had to know three things: his direction, his position, and the identity of landfalls. Direction was determined by use of the magnetic compass, invented at Amalfi in Italy before 1268. However, the deviation of the needle from the true to the magnetic pole was a difficulty not solved until 1490, when either Columbus or Cabot first discovered how to calculate by observation of the pole star.

Latitude was determined by measuring the position of the sun at noon by means of instruments derived from the astrolabe of the Arabs. Longitude was the bottleneck. The Portuguese were able to approximate this by keeping a log in which they calculated the ship's speed and plotted it against the compass course. To make this more accurate than sheer reckoning, they threw a log overboard on a long line and measured the length of time it took to begin to pull. Of course the speed of the current, if any, escaped these calculations. Although watches were invented in 1500, the chronometer set at Greenwich time was not used for determining longitude until 1735.

The question of longitude did not greatly concern the Portuguese navigators at this time, for their immediate objective was not to sail westward across the Atlantic, but to round Africa on the way to India. During the half-century before Columbus's first voyage to America, the Portuguese had pushed their way farther and farther southward along the West African coast, and Columbus himself received his early training on these voyages. He was an old Africa hand before he ventured out into the deep blue on his westward passage.

The Portuguese Sail to Africa and to India

I N 1470 the Portuguese reached the Guinea coast and began a profitable trade in pepper, ivory, gold, and slaves which enriched them and enabled them to finance more distant explorations. The cutlery, firearms, and gunpowder that they brought enabled the native West African kings to expand their territories, build up strong central governments, and make war on one another. Around the formal and highly ceremonious courts of these monarchs arose companies of skilled artisans like those of the Egyptian kings four thousand years earlier. Working in imported bronze and brass and in native woods, ivory, and ceramics, they produced highly stylized works of art of a singular beauty.

These kings obtained slaves for the trade by raiding the bush villages, by taking captives from one another in war, and by selling thousands of their own subjects who had broken some law, or violated some tabu, or fallen into debt. The pool from which this human merchandise was drawn was a varied one. The ancestors of the American Negroes came from many climatic regions, cultural levels, and social strata. Some were the sons and daughters of kings.

After Columbus's voyages, new species of cultivated plants suitable for growth in tropical forests and savannas were brought to West Africa from America, including sweet potatoes, manioc, maize, peanuts, and several kinds of beans. Thanks to these new and easily grown foodstuffs, the population rose, offsetting the loss in slaves.

In 1487 Bartolomeo Dias rounded the Cape of Good Hope, and Pero da Covilhan, traveling in disguise with Arabs, went to Calicut on the Malabar coast of India and then back to East Africa and Cairo. In his report to Lisbon, da Covilhan described Calicut, the greatest city of India of that day, as filled with Arab merchants. They had been able to monopolize the spice trade because they had conquered the shores between Arabia and India and because they knew how to sail their ships without landfalls in the path of the monsoons around the arc of the Indian Ocean.

They had even made many converts inside China, where Ibn Battuta, a native of Tangier whose works must have been known in Spain and Portugal, had traveled in the second quarter of the fourteenth century. In Amoy he had found a complete Arab city, with mosques, minarets, and suqs, as fully Arab as the French part of present-day Casablanca is European. In India the Arabs and Persians had converted to Islam the majority of the inhabitants of the Indus Valley, now West Pakistan, as well as those of East Bengal, now East Pakistan. The Malays, Javanese, and many of the Sumatrans had become Muslims before the arrival of the Europeans, as had the Moros of Mindanao in the Philippines. By arriving in southern Asia and the Far East ahead of the Europeans, the Arabs prevented large numbers of Asiatics from being converted to Christianity.

Knowledge that the Arabs could sail across oceans without landfalls must have had some influence on the decision of Columbus, who went twenty-six hundred miles from Gomera in the Canary Islands to Watling's Island in the Bahamas in five weeks in 1492, and also on da Gama, who bypassed the entire west coast of Africa in 1497 by sailing directly from the Cape Verde Islands to the Cape of Good Hope, a distance of thirty-eight hundred miles, which took him three months. Sailing up the east coast of Africa, he reached Malindi, a port in Kenya, where the resident Arabs and Hindus gave him a pilot to guide his ships directly across the Indian Ocean.

As the Portuguese were responsible for the rise of powerful kingdoms in West Africa, so the earlier monsoon trade with India and with Indonesia had profoundly affected the peoples of East Africa. At some unknown time East Indian plants, including taro and bananas, were taken to the African forests, where Negro farmers cultivated them in clearings, and the art of ironworking was introduced from India to East Africa within five hundred years of the birth of Christ. As the new food plants were suitable for cultivation in wet tropics and the new techniques of smelting and forging made it possible for native smiths to exploit the rich local sources of iron, the population of central Africa grew rapidly, exerting pressure on all sides. In 1537, nearly forty years after da Gama's first voyage, a vast horde of spear-brandishing cattle-herders, the Gallas, invaded Ethiopia and conquered half its territory. In the meantime the Bantus pushed southward along the grassy highlands of East Africa, absorbing full-sized kinsmen of the Bushmen and producing such warlike tribes as the Zulu and the Kikuyu. If some unknown group of navigators had not brought in taro and the art of blacksmithing from the eastern side of the Indian Ocean several centuries earlier, there would today be few if any Negroes in South Africa and no racial problem.

At the time that the Portuguese, having sailed around the tip of Africa, arrived on the coast of India, that sub-continent, half the size of the United States, had already become a living museum of peoples and cultures. This can be easily explained by geographical circumstances. To the north and northeast a wall of mountains, the world's highest and among the world's steepest, impose an almost impassable barrier. The coastal avenue to the southeast is narrow and heavily forested. Only to the west and northwest do natural avenues lie, and these are only relatively easy of access. Invasion after invasion, moving in over the Khyber Pass, had let in new peoples with new techniques and ideas to supplement rather than to supplant the old. Western and northern farmers and pastoralists alike found themselves more or less at home in the northwestern portions of India, where some rain falls in winter, and the summer heat, being dry, is tolerable. But to the east of the Thar Desert the winter is dry, ranging in temperature from cool to hot according to latitude and altitude, but nearly everywhere the summer is wet and hot. The rains blown in off the ocean by the southwest monsoon feed an entirely different cycle of vegetation from that on which western agriculture had been founded. It was not until the food plants of southeastern Asia, including taro and rice, had been carried in from Indo-China and Siam that most of India, including the Ganges Valley and the Peninsula, was ready for intensive cultivation.

The climate itself had imposed a series of barriers to slow down the process of conquest and assimilation. Not every bulky northerner off the cold steppe, nor even the lean desert nomad tempered to withstand dry heat, could endure the enervating wet heat of the summer monsoon. People already physiologically adapted to this most trying climate had a natural advantage over newcomers from almost anywhere. After each invasion the new conquerors reclined panting and sweating through the summer, incapable of much exertion beyond issuing commands to be fanned or to be brought cooling drinks. The conquered peoples of the Ganges Valley and the Peninsula had only to sit it out to win a bloodless victory over masters incapable of caring for themselves.

In the shady forests of the tangled southern hills small bands of curly-haired food-gatherers, shy and miniature people clad in breechclouts and armed with bows and digging sticks, moved about under the trees. There they collected roots and tubers, picked fruit, and killed small game. The climax of their annual cycle was honey-gathering after the wild bees had finished their season's work. Then the People of the Leaves would feast and celebrate. In the hills of the northeastern part of the Peninsula a people called Mundas, several million strong, cultivated taro in garden patches like those of the Polynesians, while on the cool western plateau of the Nilgiri Hills, three thousand to five thousand feet high, a special tribe of dairymen called Todas grazed buffalo and milked them to provide their farming neighbors with a smelly but imperishable form of boiled butter, called ghee. Most of the Peninsular people, like those of the Ganges Valley, were farmers dependent on rice, which yields so much grain per acre that, aside from modern industry, it supports the world's maximum number of human beings per square mile.

The Cultural History of India

THE ECONOMIC, political, and social situation of the people of India at the time of the Portuguese arrival, like that of the present inhabitants of what is now called India and Pakistan, can be understood only in the light of that sub-continent's cultural history—that is, by scanning the entire sweep of the Neolithic, Bronze, and Iron ages.

Indian history has been a record of the gradual adjustment of small local groups of economically independent peoples into an over-all system of mutually dependent units. Some of these

groups were aboriginal hunting tribes, others Neolithic and
Metal Age village communities, still others tribes of invaders.
As each came into the orbit of Indian civilization it acquired
some special task, partly drawn from its historic occupations and
partly created in response to new needs. The Aryans, whose invasion around 1700 B.C. had destroyed the cities of the Indus
Valley Bronze Age civilization, brought with them a fourfold
class system like that of other Indo-European-speaking peoples,
including the Irish. Into their relatively simple framework of
warrior-nobles, priests, craftsmen, and dependent farmers were
mortised many other categories of human beings, differing from
region to region. Each of these had its own occupation, its special duties, privileges, and tabus, and its minutely designated
level on the many-stepped social ladder.

The Indian caste system which thus developed was a product
of the interaction of history and climate. The peoples who had
been there the longest were the most competent to perform
tasks requiring a prolonged expenditure of energy, and at the
same time their cultural background was the simplest. To them
fell the more menial occupations. Those who were the least
competent physiologically had control of the most efficient means
of technology, and saved for themselves the easier tasks. The
division of labor which resulted was the most complex that the
world had seen before the Industrial Revolution. People became
immobilized in their castes not through cultural inertia, as is
commonly supposed, for the culture was constantly if slowly
changing, but because the division of labor was founded on a
physical basis. For that reason it approached in magnitude the
ecological division of labor among animal species in a natural
province.

By its means some of the Indians were able to spend their lives
in scholarly pursuits and particularly in philosophical contempla-
tion. Earlier than Christ or Dr. Einstein, they conceived the
unity of all being, and its relativity. Mathematical inquiry led
them to the concept of zero, and to the invention of the place
system, which simply means our present system of using Arabic
numerals in such combinations that the figure on the right repre-

sents units, the next to the left tens, and so on through hundreds, thousands, and millions to the edge of the paper. Realizing the importance of physiology for clear thinking as well as for sheer survival, they experimented with automatic processes of the human body, and particularly with breathing. Out of this came yoga.

Persians and Arabs carried a knowledge of these breathing exercises back to Iran and Iraq, where there arose whole brotherhoods of mystics able to commune with the infinite and with one another by controlled rhythmic breathing, a much cheaper means of satisfaction than alcohol or opium, and probably less deleterious to the system, though this has been questioned. The brotherhoods that developed around this technique spread as far as Spain and Morocco. In the world of Islam they provided a graded system of associations needed to provide structure in an otherwise gradeless society. These brotherhoods are still with us, as for example in the Ikhwan al-Muslimin in Egypt and the Fadayan Islam in Iran. The importance of this gift of India to the Middle East is easy to underestimate.

By A.D. 1500 the civilization of India had reached high peaks in many fields, having passed through the same sequence of Neolithic, Bronze Age, and Iron Age cultures as the West. Reconstructing this history, however, is difficult, for writing that can be read today did not begin before the sixth century B.C., when an alphabetic script was used for recording the sacred poetry of the Hindu religion. It came in two forms: Brahmi, derived from some early Semitic alphabet, possibly the Sabæan of southern Arabia; and Kharosthi, adapted from the Aramaic, which the Indians borrowed from scribes attached to the Persians at the time of Darius, when western India became part of the Achæmenian empire. Both are still in use. So is the Arabic alphabet, introduced in the eighth century, and the Latin, used largely for English. It is not unusual to see street signs in India in which all of these alphabets are visible.

One form of writing, however, died out long ago. That was the partly pictographic system used by the Bronze Age people of the Indus Valley, whose civilization, during the second half of the third millennium B.C., rivaled those of Iraq and Egypt. Knowledge of the existence of this ancient culture began in 1856 when John Brunton, an engineer laying out the southern section of the East Indian Railway between Karachi and Lahore, plundered the ancient city of Harrapā of hundreds of carloads of burnt brick to provide ballast for his tracks. Since then, work on this and other sites has been carried on systematically by a number of investigators, British and Indian. We know that the ancient inhabitants of the Indus Valley were advanced agriculturalists, using irrigation, that they were excellent potters, using the wheel, and that they were skilled bronze-casters and lapidaries. Their architecture in brick and stone was excellent, their drainage system the most advanced in the world, and their city-planning also unique, for they actually laid out their towns on grids instead of letting them grow around a central palace-temple compound. They had trade relations with Sumeria, as we know because of an interchange of seals. However, no Champollion has arisen to decipher their writing, and references to them in the early sacred writings of the Hindus, whose ancestors destroyed their cities, are too obscure to be useful.

The community sites that the Aryans themselves built in the Ganges Valley have not even been excavated. When systematic work is done, we can hope for little in the way of artifacts beyond stone, metal, and pottery, for the soil is too damp to preserve anything more perishable. We know from Greek evidence that cities had been built there by 300 B.C.—how much earlier we cannot be certain. Our descriptions of Indian life at this time, which was the full Iron Age, are derived from a combination of Greek accounts and an analysis of the Indian sacred literature. Later we have Roman records, and Chinese, and finally Arab, accounts. By the time of the Greeks, Indian civilization had already assumed essentially the form by which it has been known later. Although the Aryans smashed the cities of the Indus Valley, they cannot have uprooted its civilization, for the skills and attitudes of the older peoples quite manifestly survived. This is to be expected, in view of the later history of India. Nothing is ever lost; peoples and traits are merely added.

Out of this blended culture had arisen many fine skills at hand industries, particularly in metallurgy, woodworking, and the manufacture of cotton textiles. Out of it had also arisen the Hindu religion, which had a faith for everybody on every level of sophistication, providing as many sets of deities as there were castes and occupations. It also provided the subject matter for sacred poetry and a body of drama as old as that of the Greeks. Its sculptors first copied, then adapted, the Greek tradition, both for single works of art and for incorporation into a massive and elaborately decorative style of stone architecture, noted for its ornate character. Indians carried these skills to Indo-China, where the vast ruin of Angkor Vat still stands in the middle of the jungle, and out to Java, where a similar site remains at Borobodur. Despite Islam, the Javanese still put on Hindu puppet shows. The Balinese, who remain openly Hindu in religion, have kept alive the ancient forms of its drama, as thousands of Americans were able to see by means of the tour of the Balinese theatrical group in 1952 and 1953.

Out of Hinduism came Buddhism, which was carried to Afghanistan, Ceylon, Burma, Indonesia, Tibet, Mongolia, and Japan. In India itself Buddhism disappeared, possibly because of its casteless nature, and it has survived with greatest strength in countries occupied by Mongoloid peoples living east of the Altai mountain axis of Asia. Christianity was introduced into India during the fourth century of our era, if not earlier, by Syrians who claim St. Thomas as their earliest missionary. Its doctrine of equality made it unsuited to the existing social situation, and it remained the faith of a small and obscure colony in the Bombay region at the time of the Portuguese arrival. Next came Zoroastrianism, brought by the Parsees, who had left Iran at the time of the Arab invasions. They are now a rich class of merchants, scholars, and educators, concentrated in Bombay. Islam, which followed it, and which like Christianity is theoretically casteless, was imposed by a group of conquerors, yet took hold as an exclusive territorial religion only in the deserts and mountains of the northwest. For the most part Muslims became only another caste. Muslim Indians copied Persian architecture, as chaste as the Hindu is opulent, building such well-known masterpieces as the Taj Mahal. As a compromise between Hinduism and Islam, the new religion of the Sikhs arose at the very time the Portuguese were breaking the power of the Arabs and Persians in the Indian Ocean.

As the diversity of its faiths indicates, India was not then a unit like the Persian or Roman empires. It was a social *Rassenkreis* of continental dimensions in which one local culture, like one race of titmice, dovetailed into its neighbor. Political, religious, and economic institutions and associations were moderately complex. Although no super-institution had forged them into a single framework, an intricate ethnic division of labor made the most of local sources of energy—human muscle, animal muscle, simple furnaces, and direct wind- and water-power. The introduction of railroads, automobiles, airplanes, printing presses, radio stations, motion-picture studios, and factories in later ages have brought about rapid change in the direction of unity.

Chinese Civilization

I n 1511 Alfonso de Albuquerque, bearing the Portuguese title of Governor of India, took Malacca, near the modern Singapore, thus commanding the sea route to China. In Malacca the Portuguese saw Chinese merchants in their curious clothing, and in the harbor they were able to inspect a new type of ship, the Chinese junk, at which they at first laughed, thinking it clumsy. Later they were to find how seaworthy these vessels are. They had known about China from the accounts of the Polo brothers, and of the missionaries Carpini and Rubruck, all of whom had crossed Asia overland nearly two centuries earlier, in the first days of the Mongol empire. It is possible that they may have also read the detailed Arabic account of China in the travels of Ibn Battuta. More recent information must have been obtained from the Chinese merchants at Malacca, whom they allowed to continue to trade.

The Chinese at home were suspicious of all Europeans, and the

Arab traders in the Chinese ports told their hosts that the Portuguese were bloodthirsty barbarians, and were believed. The Chinese were so isolated that they had come to regard themselves as superior to all foreigners, whom they looked upon with distrust and contempt. Race prejudice reached a peak in China. Deep-set eyes, red faces, blond beards, and prominent noses were as repulsive to the Chinese visually as the body odor of Europeans was to their sense of smell. To the Chinese all Europeans looked alike, and all stank.

In 1557, after initial failure, the Portuguese were allowed to set up a trading post at Macao on a peninsula on the southern bank of the Canton River. From this foothold they dealt with a large, well-organized, and powerful empire, that of the Ming Dynasty. In 1368, the Chinese had driven the Mongols beyond the Great Wall, and by this action had broken off overland trade connections with Europe. The new dynasty, being purely Chinese, concentrated on internal affairs. Its emperors restored the old system of holding competitive examinations for the civil service, and sent officials to provinces distant from their homes. Paper money was kept at par by the requirement that at least seventy per cent of all taxes must be paid in it. The soldiers were employed to carry the rice tribute from the provinces to the capital, thus halving expenses. Newly appointed commissioners inspected the waterways. Channels were dredged, dikes raised against floods, and the whole system of inland transport and communication improved. Not only did trade between the provinces increase, but also Chinese shipmasters sailed to Java, Sumatra, Malacca, the Philippines, Indo-China, and Japan. Architecture flourished, and great skill was reached in painting and in the manufacture of bronzes and porcelain. The Chinese had much to give, but they wanted in return little that the Portuguese had to offer, at least at that moment. Sharks fins, swift's nests (for bird's-nest soup), monkeys' gallstones, rhinoceros horns, and other such valuable commodities from the Persian Gulf and the East Indies could be obtained by the Chinese themselves, with the help of the Arabs. When the Europeans came to control this trade, the situation changed.

Most Americans think of Chinese civilization as a permanent fixture. When they see our guests on the *What in the World?* television program pick up a beautiful vase, rub it fondly, and exclaim "Ming," or stroke the shiny head of the glazed effigy of a court eunuch to the enunciation of the monosyllable "Han," it is easy for them to conceive the notion that China has always been an empire in which, under different names, beautiful products were made. However, this was not the case. Reliable written history in China goes back to 841 B.C., though the official compilation now in use was not written until 100 B.C. Beyond 841 B.C. the record becomes slightly fabulous. At that point archæology takes over. The combined record of archæology and history, covering the period from a little before 2000 B.C. onward, shows a steady growth, as in other parts of the world, a growth that can be understood only if treated as a whole.

In Neolithic times [2] an agricultural people who raised for meat both dogs and the *scrofa* variety of pigs, and who made a gray-colored pottery, lived in northeastern China, while at the same time or a little later people who also kept sheep and goats, and who made painted pottery, lived in the western Chinese province of Kansu. Both were succeeded by a Late Neolithic people who had horses and cattle as well, made shiny black pottery, and built a city with a pounded-earth wall a mile in circumference at a place called Ch'êng Tzŭ Yai in Shantung, northeastern China. Although it is impossible to date this material, the presumption is that it cannot be earlier than the first certain appearance of the horse in Egypt, Sumeria, and India, which would place it at about 1700 B.C.

One of the practices of these Late Neolithic people was to foretell the future by means of the shoulder blades of animals. This is a common enough practice in the world, and one that I have witnessed in Albania. Each part of the bone has a special meaning. Thus the joint socket is the house, and its depth or shallowness indicates whether the house will be empty or filled with wealth.

[2] H. G. Creel, *The Birth of China*, John Day Company, New York, 1937, and C. W. Bishop, "The Neolithic Age in North China," *Antiquity*, Vol. 7, 1933, pp. 389–404.

Small holes on the blade are cradles, and the diviner can tell how close to the house the next birth will be by their distance from the socket. Opaque white spots mean death, and their position again indicates whether it will occur within or without the household of the inquirer.

The Albanian divination, however, is done with a blade taken from a roasted sheep. The Chinese practice, like that of many American Indians, was to heat the blade and then to read the message from the cracks that followed. At a place called An Yang in the northern part of Honan Province in North China, peasants plowing their fields during the nineteenth century, if not earlier, turned out of the soil hundreds of pieces of yellowed old bone. Some of them took these ancient-looking bones to the cities and sold them for dragon bones, to be used as medicine. Many of these bones, about one in ten, bore incised characters; all had been exposed to fire. In the cities pharmacists carefully scraped off the writing, realizing that dragons could hardly have been literate. In 1899 the first lot of the unscraped specimens reached the attention of Chinese scholars, who saw in the inscriptions not only a very archaic form of Chinese writing, but also a priceless record of life in a hitherto mythical period, the Shang Dynasty, supposed to have covered the time gap from 1765 B.C. to 1123 B.C. Since 1899 over one hundred thousand such inscriptions have been recovered, and by 1945 some fifteen thousand had been published. They were questions that some king or private citizen asked a god. An oracle priest read the cracks on the bone after holding it over the fire. The information carried on them must have been given in good faith, without exaggeration, unlike the boasting inscriptions of Bronze Age and Iron Age kings on the monuments of the Middle East. One does not exaggerate when seeking advice from one's god.

From this same region, An Yang, grave-robbers had long been digging up bronze vessels of several types, some with three long legs and a double open spout, others in the form of long narrow vases. These were eagerly bought up by collectors, particularly foreigners. Experts in both art and metallurgy considered them the finest examples of bronze-casting in the world, from any place or period. Some have brought as much as $60,000 apiece. Thus when Harvard-trained Dr. Li Chi, in 1928, began to excavate the site of An Yang for the Chinese government, he had to face the resistance of the powerfully organized grave-robbing profession. These men did not hesitate to use firearms to protect their monopoly. However, Li Chi succeeded in excavating part of the site, and the work has since been resumed.

An Yang was the capital of the Shang kingdom, dated at about 1400 B.C. Li Chi found a palace ninety-two feet long on a pounded-earth platform in the middle of a city whose outer walls he failed to locate. Next to the palace were royal workshops, just as in Bronze Age Egypt and Sumeria, for bronze-workers, stone-workers, and arrowsmiths working in bone. Royal tombs yielded bronze vessels in abundance, as well as bronze weapons and chariot fittings. Communist excavations have revealed eleven chariots in which the exact structure of the wooden parts can be seen. They were buried in clay. As the wood decayed, another kind of clay seeped in, exactly replacing it.

The bronze from which vessels, weapons, and chariot fittings were cast was smelted on the spot. Malachite ore and slag have been found. Where the ore came from we do not know, nor whence they obtained the tin, which amounts to seventeen per cent in the mixture. The nearest known sources of tin are Yunnan and Malaya. Most cutting tools were made of stone, as during the Neolithic. One distinctive knife type is the semi-lunar saddler's knife, identical with the Eskimo *ulu,* a type not found in European or western Asiatic sites. No agricultural tools have been found, which leaves one to believe that in China as in Egypt they were made of wood.

The animal bones from An Yang include those of the ox, water buffalo, horse, two kinds of pig, elephant, whales, monkey, sheep and/or goat, dog, and domestic fowl. Further evidence about these animals comes from the inscriptions themselves, in which the characters for the animals take the form of drawings. The elephant is shown with a man's hand on his trunk, possibly indicating domestication. This faunal roster indicates that the animals came from two directions. Horse, ox, sheep, goat, and one kind of pig, *Sus scrofa*, appear to be of western provenance, while the water buffalo, the fowl, and the other kind of pig, *Sus vittatus*, originated in the southeast. If the ox was humped, it was also southeastern. So was the elephant, if it was domesticated. However, there is some evidence that the climate was warmer in northern China then than it is now, and that elephants formed part of the wild fauna. Certainly the present denuded character of the terrain gives little indication of its earlier flora or its fauna. Forests must have been abundant, for the buildings were of wood, and large pillars and beams were employed. Some of this wood is still in good enough condition to permit carbon-14 analysis, which we hope can be made if ever the state of the world permits.

The principal cereal of the An Yang people was millet in two varieties. From it they made beer, important in ritual. Wheat they also cultivated. We are not sure of rice, which is dubiously indicated by a character on an oracle bone. Silk they probably had, but we are not certain. Hemp furnished a coarse textile material. That they traded over great distances is indicated by the presence of whalebone and by their use of strings of cowrie shells as money. The cowrie is a kind of snail that lives only in warm waters. Some conchologists say that the Shang cowries came from the Chinese coast south of the Yangtze, others that they had to come from the Indian Ocean west of Singapore. In either case, the presence of these shells shows that the Shang people maintained contact with the very region in which the water buffalo, vitatus pig, and common hen had been domesticated.

One of the practices of the Shang people, not unknown elsewhere, was to sacrifice a large number of human victims on the occasion of a royal funeral. This and the normal course of life and death account for the vast number of skeletons unearthed both by the legitimate and illegitimate excavators of An Yang. By the middle of 1939 the former had obtained over eleven hundred skeletons from the Shang period, not including those of the kings, which had been destroyed by grave robbers.

Li Chi turned over the An Yang skulls to Dr. T. L. Woo, a British-trained anatomist. Woo worked on this collection for over ten years without publishing the results. Then when the Japanese occupied North China Li Chi moved the skulls, along with his precious bronzes, from one temporary capital to another until they finally arrived in Taipei.

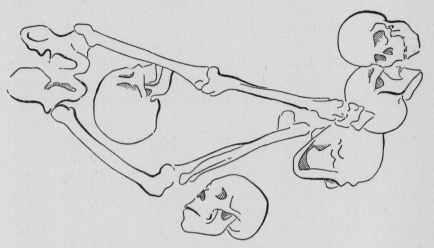

SKELETONS IN THE BURIAL PIT AT AN YANG.

In unpacking one of the skull boxes in 1953 Li Chi found a notebook in Woo's hand, containing figures for seven measurements on 161 skulls. In 1956 Li Chi showed me the skulls and I measured nine completely.

The sacrificial victims were not racially homogenous. While most had the moderately long head form of the living North Chinese, sixteen per cent were round-headed and very flat-faced, resembling some of the modern Siberian tribesmen. One male and one female skull seemed Caucasoid. A picture in a Communist Chinese magazine [3] shows long bones as well as skulls, and these bones are slender, like those of the North Chinese today.

It is a matter of pride with many Chinese, particularly with those now in power, to claim that both they and their culture are indigenous. If this is true, they are unique in the world. All people are the result of genetic mixture and selection. All cultures are the products of a combination of invention and borrow-

[3] Hsia Nai, "New Archaeological Discoveries," in *China Reconstructs*, No. 4, pp. 13–18, Peking, July–August 1952.

ing. However, China is more geographically isolated than most major provinces of the Old World. The highlands of Tibet effectively cut her off from the southwest, and the mountain spine of the Altai continues this barrier, less efficiently, northward. From time to time, invaders have moved across it in both directions. Huns and Mongols traveled westward across it until they reached Europe. There is no reason why horsemen, in earlier times, cannot have breached it in the other direction, as the earliest Neolithic peoples did.

However, the vittatus pig, the water buffalo, the domestic fowl, and the elephant all point to the southeast, and so do many of the plants that the Chinese were cultivating at the time when the historical record began. By general agreement among botanists, which is a rare thing, we are told that both dry and wet rice were first cultivated somewhere in Indo-China, Burma, Siam, or eastern India, in the tropical monsoon forest. This is also the home of the animals in question. Tropical forest conditions extend, or extended, up the southern coast of China to the Canton River. Without much doubt, southeastern China participated in the Neolithic culture that produced the banana, breadfruit, pandanus, taro, mulberry, and other plants which were carried out to Polynesia at some unknown period.

After the Shang period, Chinese history consists of a succession of kingdoms, beginning with that of the Chou people, who destroyed the Shang capital at An Yang. Without doubt many kingdoms existed side by side in what is now China. Some of the various peoples were pushed out as the Chinese proper expanded, and that was the case with the Thais, who went down to Siam, where they still remain. Others, like the Miao, Yao, and Li, still cling on as scattered village populations subject to the Chinese in the southern provinces, and on the island of Hainan. These peoples continue to speak their old non-Chinese languages. Along the coast south of the Yangtze River, during the first millennium B.C., lived a people known as Wu, whom the Chinese particularly disliked. These people went to sea in great canoes, wore elaborate feather headdresses, and collected the heads of their enemies.[4] Their language was said to be polysyllabic, unlike all those of the linquistic stock to which Chinese belongs. The evidence is good, though circumstantial, that these Wu, or others like them, had something to do with the spread of Indonesians into the archipelago which they now inhabit, and with the origin of the Polynesians and Micronesians.

As in the West, empire did not come to China until after the introduction of iron metallurgy, cavalry, and camels. A people called the Ch'in, living in northwestern China, used all three. The iron techniques may have come from the West, from India, or from both. Cavalry was certainly western. The two-humped

WU SHIP, FROM A BRONZE RAIN DRUM. DRAWING BY ROBERT HEINE-GELDERN.

camel is as much a mystery, as far as China is concerned, as the one-humper was in the West at the beginning of the Iron Age. The earliest representations of the Bactrian (two-humped) camel known are those on monuments of Achæmenian age in Iran, dating thus from the fifth century B.C. Herodotus, writing one hundred years later, while well aware of the one-humped camels of the Near East, does not mention camels at all in his account of the Scythians and Sarmatians of the plains north of the Black Sea. As their culture was continuous with that of other Indo-European-speaking nomads all the way to the borders of China, we

---

[4] See Robert Heine-Geldern, *"Bedeutung und Herkunft der Ältesten Hinterindischen Metaltrommeln," Asia Major*, Vol. 8, 1932–3, pp. 519–37; and Bernhard Karlgren, *The Date of the Early Dong-so'n Culture*, Museum of Far Eastern Antiquities, Stockholm, Bulletin 14, 1942, pp. 1–28.

must conclude that none of these people had them, or they would have spread, being so useful. Once the Chinese acquired them, in the third century B.C., they used them to great profit in trading silks across the deserts of central Asia to the west.

With cavalry the Ch'in conquered their neighbors, and with iron tools they dug extensive canals. In 222 B.C., Chêng, the head of the Ch'in state, unified China for the first time. Dividing the country into forty-one provinces, he set up a combined hierarchy headed in each by a civil governor and a general, along with an inspector. He unified the regional laws, established a fixed scale of weights and measures, unified the system of writing, and even standardized the axle lengths of chariots and other vehicles. Under his orders, the previously erected regional border walls were tied together by connecting pieces so as to create the famous Great Wall to protect China from the western barbarians and to serve as a raised highroad. The Huns, who were living in its lee, he expelled; and they in turn invaded first central Asia and then Europe, moving constantly westward until the defeat of Attila at the battle of the Catalaunian Fields, in France, in A.D. 451.

The first emperor (*Shih-huang-ti*), as Chêng was now called, was able to maintain his power by means of improved transport and communications. He deepened the Yellow River and built a highroad along its bank, connecting a string of forts which he erected. He also built a network of post roads fifty paces wide and lined with trees, connecting the principal parts of the country, and set up a postal service over them. A twenty-mile canal that he caused to be dug connected the Yangtze with the inland waterways of the north. Although his dynasty ended with his own ineffectual son, and there were times later on when China was disunited, still empire had come to stay, and China has been a political and cultural unit ever since. Unlike India, it does not contain a living stratification of peoples. There is nothing in the climate to give any one race an advantage over another, nor is it warm enough in the remote hills in which non-Chinese peoples survive to permit the retention of a primitive food-gathering culture in isolation. The "aborigines" of China are closely similar to the Chinese themselves in race as well as in technology. Climate, which aided the growth of caste in India, fostered uniformity in China. Meanwhile the extension of waterways caused boat travel to increase at the expense of vehicular traffic, and the spread of paddy rice-cultivation not only built up the world's largest population united under a single government, but also fostered hand labor at the expense of domestic animals, particularly the horse, which decreased in importance.

As time went on, the Chinese invented or discovered an increasing number of devices, plants, and other facilities. Long and heated are the arguments as to which came first, the western or the Chinese use of each. Sinophiles are convinced that printing, gunpowder, and the compass were borrowed by Europeans from China,[5] while the most authoritative students of the history of technology state that they were invented independently in Europe.[6] To me the argument is pointless, being based on a desire for prestige, like the recent Soviet claims of priority in inventing things like the airplane, submarine, and telephone. It has been proved over and over again that an invention can be made independently in different places if the conditions are similar. It has also been proved that someone can hear of something being used in a different place, and be stimulated to try to produce a similar thing. For example, Sequoya, an illiterate half-breed who had heard of the white man's writing but had not learned it, invented an alphabet for the Cherokee Indians.

Printing did not create a revolution in Chinese culture because the Chinese use thousands of different syllabic characters in their writing and it was hard for them to make a font. The European languages, which are written alphabetically, use only twenty-six (more or less) letters. The invention of printing in Europe along with the introduction of paper-manufacturing made possible the mass production of books, and with books people of all social classes began to read. The dissemination of religious literature made possible the Protestant revolution and the Catholic counter-reformation.

[5] See Derk Bodde, *China's Gifts to the West*, Asiatic Studies in American Education, American Council on Education, Washington, D.C., 1942.
[6] See R. J. Forbes, *Man the Maker*, Henry Schuman, New York, 1950.

Chinese and European attitudes about gunpowder were characteristically different. The Europeans were divided into a series of closely competing and even mutually warring nations, so that it was well worth their while to find some way to blow one another up; while China was a self-contained unit in which gunpowder could be more usefully employed in celebrations in the form of pinwheels and firecrackers. The compass was also more useful to Europeans than to the Chinese, for the Chinese navigators who went outside the network of inland waterways had only to sail along a coastline to get to the next port. Landfalls were good enough except on foggy days. To the Portuguese, who had to sail across considerable stretches of open water in the Atlantic and Indian oceans in order to reach their objectives, the compass was a necessity.

To work out the whole story of these inventions in the East and in the West and to determine how much of each was due to diffusion, how much to independent invention, and how much to invention stimulated by rumor from abroad would require a vast amount of documentary work which does not seem worth the effort. What seems important to me is not who thought of something first, but what different peoples did with it. The history of biology is full of premature innovations that failed to survive because the background was not ready for them, and so is the history of culture.

Japan Opens and Closes Her Ports

A N O T H E R civilization was quietly growing near by in a state of partial isolation: that of Japan. Japanese archæologists, who have carefully excavated a large number of sites, have found that Neolithic culture entered their islands from two directions, from North China via Korea, and from Indonesia. The exact date of these arrivals has not been determined. In Japan the Bronze Age was completely lacking. A group of invaders coming over the Korean route brought in both iron and horses. They were riders, not chariot-drivers. This fact in itself dates them within the near half of the first millennium B.C., and nearly accords with the traditional date of the first emperor, Jimmu Tenno, placed at 660 B.C. Writing was introduced about A.D. 500, after which all dates are considered reliable. Twenty-four reigns were attributed to the preceding period, and if we allow an average of a quarter-century per reign, we obtain a figure nearer 100 B.C. The horsemen who founded the Japanese empire must have left Korea during the later Chou Dynasty in Chinese history.

From a technological point of view, the history of Japan is one of borrowing a succession of traits from the peoples of the mainland and gradually working them into local culture. For example, though the Japanese borrowed Chinese ideographs in the fifth century of our era, they came to realize that these were poorly suited to their polysyllabic, inflected language. In the ninth century they developed a special script derived from them, a syllabary of forty-eight characters with twenty-three variants. This could be done because the Japanese language contains only sixty-nine possible syllables (two syllables can each be represented by two characters). When printing was introduced, the Japanese could have disseminated literacy as widely as Europeans. They failed to do so because until the Meiji Revolution of 1868, literacy was an upper-class prerogative. In the meanwhile ideographs were generally used, with the syllabary added only for difficult readings.

Painting, sculpture, and architecture all came from China, but no art expert would ever mistake the Japanese for the Chinese product. Although both are equally good, the Japanese developed styles of their own. Similarly, weights and measures and the use of gold, silver, and copper coins were also introduced from China. In the seventh century the Japanese reorganized their government on the style of the Tang Dynasty, replacing local clan lords with imperial governors. They brought in the Chinese system of holding civil-service examinations for government offices, but they allowed only noblemen to take the examinations. In China any poor boy could take them if his relatives could get together enough money to pay for his education. Buddhism, which came to Japan from India by way of China, was molded to fit local needs, and came to differ from its continental prototype as much as Protestantism does from the faith of Rome.

The first Europeans we know of who visited Japan were three Portuguese navigators, Antonio da Mota, Francisco Zeimoto, and Antonio Peixoto, who set sail from Siam in 1542 with a cargo of goods for China. A typhoon drove them off their course and carried their junk to Japan. They were received in a friendly fashion and urged to come again. Soon a lively trade began, for the Japanese were especially eager to obtain European firearms. In 1549 St. Francis Xavier, one of the first members of the Society of Jesus, went to Japan, where he remained for two years and made hundreds of converts. Other Jesuits followed him, and by 1600 more than one hundred thousand Japanese had become Christians, including nobles as well as commoners. In that year an Englishman, Will Adams, was made official shipbuilder to the Japanese government. Before that, in 1582, four Japanese had gone to visit Lisbon, Madrid, and Rome, and had returned with stories as interesting to their countrymen as the accounts of Marco Polo had been to Europeans.

In 1615, however, the Tokugawa shogun, Ieyasu, ruling as the emperor's deputy, abruptly closed the door to foreigners, letting only the Dutch continue to trade, and then only at one small island in Nagasaki harbor. The reason for this action was probably a very complex one, in which the basic motive was a reaction against cultural change too rapid for easy assimilation; but one overt explanation which historians give is that a Spaniard in Japan had said that when his country wanted to conquer another realm, his king first sent missionaries to soften the people and then followed them with soldiers. At the same time the Inquisition was going on in Spain, and when the Japanese heard of it, their rulers feared that it would spread to their own islands if the Jesuits were not curbed. In 1637 thirty-three thousand Christians revolted and were defeated in a massacre. Christianity went underground. Japan remained a secluded nation until Commodore Perry's visit in 1853.

Since that time the Japanese have taken over Western culture, and they have adapted it to their needs as skillfully as they had earlier absorbed many elements of Chinese civilization. It has become a cliché in the West that the Japanese have no capacity for invention, but this is not true. The copying that we have observed is a consequence of the forced-draft Westernization that took place after the Seclusion. Actually the Japanese invented much in the arts, including a method of abstraction, and transformed Buddhism. Their scientists have done much creative work, particularly in biology and optics.

Until the beginning of the Industrial Revolution the British could also have been accused of a lack of originality. In a very painstaking historical study, fully documented with statistical material, Margaret T. Hodgen has showed that from the time of William the Conqueror onward all technological change in England was associated with the immigration of skilled workmen from the continent.[7] In this as in other ways the Japanese merit the name frequently given them, the British of the Far East. Like the British again, the Japanese have clung to their stratified social system, with reverence for the ruler and retention of ranks of nobility.

The civilizations of India, China, and Japan, with which the Portuguese and other Europeans came in contact in the fifteenth and sixteenth centuries, were just as "high" as those of Europe from the points of view of art, good manners, philosophy, comfortable living, and most technical processes that involved manual skills. Some pro-Asiatic enthusiasts in the West believe that they were "higher." Until the voyagers that produced these contacts had broken down the barriers between East and West, the institutions of the Asiatic peoples were as complex as those of Europeans. What then gave the Europeans an initial advantage over Indians, Chinese, and Japanese which was to lead to the later cultural Westernization of the world, comparable to the physical spread of Western man in late Pleistocene times?

The answer lies in the field of energy. The Asiatic peoples based their economies on an intensive cultivation of cereals and legumes that gave a high yield per acre and could support dense popula-

[7] Margaret T. Hodgen, *Change and History*, Viking Fund Publications in Anthropology, No. 18, New York, 1952.

tions. The cultivation of these plants, particularly rice, required intensive manual labor with a minimum of animal power and little use of machinery powered by air or water. There was no particular need of that animal which in Europe provided overland transport and heavy farm traction: the horse. In Asia shipping was developed largely for use in inland waterways, while in Europe trade followed the open sea.

The Asiatic lands each included a variety of climates, ranging from tropical or sub-tropical to temperate and cold, and contained a great variety of natural resources. International trade was not as vital to them as to Europeans, nor did warfare hold out as many promises. These peoples had reached a state of cultural equilibrium as stable as that of the hunting tribes of Australia. Once they had filled their ecological space to the limit possible under the natural restrictions of their Iron Age material culture, the accent had turned to a refinement of human relations through elaborate ritual and politeness, calculated to cause a minimum of friction. Exploration, trade, and conquest interested them little. It is no wonder that the aggressive Portuguese, driving their ships onto beachheads and swarming ashore with Bibles and cannon, seemed boisterous and barbarous to these effete (to the Portuguese) Asiatics.

Contact with the West gave the Asiatics of this period little besides trouble, but it gave the Europeans fine cotton goods, silks, porcelain, tea, and jewels, as well as a taste for further luxuries. It stimulated the production of trade goods to carry out to the East, and thus eventually fostered the two basic industries of the modern age: textile-manufacturing and steel-making. But this carries us ahead of our story. We must return to that familiar date 1492.

10

A NEW WORLD

The Discovery of America

ALTHOUGH the Portuguese touched off the Age of Gunpowder, they were not long allowed to monopolize its benefits. Their more numerous neighbors, the Spaniards, with whom they shared the Iberian peninsula, soon cut themselves in on this exciting and profitable business. While the Portuguese concentrated on Africa, India, and China, the Spaniards took over the conquest of the New World. This chapter, which deals with the events of the same period as Chapter Nine in the western hemisphere, is not a sequel to the story of Portuguese navigation, trade, and conquest, but a complement to it.

Until 1492, preoccupied with the task of ejecting the Moors from their country, the Spaniards had been too busy to think much about navigation except for local forays, and had left the research and experimentation to Prince Henry. It was more than a coincidence that the very year that they finally drove the Moors from Iberian soil was the notable date of the discovery of America by Christopher Columbus, a Genoese captain who had gained much practical experience in navigating uncharted African waters in the Portugese service.

Despite the tradition to the contrary, Columbus was not the only man of his day who believed that the earth was round. Among astronomers and navigators this was common knowledge. He was simply the only man of his day who, equipped with this knowledge, both wanted to sail to the Indies by forging across the Atlantic, and was able to raise the funds with which to do it. If he had known the true size of the earth, however, he might never have tried. Eratosthenes, about 200 B.C., had correctly calculated its circumference. However, his figure of twenty-five thousand miles had been repudiated and supplanted by that of Posidonius

THE *Santa Maria.*

(130–50 B.C.), who had set it at eighteen thousand miles. The latter was the figure that Columbus had to work with.

However, underestimating the circumference of the earth by seven thousand miles was not his only error. On the existing charts, compiled from the reports of overland travelers, as well as from those of navigators, the coast of China was placed in the neighborhood of Eniwetok. Therefore Columbus believed that the Indies lay no more than four thousand miles west of Spain, and failed to suspect that the two American continents and another and wider ocean lay in between. Hence when he made his landfall in the Bahamas and saw the brown-skinned, somewhat Mongoloid-looking natives paddle out to his ships in canoes, there was no reason in the world why he should not believe that he was somewhere in Indonesia. When he reached the coast of Cuba he sent emissaries inland to pay his respects to the Great Khan, unaware even that in China the Mongol power had been replaced by that of the Ming Dynasty.

Although he may never have understood the true meaning of his discovery, he and his numerous followers, including the conquistadors Cortés and Pizarro, succeeded in doing something every archæologist dreams of, which is to step backward in time. When Cortés and his men entered the Valley of Mexico, they marched into an Early Metal Age civilization comparable in many respects to that of Egypt in late pre-dynastic or early dynastic times, and that of earliest Sumeria. It was as if, when Sir Leonard Woolley had uncovered the ramp to a royal tomb at Ur, the kings and queens and soldiers and maidens had all come to life and offered him a cup of tea. Few events in history have even contained such drama as the adventures of Cortés and his men in the palaces, temples, and markets of the city of Tenochtitlan, capital of the great king Moctezuma, and site of present-day Mexico City.

Although Moctezuma received them in a friendly fashion and lodged them as his guests in a palace, it was inevitable that trouble should arise between the two peoples. Christian Spaniards could not be expected to condone the eating of human flesh, which formed part of the court menu, or to witness without protest the gory sacrifices of hundreds of human beings, which offended their eyes, ears, and nostrils. A proud and valiant people like the Aztecs could not stomach the visitors' insults to the gods who brought them food and victory, and they felt the need of retribution. When the clash came, a small force of Spaniards on horseback, armed with muskets and spears, faced a much larger army of Indians equipped with what seemed to be glass swords, and protected by quilts. The glass swords were composite weapons made of blades of obsidian set in grooves in the edges of laths of wood, after the fashion of Neolithic sickle blades in the Old World.

Mexico City was and is situated near an extensive quarry of this obsidian, from which the Aztec knappers obtained material for these blades as well as for other cutting tools, including untold thousands that they traded to the peoples living on the plateau to the north and in the tropical lowlands to the south. These blades, which bore a high value per unit of volume and weight, they packed out of the valley on their backs, for they lacked animals capable of bearing burdens. For short hauls in the immediate neighborhood, however, they poled and paddled boats loaded with food and other merchandise on the waterways of the lakes on which the city was built, and through its many canals. The population of the city, about three hundred thousand, could certainly compare with that of Memphis during the early dynastic period, and was probably greater than that of any city in Sumeria before Babylonian times. Without easy access by water, such a large number of human beings could not have found it possible to live together.

Each of the wards into which the city was divided was inhabited by a group of related craftsmen or traders and their families. The obsidian-knappers were numerous, as were the workers in jade. Goldsmiths melted gold dust, brought to them in quills, over charcoal fires around which human sets of bellows sat, blowing into tubes to fan the flames, just as in early Egypt. Casting the gold in simple molds and also lost wax molds, and etching and chasing it, they produced jewelry that the late George Vaillant, one of our greatest archæologists and connoisseurs of early American art, considered to have been the finest in the New World. Unfortunately for us, most of it went into the Spanish melting pots, then into ingots, and finally into coinage. However, a few modern finds, such as that of an unlooted tomb opened by Alfonso Caso at Monte Albán in 1923, have produced original works. Museums, including the University Museum in Philadelphia, the National Museum in Mexico City, and the Monte Albán Museum in Oaxaca, display these pieces.

Mexican craftsmen also melted and cast copper, mostly in the form of bells. Copper intended for use as tools, particularly in the form of saddler's knives, was beaten cold. At the time of Cortés it had not yet begun to replace obsidian and polished stone. Judging by the reconstruction of Mexican prehistory made by Vaillant and others, it is safe to say that metalwork in the Valley of Mexico was then no more than three hundred years old. Knowledge of this is useful to archæologists working in Egypt and Iraq as a basis of calculation of the possible length of the pre-dynastic periods.

As in Egypt, massive blocks of stone were quarried, shaped, and fitted into more massive monuments. The pyramid of the Valley of Mexico was not a tomb, but a theater in reverse, like the Sumerian ziggurat. At the summit stood an altar and idols to the gods. From this elevated position, priests conducted human sacrifices as dramatic and as numerous as those recorded anywhere in the world, deftly opening the chests of victims with obsidian knives, and quickly removing the still quivering hearts to hold them up within sight of vast crowds.

The pyramids and the idols were carved by using stone on stone, with little if any use of metal tools. This was equally true in early Egypt. The Maya of the jungles of Yucatán, Guatemala, and Honduras, whose civilization was on the way out when the Spaniards came, had had no metal at all except a few gold and copper ornaments. All of the elaborate temples and pyramids that they built, and the tall stelæ covered with hieroglyphs and bas-reliefs, were made with stone tools.

Both the Aztecs and the Maya, as well as certain other Indians of Mexico, made books of deerskin, on which they wrote. Moctezuma had a whole house full of these books just for his kitchen accounts. Like the Egyptian hieroglyphs, their writing took the form of pictographs. Unlike the Egyptian, it contained no single consonant signs. Like the Sumerian, it was rebus writing, in which syllables that sounded alike were substituted for each other. The Mexican numeral system was different from any in the Old World, for it went not by tens, or dozens, but by twenties, with one exception; in the second row the unit was eighteen. This correction gave three hundred and sixty, the base for the calculation of a calendar. Both the place system and zero, unknown in the West until the Arabs brought them from India, had long been used by these peoples of Mexico, who worked out calendars as advanced as any in the world.

The basis of life in Mexico, as elsewhere in Central America, and in over half of the rest of North America, was agriculture.

Three staples—maize, beans, and squash—gave the carbohydrates and proteins needed for a balanced diet. These were all garden plants set out in hills in such a fashion that they provided one another with shade and support, particularly when combined with perennials such as avocado trees. Gardening was intense work, and the principal implement was the hoe. Irrigation and terraces made possible the utilization of hill slopes.

Two facts differentiated New World from Western Old World agriculture. None of the New World plants was particularly suited for such bulk treatment as sowing broadcast, reaping, and threshing. The New World farmers north of Panama lacked domestic animals suitable for plowing, carrying loads, and producing milk, manure, wool, and meat. Without any particular use for it, the American Indians failed to develop the wheel for economic purposes, though they made wheeled carts as toys for children. Hence they never could mass-produce pottery or harness the power of the wind and streams. They never approached the threshold of iron metallurgy.

In Peru, however, a full Bronze Age had begun when Pizarro first arrived. The craftsmen of the Inca empire were making knives, axes, and chisels of a good mixture of copper and tin. In their special plateau environment they had learned to cultivate plants such as the potato and a grain, quinoa, unknown in North America. They had domesticated two small members of the camel family, the llama and alpaca, which provided burden transport as well as fine wool, manure, and meat, and also the guinea pig. Along the whole extent of the plateau, and on the coast as well, they had built a network of roads as good as those of the Romans. In the mountains these were narrow and built of stone. The coastal road was thirty feet wide, banked with high clay walls to keep out the sand. Over deep chasms they had slung suspension bridges of rope. Over these roads the officials of the Inca empire traveled to keep order in the land, to collect taxes, and to see that goods could be moved and exchanged. In the coastal cities, some of which have still to be explored, the Indians worked at whole rows of looms, indicating that the Peruvians mass-produced textiles. Those of wool and cotton found in thousands of graves in the waterless coastal plain are among the finest ever woven anywhere in the world.

Politically the Aztecs were still in the stage of the Early Bronze Age peoples of the Old World. When a vigorous city state such as Tenochtitlan (Mexico City) expanded and conquered a neighboring city state, it slaughtered or enslaved the inhabitants. Many of the captives were sacrificed in huge ceremonies that kept the three hundred thousand inhabitants of Tenochtitlan as occupied as games and circuses had the Romans. The Incas, however, had reached the stage of empire, like the Persians of the days of Cyrus. With good roads and an imperial messenger system, as well as an army, they governed a number of peoples of different origins, speaking different languages and worshipping, if not different gods, at least different aspects of the sun god, with whom the emperor was identified.

This is excellent evidence that what is needed for the establishment of an empire is not specific things such as iron and horses, but any efficient means of transport and communication. The geographical realm of the Incas was protected by isolation. The Indians from the steamy jungles to the east could not hope to molest the far more numerous inhabitants of the cool, open uplands. The Incas' method of obtaining food was as efficient at that time, in terms of the number of people who could be supported per acre, as any in the world except that used in the Asiatic ricelands. What is even more important, the Indians of the high Andes, as recent tests have showed, are acclimated to high altitudes. They can work in full vigor in Chilean tin mines seventeen thousand feet up, where few white men can even exist for any period of time. The coastal strip was too narrow and too dry to permit the local city states to defy the highlanders and to remain independent once the highlanders had become fully organized. Furthermore, the exchange of goods between the highlands and coast was essential to the economy of both regions. The Inca state had few enemies outside its borders, and needed its army more for policing than for guarding or foreign wars. Peru and Bolivia were easier for the Spaniards to take than Mexico; but today, over four centuries later, of the two Mexico is by far the more Spanish, the

Andean countries are the more Indian. For this we may credit, or blame, the difference in altitude.

Mexico and the Andes are but two of the many regions that the Spaniards took in the Americas, and the Aztec and Inca but two of the agricultural, Early Metal Age civilizations they encountered. The Portuguese, through an edict of the Pope, were given colonial rights in those New World lands lying east of 46° west latitude, which includes the eastern bulge of Brazil, roughly from Belém to Rio de Janeiro. Owing to the short distance between Natal and the Cape Verde Islands, and the direction of the prevailing winds in the South Atlantic, many of the Portuguese captains called in at Brazil on their way to the Cape of Good Hope and India. In this vast new country, as in Africa and the East Indies, they entered a realm of tropical forests, more difficult by far to explore and to conquer than the open highlands and plateaus of the Spanish domain. The Indians whom they encountered, such as the Tupinamba and numerous other tribes of the Amazon and of the coastal waterways, were not in the metal ages at all, but still fully Neolithic. Because there is no flint or obsidian in the tropical rain-forest, their cutting tools were made of fish teeth, bamboo slivers, and hard, fibrous palm wood, as well as of polished stone. Some of them made huge pottery vessels, which they decorated with a vegetable glaze. Marajó Island, in the mouth of the Amazon, was the center for the manufacture of this pottery, a prize in many museums. The tropical birds of the forest supplied them with large, brightly colored feathers, which they converted into headdresses and other ornaments; on some occasions they stuck these to their bodies with gum. Members of certain tribes also painted themselves with the juice of berries which turned them bright red. Such Indians were called Colorados. Those with crown-like headdresses were dubbed Coronados, and ear-plug peoples Orejones.

To the maize and beans of the highlands, the forest Indians had added a root staple, manioc, which came in poisonous and sweet varieties. They ate both. After grating the flesh of the poisonous variety, they crammed it into a tube of diagonally plaited basketry hanging from the limb of a tree. To the bottom of this device was

attached a log. When Indians sat on the log, the meshes of the
tube contracted, and the poisonous juice was squeezed out.
Manioc was made into cakes called cassava. Like maize, this cannot be raised with yeast.

Modern explorers who visit tropical forests find overland travel
difficult, and go about by boat. The same was true of the Indians.
They were all riverine people living in long community houses
built on piles on the riverbanks and mutually accessible by canoe.
Each community was, as one would expect, independent. Although the population density of the country as a whole was not
great, there was reason for competition for the narrow zone along
the banks, which the Indians tilled by their wasteful method of
slash-and-burn agriculture. Like other Neolithic farmers without
herd animals, the men had little work to do, and hence went on
annual hunting expeditions and raided their neighbors. Those
who were successful brought home prisoners whom they kept
around the village for a while and finally executed in elaborate
ceremonies. The Indians who lived near the site of modern Rio de
Janeiro tethered their victims to the ends of long ropes and let
them fight their captors with clubs.

Jungle ambushes, wild beasts, and disease haunted the steamy,
sour-smelling interior river basins, where anthropologists can still
find Indians living in nearly the same fashion as when the Portuguese first arrived. In the more accessible and healthier regions
around Rio de Janeiro and São Paulo the conquerors set up a
colonial version of their own civilization, marked by the same
piety, splendid architecture, and racial tolerance that they showed
everywhere.

Reports from the New World by Columbus and his successors
from Spain and Portugal took the people of western Europe completely by surprise. Yet they were not the first to visit it. As everyone knows, Leif Eriksson, the son of the founder of the Norse
colony in Greenland, Erik the Red, made a voyage in the year
A.D. 1001 to an unidentified section of coast which he called Vin-
land, located somewhere between New Jersey and Labrador, and
this was followed by the voyages of Thorfinn Karlsefne, and by
the actual colonization of a harbor for two years. Yet this series of

events not only failed to reach the attention, as far as we know, of the experts in the Academy at Sagres, but it also failed to make any impact on the American Indians whom the Norsemen met, and who drove them out. This leads one to believe that other voyagers who failed to come back, from the time of the Phœnicians onward, may have made similar landfalls; they need not have impressed the Indians any more than the Vikings did.

Another instance of the same thing is the de Soto expedition of 1539–43. This intrepid commander visited several towns of Indians on the banks of the Mississippi River near Memphis. After his death his men were attacked by the Natchez Indians farther south. These people erected elaborate mounds, and their king, who was a representative of the sun god, lived on the top of one of these edifices, whence he descended on ceremonial occasions to form the central attraction in processions in which he was borne, like Pharaoh, on a litter.

De Soto and his men came and went. Two centuries later, when the French explored and settled the low Mississippi Valley, they found a similar tribe of Natchez Indians living the same elaborate pre-dynastic kind of life, but they had forgotten all about poor de Soto. Two plates of brass, marked AE, which their neighbors the Creeks of Tukabahchee carefully guarded in their sacred holy of holies, were the only proof that Spaniards had ever been there, other than the literary accounts written by members of the expedition, one of whom called himself "A Gentleman from Elvas."

The point is that such unrepeated visits and short-lived settlements produced no permanent effects on native American peoples, except to introduce new diseases. Hundreds of books have been written to prove that the Indians are the descendants of the lost tribes of Israel, or shipwrecked Welshmen, or that the Maya civilization of Yucatán was brought by Mandingo Negroes crossing the Atlantic from Africa in canoes. Atlantis, the Lost Continent of Mu, and other fictitious drowned lands in the Atlantic and Pacific have been concocted to explain American Indian civilization, but it needs no *deus ex machina*. Almost every element in the culture of the New World can be explained on the basis of a purely local growth. Anthropologists who have patiently un-

earthed the evidence that makes cultural isolationists of most of
them become very impatient with the flimsy explanations that
non-professional diffusionists continuously produce. For that reason the anthropologists may have become a little too intolerant of
some of the evidence.

We know now that man came to America from Asia during the
fourth glacial period, or immediately after it. My interpretation
of the presently available evidence is that human beings crossed
Bering Strait dry-footed when the sea level was lowered by the
immobilization of much of the world's water in glaciers. The
Yukon Valley was then unglaciated. After the ice melted, the
strait was flooded, while the avenues southward along both the
Pacific coast and the eastern slopes of the Rockies were opened.
We now have enough early post-glacial sites, from Wyoming to
Mexico, to make it certain that American Indians were hunting on
the eastern flank of the plains and on the plateaus as early as
8000 B.C. The work of Junius Bird in South America makes it
probable that the tip of that continent was reached some three
thousand years later.

The Transpacific Problem

B Y 5000 B.C. all the New World except the Eskimo country
had been occupied by the descendants of one or more small
groups of immigrants from Siberia, who found vast forests and
prairies swarming with game, fish-filled lakes and streams,
and no rival primates bigger than a spider monkey. Physical
variations in size, form, and coloring which differentiate the various regional populations of American Indians can be explained
on the basis of a physiological response to extreme differences of
environmental stress, according to the rules stated in Chapter Six.
Hence we need no genetic *deus ex machina* to explain the American Indian. A single and unrepeated migration from Siberia is
enough. If people other than the Norse visited America before
Columbus, as they may well have, they left no visible imprint on
the racial composition of the inhabitants of these two continents.

The possibility of extensive mixture from outside the Americas is rendered improbable by the evidence of blood groups. Nearly all American Indians belong to the recessive group O, either because they left Asia before the A and B groups had arisen, or because some genetic mechanism, as yet unknown, may have eliminated the other two after their arrival. While several tribes show some A and a very few B, the geographical distribution of these atypical tribes follows no special pattern, as it would if these factors had been introduced from Asia, Africa, or Europe by sea.

Hence we find a dilemma: if people visited America from elsewhere, they were transients, and transients have little effect on local cultures. Yet we know that cultural transfers must have been made at some time, presumably across the Pacific. The evidence for that is botanical. In the meanwhile we have seen enough of the development of civilization in the Old World to know the difference between cultures that have grown up by gradual stages and those which have been violently altered by outside influences. American civilizations assume the former pattern.

Careful excavations in the Valley of Mexico show that a long period of simple Neolithic agriculture preceded the rise of literate city states such as Cortés discovered. A sequence of carbon-14 dates from Bat Cave, New Mexico, which is on the periphery of this Neolithic culture, indicates that American Indians were growing maize by 4000 B.C. As far as we know now, agriculture is just as old in the New World as in the Old, but we still have much to learn. In South America the coastal sites, in which plant materials are preserved by the dry climate, have also yielded valuable evidence. Junius Bird, excavating in 1946 at Huaca Prieta, a mound at the mouth of the Chicama River on the Peruvian coast, found evidence of the continuous occupation of this site by a group of fishermen and farmers from 2500 B.C. to 1200 B.C. They cultivated squashes, gourds, peppers, and the cotton plant. From the cotton they finger-wove great quantities of cloth, of which thousands of pieces were recovered. Their occupation of the site was ended when a new people invaded it, bringing with them pottery, maize, and true weaving. These new people may have come from the highlands or from some other point along the coast.

The botanical evidence that is used to dispute the ancient im-pregnability of America can be boiled down to four principal plants: the gourd, cotton, the sweet potato, and Indian corn. The gourd, *Lagenaria siceraria,* has been grown in both hemispheres for a long time. The ancient Egyptians knew it, and the Romans ate its immature fruit. In India and southeastern Asia it was used for bottles and dishes, as it was in Central and South America. Junius Bird found gourds in the earliest levels at Huaca Prieta. Botanists believe that it was originally domesticated in Africa or India, probably the latter, and that it was not native to the west-ern hemisphere. It seems to have been cultivated in both the Old and New Worlds before 2000 B.C. How did it get from one to the other?

Two routes suggest themselves: across the narrow waist of the South Atlantic from Black Africa to Brazil, and across the Pacific. In the case of either route, two means are possible, drifting on ocean currents, or being carried by the hand of man. An experi-mental botanist who soaked some gourds in salt water to see how long their seeds will remain viable under ocean conditions found that the seeds will still germinate after an immersion long enough to carry them across either ocean by prevailing currents, judging from the time it takes messages in bottles to make the same jour-neys. So they could have gone either way, if we grant that some-one on shore would pick up such a specimen, break it open, and plant the seeds, for they cannot reproduce unless opened and re-moved from the neighborhood of salt water.

It is possible that some unknown sailor drifting in a canoe from Africa brought the gourds to Brazil, but it is unlikely. Although we know little about the prehistory of West Africa, we feel fairly sure that agriculture developed there too late to permit a passage at a time equivalent to the Old Kingdom in Egypt. If the gourd was carried by human hands across the Pacific, this happened before the probable time of settlement of the islands by Polyne-sians. Of the four possibilities, all are unlikely.

Cotton, a genus known as *Gossypium,* was cultivated as early as 2500 B.C. in both Peru and the Indus Valley country. Archæo-logical evidence, including the new discoveries of Junius Bird at

Huaca Prieta, makes this certain. Unlike the gourd, however, cotton is not all one species. Indian wild cotton, *Gossypium arboreum*, has thirteen small chromosomes. American wild cotton, including *Gossypium raimondii*, from which many botanists believe the domestic forms to be in part derived, has thirteen large chromosomes. The cultivated East Indian cotton is merely an improved form of the local wild species, with the same chromosome count. The evidence for its local origin is therefore impeccable. The cultivated American cotton of the later Peruvian levels, *Gossypium barbadense*, contains twenty-six chromosomes, thirteen large and thirteen small. Specialists in commercial cotton-breeding believe that *barbadense* is a hybrid between wild American and cultivated East Indian cottons. If this is so, someone brought cotton on a ship across the Pacific before 2500 B.C., for the cotton from the lowest levels in Huaca Prieta is the same in color and other characteristics as that of higher levels. The alternate hypothesis, that someone carried it across the Atlantic, is equally difficult to defend. The drift theory need not be considered, for cotton seed will not survive immersion in salt water.

The third critical species is Indian corn, *Zea mays*, or maize. It is a water-loving grass related to millet and sorghum. Instead of having separate capsules of spikelets and glumes to enclose each seed, as in other grasses, it has a whole cob enclosed by a husk. Because the husks will not open naturally on ripening, maize would die out but for the hand of man. This husk is a combination of four leaf-sheaths. The wild ancestor of maize may be presumed not to have had this suicidal feature.

Mangelsdorf has found in Paraguay and eastern Bolivia a variety of domestic maize called pod corn, which is a popcorn in which the four leaf-sheaths form a sort of nest around the base, but fail to enclose the ear. The earliest corn from Bat Cave, New Mexico, dated at about 4000 B.C. by carbon-14, has this same characteristic. Because the Bat Cave and contemporary pod-corn varieties are essentially the same, Mangelsdorf thinks that this was the earliest form of domestic maize grown in America, as far as can yet be determined. In Layer 4 of Bat Cave, dated at about the time of Christ, a new kind of maize appears. This has larger cobs and

kernels than the earlier specimens, and the modern type of husk.
Mangelsdorf believes that the earlier type may have been a descendant of a wild pod-corn ancestor, while the later variety shows
hybridization with *teocentli,* a wild Mexican grass itself probably
a hybrid of maize and another wild grass, *Tripsacum.*

While Mangelsdorf's reconstruction is based on much careful
work, he does not claim to have found the wild ancestor of maize,

POD CORN, AFTER MANGELSDORF.

nor does any kind of maize occur in the oldest agricultural levels
in the Peruvian coastal sites. Edgar Anderson, after studying
some small-eared varieties grown in the Naga Hills of Assam by
tribes of head-hunters, and some Chinese historical records, believes that maize was grown in the highlands of southeastern Asia
within a few decades after Magellan's trip around the world. On
this basis, as well as on the basis of technical aspects of the maize
itself, he claims that maize must have been grown in the Old
World before Columbus. Mangelsdorf refutes this claim on both
technical and historical grounds. A botanical war is on.

Species number four on the critical list is the sweet potato,
Ipomea batatas, a member of the morning-glory family. A native
of the tropical forests of South America and unknown in Europe

before the sixteenth century, it was grown on the coast during the period that began after the introduction of maize and pottery. When the first European navigators reached Polynesia they found it cultivated there, particularly in Hawaii, Easter Island, and the most remote archipelago of all, New Zealand. The Polynesians called it by one of its South American Indian names, *kumara*. Even my old teacher, Roland B. Dixon, than whom no more conservative anthropologist ever lived, admitted that someone must have carried the sweet potato westward into the islands several centuries before the time of Columbus. So fragile a plant is it that it must have been transported with tender, loving care, perhaps, as the Polynesians said, under their women's breasts.

The case of the sweet potato is not particularly mysterious. Thor Heyerdahl, in his second and more technical book,[1] postulates that some American Indian navigators from the coast of Peru may have reached some of the Polynesian islands either before or soon after the arrival of the principal ancestors of these people. The transfer of the tubers could have been made at that time. His own famous and lucrative voyage was undertaken to prove that brave men sailing in a raft of the type on which the Peruvians plied their coastal trade could have reached the islands. He has shown that this could have been done. The only other alternative is that some of the Polynesians reached the coast of Peru, obtained sweet potatoes, and went away again. I prefer Heyerdahl's alternative as a working hypothesis because in 1953 he found pre-Columbian Peruvian pottery on one of the Galapagos Islands and in 1960 on Easter Island, where it was pre-Polynesian.

While the case of the sweet potato is no problem, the other three are not so easy to explain. It is conceivable, but hardly likely, that the gourd drifted across the Atlantic before 2500 B.C. Although the presence of maize in the Old World before Columbus has not been proved, neither has its wild prototype been found in the New. The toughest nut to crack of all is cotton. If, as many botanists believe, the thirteen small chromosomes of the

[1] Thor Heyerdahl, *American Indians in the Pacific*, George Allen and Unwin, London, 1952.

cultivated Peruvian plant must have been carried from India, it must have left there before 2500 B.C., the same time as the gourd.

It is hard to explain how cotton and gourd could have been carried straight across the Pacific at such a time, for our present knowledge indicates that the Polynesian islands were not inhabited until three thousand years later. That these plants may have been borne on ships around the arc of the North Pacific, past Japan, Kamchatka, the Aleutians, and the whole western coast of North America to South America, is extremely unlikely, but cannot be disproved. Marius Barbeau,[2] a Canadian anthropologist, has found evidence that Japanese sailors were wrecked on the northwest coast of his country and lived among the Indians before the time of the first white contact, but not before the time of Columbus. The Japanese did not make good seagoing vessels before the arrival of Will Adams in 1600. In the latter half of the thirteenth century a Chinese writer named Ma-Tuan-Lin[3] compiled a vast collection of earlier accounts of travelers to different parts of the world beyond the frontiers of his country. Among them was a story of the visit of a priest named Hoei-Chin from a country named Fu Sang to the Chinese courts, in the year A.D. 499. Fu Sang, he said, lay thirty thousand li (twelve thousand miles) to the east, and extended ten thousand li (four thousand miles) farther east, where another ocean was to be seen. The name Fu Sang came from that of a giant tree whose bark the natives used to make textiles. The civilization that he described was one of a literate urban people who used copper, gold, and silver, but no iron.

He also gave them horses, milking-reindeer, and a breed of silkworm seven feet long. Among the presents that he is said to have brought to the Chinese Emperor was a mirror of some unfamiliar substance, and some threads of the giant silkworm, which were fabulously strong. Chinese literature contains many other tales about Fu Sang, some of which were intentionally exaggerated. It is not clear whether Hoei-Chin was a Buddhist priest or a

[2] Marius Barbeau, *Totem Poles*, Bulletin No. 119, National Museum of Canada, Ottawa, 1950, Vol. 2, p. 831.

[3] Ma-Tuan-Lin, *Ethnographie des Peuples Etrangeres a la Chine*, Vol. I., tr. by le Marquis d'Hervey de St. Denys, Geneva, 1876.

cleric of some other religion, though the word used definitely implied the former. It is also far from certain that Fu Sang was America. Even if it was, Hoei-Chin's journey was far too late to have had anything to do with the botanical problems that puzzle us here.

If Indian cotton and the gourd were carried to America by sea from southeastern Asia before 2500 B.C., then the people who brought them must have been Neolithic navigators, for the Bronze Age had not yet begun in southeastern Asia at that time. Two routes may be considered. One is the northern arc of the Pacific, skirting the shores of Japan and the Aleutian Islands. Another is the long route across the Indian Ocean, around the Cape of Good Hope, and across the South Atlantic. The second is not as unlikely as it would first appear, for prevailing winds and ocean currents favor it most of the way. The Indian Ocean monsoon winds carry sailing vessels today from the tip of India to a point south of Madagascar, and past the Cape of Good Hope another set of winds blows up the African west coast to the Bight of Benin, and then westward in the lee of land, and across the Atlantic to Brazil.

The first half of the third millennium B.C. was a period of calm seas and optimum sailing weather in another part of the world. It was then that sailors from the eastern Mediterranean ventured out through the Strait of Gibraltar and up the Irish Channel to round the top of Scotland and cross the North Sea to Scandinavia, or so the archæological evidence indicates. These sailors carried with them a peculiar kind of pottery decorated by channel-like grooves, and buried their dead in long tombs made of huge stone slabs and covered with earth; these are the megalithic tombs of British and Scandinavian archæology, dated at a period just before the Bronze Age. It would have been no more difficult for Neolithic seamen, with comparable equipment, to round the Cape of Good Hope and cross the narrow waist of the South Atlantic than to have made this northern passage.

Had they done so, one would expect them to have gone ashore on the west coast of Africa as well. Had they gone ashore, they would surely have introduced their tropical food plants there also, but the evidence is against this. Sometime between 609 B.C. and 593 B.C. Phœnician sailors commissioned by the Pharaoh Necho sailed clockwise all the way around Africa. Twice they camped ashore long enough to plant crops, to wait for them to ripen, and to reap them before going on. In the third year they sailed eastward through the Strait of Gibraltar and thence home. Had they met any considerable agricultural population on the way, they would not have been obliged to wait to grow their own foodstuffs. Within the next two centuries other sailors, including Sataspes the Persian, and Hanno the Carthaginian, visited the west coast of Africa. Both reported the country sparsely inhabited by Pygmies. Their evidence weakens the transatlantic contact theory. I am neither proposing such a theory nor trying to quash it prenatally, but merely trying to show that if theories on this subject are necessary, it is better to look on both sides of the globe and to weigh all the evidence than to concentrate on one route alone.

The need for such theories arises from the conviction of some plant geneticists that neither the gourd nor domestic cotton could have been cultivated in America by 2500 B.C. without some such explanation. Mangelsdorf, himself an outstanding plant geneticist, has this to say, with Douglas Oliver, about the cotton question: "There is no more need of explaining the distribution of the Old and New World cottons in terms of man's peregrinations than there is of accounting for the range of numerous other genera which have a similar geographic distribution. Indeed, if the differentiation of cotton species is to be explained in terms of man's movements, then there are other genera which are not cultivated, in which speciation ought likewise to be so explained: a procedure which would soon reduce the thesis to an absurdity." [4]

In physical anthropology, as in botany, the last two decades have been a period of emphasis on genetics to the neglect of other aspects of biology and history. I am not convinced that our present knowledge of genetics is sufficient to explain all historical

[4] P. C. Mangelsdorf and D. L. Oliver, *Whence Came Maize to Asia?*, Botanical Museum Leaflets, Harvard University, Cambridge, Mass., April 13, 1951, Vol. 14, No. 10.

THE NEW WORLD

An Aztec sacrifice. From Zelia Nuttall's
Book of the Life of the Ancient Mexicans.

PLATE XXV

Mayan litter. From a vase. Strip shows entire circumference; actual vase at right.

PLATE XXVI

Fortress of Sacsahuamacan, protecting the Inca capital, Cuzco. Lowest of three terraces.

The Weary Traveler. A Mochica pot from the Peruvian coast, time of Christ.

PLATE XXVII

Inca treasures. Gold objects from Ecuador (ABOVE) and Colombia. Many such were melted down by the conquistadors.

PLATE XXVIII

Four Peruvian textiles. Along the coastal plain the Indians wove
fine and intricate fabrics of cotton and llama and alpaca wool.

PLATE XXIX

North American Indian art.
A wolf's head found under water at Key Largo, Florida. Twelfth or thirteenth century.

PLATE XXX

West African wooden figure.
Native impression of a French non-com with whip and rifle.

PLATE XXXI

The mighty *Mo*. A model of the U.S.S. *Missouri* made
by a Moroccan who believed that this was what he saw.

PLATE XXXII

relationships among human races, nor can I believe that it is sufficient to explain all botanical relationships. Another assumption which one is likely to make without much thought is that carbon-14 dates are always true. Archæologists prefer to have a series of dates from successive levels in a single site, or from a number of sites in one neighborhood, for checking against each other. Single dates from isolated places are considered tentative. During the 1950's great improvements were made in the techniques of radiocarbon dating, and the time span covered was doubled, but all the mysteries of C-14 have not been solved, as the physicists working on it would be the first to state. We have much to learn about all these subjects that supply the archæologist with his tools, be they geology, astronomy, or whatever.

Among these tools is the history of a pest, the rat. Now the parasitic (rather than domestic) rat is a native of Java. Two Javanese genera have become accustomed to prey off man. One reached Europe by way of China, the other by the southern route. Both arrived in America after Columbus, or with him. I cannot believe that if there had been any repeated or habitual contact by sea between the Old World and the New in pre-Columbian times the rat would have been left behind. Carrying cotton seeds requires deliberate planning and planting, but the rat is a hardy hitchhiker who has been stowing himself away on ships for a long, long time. If we can find out exactly how long, it may help with the answer. We cannot yet say to what extent the peoples of the Americas developed their native cultures unaided by the travelers from the Old World, but we can say that the cultures of the New World had no visible effect, outside of Polynesia, on those of the Old.

The transpacific problem is interesting on theoretical as well as historical grounds. It brings into sharp focus the conflict between the diffusionists and the champions of independent invention. The former believe that every cultural similarity between geographically separated peoples must be the result of contact and borrowing from a single source, the latter that men of many races and countries are capable of creative work. If the diffusionists are correct, man is indeed a sorry animal. Being an optimist and humanist, I prefer to believe that genius can arise, through the infinite genetic variability of man, in any setting, and that in no country are all the inhabitants domesticated human beings.

The Impact of the New World on the Old

AFTER Columbus's famous voyage of 1492 the relationship between the New World and the Old moved from the realm of speculation into that of modern history. The acquisition of New World products greatly benefited the peoples of the Old World, particularly in Europe. Besides a fabulous wealth in gold, silver, and emeralds, the New World furnished a large number of botanical species that radically changed the basis of life in many countries of the Old World. Tobacco and Indian corn became staple crops in the Turkish empire, and cotton in Egypt. Both tobacco and cotton became cash crops grown for export on a world market, while Indian corn became a staple food in Balkan countries.

The white potato was taken from a local species grown by the Indians of the island of Chiloé in southern Chile. There the latitude, temperature, and humidity duplicate conditions found in northwestern Europe. Consequently the white potato became a European staple, particularly in Ireland and Germany. In the west of Ireland, where potato-cultivation flourished, the human population multiplied rapidly. When the potato famine struck in the late 1840's, several million Irishmen migrated to the Americas and elsewhere. Thus we can thank the Indians of southern Chile for much of our Irish population.

In the pre-Columbian Europe, the bean family had been limited to a few rather uninteresting species suited more for fodder than for food. Explorers to the New World brought back a wealth of new legumes, such as haricot beans, kidney beans, and lima beans, which added not only new taste sensations, but also a splendid source of proteins, to the European cuisine. Tomatoes added a new sauce, and chocolate a new confection. The one animal species that the explorers brought back was the turkey, soon to be intensively bred in the country whose name it bears. It is hard to think of French cooking without fried potatoes or *haricots verts*, the Italian cuisine without tomatoes, a Swiss confectionery shop without chocolate, a Dutchman without a cigar, or a modern American Thanksgiving dinner without turkey. These new foods gave western Europeans the opportunity to feed growing populations of men and livestock cheaply, and thus to support the rise of industry. From the standpoint of food alone, the discovery of America gave western Europeans at home and in the colonies an edge over the rest of the world.

The Spanish Colonial Empire

THE CONQUEST of Central and South America gave the Spaniards the world's first overseas empire, the most complex political institution yet to arise in human history. All other empires, from the Persian to the Byzantine, and including those of Asia, had consisted of groups of countries contiguous to one another or separated by narrow bodies of water such as the English Channel, Bosporus, and the Strait of Gibraltar. The need to cross the Atlantic gave the Spaniards a new set of political problems which required the creation of new organizational machinery.

This machinery had to be powerful, because in the Americas the Spaniards had found the equivalent of a private gold mine. Just as the Athenians had minted obols and drachmas from the silver of Laurium, so the Spaniards coined doubloons from the gold idols and breastplates of the New World. By the middle of the sixteenth century, when the Spaniards were busy minting money by the cartful, their neighbors, the French, Dutch, and English, were still obliged to work for their living, and it was no wonder that piracy arose on the Spanish Main and that the Spanish government devised a powerful political and military system to help them keep this windfall to themselves.

Luckily for the Spaniards, the events of the preceding half-century had paved the way for the rise of a strong political institution. Before the marriage of Ferdinand of Aragon and Isabella of Castile in 1469, the seven and a half million Spaniards owed their allegiances to a number of separate political institutions, headed by kings, princes, and churchmen, each with its own *cortés,* or parliament. Many of the towns were sovereign states. Ferdinand and Isabella dissolved the local cortés and set up a strong central government with a graded system of royal courts of justice, down to the office of village *alcalde.* A royal officer called the *corregidor* was put in charge of the towns, and the king took over the right to make all church appointments. This strong, centralized form of government arose for a very good reason immediately before Columbus discovered America. The Spaniards needed a tight organization to fight the Moors. Once the Moors had quit Spain, there was still no chance to relax, for many doubtful characters, both Muslim and Jewish, had been left behind, hiding under a cloak of simulated Christianity. The famous Inquisition, which alarmed the Japanese and quelled the early Protestants, was actually set up not so much to harry heretics from the ranks of Christianity as to root out a real or fancied fifth column of stay-behind Moors and Jews.

In 1492 the Spaniards were tough, devout, and united.[5] The strength of Ferdinand's newly centralized government gave him the wealth with which to finance exploration as an investment toward new riches. Thus when he grubstaked Columbus, he gave the navigator a royal commission as admiral and captain general, with instructions to explore new lands, to colonize them, and to relieve them of their riches, keeping ten per cent of the proceeds for his own pocket. Columbus also was instructed to convert the natives to the Catholic faith. In the administration of this still hypothetical realm he had the right to appoint his own staff.

Once the Spanish dominions in the New World had been conquered, blanket charters of this kind were soon eliminated, and the excesses of some of the conquistadors like Pizarro were soon replaced by orderly government. In Spain itself colonial affairs were first handled by a single man, Juan de Fonseca, the Archdeacon of Seville, and his two clerks. By 1503 the press of busi-

[5] My chief source for the organization of the Spanish colonial government is David R. Moore, *A History of Latin America,* Prentice-Hall, New York, 1939.

ness had made a staff increase necessary. This staff grew into a board of trade called the Casa de Contratación, whose duties were to control all commerce and immigration. In 1524 a new body, the Council of the Indies, was set up, its members appointed by the crown. They were the most competent men available, men who had been to America and understood American problems. They screened and appointed administrative personnel for colonial service, including priests; they controlled the Casa de Contratación, created laws for colonial use, and heard appeals from colonial courts.

In the New World, four viceroyalties were blocked out: New Spain, including the original territory of Mexico and all of Central America to Panama; New Granada, including Columbia and Venezuela; Peru; and La Plata, which was the Argentine. Each viceroy had to be a Spaniard of good birth, though an exception was made later on in the case of the Irishman Ambrosio O'Higgins, a governor of Chile from 1788 to 1796, the father of the more famous liberator Bernardo O'Higgins.

A Spanish viceroy ruled in great pomp and splendor. Around him the members of a court circulated as around a king. He was supposed to control the army, the church, the royal revenue, and the welfare of the Indians, whose special protector he was. He had the power to appoint some of the officials, and to make spot decrees on certain subjects without waiting for the Council of the Indies to take action. Below him ranged a local hierarchy of *gobernadores, corregidores,* and the *alcaldes* of towns, each of which had its own council, or *regidores.*

As in the old Persian empire, the viceroy was not allowed to rule unwatched or unchallenged by agents of the central government. Each viceroyalty had its own *Audiencia,* or supreme court, responsible only to the Council of the Indies. This court, which had its own judges and prosecuting attorneys, sent its inspectors out to tour the country from time to time, and once every three years, when the viceroy was obliged to stand up for examination as a condition for reappointment, the Audiencia had much to say about his conduct in office.

In 1680 the Casa de Contratación was moved from the inland

river-port of Seville to the salt-water port of Cádiz, whence all
transatlantic shipping was conducted from then on. All ships set
out in great fleets, resembling the convoys of the last two world
wars, sailing in close packs to avoid pirates and French, Dutch,
and British privateers. Naval vessels protected them. One fleet
sailed to Vera Cruz. Some of the goods unloaded there were for
Mexican consumption, and the rest was carried overland on mules
to Acapulco, where it was reloaded on other vessels for the Philippines. These islands had been discovered by Magellan in 1521.
Being then in the Spanish service, the admiral claimed them for
Spain. The Spaniards could not colonize them until they could
find some way to cross the Pacific from west to east against the
prevailing trade winds, because the Portuguese blocked the easy
route home via India. In 1565 a Spanish navigator, Andres de
Urdaneta, discovered the great circle route along the coast of
Japan and just south of the Aleutian chain. He picked up land
at Cape Mendocino, California, and then coasted to Acapulco.
Although a long route, it was an easy one, for he had a fair wind
all the way. After this the Spaniards could sail due west to Manila
and follow Urdaneta's passage, as they called it, back again. After
1565 the Philippines were rapidly colonized.

A second fleet left Cádiz for Portobello, Panama. First it stopped
at Cartagena, in Colombia, to let post riders hasten overland to
Lima to warn the viceroy. At Portobello the cargo was unloaded
and carried across the isthmus, where it was reloaded on other
ships for Peru. Although it would have been simpler to ship
goods marked for the Argentine directly to Buenos Aires, the
Portuguese and other perils stood in the way. All goods so destined had to be carried via Panama and Peru.

For forty days after each fleet arrived in Vera Cruz or Portobello, a huge fair was held in which imports were exchanged for
exports. The imports were mainly processed goods, including cutting tools, machinery, fine textiles, shoes, clothing, elegant furniture, and wines and liquors. The exports were raw and partly
processed materials such as salts, hides, horns, cacao, coffee, tobacco, corn, sugar, and dyewoods. Local manufacturing of finished products was forbidden, for the Spaniards held to the old

principle of exchanging processed goods for raw materials which had in earlier times made the Phœnicians and the Athenians lords of the Mediterranean. By following their example the Spaniards soon became lords of the Atlantic.

The countries that the Spaniards most successfully colonized resembled Spain itself in their general environmental features, being treeless plateaus, relatively arid, and fruitful under irrigation. Horses, mules, and donkeys, the riding animals and beasts of burden to which the Spaniards were accustomed, flourished there, as did the old Neolithic barnyard foursome and the hen. Among the cargoes of the incoming ships much livestock was listed, including the ancestors of the Texas longhorns, the Plains Indians' horses, and the Navajos' sheep.

In both Mexico and Peru the Spaniards removed native kings and emperors, but did little else to disturb the common lives of the people, who were already numerous and well adjusted to their landscapes on a basis of intensive hand agriculture. The introduction of iron and steel cutting tools, domestic animals, the plow, and the cart helped these Indians to prosper and to increase, for they had already reached a technological stage where these could be easily assimilated. Indian weaving, pottery-making, and other home industries continued almost unchanged, and the daily and seasonal cycles of life continued as before for the native villagers.

In place of native chiefs, the Spaniards set themselves up as hacienda-owners. Managing large estates on which Indians worked, they duplicated in the New World the position of noblemen in Spain, with the Indians as peasants. While the clergy abolished human sacrifice and other local ritual conspicuously distasteful to Christians, they allowed their new converts to remodel their local gods into saints, to offer flowers and copal at shrines, and to stage such elaborate spectacles as the dramatic spinning of voladores from high poles. Latin American civilization, from Mexico to Peru, became a harmonious blend of native and Spanish techniques, institutions, and symbols, eminently suited to its time and place.

From the standpoint of the history of institutions, this colonial enterprise produced an expansion of the state comparable to that of Rome in early imperial days. When the Latin republics eventually peeled off from the Spanish orbit, they followed the pattern of the break-up of the Roman empire for the same reason. The peoples of the new lands had learned, despite official restrictions, to take care of themselves on a Gunpowder Age level of technology. It was easier to manufacture basic tools or to buy them on a competitive world market than to pay taxes. Political power yielded, as it usually does in time, to the law of least effort, for it is simpler and easier for each one of a group of associated countries to be self-sufficient than for one of them to prevent the others from local manufacturing and from outside relations, particularly when separated from them by an ocean.

The British and Dutch Found Incorporated Trading Companies

WHILE the Portuguese and Spaniards were dividing the new markets and colonial lands of Asia, Africa, and the Americas, the peoples of northwestern Europe were also passing through a period of change. Advances in metallurgy made it possible for them to make and use more machinery, and the abundance of water power permitted them to mechanize a number of processes, particularly in the textile industry. In northern France, Flanders, and the Low Countries in particular, large communities of clothmakers had arisen from about the eleventh century onward. Specializing in fine woolens and worsteds, they needed much wool. One of the chief sources of this staple was England. It did not take the English long to persuade skilled textile-workers to cross the Channel and start industries near the source of raw material. English worsteds are still in demand throughout the world. One may see them on the backs of prosperous people in such countries as Iran and Japan, South Africa and Chile.

A short while ago I showed A. V. Kidder, whom many professionals consider to be the dean of American archæology, a Navajo blanket that my mother-in-law had given me. It contains woolen thread of four colors—black, gray, blue, and red. Dr. Kidder pointed out that the gray yarn was spun by the Navajo from raw undyed wool sheared from sheep which their ancestors had obtained from the Spaniards, and the black was produced by native dyes. The blue was dyed with indigo, a plant native to India. This dyestuff in the Navajo blanket had either been imported directly from the East Indies, or had been grown locally in the Spanish colonies, possibly Guatemala. The red yarn was not spun from Navajo wool at all. It was English wool, sheared from English sheep, dyed in England, and spun and woven in Lancashire. The Spanish government bought it from English traders to make into lining for the blue capes of their soldiers. The soldiers wore them to America, where the Navajo eventually obtained the linings, which they carefully picked apart, until they had unwound the actual English threads. Then they spun it over again, and wove it into the blanket. Americans later supplied this red fabric by peaceful means—traders.

As the textile industry in northwestern Europe grew in response to the demands of world trade, it seemed to the English, Flemish, and Dutch unnecessary to sell their product to the Portuguese and Spaniards for them to trade. Why not do their own trading? The reason was, of course, a lack of shipping and of naval power. This situation could be remedied. Meanwhile the wide circulation of reading matter which followed the printing of the Gutenberg Bible raised the literacy of the common middle-class citizen, who was becoming an important person in the cloth towns of the north. Direct access to the Bible gave him ideas of his own about religion. The medieval structure of the Church had been built around a society of lords and knights and their agricultural retainers. The rise of a new urban middle class created a need for new symbols, which could not be readily found in the existing ritual system.

While the Church might well have made the needed adjustment, other forces prevented this. When the Spaniards invaded and held the Low Countries, they brought with them the Inquisition, which aroused the hatred of the burghers. Thus the latter identified the Church with their mortal enemies, who had not only made martyrs of some of their relatives, but who were also taking their cloth to the Indies in trade. All in all, the countries around the North Sea had developed a culture distinct from that of the Mediterranean and in particular from that of the Iberian Peninsula. The Reformation gave them the independence from this other culture area which they needed. Now they could make war on the Spaniards in the New World and try to wrest the trade of India and China from the Portuguese in defiance of ecclesiastical strictures. To them the lines of longitude by which the Popes had divided the world between Portugal and Spain could be breached in full conscience, and with spiritual sanction.

The idea of competing with Spain and Portugal on the oceans of the world was fanned in England by letters written by members of the colony of Bristol merchants who lived in Seville in order to export wine, which could not be produced in England. From 1530 on, English captains were engaged in the West African trade, in the course of which they came into frequent clashes with the Portuguese, but during this period none of them succeeded in rounding either Africa or South America. In the Caribbean they went in for raiding the Spanish colonies and shipping. Meanwhile they tried two other potential routes, the Northeast Passage around Siberia and the Northwest Passage around North America. Both attempts failed in their avowed purposes, but each succeeded in another sense. Out of the Northeast Passage venture came trade with Russia by way of the White Sea, following the same route our convoys took during World War II to Archangel, and a lively whaling industry, in which the British and Dutch slaughtered thousands of leviathans in the waters facing Spitzbergen. The promoters of this venture organized themselves into a joint-stock company, called the Merchant Adventurers, in 1553. In 1557 the name was changed to the Muscovy Company, which more accurately revealed its aims. In 1576 another company, formed to finance the search for the Northwest Passage, was called the Company of Cathay. When the search failed, this company collapsed. The Hudson's Bay Company was not created until 1670, well after the settlement of New England by the Massachusetts Bay Company.

The formation of these companies brought into the world a new kind of institution, in which private citizens invested money in a common venture from which they might profit, or in which they might lose, and in which they may or may not have participated in person. It implied faith in their own government, and in the board of directors whom they themselves were free to choose, as well as confidence in the men whom they sent out to do the company's business.

Such companies were formed in England as an outgrowth of the guild system, particularly of the clothmakers' guilds. Such guilds had been accustomed to pool their resources to buy raw materials and machinery, and to divide profits. Thus the English system of dealing with overseas trade differed fundamentally from that of Spain and Portugal, in which trade was a government monopoly, one aspect only of an extension of the political institution into newly found countries. Such companies formed the basis of our modern capitalist system.

Had England been forced to rely on the fruits of her search for northern passages to the Indies, this system might never have arisen. After the defeat of the Armada in 1588, English ships could sail around either of the two southern capes with reasonable hope of success. Meanwhile another company had been formed, the Levant Company, to trade with the Turks at Istanbul and Aleppo. From Aleppo a number of Englishmen traveled overland to the Persian Gulf and one group reached India. On December 31, 1600, the Honorable East India Company was founded in London, and in 1602 the Dutch founded their own East India Company. After a considerable struggle, the English concentrated on India proper, and the Dutch on Indonesia, though neither completely yielded to the other in either area. Both founded factories, both engaged in political machinations with the local rulers. Both grew rich. Within the next few decades both established colonies in North America, as did the French and Swedes, and the Dutch settled the Cape of Good Hope region, a convenient provisioning station on the sea route to the East Indies.

The Age of Gunpowder produced not only a new form of human organization known as the incorporated trading company, but others that went with it. In order to share the profits as well as the risk of overseas enterprises, merchants invested in insurance companies, after the pattern of Lloyd's of London, which grew up in a shop intended to dispense coffee, a new drink introduced from Ethiopia by way of the Yemen and Turkey. The family system of England and other northern European countries also fitted neatly into the new pattern. Instead of dividing estates equally among male heirs according to the Roman law, British law gave all, or nearly all, to the firstborn. In upper-class families, nevertheless, all sons were usually educated. Bright younger sons with public-school and perhaps university education were eager to go forth and make their fortunes in new worlds.

The pursuit of science, which had begun as an offshoot of the division of labor in universities, soon passed to more specialized bodies known as the learned societies. First founded in Italy in the days of Galileo, these were soon imitated in England, where the Royal Society was founded in 1662, and in France, where the Academie des Sciences followed four years later. The Royal Society in London helped judge applications for patents, which were being submitted with increasing frequency during the latter part of the seventeenth century. Before the societies began publishing bulletins, the leading scientists of Europe wrote one another frequently, exchanging ideas and discoveries. They were no more tied by national boundaries than were the navigators, who, we have seen, came from all countries from Italy to England, and who served in one another's navies and chartered companies. Discovery and exploration have been international affairs since long before the Pharaoh Necho hired Phœnicians to circumnavigate Africa.

As direct fruits of the efforts of the members of learned societies came the invention and use of the telescope, microscope, thermometer, barometer, air pump, modern clock mechanisms, and mathematical symbols, as well as logarithms and calculus. All of these things were shared by anyone competent to use them. At this time, when the world was in a sense first made one, religious people seized on the opportunity to evangelize and to attempt to turn the whole world Christian. Despite the slave trade in Africa, which arose during this period, the idea of the supremacy of one race seems not to have been overtly held. Pocahontas was well received in England, and various travelers brought home wives of various colors from Asia and Africa. The Chinese and the high-caste Hindus were the racial snobs of this period.

Raising tobacco in Virginia, though an aristocratic and profitable pursuit, was far less exciting than traveling about in India, making presents to native princes bedecked in silks and diamonds, and going on tiger shoots from the backs of elephants. Compared to either of these ways of life, the chilly toil of farming and fishing in New England was bleak and burdensome. No quick profit could be seen in the settlement of the northern colonies. A Dutchman shooting hundreds of wild ducks with his blunderbuss on the Jersey marshes could hardly have foreseen the New York skyline that now rises from across the ridge of Jersey City, or have anticipated the industrial stench that hastens the traveler across this now birdless shooting ground. English, Scots, Irish, Dutch, and Swedes are stubborn people, and the new lands resembled their homes in climate and vegetation. What they sowed was no easy crop like indigo or tobacco, but the roots of a nation greater than any other the earth has yet seen.

Meanwhile another obscure adventure was proceeding modestly in the same latitudes and higher. The Russians, having defeated the Tatars, expanded eastward as remorselessly as the Goths had moved southward more than a millennium earlier. Bypassing the powerful Muslim nations of Turkestan south of the Kizil Kum and the Hunger Waste, they crept sunward along the southern fringe of the Siberian forest, throwing up forts and trading posts and tilling the narrow belt of land similar to their own steppe until they reached the Pacific in 1639. No new institutions followed this expansion, which was primarily military in nature. Nothing like the New England town meeting arose to grant them free government. Siberia long remained a place of exile for unwanted persons and an extension of the empire that the Russians had founded on Byzantine lines. More than three centuries later, the American tail is wagging the European dog, while in Muscovy the dog still wags the Siberian tail. In 1638 few rational persons would have imagined that the greatest powers on earth today would be the United States and Russia.

11

FROM COKE TO ATOMS

The Sword of Destruction

W E H A V E at length moved forward from man's first adventure, in which he came down from the trees to master the way of the hunter, to what may turn out to be the last, in which he is forging the sword of his own destruction on a cosmic anvil. At the end of the fifty thousand or more generations during which he lived off the land like other animals, he left the face of the earth as he had found it. Nature remained in balance as before. During the ten generations that have been born since the beginning of the industrial period (a collective term covering the Coke, Oil, Hydroelectric, and Atomic ages), he has carried the mutilation of the earth's surface, which he started in the Neolithic, to a point of crisis, and he has polluted the air and the seas.

While perpetrating this wholesale destruction, human beings have made such great technical advances that the two dimensions of energy and space have become inconsequential. We can now produce heat rivaling that of the sun, and we can travel at the speed of the earth's rotation, so that a flier leaving London will arrive in New York at the hour, by the clock, at which he departed. Our medical scientists are also hard at work shattering the dimension of time by discovering drugs that will let human beings live indefinitely.

These very advances have made the world into two rival workshops in which sovereign nations are as interdependent as the departments of a factory. Actually the force that pulls these workshops together is stronger than that which keeps them apart. Old concepts of nationality are now as encumbering to efficiency in the world community as customs barriers would be if imposed between individual American states. Because it now takes less time to fly around the world than it took President Washington to travel from his home in Virginia to Independence Hall in Philadelphia, and because the people of the whole world are more familiar with President Kennedy's face and voice than contemporary Americans were with the lineaments and tones of President Washington, what prevents the peoples of the world from pooling their efforts in accordance with the law of the conservation of energy is not distance, time, or technology.

It is the retention by twentieth-century, Atom Age men of the Neolithic point of view that says: *You stay in your village and I will stay in mine. If your sheep eat our grass we will kill you, or we may kill you anyhow to get all the grass for our own sheep. Anyone who tries to make us change our ways is a witch and we will kill him. Keep out of our village.*

That some people still reason this way is a result of cultural lag. While some peoples moved rapidly forward in culture, others lagged behind, preserving every archaic cultural stage from the Mesolithic onward. As time passed, the cultural differences between living peoples grew ever greater.

An example of lag is the current cult of materialism, a by-product of nineteenth-century science, which leads some men to say: *We know all that there is to know about the universe. There is no God, no over-all principle. Man is a mechanical animal, and we can control him.*

A patent fallacy of materialism is that if man is in fact a purely mechanical animal it would require another species as much more gifted than man as man is more gifted than an ape to understand all the workings of the human nervous system. Such an understanding might reveal that no earthly power controls man's life and progress, but some force from outer space. Perhaps the cosmic radiation that causes mutation in germ plasm is one manifestation. Who knows?

Throughout history certain energetic and insensitive men have always been arrogant, in the belief that they knew all that needed knowing. This belief may have led many a hunter to his death at the claws of bears during the early phases of our ancestors' existence. In earlier ages arrogance was a self-limiting nuisance. Today it is more dangerous because the weapons we have devised are too powerful to be left in the hands of overconfident men. What to do about it is a problem that currently engages the efforts of the world's best political minds.

As we move into phase four of history, few of us can participate in the deliberations that are shaping the future. All of us can, however, play parts in this most exciting of man's adventures by realizing that now, as before, it behooves the humble to be brave. Each of us needs to be reminded that every other human being is unique and of equal importance, that more remains to be learned than has yet been revealed, and that we must continue to hold in proper respect those few forces of nature which our scientists have discovered. With these thoughts in mind we can all help our leaders find the means to pass safely through our present danger. How we arrived at this situation is the subject of this chapter.

The Story of Coke [1]

THE KEY to the sequence of events which led man from the end of the Age of Gunpowder to our present situation may be found in the story of coke, for the use of this new material made it possible for industrialists to produce an almost unlimited quantity of steel, a metal which succeeded flint, polished stone, bronze, and iron as man's principal tool-making material. Steel is as hard as flint, as plastic as bronze, and as abundant as its chief component, iron. With steel, craftsmen came for the first time to work with a substance from which they could mass-produce machinery. Now they could fabricate heavy frames, shafts, gears, wheels, pistons, and boilers for any purpose.

During the Age of Gunpowder, trade between western Europe and the newly discovered and recently colonized countries had

---

[1] Although the technological details in this chapter came from many sources, my principal guide, particularly in the story of coke, has been R. J. Forbes, *Man the Maker*, Henry Schuman, New York, 1950.

created a great demand for hardware and textiles. The British and Dutch took the overseas trade away from the Spanish and Portuguese in many countries because heavy industry had moved from Spain to England and the Rhineland. In fuel and ore these countries were the richest then known in the world. By the beginning of the eighteenth century, many trees had been cut down in the British Isles to provide timber for ships to repel the Armada, but more had been felled for charcoal to feed the rapidly growing steel industry. So much steel had been forged, mostly for the overseas trade, that the shortage of charcoal had become critical. The smelteries, which had been located in southern England, where both the forests nearest to London and the principal seaports were situated, had moved to the mountainous regions of the north and west, where some wood was still to be had, and whither ore was laboriously carted over muddy roads. As everyone at all familiar with the details of heavy industry knows, ore always follows fuel because the latter is the bulkier. It should be borne in mind that the other iron-producing countries of northern Europe, such as Germany, still had wood. Only in England did this critical shortage prevail. Only in England was the need for a substitute for charcoal desperate.

As far back as the thirteenth century, the British had found a substitute for wood as heating fuel in the coal deposits of Northumberland and Durham. This coal was useless for smelting: it released sulphur upon heating, and spoiled the iron. However, it was in considerable demand for heating houses. By 1680, two hundred and eighty thousand tons of it were shipped to London each year. Much more would have been mined, except for the fact that the galleries had a habit of flooding, drowning any miners who happened to be working at the time and preventing others from following them. This problem occupied the attention of many ingenious men until, in 1705, Thomas Newcomen invented a steam pump that, burning coal, sucked the water out of the mines efficiently enough to solve the problem. From then on, the coal industry boomed.

While this invention helped heat British houses and provided a material for export, it had no immediate effect on heavy industry, on which all other economic activities depended. Nor was the Newcomen steam pump good enough for universal application as a power-converter. However, the abundance of coal and the existence of a steam engine of sorts set many men to thinking. Among them were a citizen of Coalbrookdale named Abraham Darby, who died in 1717, and his son Abraham, Jr. These two

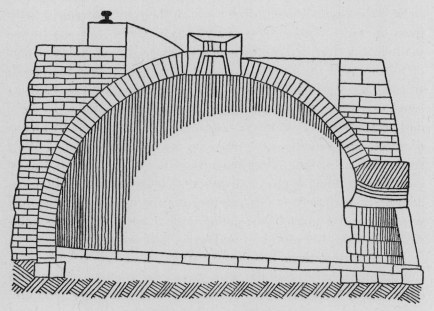

A COKING OVEN, AFTER FORBES.

men can be given credit for breaking the bottleneck that had prevented the start of the Industrial Era.

Abraham, Sr., had noticed that in place of charcoal brewers had begun to use coke as a fuel for drying malt. "Coke" is a residue of coal from which sulphur and other impurities have been removed in the form of gas. Having concluded that if coke was clean enough for malt-drying it was also pure enough for smelting, he began a lengthy series of experiments destined to culminate in his son's success in 1753. The principal reason why it took them so long was that the Darbys had been experimenting with coke made from coal which will not stack properly in the smelter.

It crushes, impeding the flow of blast air. Once they had tried bituminous coke, they were on the road to victory. Necessity was the mother not only of invention, but of the whole Industrial Revolution. Bituminous from the Appalachians, from Pennsylvania to Alabama, from the Ruhr, from the Urals, and from Manchuria is still the prime fuel around which the steel industry is built.

Now the English smelteries moved to the coalfields, less remote from the cities than the wooded glens. In 1760 someone else invented a kind of bellows in which water power operated a pair of pistons, and the heat and size of the smelters was increased. In the same year the technique of making crucible steel, an oversized extension of the old Wootz process, was added. In 1772 ball bearings, which improved the transmission of power by means of shafts and chains, were manufactured. In 1781 James Watt succeeded in making, after long trial, an efficient steam engine capable of producing power anywhere that fuel could be obtained. Almost immediately afterward, steam was used for mechanical weaving, and Arkwright's spinning mule made that process automatic. Textiles became as abundant as hardware.

The history of these inventions that depended on coke bears a significance far beyond the mere recital of names, places, and dates. From Newcomen to Watt and beyond, each man who created a basic invention did so only after long, tedious effort and much trial and error. Once the invention had been made and the device set to work, its inventor and others after him continued to experiment, adding improvement after improvement. We do not know the history of the invention of the flint blade core, the burin, copper-smelting, bronze metallurgy, ironworking, or the wheel, but we may be reasonably sure that each of them took as much time and effort as that which went into the use of coke in steel-making and into the steam engine.

Another significant fact about these inventions is that they were made by humble people. The inventors were skilled artisans without formal education in the sciences. While men like Newcomen, the Darbys, and Watt were toiling at their benches, learned scholars in wigs and lace were busy talking about physics and chemistry in abstract terms. A century was to pass before the two groups were to get together. One may presume that the basic inventions of antiquity were also made by humble people who wanted to save work by improving their tools. Certainly men like Plato and Aristotle paid little attention to what went on in the bazaars and shops of Athens. Even the inventions of the Hellenistic Greeks were largely wasted, except for a few obviously useful ones like the screw and the toothed wheel, and they did not, for reasons already mentioned, bring about an industrial revolution in antiquity. The stage had to be set for the adoption of new devices, and the trade of the Gunpowder Age had set it.

New Sources of Energy

AFTER 1800 the inventions and discoveries that Englishmen, continental Europeans, and Americans not only made but put to practical use ran into the hundreds of thousands. Except in the broadest outline, it is neither necessary nor useful to mention them here. As these inventions all depended on the utilization of energy, we are more concerned with a review of the principal sources of power used by man. Before the Coke Age these were wood, which had been burned since second-interglacial time; fodder for domestic animals, which dated from the Neolithic; the use of the wind for sailing since the Late Neolithic; charcoal since the Early Bronze Age; water power for milling and pumping, used since the medieval Iron Age; lighting by whale oil, which started commercially around the tenth century; and house-heating by coal, which had begun to assume economic importance in the fourteenth century.

After 1753 no new power source of economic importance besides coal, coke, and coal gas appeared until 1857, when Colonel Drake drilled his first oil well in western Pennsylvania. His product, however, was used first as a substitute for whale oil in lamp-lighting, and the volatile by-products such as gasoline were thrown away. In 1883 water power came to the fore again when the citizens of Appleton, Wisconsin, harnessed a local stream to generate electricity. In 1886 gasoline was sold as a fuel for horse-less carriages, and in 1898 the Curies discovered the energy-giving properties of radium. In 1926 water power passed into still another cycle when the waters of whole continental river valleys,

COLONEL DRAKE'S OIL WELL.

flooded behind dams, began to produce hydroelectric power in massive wattages. The Tennessee Valley Authority, the Hoover Dam, and the Grand Coulee followed one another in rapid succession, making possible the cheap production of aluminum and the refinement of atomic materials.

Electricity and Atomic Energy

A SUBJECT that long intrigued men of science, including Benjamin Franklin, was electricity, which is not a source of energy but a physico-chemical means of transferring it. As early as 1745 electricity was produced through the chemical decomposition of zinc in an acid bath. During the next century many improvements were made in these batteries, but chemically manufactured electricity remained too expensive for most industries. It was worth using only for communication, and then only for such high-priority devices as the telegraph and the newsprint press in which speed was at a premium.

As long as electricity could be derived only from batteries and as long as batteries depended on chemical action alone for their power, steam was the only practical source of propulsion which could be used anywhere and with both moving and stationary machines. The invention of the electric generator, about 1870, broke this bottleneck. A generator could be hitched to a steam engine, a steam turbine, or a water turbine, and could thus produce enormous quantities of electrical power. Sixteen years later the invention of the transformer made it possible to send power over long distances, and in that year the waters of Niagara Falls were harnessed and the city of Buffalo was electrified. Two years after that, the invention of the modern grid battery completed a cycle. Steam or water power from dynamos was converted in transformers in such a fashion that batteries could be charged. As far as ignition was concerned, the automobile was now feasible.

The sequence of inventions which led to the use of atomic energy began in 1895 when W. K. Röntgen found that a current passed through a vacuum tube renders near-by phosphorescent substances luminous. The principal early use of this discovery was to take X-ray pictures for medical purposes. Within three years the Curies had found that radium emits rays without electrical stimulation, and they isolated alpha, beta, and gamma rays. In 1904 Albert Einstein published his theory on the relationship between matter and energy, after which many brilliant men concerned themselves with atomic physics. In 1939 one of them, Reinhold Rüdenberg, in a race against Vladimir Zworykin, perfected the electronic microscope after fifteen years of effort, and his device greatly aided other physicists in their study of the structure of atoms. In 1945 plutonium, a heavy metal comparable to radium, was exploded over two Japanese cities. In 1952 a hydrogen bomb was detonated over a Pacific atoll, and in 1957 commercial electricity was first produced in a nuclear plant.

This rapid record of power-utilization implies more than a great increase in the world's consumption of energy. It involves three new fuels—oil, radioactive metals, and hydrogen—and three of the five known ways of converting fuel or gravity into energy. Only simple oxidation (fire) and rapid oxidation in an enclosed chamber (gunpowder) had been known before. The record also involves the participation of men of science rather than the lonely labors of artisans. The production of gunpowder was the result of the work of a man of science, Roger Bacon. All of the other basic techniques of producing energy which followed gunpowder were also the fruits of pure scientific inquiry. Only fire-making can have been discovered without the benefit of scientific specialization and abstraction.

The question now arises: why did artisans make the basic mechanical inventions while scientists discovered sources of energy? The answer to the first half of the question is that an artisan who uses a set of tools day after day has a natural interest in reducing waste effort, particularly if he is an independent workman and can earn more money by increasing production, or hopes to sell his patent to a manufacturer. He does not discover new sources of energy because his work proceeds step by step. The scientist discovers them because he is motivated by free imagination and curiosity and is interested in general problems concerning the order of the universe. It disturbs him to be unable to explain something that seems capable of discovery. Both the profit motive of the artisan and the stimulation of free inquiry among scientists are possible only in free societies like those through which the main line of human civilization has always moved.

Transportation Breaks the Sonic Barrier

B y 1700 the English, most of the western Europeans, and the British colonists in America were dependent on the sailing ship for transport by sea, and on the horse for travel by land. With the rise of heavy industry and the consequent increase in production of many kinds of consumer goods, the need for transport increased greatly. The days of sail were, however, far from over. The new manufacturing techniques made it possible to build more and larger ships and to improve the rigging, as well as to advance the art of navigation. A comparable thing happened with the horse. More and better steel meant good springs and comfortable carriages, coaching services, farmer's buggies, and the Conestoga wagons that pioneers drove over the transcontinental trails to California and Oregon.

After stationary steam engines had been perfected to the point where they could provide cheap and efficient power for industry, it took some time to make them light and efficient enough to drive ships and land vehicles. The first successful steamships were really sailing vessels with auxiliary engines, and the first railroad trains small and slow-moving. Many decades had to pass before they could replace the sailing ship and the horse-drawn coach. The history of the development of these revolutionary inventions is one of gradual growth through trial and error.

Automobiles also got off to a slow start. It was not until Henry Ford had standardized parts and devised the assembly line in order to mass-produce automobiles that individual powered vehicles became common. Similarly, though the Wright Brothers had flown in 1903, it was not until after the mass production of aluminum by means of cheap electric power, starting in 1926, that airplanes became a prime carrier of persons and of high-priority mail and goods.

Vehicles are but one aspect of transportation. Ships must have docks, and planes need landing fields as much as trains need tracks. In the 1780's, when the metal industry had grown rapidly in England, and before the rise of railroading, it was clear that road transport was not enough to carry the increasing loads of goods to and from the smelteries and forging plants, and between the processing mills and the seaports. Seaports had been located upstream not only for reasons of security, but also to be near the medieval cities. With bigger ships, deep-water ports were needed, most of which, being on the coast, would also shorten the sailing time. For all of these reasons the English broke out in a rash of canal-digging, until by 1800 the countryside was covered with liquid highways. Americans followed suit.

Owing to the competition of the railroads, shallow inland canals ceased to be dug by the middle of the last century, but deep canals connecting major bodies of salt water appeared. The Suez and Panama canals have repaid their excavation costs many times over in ship fees, and both have served Britain and America as priceless lifelines of defense, impregnable before the invention of the long-range bomber. The excavation problems of these canals stimulated the invention of earth-moving machinery, to which has been adapted the caterpillar system of propulsion used in tanks in the First World War.

By means of earth-moving machinery our engineers have been able to produce another device for moving quantities of prime materials. That is the pipeline, such as the Big and Little Inch. In the United States alone there were, early in 1953, 168,000 miles of oil pipeline through which crude oil flowed at a cost of one cent per gallon per thousand miles. The cheapness of this means of transportation keeps us on the roads. In foreign countries these pipelines create international problems. The giant Tapline, for example, through which oil is pumped eleven hundred miles from the Persian Gulf to the Mediterranean, passes through the territories of four sovereign nations, Saudi Arabia, Jordan, Syria, and Lebanon. The maintenance of such a pipeline requires the exercise of much diplomacy. This example serves to illustrate how modern technology has made the nations of the world interdependent.

Communication Nears the Speed of Light

L o n g before the beginning of the age of coke, people had devised systems of sending messages from one place to another. Even in illiterate countries like Homeric Greece, heralds carrying special insignia walked from kingdom to kingdom to bear tidings and to bring back answers. The Australian aborigines, who are Stone Age hunters, sent out similar messengers. However, the earliest formal system of organized postal service was that of the Persian emperors; from their time on, many nations have set up their own internal postal systems. At first these were for government use only, but eventually, as literacy spread and private institutions increased, they came to be public.

In 1784 the British instituted a system of special mail coaches, driven at high speed with a frequent change of post horses, and ridden by armed guards ready to repel highwaymen. Only the new roads, paved with crushed stone after the invention of macadam and the new coaches slung in springs forged by the new mass-production methods of steel-fabrication made this possible. Speedy communication between factories and London, and from both to the seaport, where the mail was put aboard packets, permitted speed-ups in manufacturing.

In 1840 the British postal service introduced the gummed postage stamp, and set its rate within the empire at one penny, whereas the lowest letter rate inside the kingdom previously had been a shilling. It is possible that this reduction was made to anticipate competition from a new system of communication. Four years later, Samuel Morse sent his famous quotation from Numbers xxiii, 23, from Washington to Baltimore. A year before the postal rate tumbled, Charles Goodyear vulcanized his first rubber, and in 1847 gutta percha came on the market. Telegraph wires could now be insulated. Battery-run telegraph systems were soon set up in all countries that participated in Coke Age civilization, and in 1866 a transatlantic cable began carrying messages between the United States and England, reducing the minimum message time from two weeks to a few minutes. In 1876 Alexander Graham Bell spoke his first message over the telephone, and within six years long-distance service was begun between Boston and New York. What has happened since is common knowledge.

While the telegraph-telephone sequence was dependent on the production of insulated wire, the techniques of wireless communication depended on the discovery of a new principle, the transmission of low-powered electrical impulses through the air by Hertzian waves. The existence of these waves was discovered by a scientist, Hertz, in 1887. By 1895 Marconi had adapted their use to the telegraph, and dot-dash stations soon became standard equipment on ocean-going vessels. Speech was not successfully transmitted by radio, however, until 1915, when De Forest perfected the radio tube after a decade of work. In 1919 radio was first used for ground-to-plane communication in airplanes, too late for World War I, but in time for the commercial aviation of the twenties and thirties and for World War II. In 1920 the first radio station in the world to produce scheduled broadcasts opened in Pittsburgh, and the news, propaganda, and entertainment that have been emitted from this and other stations have affected nearly every institution in the world.

Television began as a by-product of atomic research. Vladimir Zworykin, the inventor of the electron microscope, invented the electronic camera tube in 1923. By 1941 this and the other electronic devices used in television had been so improved that public broadcasts were initiated, and in 1954 over fifty million persons watch a single performance.

Much time and effort are saved by another set of inventions dependent on new methods of communication. Mechanical and electric typewriters, dictaphones, tape and wire recorders, microfilm cameras, photostat cameras, calculators, eighty-column punch-card cutters, tabulating and sorting machines, and electronic brains relieve not only man's muscles but the fatigue of his brain. These devices permit weekly magazines with more than one million subscribers each to keep track of their customers, and the government to issue millions of Treasury checks at a time. Our complicated civilization could not be held together without these machines.

It would be difficult to overestimate the importance of communication in the building of civilization. A superior power of speech separated man from his simian cousins and let him teach his children ancient ways. Speech made culture possible. With each new invention in the field of communication—writing, the alphabet, the printing press, the telegraph, the typewriter, the radio, and television—the range of a single man's voice was widened until it has come to echo around the world. As institutions grow outward to the limits of this range, so we have come to the threshold of the fourth phase of history and man's greatest adventure.

The Second Conquest of Climate

I N fourth-glacial times a number of human beings left their ancestral homes in the warm regions of the Old World to conquer the cold. They did this with fire, burins, and needles. In the ages from Coke to Atoms other human beings who had become adapted to cool climates found ways to live in health and comfort in all the regions of the earth. Instead of burins and needles they used a number of new inventions dependent on the new sources of energy which they had discovered. Among them, of course, were the medical advances, from Pasteur to penicillin, which have made it possible for millions of lives to be saved and millions of others prolonged, and for white men prone to the diseases of unfamiliar parts of the world to travel in impunity nearly everywhere. Among them were also processes of preserving food indefinitely, including canning and freezing, and methods of cooling entire houses and communities by air-conditioning. Now a whole city of delicate Americans stands on the hot and humid shore of the Persian Gulf, at Dhahran, and the ecological rules of Bergmann and Allen are defied by the products of the ingenuity of Messrs. Fluor and Birdseye.

Science Is International

W H I L E computing machines, electronic brains, and air-conditioning equipment are primarily American devices, the technical advances that men have made during the last two and a half centuries are not the product of any one country and it is fatuous for a single nation to claim them. In the Gunpowder Age, Arabs,

Jews, Italians, and Englishmen served Portugal and Spain in the advancement of navigation. In modern science Japanese have been outstanding in medicine and ichthyology, Chinese in mathematics; George Washington Carver, the great economic botanist, was an American Negro. The atomic physicists employed on the Manhattan project came from many countries. Anthropologists everywhere find some means to communicate with one another. Modern science is as international as Prince Henry's navigation because creative imagination and scientific curiosity belong not to nations or races but to humanity. However, the institutional climate of all nations is not equally receptive to new ideas. In some countries today as in the past the seeds of science fall on stony ground, and the institutional changes that technical inventions bring to different countries follow separate patterns.

Institutions Mushroom and Approach a Climax

T H E N E W devices invented during the last two and a half centuries have affected the entire world. One reason is global communication. Another is that the materials needed for manufacturing had to come from everywhere. The new work processes, by their very nature, required the participation of increasing numbers of people. The use of these devices and their products also required more and more space. For example, Niagara Falls could not have been harnessed without the mutual agreement of the United States and Canada. The Tapline could not have been run from the Persian Gulf to the Mediterranean without the mutual agreement of five countries, including the United States. On a more local scale, harvester combines work beautifully on the vast unfenced plains of the Dakotas, but they are of little use in the much richer wheat country of the English fens, which is broken up by nature and by man into small pieces.

In the Age of Gunpowder, European trade with Asia and the Americas produced the chartered company, with hundreds of stockholders, in England and the Netherlands. In the Age of Coke, the steel and textile industries produced still another new kind of institution, the incorporated manufacturing company, not only in England and the Netherlands, but also in many other countries, particularly Germany, Sweden, and the United States. These were predominantly Protestant nations in which the middle class, descended from the free farmers and independent guild craftsmen of a preceding age, formed the decisive element in the population.

A manufacturing company has to supply its workmen with raw materials and with power, and to sell its finished product. Thus, three departments are needed wholly apart from processing—purchasing, engineering, and sales. In processing the raw materials, several steps are always necessary, and each step requires a special category of workmen, organized into a separate department. Few of these workmen have to be as highly skilled as the craftsmen of preceding ages, for most of the precision work is done by machines. Hence no lengthy period of apprenticeship is needed. Because the machines furnish most of the energy used, the workmen do not have to be especially muscular, and women and children can perform many of the operations as well as men.

A handcraftsman does his work without outside help. He can lay it down and pick it up as he pleases. When he is tired he can rest; when hungry, he can go out for a meal. In a factory, the machines keep humming continuously, and it is costly of fuel to shut off individual looms or spinning frames while a workman goes out for a snack. If a thread breaks, the loose ends must be knotted immediately. Hence vigilance and endurance are needed in a workman, as well as quick, nimble fingers in an emergency. General education is unnecessary.

For every dozen or so workers, one foreman must be specially trained. He must be able to walk about on his section of the floor, observing everyone, patting a back here and delivering a sharp word there, keeping everyone, if not happy, at least busy. During the early days of machine industry a good workman, if he studied nights and had an outgiving personality, might rise to be a foreman, and from there on he might get to be supervisor of a department. If he was charming as well as efficient, he might hope to marry the mill-owner's homely daughter, just as a Homeric hero married the daughter of the king and eventually took the scepter into his own hands. Thus he would become a social climber, the object of the combined envy and scorn of the more anciently established gentry. In office hours he would have to be able to coordinate the activities of all the different departments, listen to complaints, and hire and fire with a combination of ruthlessness and good judgment. Business now needed executives as competent as kings and generals at handling people.

The workman who rose in this fashion was as rare as the private who becomes a field marshal. Around the mill centers in England grew up enormous populations of underprivileged human beings, underfed, uneducated, as limited in their circle of acquaintances as many lower primates, and as circumscribed in their actions as domestic animals. No science of human relations had yet arisen to complement the rapid advances in physics, chemistry, and mechanics. Few capitalists anticipated the reaction of their employees to this inhuman regimentation. Epidemics fostered by overcrowding, insanitary housing, and long hours were one result, strikes another. Workmen, under the leadership of bright but underprivileged men, organized themselves into unions.

Here was another new kind of institution, a mammoth association that included persons doing the same kind of job no matter what factory each member might work for. These unions even became international. Despite much noise and many broken heads, the management of industry was unable to put down the unions, and eventually came to recognize their worth, particularly in America, for a special reason. In England and in other countries of western Europe, manufactures were primarily for export. In order to keep prices down, wages had to be kept low. In America, as the people of our nation expanded westward, a great domestic market arose, including among the purchasers the very people who worked in the factories. A high standard of living meant increased sales and increased profits. In European countries, where the land surfaces are small and the population had been dense for centuries before the industrial boom, the birth rate rose to meet the new need, and labor was never scarce. In America, where the land had been practically empty despite a high birth rate, labor was at a premium. That is why whole communities were moved from Sicily to Massachusetts, from the Abruzzi to Pennsylvania, from Finland to Minnesota, and from Germany to Wisconsin. With labor at a premium and buying its own products, wages could be kept at a high level.

In England, northwestern Europe, and America, many services that are really public utilities came under private management, as well as foundries and factories. Railroad lines, gas companies, steamship lines, electric light plants, and even telegraph companies were privately owned. After the construction of electric power installations on a scale large enough to provide light for entire cities, which began in 1879, the specter of monopoly arose, which brings us to the threshold of the Age of Oil. In the memories of many Americans, and in the propaganda lore of the Russians, the rise of the oil industry is closely associated with the name of John D. Rockefeller, complete with his square derby and his pocketful of dimes.

The name of Rockefeller also means *corporation,* the new kind of industry which came into being with the dawn of the Age of Oil. As everyone knows, Rockefeller undersold his competitors and bought them out, one by one, until he controlled an entire basic industry with not only national but also world-wide implications. In this he was not alone. Other names such as Carnegie, Frick, Du Pont, and Armour have the same significance. In Europe the I. G. Farbenindustrie was gradually securing a world-wide monopoly in the aniline dye trade, and the Swedish Match Trust was buying monopolies from such countries as Ethiopia and Albania. In 1929 the Albanian mountaineers, who could not afford to pay five cents for a penny box of safety matches, had reverted to the outlawed method of flint and steel when they could find such devices, and were otherwise borrowing live coals from one another's fires, like the pygmies of the Andaman Islands.

Most of the men who made huge fortunes out of monopolies have left their money in trust to finance foundations devoted to public welfare. However, even this noble deed is not credited them by their foes, the Communists. In 1932 I gave a speech at a learned society in Leningrad on the progress of anthropology in

America. During the question period one Russian scientist asked me: "What good does it do to work on funds from the Rockefeller Foundation? Mr. Rockefeller will read every page and cut out every sentence that contradicts his capitalist ideology." I could not for the life of me persuade that man, or others at the meeting,

A HYDROELECTRIC DAM.

that Mr. Rockefeller really did not care what I said in my report, let alone read it.

The corporations that arose during the Oil Age had to extend their activities beyond national boundaries, not only for markets, but also for raw materials. The distribution of oil beneath the earth's surface does not follow lines of political expedience. The search for oil led Americans to Mexico and Venezuela, and the British to Iran. When the next age began in 1926 with the harnessing of hydroelectric power for the mass production of aluminum, we had plenty of bauxite in the southern Appalachians near

the sources of power. Our corporations concentrated on aluminum while the Germans specialized in magnesium, an even lighter
metal.

The Hydroelectric Age permitted the mass production of airplanes, and with airplanes world travel became commonplace. But
in the meanwhile economic institutions had developed as far as
they could go without taking over the privileges and responsibili-
ties of government. So close had they come to this that governments, in America and elsewhere, had passed anti-trust laws to
break up monopolies, to preserve free competition, and to prevent great companies from suppressing new inventions that might
necessitate expensive retooling.

The immediate result of the industrial growth of England and
the Netherlands in the early nineteenth century was the replacement of trading companies by political power in India and Indonesia. No longer could rival rajahs make war on each other or
prevent the laying of railroad tracks across their territories. With
good transportation, raw materials could be carried to the seaports, and British cutlery and cotton could be moved to the inland
cities, and thence to the villages. After their revolution and the
rise of Napoleon, the French took Algeria and began the expansion of their African empire. The British, Germans, Italians, and
Belgians carved up those portions of the Dark Continent which
the Portuguese and Spaniards could be made to relinquish. The
Germans, who had come into the theater of world trade late in
the game, and who had the most abundant natural resources of
Europe at their command, drew but a small share of Africa, and
none of Asia. Their only consolation was a piece of New Guinea,
the Bismarck archipelago, and the tiny islets of Micronesia, poor
pickings indeed when compared to India or Java or the Philippines. Their only visible outlet was to the east, into the underde-
veloped Slavic countries, and into the vacuum created by the
withdrawal of the Turkish empire. An ethnic map of Europe
drawn before World War II will show little islands of German
settlement inhabited by pipe-smoking, German-speaking farmers
and traders unassimilated by the Magyars, Rumanians, and Slavs
around them. These pioneers had been pushing eastward as an

advance guard since the eighteenth century. Linked together, they might form a fabric of empire.

The resistance of the eastern Europeans to this pressure, and Germany's lack of world trade outlets by sea, touched off the First World War. Shortly afterward, under the leadership of Woodrow Wilson, but without the support of his own government, the first international political alliance was formed, the League of Nations, itself the premature prototype of a world political institution and too weak to keep the Germans from calling another round. In the Second World War, air power began to overcome sea power. This meant that the country which could produce the most aluminum, all else equal, would win. Only two countries qualified, America and Germany. Planes require oil as well as metal, and here America held the unquestioned lead, particularly after the opening of the Arabian oil fields, and the Allies won.

In 1945 representatives of most of the nations of the world met in San Francisco to form the United Nations, a little stronger than the League of Nations, but still hampered by the retention of the veto power by Russia, and emasculated by the bickering of some inexperienced representatives of newly liberated nations, as well as by the machinations of older ones. With the collapse of the older empires, a certain amount of disorder has arisen in some of the former colonies and dominions. Without the British and Dutch to curse and to obey, it is hard for former colonial peoples to rid the roads of bandits, to keep the trains running, and to prevent political assassinations. What is even worse from the anthropologist's point of view, the marginal primitives, the People of the Leaves, the head-hunters in the jungle, are no longer prize exhibits, but troublesome poor relations to be hidden or forcibly changed. A drab uniformity is creeping over the face of the world.

By 1900 the European nations, led by England, had reached their peak. The world consisted of a group of empires, each of which had its nucleus in a small piece of the landscape of western Europe bordering on the sea, and its body in much larger pieces of the other continents and archipelagos of the world. Gradually, however, secondary nuclei were forming in the larger pieces. As Sikhs and Parsees and Brahmins and Ceylonese and Gold Coast natives went to Oxford and Cambridge in increasing numbers, larger and larger groups of Western-trained men could get together in Bombay and Calcutta and Colombo and Accra. In these centers, as in others, they built universities and shops of their own and trained their fellow countrymen on the spot. Steel mills arose, and electric power plants. Locomotives and generators could be built in Japan from Asiatic materials. As the nuclei grew, cell-division started. Just as the Roman empire broke up, so the British empire, and that of the Dutch, followed suit for the same reason.

The Rise of America

M E A N W H I L E , America rose quietly and inconspicuously to the threshold of her present position of world leadership. As pioneers migrated westward to settle the plains, the mountains, and the lands of the Pacific coast, the American Indians decreased in number. Like all open-country peoples who have never been exposed to city life, they could not cope with the diseases brought them by the descendants of the survivors of the Black Plague. Pioneers whose ancestors had lived in the filth of London and Paris and Marseille and the Rhineland cities for generations gave the Indians smallpox and tuberculosis, which cleared the land more effectively than rifles. In advance of the white man's frontier, the white man's weapons gave the Indians the means to decimate one another as the westward-moving pressure forced them into one another's hunting grounds.

Geographically the territory of the United States is ideally suited to the rise of a great nation. The broad Mississippi Valley sweeps from north to south without interruption, providing a vast, rich core. In it lay the possibility of agricultural wealth beyond measure, and the world's greatest supplies of coking coal, along with ample stocks of iron and copper ore, all located along natural inland waterways. It is second only to Africa in potential water-power, and its rivers run the year round, ensuring electrical current at all seasons. The eastern seaboard, with many harbors, was ideal for shipping and for manufacturing. The western seaboard contained the world's largest strip of mediterranean climate within any one country, capable of producing citrus fruits and other garden products in great quantity, while its northern half contained probably the world's finest stand of giant timber to survive into modern times.

Scarcity of labor made the use of labor-saving gadgets essential. The long distances stimulated the settler to repair his own tools and prevented him from settling down in a niche. Overspecialization was not profitable. With its principal market internal, American industry could afford to develop a high standard of living, and with automatic machinery ever on the increase, the need for long, tiring hours was reduced. No longer was it necessary for children to work in factories. It was much better for them to go to school. Small colleges arose as new states came into the union, and large state universities were soon established. Americans are the most educated people on earth today in terms of literacy and the average number of years in school and college. A larger percentage of Americans has college degrees than citizens of any other nation.

No country in the world has ever given rise to as many associations. The various fraternal orders, such as the Masons and Elks, charitable foundations like homes for crippled children, the Red Cross, and the Community Chest, parent-teacher associations, literally thousands of them, tie nearly every American into a mesh that holds our social system together far less painfully than any political fabric ever could. Some of them are local, others national, still others international, and even world-wide, like the International Red Cross and the Boy Scouts. They tie us together and they tie us to the rest of the world.

Another factor that gives us international feeling is our actual kinship with peoples of other countries. Many Americans have relatives in Ireland, in Portugal, in Germany, in Italy, in Lebanon, and elsewhere. It is impossible for us as a nation to become officially angry at another nation without hurting the feelings of some of us, and in disputes between other nations some of us are always emotionally linked to both sides. This is both a liability and an asset. In the period of world leadership into which America has been unwillingly launched, it should be used as the latter.

Twenty years ago the average American household consisted of a father and mother and three children, with one maid who slept in the attic and worked in the kitchen. Often a hired man mowed the lawn and tended the furnace. Market men delivered food at the back door, to which the milkman and iceman also brought their wares, while the paper boy left his daily burden at the front door. Now the family is the same, but the maid is gone and there is no attic. The choreman has also disappeared, along with the iceman, while the paper boy's successor flings the *Daily Sentinel* into the mud of the driveway from a swiftly moving automobile. Mother cooks the evening meal on an electric stove, thawing a brick of frozen peas in a few minutes and softening the asparagus in a pressure cooker in a matter of seconds. After dinner an electric dishwasher reduces kitchen work to less than half an hour, and daughter goes out to baby-sit for a neighbor while father settles down to watch the wrestling on television after he has mowed the lawn with a gasoline-motored machine.

What has this done to the American family? Mother goes out to her clubs and garden talks during the day while father is working. They spend the evening together as before. Daughter goes to college and gets a degree. When she has married she can work for a while to help put her husband through graduate school, and after the baby has arrived she is in a better position to teach her offspring useful knowledge than her grandmother was. The disappearance of servants has given the family greater privacy and intimacy. The appearance of gadgets has given women a chance to be more efficient mothers. The biological family has not suffered. On the other hand, modern living splits up brother from brother, father from son, so that the extended family has decreased in importance. This permits greater social mobility for the individual, who is no longer tied down to the level of his parents or siblings. Greater social mobility means greater efficiency of manpower.

Americans have achieved all this because we have been able to develop our natural resources, and hence our culture, in a degree of isolation. Unlike the European nations, we have not been tied to overseas lands by the need for trade. When we have taken over colonial possessions, as we did in the case of the Philippines, we have let them go voluntarily, partly because we did not want them to compete with our own sub-tropical regions in the production of duty-free materials. Now the tide has turned, and we have become an importer of basic materials such as oil and ore, and particularly of uranium and the rare metals needed for hardening steel.

Being not only an importer, but also the world's greatest power, the leader of that half of the world which has moved continuously in the main line of cultural progress, we have as our principal concern at the moment to find some way to stop what is going on in the other half. Before the Age of Gunpowder had dawned, empires could arise in different portions of the world without one even knowing of the other's existence. After that they could co-exist, though from time to time they lined up in paired sides to wage war. Now they cannot. The earth is too small for the co-existence of rival systems, particularly when the main purpose of one of them is to conquer the world. Quite patently our first task is to understand Russia, and that is what several research institutes throughout the country are amply paid to do. This is not easy, for since the opening of Japan no modern nation has shown such a disinclination toward being understood. However, we know certain basic facts, which, while self-evident, are often overlooked in favor of psychological theories and other easy cure-alls, which change from year to year, while the facts remain.

The Social Structure of the U.S.S.R.

W H I L E the territory of the U.S.S.R., including the Baltic lands annexed during the Second World War, covers eight and one half million square miles, or one sixth of the land surface of the world, excepting Antarctica, and is as large as the entire continent of South America, it possesses a very inequable distribution of kinds of climate. Ten per cent of it is in tundra, the squashy arctic swampland that we call muskeg in Alaska and Canada. This land is good only for testing atom bombs. Thirty-five per cent is in boreal forests, high-latitude land covered with spruce and larch, too cold for agriculture, and good only for lumbering, trapping, reindeer-herding, and mining. Only eight per cent, located mostly in the country between Leningrad and Moscow and in the recently acquired Baltic states, is mid-latitude forest, comparable to the landscape of most of Germany, France, and England, the kind of landscape on which industrial civilization grew up in western Europe and America. Forty-two per cent of the United States is mid-latitude forest land, both relatively and absolutely a greater area. For modern Machine Age nations, this is the best kind of land in the world.

Thirty per cent of the U.S.S.R. is grasslands, prairie or steppe; in America the percentage is twenty-three. This is grain-producing country, where many new industries are located. While California gives us five per cent of mediterranean land, Russia has less than one per cent, on the southern shore of the Crimea, centered on Yalta. Our two per cent of sub-tropics, in Florida, is unmatched; the Russians have none. They have ten per cent of mountains to our eight. Both countries are rich in minerals. However, when we consider agricultural products, and lands suited for industry, Russia comes out with the short end of the stick. What it needs to produce a well-rounded living space comparable to ours is more mid-latitude forest terrain, and more mediterranean and tropical regions not separated from the homeland by sea, as in the case of the British colonies, but hitched to it by a continuous land area.

In taking over Czechoslovakia, Hungary, eastern Germany, and Poland, the Russians have acquired the mid-latitude lands that they needed. The Caspian shore of Iran would give them a splendid piece of mediterranean climate, already growing citrus fruits, tea, tobacco, and mulberry leaves for the local silk industry. It would also give them more oil and control of the caviar that they dearly love. Expansion into North Vietnam and Laos by way of China is giving them access to tropical regions rich in oil, rubber, and tin. If they succeed in absorbing these lands, they will have duplicated in its essential boundaries the empire of Genghis Khan.

The Soviet Union is a true empire because it contains many different kinds of people. Of its two hundred and ten million inhabitants less than half are Great Russians. About fourteen per cent are Ukrainians and three per cent Byelorussians (White Russians). These two peoples speak their own Slavic languages and take pride in their own historic traditions. In the Ural Mountain country, where the new Russian industry has been built, six and a half million Tatars and native Finns make up a sizable minority in country that was exclusively their own a few decades back. The Georgians and Azerbaijani Turks each number about three million, the Uzbegs and Kazaks six million apiece, and one and a half million each is the total for the Armenians, Turkomans, Kirghiz, and Tajiks.

It must be remembered that each of these ethnic groups lives in its own country, which it has inhabited since time immemorial, that about twenty-three million of them are Muslims who do not like godlessness, and that at least sixteen millions are Turks, people with powerful kin over the mountains. When Americans moved westward, all kinds of people went to each region. Germans farmed, Jews built trading posts, English remittance men opened ranches, and Basques herded sheep, but none of these occupations was exclusive and all of the peoples were mixed together. All became and remain Americans. When the Russians moved eastward, they found little to stop them in the narrow belt of arable land between forests to the north and deserts to the south, but in Turkestan and the central Asiatic plains they encountered civilized people who occupied the land intensively, with irrigation ditches and large urban centers based on trade and hand manufactures. These peoples could not be made Russians by simple decree.

In the days of the czars, the old imperial policy of every real empire from Persian time onward was followed. Each subject people was allowed to live its own life as long as its members kept the peace and paid taxes. In the early days of the Soviet regime, the government set up institutes to encourage the local peoples of the union to take pride in their ancient civilizations, and newspapers were soon printed in dozens of outlandish languages in

phonetic alphabets devised for the occasion. In the Institute for
Northern Peoples at Leningrad, which I visited in 1932, dozens
of primers had been printed in Chukchi, Tungus, and many other
languages, showing reindeer-hunters how to brush their teeth
and praise Stalin.

A few years later the policy changed. It must have been realized
that these tribes and nations were not becoming good soviets as
rapidly as had been hoped, and an effort was made to obliterate
the native cultures where they conflicted with the Communist
ideal. Russians were then settled in numbers in critical areas, particularly along the borders of Iran and Afghanistan. After the Germans had withdrawn from the Caucasus in World War II, several
whole nations were killed off or deported, including the Volga
Germans, the Chechen and Ingush in the Caucasus, the Cri-
mean Tatars, and the Kalmucks.

The reason for this change of policy was, of course, a desire
for unity in the face of a supposedly hostile outer world, the
same desire that had led to the expulsion of the so-called *bourgeoisie* during the Bolshevik revolution. Under the efforts of
Peter the Great and other czars, tens of thousands of Germans,
Frenchmen, Englishmen, Hungarians, and other western Europeans had been attracted to the cities of Russia to set up busi-
nesses and factories, to build up the very middle-class enterprises that had been so successful in their native lands. As a
group these people had never become completely assimilated.
Nearly every Russian *émigré* who left his country at the time of
the Revolution will tell you that he is part Swedish, part Scotch,
part French, and so on; hardly one is a full Russian. Although
he thought himself Russian, the workmen and students who
started the revolt considered him an alien. Getting rid of the
bourgeoisie, a Marxist idea originally aimed at a class within a
population, was converted into a concept of xenophobia needed
for unity.

The same urge led to the adoption of godlessness. The dozens
and dozens of separate peoples, each living within the framework
of its own set of customs, language, folklore, and religion, had to
be convinced of the validity of Communism. The Russians were

not strong enough to hold them all by force, at least in the beginning. Hence they tried to make the new regime attractive to them
by giving them their own alphabets and newspapers, and encouraged them to foster national sports, arts, and costumes. But
the serious obstacle toward unity was not a question of goatskin
bagpipes versus violins, or skirts versus trousers, or even brimmed
hats versus fezzes and turbans, as Mustapha Kemal and Riza
Shah had thought in Turkey and Iran, but religion. Something had
to be done to level off religious differences between the peoples,
for religions not only divided them but also tied them to powers
outside the fence.

In a period of rapid technical and scientific change, religion
is particularly vulnerable, for the language of religion is archaic
and its symbols are rendered invalid, in a superficial and immediate sense, by modern discoveries. If the world is round, where
is heaven located? The time at which peoples living on various
levels of primitive and medieval culture begin to wake up to the
novelties of electric lights and radios and automobiles is just the
time when religious belief is at its shakiest, when it can be dealt
a solid blow, before it has had a chance to recover, as it now has
recovered in America. Hence the great anthropologist Bogoras,
who once conducted an expedition to the Chukchi of the Bering
Strait country for the American Museum of Natural History, set
up a Godless Museum in Moscow in which he arranged a collection of idols and religious paintings of all the peoples of the union
in such a way as to make them look ridiculous.

Something solid and unified in the way of a set of symbols had
to be slipped into the void thus created to replace the discredited
systems. This was obviously the worship of the state, and, as time
went on, the deification of Stalin, whose smiling face, with the
pockmarks retouched, could be seen on every wall, and was carried on a banner forty feet high in every important parade. This
was something everyone could believe in, something that would
hold them all together no matter how tyrannically they were
ruled, or to what depths their standard of living might recede.

However, a church state, which is what the Communists thus
created in the Soviet Union, can exist only in isolation. We have

seen this in the cases of Egypt and Incaic Peru, and it was equally true in Tibet and the Yemen. Egypt was blocked from outside penetration by deserts and a swampy delta; Peru, Tibet, and the Yemen by altitude. In each case the kingdom or empire collapsed once the barrier was penetrated by others: Egypt by the Hyksos, Assyrians, Persians, and Greeks; Tibet by the Chinese Communists, who crossed swampy land on the ice; and the Yemen by the Turks. As the U.S.S.R. is not isolated by geography, this condition had to be imposed by the lowering of a man-made curtain.

It was in isolation of a sort that America grew great, but we were never cut off from communication with the outside world. Our immigrants received letters from their old-country relatives, to whom some of them sent remittances. We considered ourselves fortunate people, and our government had no reason to prevent contact. Any American who did not like it here was free to go back to Europe, as some did. On the other hand, Russia's passion for isolation has handicapped its attempt at growing great because from the start it lacked trained personnel; it lacked unity; and the village pattern of community life which dates from the Neolithic persisted. While we set up huge mechanized farms, with private capital, on empty prairies, the Russians tried to achieve the same result by forcing peasants out of their villages into collectives.

Notable in Russian life is the feeble development of any institution besides the state. In comparison to our myriad of voluntarily organized clubs and associations, one finds but few organizations, and those all of government inspiration. Not only did the soviets attack the church; they soon decided to strike a mortal blow at the family by sending children to state nurseries while their mothers worked, by making divorce automatic and abortions free, and by crowding people so that they had no privacy. This did not work, but owing to the housing shortage, the lack of privacy remains. As a keen observer said: [2] "Communism seems to make people more selfish and self-centered. Individuals spend so much of their day working for the all-powerful and ever-demanding state, and for the 'good of all,' that in their private lives,

[2] Rounds, Frank, Jr., *A Window on Red Square*, Boston, Houghton Mifflin, 1953, pp. 118–19. By permission.

in their free time, in their precious off hours, they quite naturally exist only for themselves and deliberately ignore everybody else, following old animal instincts."

Materialism being the Communist ideal, it is no wonder that Russian soldiers in Europe desert when they have learned to use western plumbing. But ever since the discovery that all men must die, made somewhere in the distant reaches of our ancestors' history as hunters, materialism has been inadequate to set the human mind at rest. Materialism is the product of bad science, just as bigotry is the product of bad theology. Even Communists need a more effective spiritual palliative than the overblown picture of a living man's features, or a marble tomb on Red Square.

The Perilous Dawn of the Fourth Phase of History

ALTHOUGH it is hard for us to realize it, we are already groping our way forward in the dim light of the dawn of phase four of history. We know that dawn has broken because the trend of the third phase, which continued unabated from the Neolithic to the Age of Atoms, has turned. That trend was toward an increasing differentiation between the cultures of the world. Now we are marching in the direction of global cultural uniformity. At the dawn of phase two of history, back in the Würm glacial period, man became one species. At the dawn of phase four he is starting to become a single cultural community, though at the moment the process of unification is taking place from two centers.

Like all periods of transition, this dawn is fraught with perils. Of these the most conspicuous is the atomic race between the United States and Russia. Less spectacular and nearly as expensive to eliminate is the danger to the earth's surface and atmosphere brought about by the cumulative effect of man's labors. Long ages ago deforestation and soil erosion reduced most of Iran to a desert and much of China to a flood plain. Overcutting, overplanting, and overgrazing have brought Tobacco Roads and dust bowls to America in the span of a few generations. Air pollution is menacing the health of the citizens of Los Angeles, New York, Philadelphia, London, and even Mexico City.

As these dangers are well known, steps may be taken to relieve them. A third danger of equal gravity is more likely to escape the attention of global planners because this peril lies outside the range of most people's experience. Anthropologists are aware of it because it falls within their field of competence. It is the danger that orderly international relations will break down between the Western nations and the countries recently liberated from colonial rule before freedom and equality can be established as the order of the world. This danger stems from the failure of peoples of different cultural backgrounds to understand one another.

Fifty years ago cultural differences were taken for granted, and wise administrators, diplomats, and businessmen made allowances for them. Arabs were expected to wear flowing robes and turbans and to take time out from work several times a day for prayer. Hindus were expected to wear tight cotton trousers, to be fussy about whom they ate with, and to interlard ordinary conversations with philosophy. Today people all over the world tend to wear similar clothing, to ride in identical automobiles, and to drink similar cola beverages. This shell of uniformity, exaggerated by the western press, gives many western observers a false sense of cultural unity and thus of security.

An example of intercultural misunderstanding occurred when the British and American press poked fun at Dr. Mossadegh's habit of bursting into tears when making speeches. In Britain and America public weeping is considered unmanly. In Iran, however, ordinary people think weeping to be a sign of deep conviction and sincerity. Persian villagers weep publicly during religious services—an essential element of their Shi'a Muslim faith is grief over the martyrdom of the Prophet Mohammed's two grandsons, Hasan and Husain. Dr. Mossadegh's histrionics, which caused Westerners to underestimate his power, brought him a great popular following among his own people and rendered the Shah's task of convicting and punishing him extremely difficult. At that time the West came closer to losing Iran than most of us realized.

The difference in intercultural attitudes was brought home to me one day in 1947 when an aged mountaineer from the Spanish Zone of Morocco sought me out on the terrace of my favorite hotel in Tangier. He wanted to sell me a ship model that he had just finished carving. It was, he declared proudly, an exact replica of the U.S.S. *Missouri*, which had anchored in the harbor for several days a short time before. Unless he had told me, I never would have recognized it. The hull was copied from that of an ordinary freighter. On either side of the bow two imitation diamonds glared ahead to ward off the evil eye, as in most Mediterranean ships. In place of the bridge stood a high rectangular tower, in the form of a Moroccan minaret, and from the tower two tiny airplanes swooped overhead on wires. I congratulated the old man and bought his ship. It was put on exhibit in the University Museum in Philadelphia, in front of a profile of the U.S.S. *Missouri*. More graphically than pages of text ever could, it shows how people brought up in one culture see the handiwork of another.

A few days after the old man's visit an immaculately dressed Moor came to see me on the same terrace. He asked me to follow him out under the pine trees because he did not want our conversation to be overheard. Once we were alone, he told me that I had acquired a great reputation among the workmen at the caves as an expeller of jinns (evil spirits). Actually I had performed several ceremonies to restore their peace of mind while working in the inner recesses of the caverns. Deeply buried in his garden, he told me, lay a box filled with gold coins. He could not dig it up because it was protected by a frightful jinn. Would I please come with him to drive this jinn away? Afterward he would share the treasure with me. I thanked this kind and generous man heartily, and told him that jinn-expulsion was an arduous task that required much preparation. As we were leaving for America the next day, I could not do it. What a pity that he had not come to me sooner! He walked away saddened but satisfied. His self-esteem had not been injured.

While I would not dream of holding myself up as a model of any kind of behavior, I have told this story for a reason. Dealings between nations are nothing but dealings between individuals on a larger and more sensitive scale. In the contest now going on between the western and Communist powers for the vast populations of the former colonial empires of Asia and Africa, it is not the side that hands out the most wheat and steel that will win, nor the side that lives at home under the more liberal or humane type of government. The side that will win is the side that can keep order among its friends and associates while it permits the underprivileged peoples of the world to improve their lot and approach our standard of living by their own efforts, without loss of dignity or self-esteem. This is the most delicate and difficult of the three great perils that face us now at the dawn of the fourth phase of history.

The peoples of the world who have not yet irrevocably taken sides still have a choice as to which of the two centers of unification they will join, and that choice may determine the outcome of this colossal rivalry.

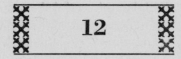

12

A VISION OF PARADISE

The Main Line of History

W E who are now alive are passing through an age of transition, the first major cultural shift since the Neolithic began about 7000 B.C. The changes going on about us are so rapid that we can see more of them in a single lifetime than generations of our ancestors ever witnessed. It is truly an exciting time to be alive.

But merely to observe what is happening is not enough. We should prepare for future events by reviewing those of the past. Our knowledge of the main episodes of history is clear enough to reveal the outlines of a regular pattern, though many of the details are shrouded in ignorance. This book has shown that ever since man began chipping pebbles his mastery of the materials of the earth's surface and of the sources of potential energy in and on it has progressed at a steady rate of increase. That is to say, man's increase in numbers, in food supply, in the complexity of his institutions, and in every other variable that we can measure with any hope of accuracy, seems to have been cumulative in a mathematical sense. In this respect man may be seen to have followed the laws of nature as automatically as inorganic materials, plants, and animals.

For the sake of convenience I have followed the conventional archæological scheme in giving the various parts of this progressive scale the names of ages, like the Paleolithic, Neolithic, Bronze, and Iron. From there on I have used another set of labels, partly original and partly borrowed, to indicate sources of energy rather than tool materials. These are the Ages of Gunpowder, Coke, Oil, Hydroelectric Power, and Atoms. The use of these arbitrary labels to designate segments of the historical scale is not meant to imply that human progress has moved through time by fits and starts. The initial events that ushered in these arbitrarily designated ages were not technical revolutions, but landmarks in the continuous progress of man. Events moved forward steadily, not jerkily, as we know from the history of invention in England in the eighteenth century. While the discovery of new sources of energy occurred at known intervals, after each such discovery it took people time to improve and perfect the mechanical means by which they controlled and used it; and when a certain level of perfection had been reached, these people were ready for a new discovery, which they then made. As time went on, the *rate* of discovery of new sources of energy and of progress in mechanical inventions to use them increased cumulatively, until now it is almost impossible for a single man to keep himself informed of these matters.

As human beings expend more and more energy from sources outside the human body, they grow in numbers, and the technical processes whereby they produce and apply this energy and keep themselves in order while so doing automatically increase the division of labor and of specialization. Out of the division of labor comes a series of births. What is born in each case is a new kind of institution, as for example the simple economic, the religious, the guild, the endowed educational, the global trading company, and the modern factory. These kinds of institutions are born, rather than are developed gradually like power-consumption and inventions, because human groupings follow the same natural rules as cells in biology. Each birth is rather painful, in the sense that it takes the human organism a little time to get used to a new set of human relationships.[1]

The number and complexity of institutions within societies regularly follow the changes in power-consumption as part of cause and effect in human life, which is merely a part of the evolution of life on earth, of the earth itself, and of the universe.

[1] Childe's use of the word *revolution* can be more nearly applied to these acts of birth than to the technological events, themselves gradual in nature, which caused them. V. Gordon Childe, *Man Makes Himself.* C. A. Watts & Co., London, 1936.

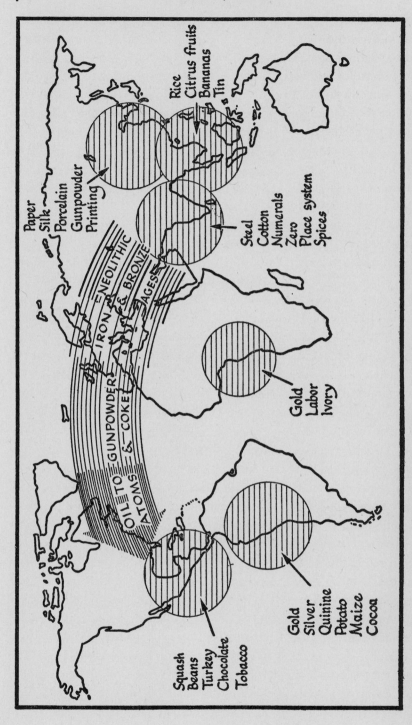

THE MAIN LINE OF CULTURAL CHANGE, AND CONTRIBUTING CENTERS

Technical knowledge has followed these changes, and out of technical knowledge science has arisen. A landmark of history was the point at which one man, Aristotle, could draw together and internally relate for the convenience of his students all existing knowledge, but even he ignored the mechanical principles used by artisans in contemporary Athenian workshops. Another was the moment when a division of labor took place among scholars who specialized in different subjects, and universities arose. A third was the point somewhere in the middle of the last century, about one hundred years ago, when science began to lead technology instead of the reverse.

It is clear that all parts of the world, all of the members of the human family, have not participated equally in the events that have marked the main line of human progress. This line of progress began in a very favorable place and has kept to favorable places, moving on from one to another as each set of technological changes has made some new spot better suited for creative living than the last. As culture has progressed, the amount of land needed for the most advanced people to work and live in has grown, until now it is the whole world. As techniques of transport and communication have improved, cultural advances made in some lands have spread to others with increasing rapidity, and cultures on the outer peripheries have been affected. More than one active center of cultural progress has existed in the world away from the main line, and these centers were long separated from one another by geographical barriers. When and where they overlapped, the exchange of products and ideas was of profit to all concerned, particularly to those centers which possessed greater power than the others.

However, there still are marginal regions where cultural diffusion has been uneven, where simple Stone Age hunters are suddenly confronted by strangers carrying rifles, where Neolithic garden-cultivators are trading their stone axes for steel ones and their pottery water jugs for discarded oil tins, and where proud citizens of ancient empires, accustomed to getting news some weeks late from camel caravans, find themselves listening to propaganda broadcasts over public radios. In the blue-and-white-tiled city square the clear call of the muezzin, bidding the faithful to prayer, is replaced one day by a tinny summons issuing not from the lips of a bearded man, but from a shiny metal cone hanging from the minaret. Out at the airport, pilgrims to the holy places climb directly from the backs of camels to seats in a DC-6. These changes in technology lead to the births of new institutions, in these places as elsewhere, but what is born from such travail is often an unfamiliar child, resembling neither the laggard nor the advanced parent, and hard for both to cope with.

I am speaking about human beings in groups rather than as individuals. A human being, no matter who his parents are, is a plastic animal. It has been demonstrated many times that a normal baby taken from any country and brought up apart from his own people will follow the cultural pattern of his adopted country like any other child in that country. The reason why a human being can be brought up in any culture is that he has a human brain, and that his ability to use this brain is inherited in the form of capacities for behavior rather than as prefabricated patterns. However, if not a single baby, but a whole family or group of families, is transferred from one cultural milieu to another, the result will be different. The parents, who have already learned one way of doing things, may have some trouble in adjusting, but their children may be even worse off. What they learn in the home is not what they are taught in school and on the playground. As our techniques of transportation continue to improve and as people move around more and more, difficulties of this kind are bound to increase.

If we follow the main line of cultural development from the point in history at which our information becomes clear enough to let us reconstruct institutions, we see that it has always moved through the medium of cultures in which individual enterprise has been at a premium, and in which the political institution has existed only in order to give structure to other institutions, such as the economic, familial, religious, and associational. In Sumer, from which we inherit more than we do from Egypt, merchants were free men and schools were private. Among the Phœnicians also private enterprise was the rule, as it was among the Greeks, who endowed private schools. The Arabs, who were primarily merchants, carried on the Greek tradition of independent schools, and the free craftsmen and traders of Venice and Genoa continued it. Universities arose in Italy, Arab Spain, England, and France. In the north of Europe the clothmakers' guilds built up a new kind of capitalism, which was transferred into private trading companies in the days of exploration, and with the rise of industry after 1750, manufacturers also became capitalists, while labor unions preserved or restored the standard of living of the laboring classes. In such countries social mobility has always been great.

During the period of accelerated industrial invention that characterized the Age of Coke, we know, for the documentation is excellent, that all kinds of men worked on new devices, experimented doggedly with old ideas, and originated a few new ones, ironing the defects out of their machines until they had made them work. They did this because they were free men and could grow rich if they succeeded. They wanted to grow rich in order to improve the lots of their families and educate their children.

The same respect for free enterprise characterized those independently growing cultures which followed paths of their own until the events of the Age of Gunpowder brought the peoples of the world together. The Chinese, with their love of learning, made government posts available to young men of any background who could pass the necessary examinations, and fostered free enterprise in manufacturing and trade. Among the Aztecs whom Cortés saw, the craftsmen were free men organized in guilds similar to those of the Arabs, and the merchants were important people who risked their lives in foreign travel, often in disguise, in order to reap wealth as a reward. These examples alone suffice to show that a capacity for steady progress is not an exclusive possession of any one race.

When we study the cultural situation which still exists in lands marooned outside the main centers of change, as we explore stagnant whirlpools of history, we soon see that if these cultures are advanced enough to have a division of labor their artisans and merchants are not esteemed, while rulers and priests receive the highest rewards. So they should, under such circumstances, for their jobs are to maintain equilibrium with a minimum expenditure of energy. A great gap separates these rulers from the ruled, and mobility is nearly nil. Peoples who live in the bonds of such cultures simply wait fearfully for the next collision with another group to shake them from outside, and when it strikes they resist it as strongly as they can because it shatters their social structure, to which they cling for survival. For this reason, stagnation is a characteristic of such cultures. Members of all races are capable of both progress and stagnation, and stagnation, like diseases, is contagious.

On the other hand, an individual drawn from a population living in cultural stagnation can migrate to another country and participate in its advances. This has frequently been done. So has the reverse. Individuals from culturally mobile countries have moved to places where the pace is sluggish, and they have stirred things up by the introduction of new ideas if the local situation was ripe for such change. We saw this happen in the period of exploration and discovery in the fifteenth and sixteenth centuries, and it is happening today. Nevertheless, it is important to remember that the individual human being lives a life of his own which does not necessarily have to follow that of his community.

Communication, Institutions, and Science

A s the main line of cultural progress moved westward from its Neolithic center in Turkestan and the Iranian highlands across the Mediterranean countries to western Europe and to America, cumulative changes took place in several of its aspects which are capable of measurement. These are, for example, the amount of energy expended in mechanical enterprises, from the momentum of the obelisk boats floated down the Nile by the Egyptians of the Old Kingdom to the explosive force of an atom bomb; the highest temperatures produced at different periods, from the first smelting of copper with charcoal to our present imitation of the heat of the sun; and the speed of travel from that of a man running to supersonic air speeds. All of these inventions and energy conversions produced, in the final analysis, progressive changes in the techniques of communication. Through the agency of communication these increases in energy-consumption made possible the growth of new, larger, more complex institutions, because the size of an institution depends on the ability of men to work together. This is possible only if they can communicate with one another.

Writing began about 3000 B.C., the first postal service around 700 B.C., printing about A.D. 1450, the telegraph in 1835, the telephone in 1876, the common use of radio in 1915, and of television in 1941. These are probably the most vital dates in the history of technology, for though they do not represent stages of energy-consumption which can be readily put on a chart, they are in each case an end product of the general pattern of rising energy-consumption.

Each of these dates can be said to have marked the beginnings of a new kind of institution. In 3000 B.C. we see our first evidence of kingdoms, with complex political and religious hierarchies. About 700 B.C. the first empire appeared. Shortly after the invention of printing, in the middle of the fifteenth century, the world's first overseas trading companies owned by stockholders were incorporated, and along with the telegraph, complex manufacturing plants came into existence. Cartels appeared with the telephone, World War I and the League of Nations with the radio, and World War II and the United Nations with television. These coincidences, like the structure of human institutions, occurred naturally.

Improvements in communication and the growth of more and more specialized institutions also made possible the growth of science, which arose from very humble beginnings. Ever since man began to talk it is likely that he has wondered about the nature of the universe, and his ignorance disturbed him, particularly when a brother was struck by lightning or an uncle drowned in a freshet while fording a river. The mere fact of death by disease was enough to wed scientific curiosity to ritual. The earliest science of which we know dealt not with the universe itself, which remained the bailiwick of priests, but with the measurement of distances, weights, and the passage of time. It was not until the days of the Greeks that the study of the nature of the universe was divorced from its religious context. From then on, brave souls in one place or another, often within the church itself, kept science alive and increased its compass until the rise of universities and learned societies permitted further growth setting both science and religion free. In the fourteenth century a prince employed scientists to improve navigation, and by 1850 manufacturers themselves became scientists. Today not only are navigation and industry dependent on science, but our greatest shortage is in scientific personnel.

We need not only men who can handle complicated machinery and read dials, but also men who can think in large terms. The more specialized branches of learning become, the harder it is for individual men to master the essentials of them all, but the problem is not insoluble. In response to this need, science writers are being trained in considerable numbers, and publications like *Science, Natural History,* and the new *Scientific American* have arisen. Such writers and magazines are essential to make it possible for the heads of state to direct intelligent planning. Until recently the world has gone its own way innocent of planning except for the most essential rules of human relations as expressed in the most fundamental doctrines of religion. Now it can no longer leave things to chance because with the dawn of phase four a climax in history has been reached.

Man Approaches a Climax in Cosmic History

THIS climax is not simply the business of atomic bombs. If we blow ourselves up, that will merely mean that the climax is a grand finale rather than a gate to a new life. Harlow Shapley estimates that the universe contains about one hundred thousand planets capable of having life.[2] It is possible that each such

---

[2] Harlow Shapley, *On Climate and Life,* Harvard University Press, Cambridge, Mass., 1953, pp. 2–4.

planet goes up in atomic clouds after a critical stage in the relation of matter to energy has been reached by the living organisms
which inhabit it. If that is our destiny, then we may also disappear, but the whole history of man indicates that we have the
power to preserve as well as to destroy our environment and ourselves.

We have reached the threshold of a climax for a simpler and
less speculative reason, because the mass of the earth is finite. Man
has destroyed vast stores of its energy potential at an increasing
rate, so that unless new sources are discovered, the bottom of the
barrel is in sight. Eventually we will probably find the means to
use solar energy, which is self-renewing and, for our purposes,
limitless. When solar energy has replaced coal and oil, the dangerous pollution of our atmosphere may be ended and we will
cease to worry about the debatable danger to higher forms of life
wrought by an unrestrained use of atomic energy. Until solar
energy is a household commodity, the world needs a co-ordinator
of energy because it is wasteful for rival nations to expend it
competitively. International energy-control can be set up only
when we have eliminated the current rivalry between the world's
two great centers of cultural unification. This rivalry is the most
serious impediment in the way of our full transition into phase
four of history.

Our power-consumption requirements have led us to the point
where it is more economical for mankind to be joined into a single
super-institution than to remain split in a pair of warring halves,
each consisting of a major power and its satellites or friends. It
seems unlikely that man, after he has been so successful to date,
will be foolish enough to defy the law of least effort which has
guided his progress this far and is patently more powerful than
he is.

The Land of Youth

O N C E we have lived through the rapid changes that are now
marking our transition from the third to the fourth phase of history, from a period of diversification into one of unification, we

shall be squarely faced with a number of serious problems. These
are food supply, conservation, population-control, longevity, and
education, and the product of all the others—organization. Without doubt improvements in food-production will momentarily
offset the current destruction of the world's forests and erosion
of its soils. But even if we succeed in making food out of sea
water, sunlight, soil, and air by synthetic means, and in distribut-
ing it to the earth's hungry hundreds of millions, we shall have
returned to the beginning of the third phase of history, to a new
Neolithic, if we do not solve other problems.

The earth's surface will be rapidly destroyed, if not by agriculture, then by our efforts to manufacture the tools, clothing, houses,
vehicles, and highways needed by an ever growing population.
The remaining forests will be felled, the deserts flooded, and the
few wild animals to survive man's final encroachment of their
realms will flee to the mountaintops. As synthetically nourished
human beings crowd one another on the same land surface that
held a few million hunters only eight thousand years ago, the
problem of social organization will grow too complex for solution
without loss of the freedom for which we now struggle.

One can never return completely to a previous stage of existence. We shall never be able to recapture the life of our ancestors
of Upper Paleolithic and Mesolithic times, nor would we want to,
because we could not bear to lose the scientific knowledge that
we have slowly accumulated during the intervening centuries.
We would do well, however, if some of us recaptured certain
aspects of the hunting life which others of us have never lost. All
anthropologists who have lived with primitive hunters report
that they are sportsmen, gentlemen, and conservationists. Good
manners, co-operation, and a respect for the plants and animals
among which they live and from which they derive their food are
basic hunting patterns of behavior.

The state of being underprivileged came in at the dawn of the
third phase of history. From Neolithic times onward it grew like
a noisome tumor as rabble, mobs, and masses arose in villages
and slums, as a product of the widening gap between rich and
poor, between noble and slave. In the future no one needs to be

underprivileged in the sense that an Asiatic tenant farmer is to-day. An equality of opportunity like that which exists among hunters can be restored, but only by raising the standards of everyone. This implies a limitation of population, which in turn depends on a general rise in the level of world education.

The optimum number of persons who can live on the earth should be determined not in terms of materials and energy-consumption, but in terms of the requirements of human nature. Although we will not again be hunters, our biological make-up is the same as theirs and our biological needs were determined by natural selection over hundreds of thousands of years. We can

WOMAN GATHERING HONEY, SPANISH MESOLITHIC CAVE ART.

live and work most happily and efficiently if we reproduce, with modern improvements, some approximation to our ancestors' living conditions. A hunter needs space to move around in. He needs trees and grass and rocks and streams; he needs the presence of birds and animals, and the opportunity for exercise and recreation. He needs a job which is at times dangerous, and at all times sharpens his wits. He needs to be able to seclude himself with a small group of intimate relatives and friends with whom he interacts face to face, and his more formal interactions with larger groups must be kept within limits which vary with the individual temperament, but which are often exceeded in modern living. Above all, he needs to be able to make decisions on his own, and not to have his opinions molded into a rackful of rubber stamps.

If men are to be able to live in this fashion, the size of the earth's population needs to be sharply limited. Technical processes must be devised to manufacture the consumer goods that

MESOLITHIC SPANISH CAVE ART.

we need without further destruction of the earth's surface, and the biosphere as it existed about 6000 B.C. during the post-glacial optimum must be restored as nearly as possible. This means reforestation, cleaning and stocking streams, and an end of air-pollution. Cities must be decentralized, industries scattered, and everyone will live in natural surroundings.

Part of population-control is the medical problem of increasing longevity. According to actuarial statistics, children born in Connecticut in 1900 had a life expectancy of 50.4 years; in 1950 of 70.6 years. If medical scientists find means to defeat heart disease and cancer, the chances are good that a few of us now living may become Methuselahs. If the medical researchers also learn the secrets of all the endocrine glands, we may not only live indefinitely but we may be eternally young. Then the old Irish paradise, *Tír na nÓg*, the Land of Youth, may come into being.

If men are allowed to live in a world without want where there is work and space for all, there can be no division between rich and poor, dignified and undignified, educated and ignorant, beyond those resulting from the differences in capacities which individual human beings inherit genetically. Creative and administrative kinds of superior intelligence will be at a premium everywhere. The shortage of high-level brainpower in every country will make it necessary for the world community to conserve this most precious of all its commodities and to see that everyone is educated at least to the point where his capacities for intellectual work and leadership shall have been objectively evaluated.

Educating young people should take less time than it does now because, as Wilder Penfield [3] has shown, we try to teach children the wrong subjects at the right times. For example, when a child is beginning to speak, it can learn four languages as easily as one. The ages of four to ten could be devoted to languages, which would come back later when needed. But even if we make our process of education more efficient than at present and persuade more competent people to become teachers by offering higher rewards, it is by no means certain that many of us are potentially competent to assume leadership in a one-piece world. Our brainpower needs to be pooled, and the danger of a shortage of it is another reason for world-unification.

It has been shown by many social experiments that man cannot control every facet of life. All that we can do is to try to isolate the factors that are the keys to the entire structure, and to work on them. These are basically: the conservation of natural re-

[3] Wilder Penfield, "A Consideration of the Neurophysiological Mechanisms of Speech, and Some Educational Consequences," *Proceedings of the American Academy of Science*, Vol. 82, No. 5, Boston, 1953.

sources; power-production; population-control; the full utilization of brainpower; and education. The details of social structure will fall into place automatically as the end product of all these forces, as they always have done.

Our overwhelming problem is not to plan the future in detail, but to tackle these key problems and to follow each of them through to its natural conclusion. The international protection of migratory birds may seem to some people a trivial matter, but it is a step forward. So is the concept of an atomic pool for peaceful use; so is the international birth-control movement, which is having the most success in Japan; so are international scholarships, particularly at the preparatory-school level.

No reasonable person wants to surrender his country's sovereignty any more than he wishes to give up his personal liberties, but by the time the goals I have outlined have been attained, the protection of sovereignty throughout the world will have become as unnecessary as fortifications on the border between the United States and Canada. Political unification of the world is not the first necessary step. By the time it has become possible without turmoil, it will also have become unnecessary.

While we work on these problems—and some of them are before our eyes—some men have already embarked on a bold new adventure, the conquest of outer space. This is a healthy sign, a clear indication that some of us are still feral men, unwilling to domesticate ourselves by any kind of bondage, even that of the spatial limitations of our planet's surface. While our ancestors conquered many plants and animals during the Neolithic and later ages, and while at various times during the third phase of history some men enslaved one another, the human spirit was nowhere permanently broken. Had it been, our hope of success in present and future adventures would be less than it is.

As President Eisenhower once said: "We live not in an instant of danger but in an age of danger." An age of danger requires the leadership and obedience of men as wise, as cunning, and as brave, as competitive, and as co-operative as he who killed the first mammoth.

A half-million years of experience in outwitting beasts on mountains and plains, in heat and cold, in light and darkness, gave our ancestors the equipment that we still desperately need if we are to slay the dragon that roams the earth today, marry the princess of outer space, and live happily ever after in the deer-filled glades of a world in which everyone is young and beautiful forever.

One final doubt mars this vision of paradise. The hunters who killed the mammoths and outwitted the beasts were young men, in their prime. Few lived to be fifty. Those who had reached that ancient age spent their days by the campfire while their sons and grandsons carried in the meat. Their business was to teach young men the wisdom of ancient ways devised by ancestors who had become gods and tested and perfected over hundreds of generations. They did not need flexible minds.

Their descendants do. The graybeards who sit around the council fires of nations today need more than ancient wisdom. They must be able to shed the thought patterns of their youth as quickly as an Ona drops his robe when he kneels to shoot. They were brought up in an earlier age when America could hide behind her oceans, when Britons believed that Gibraltar and Suez were impregnable, and Muscovites felt as safe as squirrels in a nest in the shelter of their barren steppes.

Cannot these old men bring themselves to realize, and persuade their followers and supporters, that the passport to a new life is theirs for the asking, but only if they will discard the traditional caution of statesmen, complete with homburgs, umbrellas, and filibusters, and develop minds as bold and flexible as that of a hunter tracking a bear?

Can they not realize that the alternative to cultural change is not a perpetuation of the status quo, but the failure of a cosmic experiment, the end of man's great adventures? I think that they can. I think that despite man's increase in longevity, he will conquer this last obstacle as he has so many others, and that he will move forward according to schedule.

GLOSSARY

NOTE: *This glossary had to be prepared while I was in Afghanistan. I am deeply indebted to my expedition companion, Dr. Henry Coulter, for help with the geological and climatic terms. Revised in 1961.*

ACADEMY   Plato's endowed school of higher education.

ACHÆMENIAN   The first Persian empire, that of Darius, Cyrus, and Xerxes.

AINUS   Caucasoid aborigines of northern Japan.

AKKADIANS   A Semitic-speaking people of Bronze Age Mesopotamia who took over Sumerian culture.

AL-AZHAR   A Muslim university in Cairo, opened in A.D. 972.

ALCALDE   Spanish for village mayor.

ALLEN'S RULE   Animals living in deserts and arid grasslands have longer extremities than those of the same or closely related species living in forests or on mountains.

ANGKOR VAT   A ruined-temple site in Cambodia.

ANGSTROM   One one-hundred millionth of a centimeter.

ANNEALING   A process of hardening copper by repetitive heating and pounding.

ANTHROPOMETRY   The technical discipline of measuring human bodies.

APE-MEN   Extinct primates that had acquired the erect posture and human tooth form without evidence of speech, tools, or fire.

ARGAL   A wild sheep of northern Iran.

ARI-RI   High king of Tara, monarch of all Ireland.

ARTIFACT   Any object fashioned for use by man.

ASSOCIATION   A class of institution composed of individuals drawn from other institutions and brought together by participation in some common activity or interest.

ASSYRIANS   A Semitic-speaking people of northern Mesopotamia of Late Bronze Age and Early Iron Age times.

ASTROLABE   An astronomical instrument perfected by the Arabs, used for determining latitude.

AUDIENCIA   A Spanish colonial supreme court.

AURIGNACIAN   A series of three closely related Upper Paleolithic cultures found in western Europe, covering the time span of the first warm oscillation and second advance of the Würm glaciation.

AUSTRALOPITHECINES   The entire group of fossil ape-men found in Africa, Palestine, and Java.

BACTRIAN CAMEL   A two-humped camel of central Asia.

BAIRAKTAR   An Albanian clan chief.

BAKHTIARIS   A federation of Persian-speaking nomads of the central Zagros Mountains.

BALLY   An Irish township.

BANTU   East African Negroes who speak languages of a single stock, so named.

BARBARY APES   A species of ground-living monkey inhabiting rocky places in North Africa and Gibraltar.

BEAKED TOOL   A crude tool, made of a flint nodule or a pebble, in which one end is retouched into the form of a beak.

BERBERS   Hamitic-speaking inhabitants of North Africa.

BERGMANN'S RULE   Warm-blooded animals of a given species are larger in colder regions and smaller in warmer ones.

BLADE   A parallel-sided blank of flint of nearly uniform thickness, struck off a prepared core of generally tubular shape.

BLADE CORE   A carefully prepared flint core, with a striking platform, and of roughly tubular form, from which blades are removed by expertly placed blows, usually cushioned from direct contact with the hammer by a divot of some elastic material.

BLOOM   The spongy mass of iron that oozes from the ore in smelting.

BLOOMERY   A special furnace for smelting iron.

BO-AÏRE   A cattle chief, free farmer of class three of ancient Ireland. He owned buildings and cattle, but rented tillage from nobles.

BOND CLASSES   Slaves and landless, propertyless freemen in ancient Ireland.

BOOK OF THE COMING FORTH BY DAY, OR OF THE DEAD   A sacred book of the ancient Egyptians which contained a guide for the soul of the dead to the land of Osiris.

BOS BRACHYCEROS   A small, short-horned breed of Neolithic cattle.

BOS PRIMIGENIUS   The wild ox, probable ancestor of most breeds of modern cattle.

BRACHIATING   The method of arboreal locomotion employed by apes, howler monkeys, and spider monkeys—swinging through the trees hand over hand.

BRAHMI   An Indian alphabet derived from an early South Arabian model.

BRAINSTEM   The lower portion of the brain, extending into the medullary cavity, in which automatic actions are controlled.

BROW RIDGES   Bony prominences marking the transition from forehead to face in man.

BURIN   A flint chisel made by removing a spall from one side of the end of a blade.

BUSHMEN   Aboriginal hunters of South Africa.

CARBON-14 DATING   A method of determining the age of an archæological specimen or group of specimens of organic origin by measuring the degree of disintegration of its carbon-14 atoms.

CASA DE CONTRATACIÓN   A Spanish board of trade organized in 1503 to deal with the American colonies.

CAUCASOID   The white race.

CENOZOIC   The last seventy million years of geologic time.

CEREBELLUM   A special part of the brain, covered in man by the cerebral hemispheres, which governs balance.

CHAPELLE-AUX-SAINTS, LA   The best-known and most commonly illustrated specimen of Neanderthal.

CHERTY PLAIN   A flint-strewn area of the Arabian Desert.

CH'IN   An Iron Age people of China who unified that country for the first time. Their dynasty dated from 222 B.C. to 206 B.C.

CHOPPER   A crude core of flint or other material sharpened by retouching along a single edge.

CHOPPING-TOOL   The same as above, but retouched by striking alternate blows from either side.

CHOU   A Chinese people who destroyed the Shang capital of An Yang and set up a second Bronze Age dynasty.

CHROMOSOME   A microscopic fibrous element inside the nucleus of a cell.

CHURINGA   An object of stone or wood made by Australian aborigines and regarded by them as sacred. Some churingas can be whirled and made to produce a roaring sound, useful in ceremonies.

CŒLACANTH   A very primitive fish recently discovered in African waters —a living fossil.

CONTAGIOUS MAGIC   A type of magic based on a belief in guilt by association, or the transfer of qualities and characteristics from one object or person to another by physical contact.

COPAL   A native incense gum of aboriginal Middle America.

CORE (FLINT)   The central portion or nucleus of a flint nodule, formed by the removal of flakes, flake-blades, or blades.

CORREGIDOR   Spanish for mayor of a city.

CORTÉS   Spanish for parliament; also the name of the conqueror of Mexico.

COUNCIL OF THE INDIES   A Spanish governmental department set up in 1524 to handle colonial affairs.

COUNT OF PRIVATE ESTATES   Manager of estates confiscated by the Byzantine emperors.

COUNT OF THE SACRED LARGESSES   Treasurer of the Byzantine empire.

CULTURE   The sum total of the procedures by which human beings live, transmitted from generation to generation. A specific culture is a set of procedures followed by a given people over a given period. Archæologically speaking, the word culture is sometimes used to signify the tool assemblage of a specific period and people.

CUNEIFORM   A system of writing introduced by the Sumerians in which characters are incised on soft clay tablets or seals with a wedge-shaped stylus.

DANKALIS   A group of desert Hamites living between the Ethiopian plateau and the Red Sea.

DANUBIANS   Neolithic people of Central Europe.

DIFFUSIONIST   One who believes that no cultural trait is invented more than once and that all cultural similarities are due to contact.

DRUID   A pagan Celtic priest.

ECOLOGY   The science of the balance in nature existing between the sum total of animal and vegetable species in any environment.

EMMER   An early form of cultivated wheat.

EMPIRE   A complex political institution in which one people rules a number of others, permitting each to retain its own language, laws, and customs.

ERGESTEROL   One of the components in the subcutaneous fat of the human body.

ETA   A class of Japanese outcastes.

EXARCH   Commander in chief of the Byzantine army.

EXTERNAL PTERYGOID MUSCLES   A pair of muscles extending from the palate to attachments covering the articulating condyles of the lower jaw. It moves the lower jaw forward and helps open the mouth.

FACE-TO-FACE GROUP   The basic unit of society—a group of people who meet regularly and intimately, as for example the members of a family. The face-to-face group is the simplest form of institution. Complex institutions are networks of face-to-face groups.

FACETED PLATFORM   A striking platform, q.v., made by the removal of a series of small flakes.

FADAYAN ISLAM   A politico-religious brotherhood in modern Iran.

FERRASSIE, LA   A relatively advanced French Neanderthal skeleton.

FLINT   A rock composed of cryptocrystalline silica, used by early man for tools. Also: "A variety of chert composed of chalcedony and extremely fine grained quartz"—L. B. Pirsson and A. Knopf, *Rocks and Minerals*, John Wiley and Sons, New York, 1948, p. 274.

FONTÉCHEVADE   Remains of two specimens of Homo sapiens found in a French cave of third-interglacial date and stratigraphically below and sealed from the cultural remains of Neanderthal man, which they thus demonstrably antedated.

FORAMEN MAGNUM   The hole at the base of the skull through which the brain stem passes.

FOURTH GLACIAL ADVANCE   The latest of four major Pleistocene ice advances.

FU SANG   An unidentified country said to lie 4000 miles east of China, according to an account said to be dated at A.D. 499.

FULL-BRAINED MEN   Hominid primates at the same brain-size level as modern man and including extinct as well as living races of Homo sapiens.

GENE   A protein particle, forming part of a chromosome, q.v., by means of which a hereditary character is thought to be transmitted.

GHEE   Boiled butter made of water-buffalo milk.

GIBBON   A genus of small apes inhabiting parts of southeast Asia and Indonesia.

GIGANTOPITHECUS   A Pleistocene fossil ape from South China.

GLACIAL PERIOD   In this context, a time span encompassed by any one of the four major glacial advances of the Pleistocene.

GLOGER'S RULE   Animals living in wet forests tend to have black or red coats; those in arid regions buff or gray ones.

GOSSYPIUM   A genus of cotton cultivated in Peru and India as early as 2500 B.C. G. *arboreum* is the wild Indian prototype, G. *raimondii* the American. The Peruvian cultivated cotton is G. *barbadense*, believed by some experts to be a hybrid between the two.

GREASE STONE   A smooth flat stone used by primitive food-gatherers as a receptacle for animal fats and seeds.

HALF-BRAINED MEN   Extinct man-like primates for whom culture may be demonstrated or postulated. Anatomically they differ from modern man chiefly in the possession of a brain size one evolutionary level below that of Homo sapiens. *Homo erectus.*

HAMITIC   A family of languages spoken in North and East Africa.

HAN   A Chinese dynasty reigning from about 202 B.C. to about A.D. 220.

HAND AX   An almond-shaped core implement of quartzite or flint, symmetrical both bilaterally and bifacially, and retouched on both borders.

HARRAPĀ   A city site of the Indus Valley Bronze Age civilization.

HEIDELBERG MAN   See *H. heidelbergensis.*

HIERATIC   A form of ancient Egyptian writing devised for use with a brush on papyrus.

HITTITES   A people of Anatolia who may have been the first ironworkers.

HOEI-CHIN   A priest of Fu Sang, q.v.

HOMO   The genus that includes all men. It has two species, H. erectus and H. sapiens.

H. ERECTUS   An extinct species of man from which Homo sapiens evolved.

H. HEIDELBERGENSIS   A fossil man identified by a single lower jaw found in first-interglacial gravels in Germany.

H. NEANDERTHALENSIS   A subspecies of fossil men characterized by a low skull vault, a long, muzzle-like, chinless face, and heavy long-bone structure.

H. RHODESIENSIS   A subspecies of fossil men found in Rhodesia and South Africa, characterized by a low vault and enormous brow ridges.

H. SAPIENS   The species to which all living human beings belong.

H. SOLOENSIS   A subspecies of fossil men found in Java, in the Upper Pleistocene.

HOTTENTOTS   A cattle-breeding people of South Africa racially and linguistically akin to the Bushmen.

HOUR PRIESTS   Volunteer lay priests serving a month at a time in ancient Egyptian rural temples.

HUACA PRIETA   A Peruvian coastal site excavated by Junius Bird.

HYKSOS   A horse-using people who invaded Egypt about 1700 B.C.

ICE AGE   The Pleistocene Period, q.v.

IKHWAN AL-MUSLIMIN   A politico-religious brotherhood in modern Egypt.

INSTITUTION   A group of people which is organized for some purpose, follows rules of procedure, and has a structure of varying degrees of complexity. An individual may belong to a number of different institutions.

INTERGLACIAL PERIOD   The time span between any two of the four successive advances of the ice during the Pleistocene.

INTERNAL PTERYGOID MUSCLES   A pair of muscles extending from the palate to attachments on the insides of the lower rear corners of the lower jaw. It provides the jaw with side-to-side motion.

IPOMEA BATATAS   The sweet potato.

JARMO   An early Neolithic site in Iraq excavated by Robert Braidwood.

JINN (ARABIC)   An evil spirit.

JOMON   A Mesolithic and Neolithic culture of Japan, noted for its early pottery.

KABYLES   Central Algerian Berbers.

KAMEHAMEHA I   First king of the entire Hawaiian Islands, unified in 1795.

KANALOA   A Hawaiian god identified with the ancestor cult and kava-drinking.

KANAM MANDIBLE   A piece of a sapiens jaw found in Kenya, dated at the beginning of the Pleistocene.

KANE   The Hawaiian high god—the creator.

KANJERA MAN   Specimens of Homo sapiens found in Kenya and attributed to the Upper Pleistocene.

KASSITES   An Indo-European-speaking people who invaded Mesopotamia about 1700 B.C.

KAVA   A Polynesian beverage made from a kind of pepper root.

KHAROTHI   An Indian alphabet derived from the Aramaic.

KING OF THE HILLS AND PEAKS   Head of an Irish county.

KU   The Hawaiian war god.

KUKUI-NUT   A Hawaiian nut used as a candle.

KUMARA   A name for the sweet potato used both in South America and Polynesia.

KURDS   Indo-European-speaking mountaineers inhabiting contiguous portions of Iran, Iraq, Turkey, and Syria.

LAGENARIA SICERARIA   The common gourd.

LAW OF ACCELERATION   Newton's law; the principle governing the accumulative increase of the rate of progression of bodies in motion.

LAW OF LEAST EFFORT   The second law of thermodynamics or the law of the conservation of energy; the natural principle on which the cohesion and equilibrium of individuals and groups is based.

LI   An aboriginal people of southern China.

LOESS   A fine, wind-deposited soil composed of silt-sized particles.

LONGO   The Hawaiian god of agriculture.

LOST WAX   A process of casting metal objects in which a model of the object is first made of wax, then covered with clay, and finally melted out through holes to form a mold.

LYCEUM   Aristotle's endowed school of higher education.

MAGDALENIAN   The last of three classic Upper Paleolithic cultures of western Europe characterized by reindeer-hunting and the manufacture of bone and antler tools along with unretouched blades.

MAKAHIKI   A Hawaiian sacred emblem.

MAN-APES   Australopithecines, q.v. Same as ape-men.

MAPA MAN   A late Middle Pleistocene skeleton from South China.

MASSETER MUSCLES   A pair of muscles extending from the zygomatic arches and malars to the lower rear angles of the lower jaw. Its contraction helps the temporals draw the jaw upward.

MASTER OF OFFICES   Byzantine prime minister.

MATABELE   A South African Bantu tribe.

MA-TUAN-LIN   A Chinese writer of the thirteenth century who collected a set of travelers' tales.

MEDES   A people of ancient Persia whose capital was Ecbatana, the modern Hamadan.

MEGALITHIC TOMBS   A type of tomb built of large stones, especially those of northwestern Europe dating from Late Neolithic and Early Bronze Age times.

MEGANTHROPUS PALÆOJAVANICUS   An Australopithecine, identified on the basis of fragments of a jaw from Java.

MELANIN   Granular pigment in human and animal tissue.

MENES   Traditional founder of the first dynasty of Egypt.

MESOLITHIC   The cultures of the hunting peoples who lived between the end of the Würm glaciation and the time of the introduction of agriculture and animal husbandry.

METIC   A free foreigner living in Athens without political franchise.

MIAO   An aboriginal people of southern China.

MING   A Chinese dynasty reigning from A.D. 1368 to 1644.

MINOAN   The Bronze Age culture of Crete.

MIOCENE   The fourth of seven divisions of the Cenozoic era.

MONGOLOID   The so-called yellow race.

MOR-TUATH   An Irish county.

MOUSTERIAN   A Middle Paleolithic cultural assemblage, in some areas attributable to Neanderthal man.

MU   A fictitious lost continent in the Pacific.

MULLAH   A Muslim clergyman.

MUSEUM   An endowed school of higher education founded in Alexandria in 323 B.C. by Ptolemy I.

MYSTERY   An ancient Greek religious association and its practices.

NEANDERTHAL MAN   See *H. neanderthalensis.*

NEOLITHIC   A way of life involving the use of polished-stone tools, agriculture, and animal husbandry, or some combination of these traits. Any period in any part of the world in which people lived or live in this fashion.

NEOLITHIC BARNYARD FOURSOME   The sheep, goat, pig, and ox.

NEW STONE AGE   The Neolithic.

NISEAN HORSES   Large riding-horses bred in Iron Age Persia.

NOMARCH   Governor of an ancient Egyptian province.

NOME   An Ancient Egyptian province.

NOTHOI   Children of concubines in Homeric Greece.

ŒSTRUAL CYCLE   The cycle of sexual periodicity in female primates which reaches its climax at the time of ovulation.

OLDUVAI   A four-hundred-foot gorge in Tanganyika in which Lewis Leakey found the Olduvai child, Zinjanthropus, and an early Homo erectus skull, and in which Hans Reck earlier found a Mesolithic skeleton.

OLDUVAI CHILD   Parts of a skeleton of an Australopithecine found below and presumably older than Zinjanthropus.

ONAGER   A western Asiatic wild ass.

OREOPITHECUS   A Miocene-Pliocene primate from Italy which some paleontologists think ancestral to man.

PALEARCTIC FAUNA   The characteristic assemblage of animals of the colder regions of the northern hemisphere.

PEBBLE TOOL   A crude tool made by breaking or splitting a water-rounded pebble.

PEDAGOGUE   A Greek slave who led a boy to school and home again, and disciplined him.

PEOPLE OF THE BOOK   A Muslim term to designate Christians, Jews, and sometimes also Zoroastrians.

PERMAFROST   Permanently frozen ground.

PITHECANTHROPUS ERECTUS   A species of fossil half-brained men found in Java.

PITHECANTHROPUS ROBUSTUS   A species of Pithecanthropus identified on the basis of one massive and brutal skull from Java.

PLACE SYSTEM   A system of numerical notation in which the position of a symbol indicates its order of magnitude.

PLEISTOCENE   The sixth subdivision of the Cenozoic era, extending from nearly a million years ago to about 8000 B.C. Some geologists believe that we are still in the Pleistocene, or "That part of late Cenozoic time which is characterized by repeated climatic cooling, involving repeated conspicuous glaciation in high and middle latitudes, and related worldwide fluctuations of sea-level. It is also marked by the appearance and intercontinental migrations of the modern horse, cattle, mammoths, camels, and man." Richard F. Flint, *Glacial Geology and the Pleistocene Epoch*, John Wiley and Sons, New York, 1947, p. 208.

PLIOCENE   The fifth of seven subdivisions of the Cenozoic era.

POD CORN   A primitive type of maize in which each seed is separately sheathed.

POLISHED-STONE AX   An ax blade made of some hard, compact stone by a process of pecking, grinding, and polishing.

POST-GLACIAL OPTIMUM   A period of relatively warm climate about 6000 B.C.

PRÆTORIAN PREFECT   A governor of one of the four prefects of the Byzantine empire.

PRESSURE FLAKING   The technique of retouching flint implements by pressing the edge with a piece of wood or bone, or with the teeth, instead of striking blows.

PRIMATES   An order of mammals which includes lemurs, tarsiers, monkeys, apes, and man.

PROCONSUL   An extinct East African primate which may have been ancestral to apes, Australopithecines, and men.

QASHQAIS   A confederation of Turkish-speaking nomads inhabiting the southern Zagros Mountains in Iran.

QUERN   A simple stone milling device.
> rotary—a pivoted circular stone grain mill that is rotated by hand.
> saddle—a rectangular stone grain mill with a concave upper surface operated by rubbing an upper stone back and forth by hand.

RACIAL SYSTEM   See *Rassenkreis.*

RASSENKREIS   A racial system composed of all of the geographical races of a species of animal occupying a continuous geographical area.

REBUS   A form of pictographic writing in which syllables that sound alike are substituted for each other.

REGIDORES   Members of a Spanish colonial town council.

RENSCH'S DESERT FAT RULE   Desert animals that store fat store it in lumps.

RENSCH'S HAIR RULE   Animals of a given species living in cold regions have longer hair than those living in hot regions.

RETOUCHING   The process of sharpening flint implements by the removal of small spalls.

RHODESIAN MAN   See *H. rhodesiensis.*

RIFFIANS   Members of a confederation of fourteen Berber tribes inhabiting part of northern Morocco.

SABÆAN   A South Arabian Iron Age culture, and its alphabet.

SABRAS   Jews born in Palestine of immigrant parents.

SALDANHA BAY MAN   A skullcap and piece of jaw from near Cape Town.

SALUKI   A greyhound type of dog which hunts by sight rather than by smell; native to the desert regions from Afghanistan to Arabia.

SATRAPY   An ancient Persian province.

SAVANNAS   Low-latitude grasslands studded with trees.

SEDNA   An Eskimo deity.

SESREACH   An Irish plowland; 120 Irish acres.

SHADUF   An Egyptian water-raising device.

SHAMAN   An all-purpose religious specialist among hunters and other simply organized peoples who restores equilibrium to the individuals and groups among whom he practices after it has been disturbed by illness, bad weather, or some other misfortune.

SHANG   A Chinese dynasty of the Bronze Age, supposed to have lasted from 1765 B.C. to 1123 B.C.

SHATTERING   A genetic capacity of grasses and legumes by which, at the time of ripening, the husks or pods open automatically, scattering the seeds and permitting self-sowing; the mutation that destroys this capacity prevents reproduction, except by human agency, and permits reaping.

SHEKEL   A Mesopotamian Bronze Age unit of weight in which gold equals eight times its weight in silver.

SHIH-HUANG-TI   Title of the Ch'in ruler Chêng, meaning "First Emperor."

SHLUH   Berbers of the Moroccan Grand Atlas and Sous Valley.

SHOGUN   A Japanese feudal military lord.

SIAMANG   A large ape closely related to the gibbon.

SINANTHROPUS PEKINENSIS   A race of Homo erectus whose remains were found in the cave of Chou-kou-tien near Peking.

SIVAPITHECUS   An extinct primate of northern India with short canines and a chin.

SLIP   A surface layer on pottery produced by washing it with a fine clay solution before firing.

SLOW GAME   A class of animals, such as tortoises, snails, gophers, and moles, which can be collected for food by women and children as well as by men. The collection of slow game may have preceded hunting as a means of livelihood in the history of man-like creatures.

SNOWMAN   The *yeti,* a cold-adapted, altitude-adapted bipedal primate which may or may not exist in the Himalayas.

SOLO MAN   See *H. soloensis.*

SOLUTREAN   An Upper Paleolithic culture that followed the Aurignacian in France and central Europe; characterized by mammoth-hunting and the manufacture of long, pressure-flaked, bifacial blade tools.

SOMALIS   A heat-adapted people of Hamitic speech and Muslim religion living in the Horn of Africa.

SPEAR-THROWER   A wooden device used to increase the length of the arm and hence its leverage in casting spears.

STEINHEIM   A female Homo sapiens skull found in Germany and dated at the second interglacial.

STEREOSCOPIC VISION   The kind of vision enjoyed by monkeys, apes, and men in which overlapping images permit three-dimensional perception at a short distance—e.g., at hand's length.

STRATEGOS   A Byzantine general.

STRIKING PLATFORM   A smooth surface made on a flint core by removing a flattish flake. From it other flakes, flake-blades, or blades may be struck successively.

SUMERIANS   A Bronze Age people who introduced metallurgy and writing to Mesopotamia.

SUMMER SLED   An animal-drawn sled used on dry land.

SUQ   An Arab market or bazaar.

SUS SCROFA   The Palearctic wild boar.

SUS VITTATUS   A wild pig of southeast Asia.

SWANSCOMBE MAN   A fragmentary Homo sapiens skull of second-interglacial date found in England.

SYMBIOSIS   A way of life in which animals of two species live together to their mutual benefit.

SYMBOL   Anything that represents something else.

TANG   A Chinese dynasty reigning from about A.D. 907 to about 960.

TAPA   Polynesian bark cloth.

TAPA LOG   A log on which tapa cloth is prepared by beating bark.

TARPAN   A wild horse of eastern Europe and west-central Asia.

TEMPORAL MUSCLES   A pair of muscles extending from the side of the skull under the zygomatic arches to the coracoid processes of the lower jaw. Its contraction draws the lower jaw upward against the upper jaw.

TEOCENTLI   A wild grass believed to be involved in the evolution of some forms of cultivated maize.

TÍR NA NÓG   The Land of Youth—the ancient Irish concept of paradise.

TOGGLE   A mechanical device that holds fast under tension but comes free when loose.

TRIDACNA   A giant clam of the Pacific whose shell was used as tool material by Micronesians and Polynesians.

TRIPSACUM   A wild grass believed to be involved in the evolution of many kinds of cultivated maize.

TUAREG   A group of Saharan camel nomads of Berber speech.

TUATH   A division of land in ancient Ireland; originally, "people."

TUMBLE-HOME   The bell-bottomed hull construction of a sailing vessel of the Age of Gunpowder, permitting the firing of broadsides without capsizing.

TUNDRA   Arctic swampland overlying permanently frozen ground.

TZE YANG MAN   An early Upper Pleistocene skeleton from South China.

ULU   An Eskimo term for a half-moon-shaped knife used by women for cutting skins.

UNGULATE   A hoofed mammal.

UNIVERSITY   An institution of higher education in which a division of labor exists between professors.

UPPER PALEOLITHIC   The cultures of the hunting peoples who lived between the time of man's first successful invasion of frozen regions and the end of the Würm ice.

URÆUS   A forehead decoration in the form of a snake, worn by ancient Egyptian kings as a symbol of sovereignty.

URDANETA'S PASSAGE   The easterly great circle route around the North Pacific by which the Spaniards sailed with following winds from the Philippines to Mexico.

VICAR   Governor of a diocese (sub-prefecture) of the Byzantine empire.

VOLADORES   Tarascan Indians who swing on ropes from high poles in a spectacular ceremony.

WATTLE-AND-DAUB, WATTLING   A technique of wall-building in which withes are woven between poles set in a row, and the surface sealed with a coat of mud or clay.

WATUSI   Members of a noble tribe of tall and narrow-faced pastoralists in Uranda-Urundi.

WOOTZ   A kind of fine steel made in India in small cakes as early as 500 B.C.

WU   A non-Chinese people who inhabited the coast south of the Yangtze River during the first millennium B.C.

WÜRM   In the European time scale, the fourth glacial advance of the Pleistocene, comparable to the Wisconsin in America.

YAO   An aboriginal people of southern China.

ZEA MAYS   Indian corn, maize.

ZINJANTHROPUS   A large Australopithecine from Olduvai Gorge, Tanganyika.

ZOROASTRIANS   Members of a Persian religious sect of fire-worshippers.

INDEX

A NOTE ABOUT THE AUTHOR

CARLETON STEVENS COON, curator of ethnology and professor of anthropology at the University Museum in Philadelphia since 1948, was born in Wakefield, Massachusetts, and received his A.B., A.M., and Ph.D. from Harvard University. He has divided his time between field work and teaching, first at Harvard, then at the University of Pennsylvania. In connection with his work he has traveled extensively in Africa, Asia, and Europe. He arranged the famous "Hall of Man" exhibit at the University Museum, and is a regular panel member on the Peabody Award-winning television program *What in the World?* Dr. Coon is President of the American Association of Physical Anthropologists. He has written many books, including *Caravan: The Story of the Middle East* (1951, 1958); *The Story of Man* (1954, Revised Edition 1962); and *The Seven Caves* (1957). Dr. Coon has two sons and five grandchildren. He and Mrs. Coon, the former Lisa Dougherty, make their home in Devon, Pennsylvania and West Gloucester, Massachusetts.

A NOTE ON THE TYPE
IN WHICH THIS BOOK IS SET

The text of this book is set in Caledonia, *a Lino-type face that belongs to the family of printing types called "modern face" by printers—a term used to mark the change in style of type-letters that occurred about 1800. Caledonia borders on the general design of Scotch Modern, but is more freely drawn than that letter.*

The book was composed by The Plimpton Press, Norwood, Massachusetts, and printed and bound by Kingsport Press, Inc., Kingsport, Tennessee. The typography and binding design are based on originals by W. A. Dwiggins.